The Dictionary of
AMERICAN
HISTORY

Sol Holt, B.A., M.A., LL.B.

OCEANA PUBLICATIONS, INC.

Dobbs Ferry, New York

1963

Library of Congress Catalog Card Number: 63-15623

Printed in the U. S. A.

ABOUT THE AUTHOR:

Sol Holt has been a teacher in the New York City public school system for thirty years, and is presently Chairman of the Department of Social Studies at Clara Barton Vocational High School in New York City. He is the author of several textbooks and student manuals, many of them dealing with world and American history.

As a teacher, Mr. Holt has long felt the need of a concise, handy reference book for his history students. He also believes the present volume will be of great value to adults who once knew their country's history but have now forgotten most of the details.

Mr. Holt holds a B.A. from City College of New York, an M.A. from Columbia University and an LL.B. from Brooklyn Law School.

To Jeanne

The Dictionary of
AMERICAN HISTORY

CHRONOLOGY OF AMERICAN HISTORY

CAPITALIZED ITEMS are listed in the dictionary

1492 COLUMBUS discovers the New World
1493 PAPAL LINE OF DEMARCATION
1497 JOHN CABOT explores Labrador coast
1498 VASCO DA GAMA sails to India
1500 CABRAL reaches Brazil
1513 PONCE DE LEON explores Florida
      BALBOA finds the Pacific Ocean
1519 CORTEZ conquers Mexico
1520 MONTEZUMA killed by Spaniards
1522 MAGELLAN'S ship completes voyage around the
      world
1532 PIZARRO conquers the Incas
1534 CARTIER discovers the St. Lawrence River
1539 DE SOTO explores Mississippi River region
1565 ST. AUGUSTINE founded in Florida
1580 DRAKE completes circumnavigation of globe
1587 Roanoke Colony (LOST COLONY) founded
1588 English defeat SPANISH ARMADA
1606 VIRGINIA COMPANY OF LONDON chartered
      PLYMOUTH COMPANY organized
1607 JAMESTOWN settled by English
1608 QUEBEC settled by French
1609 HENRY HUDSON explores Hudson River
1619 First slaves arrive in Virginia (SLAVE TRADE)
      Virginia HOUSE OF BURGESSES meets
1620 MAYFLOWER COMPACT signed
      PLYMOUTH COLONY established
1621 DUTCH WEST INDIA COMPANY chartered
1624 NEW NETHERLAND colony established
1627 COMPANY OF NEW FRANCE chartered
1628 NEW HAMPSHIRE COLONY established
1629 MASSACHUSETTS BAY COMPANY chartered
1630 MASSACHUSETTS BAY COLONY established
1631 DELAWARE COLONY settled by Dutch
1634 MARYLAND Colony established
1636 RHODE ISLAND COLONY founded

CONNECTICUT Colony founded
HARVARD COLLEGE established
1638 JOHN DAVENPORT settles New Haven
1639 FUNDAMENTAL ORDERS OF CONNECTICUT adopted
1642 Beginning of IROQUOIS WAR
1643 NEW ENGLAND CONFEDERATION organized
1649 Maryland TOLERATION ACT
1653 End of IROQUOIS WAR
1660 British NAVIGATION ACT
1663 British NAVIGATION ACT
1664 English capture NEW NETHERLAND
1673 MARQUETTE and Joliet explore Mississippi River
1674 SIR EDMOND ANDROS appointed governor of New York
1675 Beginning of KING PHILIP'S WAR
1676 BACON'S REBELLION
End of KING PHILIP'S WAR
1677 CULPEPPER'S REBELLION
1678 BOLTING ACT
1682 PENNSYLVANIA COLONY established
William Penn's FRAME OF GOVERNMENT drawn up
1686 DOMINION OF NEW ENGLAND established
DONGAN CHARTER granted
1689 End of DOMINION OF NEW ENGLAND
Beginning of King William's War (FRENCH AND INDIAN WARS)
LEISLER'S REBELLION
1692 Salem WITCHCRAFT TRIALS
1697 End of King William's War (FRENCH AND INDIAN WARS)
1699 WOOLENS ACT
1701 Pennsylvania CHARTER OF LIBERTIES
Beginning of Queen Anne's War (FRENCH AND INDIAN WARS)
1704 DELAWARE COLONY established
1713 End of Queen Anne's War (FRENCH AND INDIAN WARS)
1732 HAT ACT
1733 MOLASSES ACT
GEORGIA COLONY established
1735 Trial of JOHN PETER ZENGER
1739 CATO CONSPIRACY

10

1744 Beginning of King George's War (FRENCH AND INDIAN WARS)

1748 End of King George's War (FRENCH AND INDIAN WARS)

1750 IRON ACT

1754 Beginning of FRENCH AND INDIAN WAR
ALBANY PLAN OF UNION
KINGS COLLEGE (Columbia) established
PAXTON BOYS organized

1755 GENERAL BRADDOCK defeated

1758 FORBES EXPEDITION

1759 British capture TICONDEROGA and QUEBEC

1763 Conestoga Massacre (PAXTON BOYS)
Conspiracy of PONTIAC
End of FRENCH AND INDIAN WAR
TREATY OF PARIS
PARSON'S CAUSE
British Royal PROCLAMATION

1764 CURRENCY ACT
SUGAR ACT

1765 QUARTERING ACT
STAMP ACT
STAMP ACT CONGRESS meets

1766 STAMP ACT repealed
DECLARATORY ACT

1767 TOWNSHEND ACTS

1768 CIRCULAR LETTER

1770 BOSTON MASSACRE
TEA ACT

1771 BATTLE OF ALAMANCE
GOLDEN HILL RIOT

1772 COMMITTEES OF CORRESPONDENCE organized
BURNING OF THE "GASPEE"
WATAUGA ASSOCIATION organized

1773 BOSTON TEA PARTY

1774 BOSTON PORT BILL
INTOLERABLE ACTS
CONTINENTAL ASSOCIATION organized
First CONTINENTAL CONGRESS meets
QUEBEC ACT

1775 SECOND CONTINENTAL CONGRESS meets
AMERICAN REVOLUTION begins
PAUL REVERE'S ride
OLIVE BRANCH PETITION

NEW ENGLAND RESTRAINING ACT
BATTLES OF LEXINGTON, CONCORD and BUNKER HILL
Capture of TICONDEROGA
1776 DECLARATION OF INDEPENDENCE signed
THOMAS PAINE'S "Common Sense" published
NATHAN HALE executed
BATTLES OF TRENTON and LONG ISLAND
1777 BATTLES OF BENNINGTON, SARATOGA, ORISKANY, GERMANTOWN, and BRANDYWINE
CONWAY CABAL
1778 French TREATY OF ALLIANCE
BATTLE OF MONMOUTH
CHERRY VALLEY MASSACRE
1780 BATTLES OF KINGS MOUNTAIN and CAMDEN
1781 BATTLES OF COWPENS, GUILFORD COURTHOUSE and YORKTOWN
ARTICLES OF CONFEDERATION ratified
1783 End of AMERICAN REVOLUTION
TREATY OF PARIS
Beginning of so-called CRITICAL PERIOD
1784 Merchantship "EMPRESS OF CHINA" reaches China
1785 LAND ORDINANCE
MOUNT VERNON CONVENTION meets
1786 SHAYS' REBELLION
Scioto Company organized (MANASSEH CUTLER)
ANNAPOLIS CONVENTION meets
OHIO COMPANY organized
1787 NORTHWEST ORDINANCE
CONSTITUTIONAL CONVENTION meets
FEDERALIST papers begun
1789 End of so-called CRITICAL PERIOD
GEORGE WASHINGTON becomes first president
JUDICIARY ACT
1790 SAMUEL SLATER builds first American factory
ASSUMPTION ACT
1791 AMERICAN BILL OF RIGHTS added to Constitution
First BANK OF UNITED STATES chartered
VERMONT admitted as a state
1792 MINT ACT
1793 GEORGE WASHINGTON begins second presidential term

COTTON GIN invented
Washington's PROCLAMATION OF NEUTRALITY
GENET AFFAIR
FUGITIVE SLAVE LAW
1794 JAY TREATY with England
NEUTRALITY ACT
WHISKEY REBELLION
BATTLE OF FALLEN TIMBERS
1795 TREATY OF GREENVILLE
NATURALIZATION ACT
PINCKNEY TREATY with Spain
1796 Washington's FAREWELL ADDRESS
1797 JOHN ADAMS becomes president
X Y Z AFFAIR
1798 VIRGINIA AND KENTUCKY RESOLUTIONS
ALIEN AND SEDITION LAWS
NATURALIZATION ACT
AMENDMENT 11 ratified
1800 CONVENTION OF 1800 with France
1801 THOMAS JEFFERSON becomes president
JOHN MARSHALL appointed Chief Justice
JUDICIARY ACT
1803 LOUISIANA PURCHASE
MARBURY V. MADISON
1804 War with BARBARY PIRATES
LEWIS AND CLARK EXPEDITION starts
AMENDMENT 12 ratified
1805 THOMAS JEFFERSON begins second presidential
term
1806 ZEBULON PIKE explores the west
NON-IMPORTATION ACT
1807 CHESAPEAKE AFFAIR
EMBARGO ACT
First successful steamboat (ROBERT FULTON)
1809 NON-INTERCOURSE ACT
JAMES MADISON becomes president
1810 FLETCHER V. PECK
MACON ACT
1811 Construction of CUMBERLAND ROAD begun
BATTLE OF TIPPECANOE
1812 Beginning of WAR OF 1812
Battle of "CONSTITUTION" AND "GUERRIERE"
1813 CREEK WAR begins
JAMES MADISON begins second presidential term

13

OLIVER H. PERRY wins Battle of Lake Erie

1814 BATTLE OF LUNDY'S LANE
HARTFORD CONVENTION
End of CREEK WAR
End of WAR OF 1812
TREATY OF GHENT

1815 BATTLE OF NEW ORLEANS

1816 First protective tariff (TARIFF OF 1816)
Second BANK OF UNITED STATES chartered
MARTIN V. HUNTER'S LESSEE

1817 Beginning of First SEMINOLE WAR
JAMES MONROE becomes president
Beginning of ERA OF GOOD FEELINGS
BONUS BILL
RUSH-BAGOT AGREEMENT

1818 Canadian boundary dispute settled (TREATY OF 1818)

1819 TALLMAGE AMENDMENT
MC CULLOCH V. MARYLAND
Financial PANIC
FLORIDA PURCHASE from Spain
DARTMOUTH COLLEGE CASE

1820 MISSOURI COMPROMISE

1821 COHENS V. VIRGINIA
JAMES MONROE begins second presidential term

1823 MONROE DOCTRINE

1824 Henry Clay's AMERICAN SYSTEM
GIBBONS V. OGDEN

1825 JOHN QUINCY ADAMS becomes president
ERIE CANAL opened

1828 TARIFF OF ABOMINATIONS
EXPOSITION AND PROTEST
WORKINGMEN'S PARTY organized

1829 ANDREW JACKSON becomes president

1830 MAYSVILLE ROAD BILL
WEBSTER-HAYNE DEBATE
NAT TURNER'S REBELLION
BLACK HAWK WAR begins

1832 Samuel Francis Smith writes "AMERICA"
President Jackson's NULLIFICATION PROCLAMATION
Worcester v. Georgia (CHEROKEE INDIANS)
SOUTH CAROLINA Ordinance of Nullification

1833 COMPROMISE TARIFF

ANDREW JACKSON begins second presidential term
FORCE ACT
1834 CURRENCY ACT
1835 SAMUEL COLT patents the revolver
New York Herald starts publication (JAMES GORDON BENNETT)
Beginning of second SEMINOLE WAR
1836 Beginning of TEXAS WAR OF INDEPENDENCE
JOHN ERICSSON invents Screw Propeller
The ALAMO disaster
DEPOSIT ACT
SPECIE CIRCULAR
BATTLE OF SAN JACINTO
1837 MARTIN VAN BUREN becomes president
"CAROLINE" AFFAIR
MARY LYON founds Holyoke Female Seminary
Financial PANIC
1838 AROOSTOOK WAR
1839 ANTI RENT WAR begins in New York
CHARLES GOODYEAR develops vulcanized rubber
1840 INDEPENDENT TREASURY SYSTEM
1841 WILLIAM HENRY HARRISON becomes president
JOHN TYLER becomes president when Harrison dies
BROOK FARM established
1842 WEBSTER-ASHBURTON TREATY
CREOLE CASE
DORR'S REBELLION
1844 SAMUEL F. B. MORSE invents the telegraph
1845 JAMES K. POLK becomes president
End of TEXAS WAR OF INDEPENDENCE
TEXAS ANNEXATION
SLIDELL MISSION
1846 ELIAS HOWE invents sewing machine
RICHARD HOE invents steam cylinder press
MEXICAN WAR begins
BATTLES OF MONTEREY, PALO ALTO and RESACA DE LA PALMA
BEAR REPUBLIC established in California
OREGON TREATY with England
WILMOT PROVISO
WALKER TARIFF
1847 BATTLE OF BUENA VISTA
MORMONS migrate to Utah
1848 Seneca Falls Convention (FEMINIST MOVEMENT)

15

End of MEXICAN WAR
TREATY OF GUADALUPE HIDALGO
Gold discovered in CALIFORNIA
FREE SOIL PARTY organized
1849 California GOLD RUSH
ZACHARY TAYLOR becomes president
1850 MILLARD FILLMORE becomes president when Taylor dies
COMPROMISE OF 1850
CLAYTON-BULWER TREATY
GEORGIA PLATFORM
FUGITIVE SLAVE LAW
Webster's "SEVENTH OF MARCH" SPEECH
1852 HARRIET BEECHER STOWE'S *Uncle Tom's Cabin* appears
1853 FRANKLIN PIERCE becomes president
GADSDEN PURCHASE
1854 COMMODORE MATTHEW C. PERRY opens Japan
BLACK WARRIOR INCIDENT
KANSAS-NEBRASKA ACT
OSTEND MANIFESTO
REPUBLICAN PARTY organized
1856 Civil War in BLEEDING KANSAS
POTTAWATOMIE MASSACRE
BESSEMER PROCESS developed
1857 JAMES BUCHANAN becomes president
DRED SCOTT DECISION
"IMPENDING CRISIS" published
HARPER'S WEEKLY begins publication
Financial PANIC
1858 Lincoln's "HOUSE DIVIDED" SPEECH
LINCOLN-DOUGLAS DEBATES
FREEPORT DOCTRINE
1859 COMSTOCK LODE discovered
EDWIN L. DRAKE drills first oil well
JOHN BROWN'S RAID
1860 South Carolina's ORDINANCE OF SECESSION
CRITTENDEN AMENDMENTS
PONY EXPRESS organized
1861 CONFEDERATE CONSTITUTION drawn up
CONFEDERATE STATES OF AMERICA organized
ABRAHAM LINCOLN becomes president
Beginning of WAR BETWEEN THE STATES
Firing on FORT SUMTER

16

First BATTLE OF BULL RUN
Ex Parte Merryman (HABEAS CORPUS)
MORRILL TARIFF
TRENT AFFAIR
1862 Battle of "MONITOR" AND "MERRIMAC"
PENINSULAR CAMPAIGN
MORRILL ACT
HOMESTEAD ACT
GREENBACKS issued under Legal Tender Act
BATTLES OF SHILOH, FREDERICKSBURG, AN-
TIETAM, MURFREESBORO and FORT DONEL-
SON
1863 GETTYSBURG ADDRESS
EMANCIPATION PROCLAMATION
DRAFT RIOTS in New York
NATIONAL BANKING ACT
BATTLES OF GETTYSBURG, VICKSBURG,
CHANCELLORSVILLE, CHICKAMAUGA and
MISSIONARY RIDGE
1864 WADE-DAVIS BILL
Massacre of Sandy Creek (CHEYENNE INDIANS)
BATTLES OF PETERSBURG and NASHVILLE
ATLANTA CAMPAIGN
1865 ABRAHAM LINCOLN begins second presidential
term
WILDERNESS CAMPAIGN
Surrender at APPOMATTOX COURTHOUSE
HAMPTON ROADS CONFERENCE
End of WAR BETWEEN THE STATES
FREEDMEN'S BUREAU established
President ABRAHAM LINCOLN assassinated
ANDREW JOHNSON becomes president
Beginning of RECONSTRUCTION ERA
AMENDMENT 13 ratified
PATRONS OF HUSBANDRY organized
MAXIMILIAN AFFAIR in Mexico
1866 Atlantic Cable laid by CYRUS FIELD
NATIONAL LABOR UNION organized
KU KLUX KLAN organized
NATIONAL UNION PARTY formed
CIVIL RIGHTS BILL
1867 IMPEACHMENT OF PRESIDENT JOHNSON
RECONSTRUCTION ACT
TENURE OF OFFICE ACT

17

	ALASKA PURCHASE
1868	COVODE RESOLUTION
	AMENDMENT 14 ratified
	BURLINGAME TREATY
1869	ULYSSES S. GRANT becomes president
	BLACK FRIDAY
	PROHIBITION PARTY organized
	UNION PACIFIC RAILROAD completed
	KNIGHTS OF LABOR organized
1870	AMENDMENT 15 ratified
1871	ALABAMA CLAIMS dispute settled
	Beginning of Apache War (COCHISE)
1872	AMNESTY ACT
	CREDIT MOBILIER scandal
	LIBERAL REPUBLICAN PARTY organized
1873	ULYSSES S. GRANT begins second presidential term
	Financial PANIC
	DEMONETIZATION ACT
	"VIRGINIUS" AFFAIR
1874	KALAMAZOO CASE
	GREENBACK PARTY organized
	BARBED WIRE invented
1875	CIVIL RIGHTS BILL
	Beginning of SIOUX WAR
	WHISKEY RING scandal
	RESUMPTION ACT
1876	Disputed ELECTION OF 1876
	ELECTORAL COMMISSION ACT
	MULLIGAN LETTERS
	BATTLE OF LITTLE BIG HORN
	End of SIOUX WAR
	ALEXANDER GRAHAM BELL invents the telephone
	BELKNAP SCANDAL
1877	RUTHERFORD B. HAYES becomes president
	THOMAS A. EDISON invents the phonograph
	End of RECONSTRUCTION ERA
	DESERT LAND ACT
1878	BLAND-ALLISON ACT
1879	THOMAS A. EDISON invents the electric light
1881	JAMES A. GARFIELD becomes president
	JAMES A. GARFIELD assassinated
	CHESTER A. ARTHUR becomes president
	CLARA BARTON founds American Red Cross

1882 CHINESE EXCLUSION ACT
JOHN D. ROCKEFELLER organizes the Standard Oil Trust
1883 PENDLETON ACT
PRESIDENTIAL SUCCESSION ACT
Civil Rights Cases (CIVIL RIGHTS BILLS)
1884 TREATY OF WANGHIA
1885 GROVER CLEVELAND becomes president
CONTRACT LABOR LAW
OTTMAR MERGENTHALER invents the linotype machine
1886 HAYMARKET RIOTS
End of Apache War (COCHISE)
PRESIDENTIAL SUCCESSION ACT
AMERICAN FEDERATION OF LABOR founded
Granger Laws unconstitutional (GRANGER CASES)
1887 INTERSTATE COMMERCE ACT
DAWES ACT
ELECTORAL COUNT ACT
BAYARD-CHAMBERLAIN TREATY
1889 BENJAMIN HARRISON becomes president
First PAN AMERICAN CONFERENCE held
JANE ADDAMS establishes Hull House
1890 MAFIA INCIDENT
MC KINLEY TARIFF
SHERMAN ANTI-TRUST ACT
SHERMAN SILVER PURCHASE ACT
FRONTIER comes to an end
1891 BALTIMORE INCIDENT
FOREST RESERVE ACT
POPULIST PARTY organized
1892 HOMESTEAD STRIKE
Populist Party draws up OMAHA PLATFORM
1893 GROVER CLEVELAND becomes president for a second time
Financial PANIC
BERING SEA DISPUTE
SHERMAN SILVER PURCHASE ACT repealed
JACOB COXEY leads march on Washington
MC CLURE'S MAGAZINE founded
1894 PULLMAN STRIKE
CAREY ACT
WILSON-GORMAN TARIFF
THOMAS A. EDISON invents motion pictures

19

1895   VENEZUELA BOUNDARY DISPUTE
U. S. V. KNIGHT
Pollock V. Farmers' Loan and Trust Co. (INCOME TAX)

1896   "CROSS OF GOLD" SPEECH
Plessy V. Ferguson (SEGREGATION)

1897   WILLIAM MC KINLEY becomes president
DINGLEY TARIFF
KLONDIKE GOLD RUSH

1898   DE LOME LETTER
SPANISH-AMERICAN WAR
BATTLE OF MANILA BAY
TELLER RESOLUTION
TREATY OF PARIS
HAWAIIAN ISLANDS acquired
Erdman Act (YELLOW DOG CONTRACTS)

1899   ADDYSTON PIPE AND STEEL CO. V. U. S.
HAGUE COURT established
OPEN DOOR POLICY

1900   BOXER REBELLION
GOLD STANDARD ACT
FORAKER ACT
SOCIALIST PARTY organized

1901   WILLIAM MC KINLEY begins second presidential term
President WILLIAM MC KINLEY assassinated
THEODORE ROOSEVELT becomes president
JOHN P. MORGAN organizes the U. S. Steel Corporation
INSULAR CASES
PLATT AMENDMENT
HAY-PAUNCEFOTE TREATY

1902   VENEZUELA DEBT DISPUTE
PHILIPPINE GOVERNMENT ACT
NEWLANDS RECLAMATION ACT
ANTHRACITE COAL STRIKE

1903   WRIGHT BROTHERS make first airplane flight
HAY-HERRAN TREATY
ELKINS ACT
Canal Zone acquired by HAY BUNAU-VARILLA TREATY
ALASKA BOUNDARY DISPUTE settled

1904   Construction of PANAMA CANAL begins
THEODORE ROOSEVELT elected president

ROOSEVELT COROLLARY announced
1905 LOCHNER V. NEW YORK
SANTO DOMINGO DEBT DISPUTE
1906 HEPBURN ACT
MEAT INSPECTION ACT
PURE FOOD AND DRUG ACT
1907 GENTLEMEN'S AGREEMENT
DRAGO DOCTRINE
Financial PANIC
1908 DANBURY HATTERS CASE
ALDRICH-VREELAND ACT
ROOT-TAKAHIRA AGREEMENT
NATIONAL CONSERVATION COMMISSION established
1909 WILLIAM HOWARD TAFT becomes president
PAYNE-ALDRICH TARIFF
VENEZUELA DEBT DISPUTE
1910 BALLINGER-PINCHOT CONTROVERSY
MANN-ELKINS ACT
1911 Supreme Court applies RULE OF REASON
1912 MAGDALENA BAY INCIDENT
Tolls Exemption Act leads to CANAL TOLLS CONTROVERSY
PROGRESSIVE PARTY organized
1913 WOODROW WILSON becomes president
FEDERAL RESERVE ACT
WATCHFUL WAITING policy
UNDERWOOD TARIFF
PUJO COMMITTEE meets
INCOME TAX amendment ratified
AMENDMENT 17 ratified
1914 SMITH-LEVER ACT
TAMPICO INCIDENT
PROCLAMATION OF NEUTRALITY at outbreak of World War I
PANAMA CANAL completed
FEDERAL TRADE COMMISSION ACT
CLAYTON ANTI-TRUST ACT
1915 Japan's TWENTY-ONE DEMANDS
"LUSITANIA" sunk
LA FOLLETTE SEAMEN'S ACT
1916 JONES ACT for Philippine Islands
ADAMSON ACT
Sussex Pledge (SUBMARINE WARFARE)

FEDERAL FARM LOAN ACT
Keating-Owen Act (CHILD LABOR)
BLACK TOM EXPLOSION

1917 WOODROW WILSON begins second presidential term
ZIMMERMAN NOTE
U. S. enters WORLD WAR I
JONES ACT for Puerto Rico
LITERACY TEST ACT
SELECTIVE SERVICE ACT
ESPIONAGE ACT
LANSING-ISHII AGREEMENT
VIRGIN ISLANDS PURCHASE

1918 President Wilson's FOURTEEN POINTS
Hammer v. Dagenhart (CHILD LABOR)
SEDITION ACT
BATTLES OF BELLEAU WOOD, MARNE, ST.
MIHIEL, and CHATEAU THIERRY
ARMISTICE ending World War I

1919 PARIS PEACE CONFERENCE
VERSAILLES TREATY drawn up
PROHIBITION amendment ratified
BOSTON POLICE STRIKE
ABRAMS V. U. S.
COMMUNIST PARTY organized in U. S.
SCHENCK V. U. S.

1920 WORLD COURT established
WATER POWER ACT
ESCH-CUMMINS TRANSPORTATION ACT
AMENDMENT 19 ratified

1921 WARREN G. HARDING becomes president
DILLINGHAM IMMIGRATION ACT
EMERGENCY TARIFF ACT
BUDGET AND ACCOUNTING ACT
WASHINGTON DISARMAMENT CONFERENCE
begins

1922 Bailey v. Drexel Furniture Co. (CHILD LABOR)
FORDNEY MC CUMBER TARIFF ACT
CAPPER-VOLSTEAD ACT
CABLE ACT

1923 CALVIN COOLIDGE becomes president
ADKINS V. CHILDREN'S HOSPITAL

1924 BONUS BILL
CALVIN COOLIDGE elected president
JOHNSON-REED IMMIGRATION ACT

DAWES PLAN
TEAPOT DOME SCANDAL
1925 SCOPES TRIAL in Tennessee
1926 WATSON-PARKER ACT
1927 COTTON PICKER invented
1928 KELLOGG-BRIAND PACT
1929 HERBERT HOOVER becomes president
NATIONAL ORIGINS ACT
Root Formula (ELIHU ROOT)
Beginning of GREAT DEPRESSION
YOUNG PLAN
AGRICULTURAL MARKETING ACT
1930 HAWLEY-SMOOT TARIFF
LONDON NAVAL CONFERENCE
1931 Hoover Moratorium (WAR DEBTS)
1932 STIMSON DOCTRINE
RECONSTRUCTION FINANCE CORPORATION
established
NORRIS-LA GUARDIA ANTI-INJUNCTION ACT
GLASS-STEAGALL ACT
BONUS ARMY marches on Washington, D. C.
1933 FRANKLIN D. ROOSEVELT becomes president
BANK HOLIDAY
Beginning of NEW DEAL
NATIONAL INDUSTRIAL RECOVERY ACT
AGRICULTURAL ADJUSTMENT ACT
BANKING ACT
Emergency Railroad Transportation Act (RAILROAD
LEGISLATION)
Home Owners Loan Act (HOUSING LEGISLA-
TION)
GOLD REPEAL RESOLUTION
TENNESSEE VALLEY AUTHORITY ACT
CIVILIAN CONSERVATION CORPS established
FARM CREDIT ADMINISTRATION established
Lame Duck Amendment (AMENDMENT 20) ratified
PROHIBITION ends when Amendment 21 is ratified
Beginning of GOOD NEIGHBOR POLICY
Philippine Independence Act (PHILIPPINE IS-
LANDS)
Hawes-Cutting Act (PHILIPPINE ISLANDS)
1934 SILVER PURCHASE ACT
SECURITIES AND EXCHANGE ACT

23

FEDERAL COMMUNICATIONS ACT
RECIPROCAL TARIFF ACT
GOLD RESERVE ACT
JOHNSON DEBT DEFAULT ACT
First FARM MORTGAGE MORATORIUM ACT
RAILROAD RETIREMENT ACT
National Housing Act (HOUSING LEGISLATION)
1934 EXPORT-IMPORT BANK established
TYDINGS-MC DUFFIE ACT
1935 SOCIAL SECURITY ACT
MOTOR CARRIER ACT
NATIONAL LABOR RELATIONS ACT
GOLD CLAUSE CASES
WHEELER-RAYBURN ACT
BANKING ACT
CONNALLY ACT
Second FARM MORTGAGE MORATORIUM ACT
RAILROAD RETIREMENT ACT
RURAL ELECTRIFICATION ADMINISTRATION established
SCHECTER V. U. S.
SOIL CONSERVATION ACT
1936 U. S. v. Butler (AGRICULTURAL ADJUSTMENT ACT, 1933)
SOIL CONSERVATION AND DOMESTIC ALLOTMENT ACT
MERCHANT MARINE ACT
ROBINSON-PATMAN ACT
ASHWANDER V. T.V.A.
1937 FRANKLIN D. ROOSEVELT begins second presidential term
BANKHEAD-JONES FARM TENANT ACT
RAILROAD RETIREMENT ACT
WEST COAST HOTEL V. PARRISH
Wagner-Steagall Housing Act (HOUSING LEGISLATION)
Cash and Carry NEUTRALITY ACT
JUDICIARY REORGANIZATION BILL
Helvering v. Davis (SOCIAL SECURITY ACT)
1938 CONGRESS OF INDUSTRIAL ORGANIZATIONS formed
PURE FOOD DRUG AND COSMETIC ACT
FAIR LABOR STANDARDS ACT
Second AGRICULTURAL ADJUSTMENT ACT

CIVIL AERONAUTICS ACT
Steagall National Housing Act (HOUSING LEGISLA-
TION)
VINSON NAVAL ACT
1939 NEUTRALITY ACT
WORLD WAR II begins in Europe
BELL ACT
HATCH ACT
1940 Burke-Wadsworth Act (CONSCRIPTION)
NATIONALITY ACT
DESTROYER-MILITARY BASE EXCHANGE
TRANSPORTATION ACT
SMITH ACT
1941 FRANKLIN D. ROOSEVELT begins third presiden-
tial term
LEND-LEASE ACT
FOUR FREEDOMS address by Franklin D. Roosevelt
Churchill and Roosevelt draw up ATLANTIC CHAR-
TER
PEARL HARBOR ATTACK
U. S. enters WORLD WAR II
United States v. Darby Lumber Co. (CHILD LABOR)
1942 Surrender of CORREGIDOR
BATTLES OF BATAAN, CORAL SEA, GUADAL-
CANAL, JAVA SEA and MACASSAR STRAIT
U. S. forces invade Africa (AFRICAN CAMPAIGN)
1943 FULBRIGHT RESOLUTION
CAIRO CONFERENCE
WAR LABOR DISPUTES ACT
1944 BATTLES OF THE BULGE, LEYTE GULF and
PHILIPPINE SEA
G. I. BILL OF RIGHTS
D DAY in Europe
DUMBARTON OAKS CONFERENCE
1945 FRANKLIN D. ROOSEVELT begins fourth presi-
dential term
HARRY S. TRUMAN becomes president
First ATOM BOMB exploded
ACT OF CHAPULTEPEC
BATTLES OF IWO JIMA and OKINAWA
POTSDAM AGREEMENT
YALTA CONFERENCE
SAN FRANCISCO CONFERENCE
UNITED NATIONS organized

118216

WORLD WAR II ends with surrender of Germany and Japan

1946 PHILIPPINE ISLANDS become independent
LOBBYING ACT
EMPLOYMENT ACT
ATOMIC ENERGY COMMISSION established

1947 NATIONAL SECURITY ACT
New PRESIDENTIAL SUCCESSION ACT
RIO PACT
TAFT-HARTLEY ACT
MARSHALL PLAN
TRUMAN DOCTRINE

1948 DISPLACED PERSONS ACT
BERLIN BLOCKADE
HARRY S. TRUMAN elected president
SELECTIVE SERVICE ACT

1949 NORTH ATLANTIC TREATY ORGANIZATION formed
Point Four Program (FOREIGN AID PROGRAM)

1950 Beginning of KOREAN WAR

1951 AMENDMENT 22 ratified
MC CARRAN INTERNAL SECURITY ACT

1952 MC CARRAN-WALTER IMMIGRATION ACT
EUROPEAN DEFENSE COMMUNITY established

1953 DWIGHT D. EISENHOWER becomes president
End of KOREAN WAR

1954 BRICKER AMENDMENT proposed
SOUTHEAST ASIA TREATY ORGANIZATION formed
WILEY-DONDERO ACT
Brown v. Board of Education (SEGREGATION)

1955 A.F.L.-C.I.O. organized

1957 EISENHOWER DOCTRINE

1959 ST. LAWRENCE SEAWAY opened
L A B O R MANAGEMENT REPORTING AND DISCLOSURE ACT

1961 JOHN F. KENNEDY becomes president
PEACE CORPS organized
AMENDMENT 23 ratified

1962 PRAYER BAN IN PUBLIC SCHOOLS
SATELLITE COMMUNICATIONS ACT
CUBAN QUARANTINE
TRADE EXPANSION ACT

ABC POWERS. See TAMPICO INCIDENT

ABOLITIONISTS. Northerners before the WAR BETWEEN THE STATES (1861) who advocated the immediate abolition of slavery in the U. S. Among the Abolitionist leaders were such extremists as WILLIAM LLOYD GARRISON, ELIJAH P. LOVEJOY and JOHN BROWN, as well as more moderate reformers such as John Greenleaf Whittier, James Russell Lowell and Theodore Weld.

ABRAMS V. U. S. (1919). U. S. Supreme Court decision upholding the constitutionality of the SEDITION ACT (1918) which made it a crime to speak disloyally of the U. S. government or interfere with the war effort (World War I). Justice OLIVER WENDELL HOLMES, JR., dissented in the decision, holding that the Sedition Act was a violation of freedom of speech guaranteed under Amendment 1 of the U. S. Constitution.

ACT OF CHAPULTEPEC (1945). Agreement signed by all republics in the Western Hemisphere (except Argentina) at Chapultepec Castle in Mexico City, while WORLD WAR II (1941-45) was still in progress. The agreement provided that military aggression against any one of the American republics would be considered military aggression against all the signers.

ADAIR V. U. S. (1908). See YELLOW DOG CONTRACTS

ADAMS, JOHN (1735-1826). Second president of the U. S. He was one of the Boston leaders who protested against the STAMP ACT (1765) and one of the men chosen to draft the DECLARATION OF INDEPENDENCE (1776). In 1789 he was elected vice-president of the U. S. and was re-elected to the position four years later. In 1797 he became president (ELECTION OF 1796) but was defeated for a second term (ELECTION OF 1800) by THOMAS JEFFERSON.

27

During Adam's term as president, the ALIEN AND SEDITION LAWS (1798) were enacted and were then sharply criticized in the VIRGINIA AND KENTUCKY RESOLUTIONS (1798). The XYZ AFFAIR (1798) with France stirred the nation and gave Adams momentary popularity. Adams appointed JOHN MARSHALL Chief Justice of the Supreme Court in 1801.

ADAMS, JOHN QUINCY (1767-1848). Sixth president of the U. S. In 1814 he helped to negotiate the TREATY OF GHENT ending the WAR OF 1812. President JAMES MONROE appointed him Secretary of State (1817) and in that capacity he played an important role in the writing of the MONROE DOCTRINE (1823). In the ELECTION OF 1824 he ran for president against ANDREW JACKSON, HENRY CLAY and WILLIAM H. CRAWFORD. Since no candidate received a majority vote in the election, the House of Representatives chose John Quincy Adams as president. This was the only instance in our history where both father (JOHN ADAMS) and son held the office of president.

During John Quincy Adams' term as president, the ERIE CANAL was opened (1825), and Congress passed the so-called TARIFF OF ABOMINATIONS (1828), a strongly-worded denunciation of the tariff. John Quincy Adams was defeated for a second presidential term by Andrew Jackson in the ELECTION OF 1828. After leaving the presidency, Adams served in Congress for 17 years (1831-48) and fought for repeal of the GAG RULE which forbad the reading of anti-slavery petitions in Congress.

ADAMSON ACT (1916). Forestalled a threatened strike of railroad workers and established an eight-hour day for employees on all interstate railroads. (See RAILROAD LEGISLATION)

ADAMS-ONIS TREATY (1819). See FLORIDA PURCHASE

ADAMS, SAMUEL (1722-1803). Leader of colonial resistance to England before and during the American Revolution. He prepared a protest against the STAMP ACT (1765), helped organize the SONS OF LIBERTY and the COMMITTEES OF CORRESPONDENCE, and was involved in the BOSTON TEA PARTY.

ADDAMS, JANE (1860-1935). Established a neighborhood settlement center (1889) called Hull House, which became world famous for its work with the poor. She was also a leader in the world peace movement and in 1931 was awarded the NOBEL PRIZE for work in promoting world peace.

ADDYSTON PIPE AND STEEL CO. v. U. S. (1899). After the government failure to dissolve the sugar trust (see U. S. v. KNIGHT), another lawsuit was brought against a steel manufacturer on the ground that an illegal market allocation agreement had been formed. The court held that the SHERMAN ANTI-TRUST ACT applied and the pooling agreement was illegal.

ADKINS V. CHILDREN'S HOSPITAL (1923). In 1918 Congress passed a law establishing a minimum wage scale for women working in the District of Columbia. The Supreme Court held the law unconstitutional because it violated AMENDMENT 5 of the Constitution which prohibited the federal government from passing any law that deprived a person of "life, liberty, or property without DUE PROCESS OF LAW."

A.F.L.-C.I.O. National labor federation formed in 1955 by a merger of the AMERICAN FEDERATION OF LABOR (A.F.L.) and the CONGRESS OF INDUSTRIAL ORGANIZATIONS (C.I.O.). The first president of the new organization was George Meany. In 1962 the A.F.L.-C.I.O. claimed a total membership of 16,000,000 workers.

AFRICAN CAMPAIGN: WORLD WAR II (1940-43). During World War II a German Army attempted to capture Egypt and the Suez Canal by moving east along the North African coast (1940). German forces penetrated deep into Egypt before they were stopped by the British. In 1942, U. S. forces landed in west North Africa. The combined British forces in the east and American forces in the west finally forced the surrender of the German Armies in North Africa in 1943 and put an end to the African campaign.

AGRICULTURAL ADJUSTMENT ACT (1933). One of the first laws passed by the NEW DEAL Congress, it provided that farmers were to reduce the size of their farm crops

29

voluntarily. Farmers who accepted this plan were to be paid by the government for each acre of land not cultivated. In 1936 the Supreme Court declared the law unconstitutional (U. S. v. Butler).

AGRICULTURAL ADJUSTMENT ACT (1938). Also known as the second A.A.A. or the Jones Agricultural Adjustment Act. It replaced the AGRICULTURAL ADJUSTMENT ACT of 1933 which the Supreme Court had declared unconstitutional. The new act provided for a plan under which the Secretary of Agriculture was to establish annual marketing quotas for corn, wheat, cotton, rice and tobacco equal to the nation's needs for one year, provided that two-thirds of the farmers growing these crops voluntarily agreed to the plan. Parity payments were to be made to farmers by the government if the prices for their crops fell below the pre-World War I levels (1909-1914). The law also provided for government loans to farmers for stored crops that were kept off the market as part of an Ever Normal Granary Plan. Farm loans were to be administered by the Commodity Credit Corporation (C.C.C). In addition, payments were to be made to farmers for soil conservation work on farm land taken out of production and put into the so-called Soil Bank. A Federal Crop Insurance Corporation (F.C.I.C.) was to provide insurance protection to farmers against crop losses resulting from drought, floods, insects, plant diseases and other natural causes. The Supreme Court held this comprehensive law to be constitutional (1939) because it regulated the *marketing* rather than the production of crops.

AGRICULTURAL LEGISLATION. See FARM LEGISLATION

AGRICULTURAL MARKETING ACT (1929). Established a Federal Farm Board with power to buy surplus crops and put them in storage and to lend money to farmer co-operatives so that they could pay for storage of surplus crops until prices rose. (See FARM LEGISLATION)

AGRICULTURAL REVOLUTION. Name applied to the changes in methods of farming that occurred in the 19th and 20th centuries in Europe and in the U. S. The agricultural revolution resulted in widespread use of farm machinery, such as harvesters, reapers, seed drills, combines and tractors, and the application of scientific methods of farming such as artificial fertilization, crop rotation and contour plowing.

AGUINALDO, EMILIO (c.1869-   ). See PHILIPPINE ISLANDS

ALABAMA CLAIMS. During the WAR BETWEEN THE STATES, a number of Confederate vessels such as the *Alabama* and the *Shenandoah* were built in British shipyards and were used by the CONFEDERATE STATES to attack and destroy large numbers of Northern ships. At the end of the war the U. S. asked Great Britain to pay for the damages inflicted by these British-built vessels. Impending war in Europe between France and Prussia led Great Britain to agree to a settlement of the Alabama Claims. In 1871 Great Britain and the U. S. signed the Treaty of Washington by which both nations agreed to let a court of arbitration establish the amount of damages. The court awarded $15,500,000 to the U. S.

ALAMANCE, BATTLE OF (1771). A number of colonial settlers in the western part of North Carolina rebelled because they were not adequately represented in the colonial assembly and because colonial laws favored the seaboard rather than the western Piedmont region. William Tryon, the colonial governor, led the colonial militia against the rebels and crushed them at Alamance Creek. The ringleaders were tried for treason and were executed.

ALAMO, THE. A church mission in San Antonio, Texas. It was at this mission that a small force of about 200 Texans held off an army of 3,000 Mexicans during the TEXAS WAR OF INDEPENDENCE (1836). After a 12-day siege the Alamo was taken by the Mexicans (1836) and not a single Texan was left alive. DAVY CROCKETT, one of the Alamo defenders, left a diary describing the siege. During the remainder of the TEXAS WAR OF INDEPENDENCE "Remember the Alamo" became the rallying cry of the Texan fighters.

ALASKA BOUNDARY DISPUTE (1903). When the U. S. purchased Alaska from Russia in 1867 (see ALASKA PURCHASE) the treaty of purchase did not clearly define

31

the boundary between Alaska and Canada. After the discovery of gold in the Klondike region (see KLONDIKE GOLD RUSH), the determination of the exact boundary assumed major importance. In 1903 the dispute was settled by arbitration. (See BIG STICK POLICY)

ALASKA PURCHASE (1867). Secretary of state WILLIAM H. SEWARD arranged a treaty by which the U. S. purchased Alaska from Russia for $7,200,000. Seward's purposes were to expand American territory, eliminate Russia from the Western Hemisphere, show our appreciation to Russia for her friendship to the North during the War Between the States and stop any further expansion of British territory in North America. Many Americans opposed the purchase and called it "Seward's Folly" and "Seward's Icebox."

ALBANY PLAN OF UNION (1754). Drawn up by BENJAMIN FRANKLIN, it provided that seven English colonies were to join to defend themselves against the Indians and the French on the western border. Although the plan was rejected, it was one of the first attempts to unite the colonies for their common welfare.

ALBANY REGENCY. Powerful faction of DEMOCRATIC PARTY political leaders in New York State politics from about 1820 to 1850. Among its notable members were MARTIN VAN BUREN, WILLIAM L. MARCY, Benjamin F. Butler and Silas Wright. The power of the Albany Regency was broken after 1848 as a result of party differences over Jackson's radical reforms, the slavery issue and the split between HUNKERS and BARNBURNERS in the state.

ALDRICH-VREELAND ACT (1908). Permitted National Banks to issue a limited amount of paper currency based on nongovernment securities. (See BANKING LEGISLATION)

ALGONQUIN INDIANS. A small tribe of Canadian Indians with whom the early French explorers of Canada formed alliances. For example, CHAMPLAIN formed an alliance with the Algonquin Indians in 1609 and fought a war with the IROQUOIS INDIAN tribe, traditional enemy of the

Algonquins. Eventually the Iroquois defeated the Algonquins and the latter were scattered in eastern Canada.

ALIEN ACTS (1798). Part of the FEDERALIST PARTY program during President JOHN ADAMS' administration to weaken THOMAS JEFFERSON's new REPUBLICAN PARTY. Two Alien Acts passed by Congress gave the president power to deport aliens whom he judged dangerous to the peace and safety of the nation, and to imprison dangerous aliens in time of war. Since most recent immigrants to the U. S. favored Republican Party principles, the laws were aimed at Jefferson's supporters. The Alien Acts expired before Jefferson became president in 1801.

ALIEN AND SEDITION ACTS. See ALIEN ACTS and SEDITION ACT

ALIEN PROPERTY CUSTODIAN. Federal agency established in 1917 during World War I and re-established in 1942 during World War II to hold and dispose of property in the U. S. owned by persons or corporations residing in enemy countries. A number of scandals resulted from the maladministration of the Alien Property Custodian's Office during the administration of President WARREN G. HARDING after World War I.

ALIEN REGISTRATION ACT (1940). See SMITH ACT

ALLEN, ETHAN (1738-89). During the AMERICAN REVOLUTION, Allen led his "Green Mountain Boys" of Vermont in the successful capture of the British forts at TICONDEROGA and Crown Point on Lake Champlain (1775). In the same year he was a member of a patriot army that set out to capture Montreal. Allen was taken prisoner by the British but was released in an exchange of prisoners.

ALTGELD, JOHN P. (1847-1902). Governor of Illinois (1892-96). In 1893 he pardoned three of the men who had been convicted in the HAYMARKET RIOTS of 1886. This act of amnesty aroused nationwide criticism. During the Chicago PULLMAN STRIKE (1894), Altgeld protested the use of federal troops sent by President GROVER CLEVELAND to protect the movement of U. S. mail.

AMENDMENT 1

AMENDMENT 1 (1791). Prohibits Congress from passing any law abridging freedom of religion, freedom of speech, freedom of the press, freedom of assembly, or freedom to petition the government.

AMENDMENT 5 (1791). Provides that no person accused of a crime may be brought to trial except through indictment by a grand jury. He may not be tried twice for the same crime, be forced to testify against himself or be deprived of life, liberty, or property without DUE PROCESS OF LAW. No person may be deprived of his property by the government unless he receives just payment.

AMENDMENT 10 (1791). Provides that any power not given to the federal government or prohibited to the states by the Constitution is a reserved power of the states or of the people.

AMENDMENT 11 (1798). In 1793 a case was brought before the U. S. Supreme Court in which a citizen of another state sued the state of Georgia (Chisholm V. Georgia). This case resulted in protests from the legislature of Georgia and other states and the adoption of this amendment. Under Amendment 11, a state cannot be sued without its consent in a federal court by a citizen of another state or a citizen of a foreign country.

AMENDMENT 12 (1804). In the ELECTION of 1800, the Electoral College cast 73 votes for both JEFFERSON and BURR but failed to indicate which votes were for the presidency and which were for the vice-presidency. The House of Representatives finally chose Jefferson for the presidency. To avoid similar confusion in the future, the 12th Amendment provided that the Electoral College shall clearly indicate which of their votes are for the presidency and which are for the vice-presidency.

AMENDMENT 13 (1865). Prohibited slavery or involuntary servitude except as a punishment for crime in the U. S. (See EMANCIPATION PROCLAMATION)

AMENDMENT 14 (1868). Defines citizens as persons born or naturalized in the U. S. The amendment also forbids a *state* from depriving any person of life, liberty, or property

34

without DUE PROCESS OF LAW or depriving any person of equal protection of the laws. If a state deprives any citizen of the right to vote, its Congressional representation shall be reduced. The amendment also bars from public office all Southerners who participated in the War Between the States and forbids the payment of any part of the Confederate debt or of compensation for the emancipation of slaves. Although originally passed to protect the rights of the newly emancipated Negro, the "due process" and "equal protection" clauses of the amendment have frequently been used as a defense against regulation and control of corporations by state laws.

AMENDMENT 15 (1870). Provides that the right of a citizen to vote shall not be denied because of race, color, or previous condition of servitude. In spite of this amendment, however, many Southern states continue to use various devices to disfranchise the Negro. (See POLL TAX and LITERACY TESTS FOR VOTING)

AMENDMENT 16 (1913). Provided that direct taxes may be levied on the basis of earned income, thus legalizing the INCOME TAX.

AMENDMENT 17 (1913). Eliminated the process of electing senators by state legislatures and provided for the election of senators directly by the voters.

AMENDMENT 18 (1919). See PROHIBITION ERA

AMENDMENT 19 (1920). Provided that no state could deprive a person of the right to vote because of sex. (See WOMAN SUFFRAGE)

AMENDMENT 20 (1933). Also known as the "Lame Duck" Amendment. It provided for a change of dates for the inauguration of the president from March 4 to January 20 and for the meeting of the short session of Congress during a presidential election year from March 4 to January 3. This change of date eliminated the so-called LAME DUCK CONGRESSES. The amendment also gave Congress the power to decide who shall be president in the event that the elected president or vice-president fails to qualify, or both die before the date of inauguration.

AMENDMENT 22 (1951). Provided that no candidate could be elected to the presidency for more than two terms or hold the office of president for more than ten years. (See ROOSEVELT, FRANKLIN D.)

AMENDMENT 23 (1961). Prior to the enactment of this amendment, citizen residents of Washington D. C. could not vote in national presidential elections. Under the amendment the right to vote was granted to them.

AMERICA. Name given to the New World (see VESPUCCI, AMERIGO). It is also the name of a patriotic song written by Samuel Francis Smith in 1832 to the tune of the British hymn *God Save the King.*

AMERICAN COLONIZATION SOCIETY. Formed in 1817 for the purpose of resettling emancipated American Negroes in Africa. The Republic of Liberia was established in Africa (1822) as an independent country for them. Before the War Between the States (1861), the society transported more than 11,000 Negroes to Liberia.

AMERICAN EXPEDITIONARY FORCES (A.E.F.). Name applied to the American army sent to Europe during WORLD WAR I (1917-18). The entire A.E.F. was under the supreme command of General JOHN J. PERSHING. More than 2,000,000 Americans were landed in Europe before the war came to an end.

AMERICAN FEDERATION OF LABOR (A.F.L.). One of the oldest and most important national labor organizations, founded in 1886. One of its founders, SAMUEL GOMPERS, became president of the A.F.L. in 1886 and remained president (with the exception of one year) until his death in 1924. The early aims of the A.F.L. were wage increases, shorter working hours, a six-day work week, and abolition of child labor. The A.F.L. endorsed no political party and nominated no candidates for political office, and restricted its membership to skilled craft unions. Its membership grew from 300,000 in 1890 to more than 8,000,000 in 1950. In 1937 one wing of the A.F.L., led by JOHN L. LEWIS, split from the organization over the question of organizing unskilled labor in mass-production industries. Lewis organized

(1938) the rival CONGRESS OF INDUSTRIAL ORGAN-IZATIONS (C.I.O.) which grew rapidly in membership. In 1955 the two organizations were reunited to form the A.F.L.-C.I.O., under the presidency of George Meany.

AMERICAN PARTY. See KNOW-NOTHING PARTY

AMERICAN REVOLUTION (1775-1783). Conflict between the thirteen American colonies and Great Britain by which the colonies gained their independence. The Revolution began because of burdensome taxes levied by the British Parliament (see STAMP ACT, SUGAR ACT, TOWN-SHEND ACTS), restrictions on trade, commerce (see NAVIGATION ACTS) and manufacturing (see HAT ACT, IRON ACT), denial of personal liberties (see WRITS OF ASSISTANCE) and interference with colonial self-government (see INTOLERABLE ACTS). During the war there were numerous military engagements, beginning with the BATTLE OF LEXINGTON (1775), reaching a climax at the BATTLE OF SARATOGA (1777), and ending with the BATTLE OF YORKTOWN (1787), the last major engagement of the war.

The most important provisions of the TREATY OF PARIS (1787) ending the war gave the Thirteen Colonies their independence and established the western boundary of the U. S. at the Mississippi River.

AMERICAN SYSTEM. Name applied by HENRY CLAY to his legislative program in 1824. His American System provided for the construction of internal improvements (roads and canals) financed by the national government, and a protective tariff to provide revenue to build the internal improvements and at the same time protect American manufacturers from foreign competition.

AMHERST, JEFFREY (1717-97). British general sent to the American colonies to fight in the FRENCH AND INDIAN WAR (1754-63). Amherst was one of the most successful British generals in the war. He captured Crown Point and TICONDEROGA (1759) and directed the capture of Montreal (1760).

AMISH. See MENNONITES

AMNESTY ACT (1872). Pardoned all Southern whites who had participated in the WAR BETWEEN THE STATES (1861-65) except for a few hundred leaders. This act restored the right to vote to most Southern white citizens and gradually led to the ending of CARPETBAG GOVERNMENTS in Southern states.

ANDERSONVILLE. Confederate prison for captured Union soldiers during the WAR BETWEEN THE STATES (1861-65). More than 12,000 Union soldiers imprisoned at Andersonville, Georgia, during the war died of disease, mistreatment, malnutrition, and unsanitary conditions.

ANDRÉ, MAJOR JOHN (1751-80). British officer who plotted with BENEDICT ARNOLD, a general in the American Revolutionary Army, to let the British seize West Point. The traitorous plot was discovered and Benedict Arnold fled to England. Major André, however, was captured by the Americans and hanged as a spy.

ANDROS, SIR EDMOND (1637-1714). Royal governor of the New York colony (1674-81) and later royal governor of the DOMINION OF NEW ENGLAND (1686-89). Andros tried to restrict the liberties of the colonists (see CHARTER OAK) and at the same time increase taxes. When the Glorious Revolution (1688) in England put an end to the reign of King James II, Andros' rule ended abruptly (1689).

ANNAPOLIS CONVENTION (1786). Meeting of delegates from five states, called by the state of Virginia to consider changes and improvements in trade regulations between states. An outgrowth of the Annapolis Convention was a resolution asking Congress to call another convention to meet in Philadelphia in 1787 for the purpose of amending the ARTICLES OF CONFEDERATION.

ANTHONY, SUSAN B. (1820-1906). One of the important figures in the 19th century FEMINIST MOVEMENT to obtain women suffrage and equal rights for women in business, professions and property ownership. In 1872 she was arrested and jailed because she insisted on voting.

ANTHRACITE COAL STRIKE (1902). Bitter industrial-labor-conflict between the UNITED MINE WORKERS union, led by JOHN MITCHELL, and the anthracite mine owners. President THEODORE ROOSEVELT intervened in the strike and appointed a mediation commission which granted the miners a wage increase and improved working conditions, but did not provide for union recognition.

ANTIETAM, BATTLE OF (1862). One of the major military engagements of the WAR BETWEEN THE STATES. A Confederate army led by General Lee invaded Maryland and was met at Antietam by the Union forces under the command of General McClellan. This was one of the bloodiest battles of the war. Neither side could claim victory, but Lee was forced to retreat to Virginia.

ANTI-FEDERALIST PARTY. Those who opposed the ratification of the U. S. Constitution when it was presented to the states for adoption (1788-9) were called Anti-Federalists. This group included small farmers, city laborers, debtors and paper money advocates. After the Constitution was adopted and put into effect (1789) these Anti-Federalists became a political party whose principles included a strict interpretation of the Constitution, and strong state governments as opposed to a strong national government. Under the leadership of THOMAS JEFFERSON, the Anti-Federalists changed their name to DEMOCRATIC REPUBLICAN PARTY and later to REPUBLICAN PARTY. This is *not* the Republican Party that is in national politics today.

ANTI-MASON PARTY. Minor political party organized before the War Between the States (1861) to oppose the existence of secret societies such as the Order of Masons. The Anti-Mason Party held a national convention in 1831 and nominated a candidate for president. The Anti-Masons disappeared as a party soon after the ELECTION OF 1832 and most of their members joined the WHIG PARTY.

39

ANTI-MONOPOLY LEGISLATION. The growth of trusts and monopolies in the latter half of the 19th and in the 20th century led Congress to enact a series of laws aimed at maintaining competition in business. These included the SHERMAN ANTI-TRUST ACT (1890), the CLAYTON ANTI-TRUST ACT (1914), the FEDERAL TRADE COMMISSION ACT (1914), the ROBINSON-PATMAN ACT (1936) and others. The decisions of the U. S. Supreme Court in interpreting these laws have had an important effect on the growth of American industry. (See RULE OF REASON)

ANTI-RENT WAR. Also known as the "Helderberg War." In colonial times, Dutch patroons (see PATROON SYSTEM) and rich English landowners granted settlers tracts of land under perpetual leases. Although the settlers considered themselves owners of the land, they were required to pay a small annual rent to the heirs of the original grantors. Between 1839 and 1846 a series of disturbances developed in upper New York State when the small landowners refused to pay the back rent. The state militia was called out by Governor WILLIAM H. SEWARD and the violence was suppressed. Under the new state constitution adopted in 1846 perpetual leases were abolished in New York State.

ANTI-SALOON LEAGUE (1893). See PROHIBITION

ANTI-TRUST LEGISLATION. See ANTI-MONOPOLY LEGISLATION

APACHE INDIANS. See COCHISE and GERONIMO

APPOMATTOX COURTHOUSE. Place where General ROBERT E. LEE, the Confederate commander, surrendered to General ULYSSES S. GRANT, the Union Army leader, on April 9, 1865. The surrender brought the WAR BETWEEN THE STATES to an end. (See WILDERNESS CAMPAIGN)

ARAPAHO INDIANS. See PLAINS INDIANS

ARMISTICE. On November 11, 1918, the German armies ceased fighting in WORLD WAR I on terms dictated by

Marshal Foch, commander of the Allied forces in Europe. Armistice Day was celebrated in all Allied countries with wild enthusiasm. The armistice provided for Allied occupation of the German Rhineland, the surrender of most of Germany's military and naval equipment, the revocation of treaties signed by Russia and Rumania (whom Germany had defeated during the war), and the return of Allied war prisoners.

ARNOLD, BENEDICT (1741-1801). American commander during the AMERICAN REVOLUTION. He led an unsuccessful expedition to capture Quebec. In 1777 he helped defeat the British at the BATTLE OF SARATOGA. In 1780 he turned traitor and, together with Major JOHN ANDRÉ of the British Army, plotted to turn over the American fortification at West Point to the British. The plot was discovered, Major André was hanged as a spy, but Arnold escaped to England, where he remained until his death.

AROOSTOOK WAR. The TREATY OF PARIS (1783) ending the American Revolution did not clearly define the boundary between Canada and Maine. In 1838 a number of Canadians entered the disputed area called the Aroostook Valley. President Van Buren sent General Winfield Scott to the region and Congress appropriated money for a possible war. Both sides, however, agreed to have the boundary dispute settled by a commission. In 1842 the dispute was settled by the WEBSTER-ASHBURTON TREATY.

ARTHUR, CHESTER A. (1830-1886). Twenty-first president of the U. S. After the War Between the States (1865) President Grant appointed Arthur Collector of the Port of New York, but Arthur was removed by President Hayes. Arthur was a member of the STALWART wing of the REPUBLICAN PARTY. In 1880 the Republicans named Arthur for the vice-presidency in order to satisfy the Stalwart wing of the party. Arthur was elected, together with JAMES A. GARFIELD, the Republican candidate for the presidency. As vice-president, Arthur was involved in political party bickering over the distribution of federal patronage in New York State. After Garfield's assassination (1881) Arthur was elevated to the presidency and completed the term. As president, Arthur opposed many of the

41

proposals of the conservative wing of the Republican Party and thereby destroyed his chances of getting the presidential nomination in 1884.

During Arthur's term of office as president, Congress passed the CHINESE EXCLUSION ACT (1882), over the president's veto, and the PENDLETON ACT (1883), establishing the Civil Service.

ARTICLES OF CONFEDERATION. The document adopted by the SECOND CONTINENTAL CONGRESS and ratified by the thirteen states (1781). It outlined the form of central government under which the new nation was to be ruled. The Articles of Confederation remained in effect from 1781 to 1789, when they were superseded by the Constitution. The Articles provided for a Congress in which each state had one vote, a vote of nine states was needed to pass an important law, and a unanimous vote was needed to amend the Articles. Congress did not have the power to levy taxes, regulate interstate commerce or coin money. Under the Articles there was no single national executive or president and no Supreme Court or national system of law courts.

ASHWANDER V. T.V.A. (1936). U.S. Supreme Court decision upholding the constitutionality of the TENNESSEE VALLEY AUTHORITY ACT (1933). The court held that the construction of dams was a constitutional exercise of federal power over navigable rivers. The construction of power plants and electric transmission lines to use the power resulting from dam construction was also held to be a legitimate exercise of Congressional power.

ASSASSINATION, PRESIDENTIAL. Attempts to kill the president of the U. S. have occurred a number of times. In 1835 a demented person named Lawrence tried to shoot President ANDREW JACKSON but failed. In 1865 President ABRAHAM LINCOLN was shot and killed by JOHN WILKES BOOTH, a Southern sympathizer. President JAMES A. GARFIELD was shot and killed by Charles Guiteau, a disappointed job seeker, in 1881. President WILLIAM MC KINLEY was killed by an anarchist assassin named Leon Czolgosz, in 1901. Unsuccessful assassination attempts were made to kill President FRANKLIN

D. ROOSEVELT in 1933 and President HARRY S. TRUMAN in 1950.

ASSUMPTION ACT (1790). Passed by Congress as part of ALEXANDER HAMILTON'S Financial Plan during President GEORGE WASHINGTON'S first term in office. The act provided that the federal government was to pay the Revolutionary War debts owed by the separate states. Although the act met much opposition, it was passed when THOMAS JEFFERSON, Secretary of State at that time, gave his support to the bill in return for Hamilton's support for a bill establishing the permanent capital of the U. S. farther south along the Potomac River. (See WASHINGTON, D. C.)

ASTOR, JOHN JACOB (1763-1848). American merchant, fur trader, and financier. Astor engaged in the China shipping trade, invested in New York City real estate, and established fur trading posts along the Great Lakes and on the Columbia River in the OREGON TERRITORY. Astor's fur trading post at Astoria, Oregon (1811) was one of the bases on which the U. S. subsequently claimed the Oregon Territory.

ATAHUALPA. Ruler of the Inca Indians in Peru at the time of the Spanish conquest of Peru (1532). He tried but failed to get PIZARRO, the Spanish Conquistador, to leave Peru by offering gold and silver gifts. Atahualpa was captured and imprisoned by the Spaniards. He offered to fill a room full of gold as high as he could reach if Pizarro would free him. The huge ransom was paid, but Pizarro had Atahualpa strangled to death before the eyes of his own people (1533).

ATCHISON, TOPEKA AND SANTA FE RAILROAD. One of the major western railroad lines to the Pacific Ocean built after the War Between the States. Cyrus K. Holliday (1826-1900), promoter of the rail line, received a vast grant of public land from Congress (1863) to help in part to finance construction of the line. (See RAILROAD LAND GRANTS)

ATLANTA CAMPAIGN (1864). One of the last major campaigns of the WAR BETWEEN THE STATES (1861-65).

43

General WILLIAM T. SHERMAN, leading a Union Army, began a march from Chattanooga, Tennessee to Atlanta, Georgia. The city of Atlanta was practically destroyed by Union bombardment. From Atlanta the Union Army marched across Georgia to Savannah on the coast. Sherman's Army followed a "scorched earth" policy of destroying everything of value in its path. The destruction wrought by Sherman's Atlanta Campaign and "march to the sea" was a major disaster to the Southern Confederacy.

ATLANTIC, BATTLE OF THE (1941-45). During WORLD WAR II, submarine warfare conducted by Germany had as its objective the sinking of every merchant ship bringing supplies to the Allies in Europe. The Battle of the Atlantic between German submarines and Allied shipping began in 1941 before the U. S. entered the war and continued for the duration of the war. (See SUBMARINE WARFARE)

ATLANTIC CABLE. See FIELD, CYRUS W. and COOPER, PETER

ATLANTIC CHARTER (1941). A statement of principles for world peace prepared by President FRANKLIN D. ROOSEVELT and British Prime Minister Winston Churchill in August 1941. The Atlantic Charter consisted of eight principles, including no territorial aggression, respect for rights of all nationalities, the right of self-government for all people, economic advancement of all people, access of all nations to raw materials, freedom from fear and want, freedom of the seas, and the establishment of a system of international security based on disarmament.

ATOM BOMB. In 1939 Dr. Albert Einstein and other scientists suggested to President FRANKLIN D. ROOSEVELT the possibility of developing a powerful and destructive weapon based on the release of atomic energy. In 1942 work was begun on this highly secret "Manhattan Project." In July, 1945 the first atomic bomb was successfully exploded at Alamogordo, New Mexico, and three weeks later the first A Bomb was dropped on the Japanese city of HIROSHIMA in the last year of WORLD WAR II. Modern nuclear weapons are far more destructive than the original A Bomb.

44

ATOMIC ENERGY COMMISSION (1946). Federal agency established to regulate the development and use of atomic power both for war and peace. A commission of the same name, also established in 1946, was set up as an agency of the UNITED NATIONS. Its function is to recommend methods of controlling the use of nuclear weapons in wartime and encouraging the development of peacetime uses of atomic energy.

ATTUCKS, CRISPUS (1723-1770). One of the members of the Boston mob fired upon by British soldiers in 1770. This became known as the BOSTON MASSACRE. Attucks, a Negro, was one of the five Americans who was killed by the British fire.

AUSTIN, MOSES (1761-1821). Connecticut land promoter who, together with other men, received a huge grant of land in Texas from the Mexican government in return for an agreement to bring settlers to Texas. Moses Austin died before he could fulfill his contract but his son STEPHEN AUSTIN carried out his plans.

AUSTIN, STEPHEN (1793-1836). After the death of his father, MOSES AUSTIN, Stephen carried out the latter's plan and established a thriving settlement in Texas, with the approval of the Mexican government. When TEXAS gained its independence, Stephen Austin ran for the presidency of the Lone Star Republic but was defeated by SAM HOUSTON (1836).

AUTOMATION. Elimination of human labor through the use of automatic machinery in industrial processes. This has been made possible by the development of electronic brains, data processing machines, and other electronic equipment.

AZTECS. Indians of central Mexico who had established a highly developed civilization in the 14th and 15th centuries before the coming of the white man. The Aztecs knew how to weave textiles, dig canals, raise crops, maintain a calendar, use picture writing, and make gold and silver ornaments. In addition they knew something about astronomy and mathematics. However, a part of their religious ceremonies included the practice of human sacrifice. From 1519 to 1521 HERNANDO CORTEZ, the Spanish Conquistador, conquered and destroyed the Aztec kingdom, killed the last of the independent Aztec chiefs (MONTEZUMA) and made Mexico a part of the Spanish Empire in the New World.

"BACK TO NORMALCY" or **"RETURN TO NORMAL-CY."** See HARDING, WARREN G.

BACON'S REBELLION (1676). Revolt in the Virginia Colony led by Nathaniel Bacon, a planter. The rebels were mainly frontier planters who protested against the failure of the Virginia governor to provide them with adequate protection against the Indians. The rebellion collapsed when Bacon died of malaria (1676). This was the earliest revolt against British authority recorded in the American colonies.

BAILEY V. DREXEL FURNITURE CO (1922). See CHILD LABOR

BALBOA, VASCO NUNEZ DE (c.1475-c.1519). One of the great Spanish explorers who in 1513 crossed the jungles and swamps of Panama and reached the Pacific Ocean. He called the new ocean the "South Sea." His discovery demonstrated that the New World was a land barrier standing in the way of vessels seeking to reach the Far East by sailing west.

BALLINGER-PINCHOT CONTROVERSY (1910). Richard A. Ballinger, Secretary of Interior under President TAFT, refused to permit the withdrawal of certain valuable public lands from sale to private business interests. GIFFORD PINCHOT, chairman of the National Conservation Commission, accused Ballinger of obstructing the CONSERVATION MOVEMENT by favoring private business interests. When President Taft removed Pinchot from his government post, many Americans accused Taft and Ballinger of putting the profits of private industry above the interests of the nation.

BALTIMORE INCIDENT (1891). The U. S. detained a vessel carrying munitions from California to revolutionists in Chile. The incident caused hostility among Chileans and led to an attack on American sailors from the cruiser

Baltimore, on shore leave in Valparaiso, Chile. A number of American sailors were killed and wounded. The U. S. asked for and received an apology and payment of an indemnity.

BANKHEAD-JONES FARM TENANT ACT (1937). Established the Farm Security Administration (F.S.A.) with power to provide low-cost 40-year loans to tenant farmers, SHARE CROPPERS and farm workers who wished to purchase their own farms. (See FARM LEGISLATION)

BANK HOLIDAY (1933). The GREAT DEPRESSION which began with the stock market crash of 1929 reached its lowest point in March, 1933. Runs on banks by depositors forced more than 5,000 banks to close their doors. After FRANKLIN D. ROOSEVELT took office on March 4, 1933, one of his first emergency measures was to declare a four-day National Bank Holiday closing all banks in the country. On March 9, 1933, Congress passed an Emergency Banking Act (see BANKING LEGISLATION) authorizing the president to continue the bank holiday but to arrange for the reopening of those banks that were examined and found to be solvent. By April 1, most of the nation's banks were back to normal again.

BANKING ACT (June, 1933). Passed by Congress during the early months of the NEW DEAL, it is also known as the Second GLASS-STEAGALL Banking Act. This law established the Federal Deposit Insurance Corporation which was to insure bank deposits up to $5,000 (later raised to $10,000). The act also forbad the affiliation of banks with companies selling securities.

BANKING ACT (1935). Also known as the third GLASS-STEAGALL Banking Act. Under this act the FEDERAL DEPOSIT INSURANCE CORPORATION (F.D.I.C.), first established under the BANKING ACT of June, 1933, was made permanent. The Federal Reserve Board was reorganized and its name was changed to the Board of Governors of the Federal Reserve System. Broader powers for the control of credit were given to the Federal Reserve Banks and to the new Board of Governors. (See BANKING LEGISLATION)

BANKING LEGISLATION. HAMILTON'S FINANCIAL PLANS included the organization of the First BANK OF U. S. (1791). After the expiration of its 20-year charter, a Second BANK OF U. S. (1816) was authorized by Congress. President ANDREW JACKSON's opposition to the bank resulted in the nonrenewal of the bank charter, which expired in 1836. To replace the Bank of U. S., Congress established the INDEPENDENT TREASURY SYSTEM (1840). During the WAR BETWEEN THE STATES (1861-65) Congress passed the NATIONAL BANKING ACT (1863) providing for the establishment of private national banks with power to issue currency. This power was extended by the ALDRICH-VREELAND ACT (1908). The repeated financial PANICS resulting from an inflexible currency system and an uncoordinated banking system led Congress to enact the comprehensive FEDERAL RESERVE ACT (1913). During the GREAT DEPRESSION (1929-35) the many bank failures (see BANK HOLIDAY) and runs on banks resulted in the Congressional enactment of the EMERGENCY BANKING ACT (March, 1933), the BANKING ACT of June 1933, and the BANKING ACT of 1935.

BANK OF UNITED STATES, FIRST (1791). Chartered by Congress for a 20-year period as part of Alexander HAMILTON'S FINANCIAL PLANS. The U. S. government owned one-fifth of the bank stock. The bank was privately, not government, managed. It had power to issue paper banknotes redeemable in gold and silver. The charter of this bank expired in 1811 and was not renewed by Congress. (See BANK OF UNITED STATES, SECOND)

BANK OF UNITED STATES, SECOND (1816). Influenced by monetary confusion during and after the WAR OF 1812, Congress chartered a Second Bank of U. S. for a 20-year period. A bill to give a new charter to the bank was passed by Congress in 1832 but was vetoed by ANDREW JACKSON. In 1836 the Second Bank of U. S. came to an end.

BARBARY COAST. Name of the waterfront area of San Francisco during the GOLD RUSH days following 1849. The Barbary Coast attracted a motley crowd of disreputable people, including gamblers, adventurers, and gangsters. (See VIGILANTES)

BARBARY PIRATES. In the early 19th century the Moham-
medan rulers of the Barbary States of North Africa (including Morocco, Fez, Algiers, Tunis and Tripoli) were
hostile to all Christians. Consequently they made it their
policy to seize ships of Christian nations, including those
of the U. S., and holding the crews for ransom. In 1801
President JEFFERSON decided to end these annoying
piracies by sending a squadron of American ships to the
Mediterranean. War was not declared, but a number of
naval skirmishes occurred. In 1805 the ruler of Tripoli
signed a treaty guaranteeing the safety of American ships.
The rulers of other North African states did the same, after
a number of years.

BARBARY STATES. See BARBARY PIRATES

BARBED WIRE. Invented by Joseph F. Glidden and patented
in 1874. The widespread use of barbed-wire fences by landowners of the Great Plains in the last quarter of the 19th
century put an end to the open cattle ranges of the west.
Thereafter each landowner fenced in his own land and
owners of cattle herds could no longer have their cattle feed
anywhere that they found grass.

BARNBURNERS. Radical wing of the DEMOCRATIC
PARTY in New York State in the 1840's, as distinguished
from the conservative or HUNKER faction. The name
"Barnburner" was derived from the story of the farmer
who burned down his barn to get rid of the rats. The Barnburners, it was said, would end up destroying the Union
in order to get rid of slavery. In 1848 the Barnburners split
from the regular Democratic Party and joined the FREE
SOIL PARTY in nominating MARTIN VAN BUREN for
the presidency. (See ELECTION OF 1848)

BARRY, JOHN (1745-1803). Brilliant U. S. naval commander during the American Revolution. As captain of the
Lexington and the *Alliance* he won a number of notable
naval victories against British vessels. Barry ranks with
JOHN PAUL JONES as one of the great naval commanders
of the American Revolution.

BARTON, CLARA (1821-1912). Served as a nurse and superintendent of nurses in the War Between the States (1861-

65). In 1881 she founded the American Red Cross, of which she was president from 1882 to 1904. During this period, the Red Cross served in the Spanish-American War (1898), the Boer War in South Africa (1899-1902) and during the Galveston tidal wave disaster (1900).

BARUCH, BERNARD M. (1870-   ). American financier and adviser of presidents. During World War I he was chairman of the WAR INDUSTRIES BOARD (1918-19). During World War II he was special adviser to President Franklin D. Roosevelt and investigated many special problems such as methods of overcoming wartime rubber shortages. In 1946 he served as U. S. representative to the United Nations ATOMIC ENERGY COMMISSION and prepared a plan for the international control of atomic energy through a system of inspection.

BATAAN, BATTLE OF (1942). During WORLD WAR II (1941-45) the Japanese invaded the Philippine Island of Luzon (1941) and the outnumbered American garrison retreated to the Bataan Peninsula, where they continued to hold out for many weeks. However, they were forced to surrender finally (1942). The American commander, General DOUGLAS MAC ARTHUR, under military orders, escaped from Bataan before its surrender.

BATTLE OF . . . . Refer to name of battle.

BAYARD-CHAMBERLAIN TREATY (1887). To settle a dispute between the U. S. and Canada over fishing rights off the Newfoundland coast (1885) a joint British-U. S. commission met (1887) and drew up this treaty plus additional arrangements to settle the fishing dispute, and the problem of U. S.-Canadian trade. The U. S. Senate rejected the treaty, but the arrangements with respect to fishing rights and the use of Canadian ports by U. S. fishing boats were followed nonetheless until 1923. In that year they were abrogated by Canada to retaliate against the high U. S. FORDNEY-MC CUMBER TARIFF ACT.

BEAR REPUBLIC. See CALIFORNIA

BEAUREGARD, GENERAL PIERRE (1818-1893). Confederate general who ordered the firing on FORT SUMTER

51

(1861) which started the WAR BETWEEN THE STATES. During the war he fought in numerous battles and directed the Confederate campaign in Tennessee, South Carolina and Georgia.

BEECHER, HENRY WARD (1813-87). ABOLITIONIST leader and eloquent Brooklyn preacher and orator. He was the brother of HARRIET BEECHER STOWE who wrote *Uncle Tom's Cabin.* Beecher made the Plymouth Church in Brooklyn nationally famous by his denunciations of slavery from the pulpit. During the Civil War in Kansas (see BLEEDING KANSAS), Beecher helped equip with rifles (see BEECHER'S BIBLES) the Free Soil emigrants moving into Kansas.

BEECHER'S BIBLES. During the Civil War in Kansas (1856) (See BLEEDING KANSAS), HENRY WARD BEECHER, a Northern abolitionist preacher, raised subscriptions to equip with rifles Free Soil emigrants moving to Kansas. Such rifles he said, would be a more convincing argument to pro-slavery men than the Bible. When the rifles reached Kansas they were nicknamed "Beecher's Bibles."

BEHAIM, MARTIN (c.1459-c.1506). German geographer who developed an improved astrolabe and prepared a globe of the earth, both of which were widely used by navigators and explorers of the 15th and 16th centuries. However his globe, completed in 1492, was quite inaccurate even for his own day.

BELKNAP SCANDAL (1876). Secretary of War Belknap, in President ULYSSES S. GRANT's administration, was accused of accepting bribes from employees in the government Indian service. He was impeached by the House of Representatives but resigned before his case came before the Senate.

BELL ACT (1939). Provided that the U.S. would not levy any tariffs on Philippine goods shipped to the U. S. for eight years after the Philippine Islands obtained their independence under the TYDINGS-MC DUFFIE ACT (1934). Thereafter the tariff rates would be raised gradually over a 20-year period.

BELL, ALEXANDER GRAHAM (1847-1922). Inventor of the telephone. After years of experimenting with the transmission of sound through wires, he perfected the first practical telephone. It was exhibited at the Philadelphia Centennial Exposition (1876) and aroused world-wide interest.

BELL, JOHN. See CONSTITUTIONAL UNION PARTY and ELECTION OF 1860

BELLEAU WOOD, BATTLE OF (1918). One of the battles of WORLD WAR I, fought in France, in which American troops won a notable victory over the Germans.

BENNETT, JAMES GORDON (1795-1872). Nineteenth century newspaper publisher and editor. He started the New York *Herald* in 1835 and made it nationally famous through its wide news coverage and sensationalism in reporting. It continued to be an important newspaper long after his death, but in 1924 was merged to form the New York *Herald-Tribune*.

BENNINGTON, BATTLE OF (1777). Important military engagement during the AMERICAN REVOLUTION. A small force of British soldiers was detached from General Burgoyne's main force in New York to gather supplies in Vermont. At Bennington this small force was met by colonial militia and defeated with heavy losses.

BENTON, THOMAS H. (1782-1858). Missouri newspaper owner and political leader before the War Between the States. He was the first senator elected from Missouri and served for 30 years (1821-51). Benton vigorously supported President JACKSON in opposing recharter of the Second BANK OF U. S. He drew up the SPECIE CIRCULAR (1836) which Jackson announced. Benton's Congressional program aimed mainly at the expansion and development of the west. He supported many of JOHN C. FREMONT'S western expeditions and became Fremont's father-in-law. Benton was defeated for a sixth senatorial term (1851) because of his opposition to the slavery provisions of the COMPROMISE OF 1850.

BERING SEA DISPUTE (1893). Indiscriminate slaughter of seals near the Pribilof Islands by unlicensed hunters threat-

53

ened to exterminate the herds. The U. S. seized a number of Canadian fishing vessels that were hunting seals in the open sea. Great Britain protested. In 1893 the dispute was settled by arbitration and regulations were drawn up to protect the seal herds from indiscriminate killing.

BERKELEY, LORD JOHN (1602-78). English nobleman who, together with Sir George Carteret, received all land between the Hudson and Delaware Rivers as a gift from the Duke of York. Berkeley and Carteret took over the small Dutch settlement in the region and established the NEW JERSEY COLONY.

BERLIN AIRLIFT. See BERLIN BLOCKADE

BERLIN AND MILAN DECREES (1806-07). Issued by Napoleon I of France during his wars with Great Britain. These and other similar decrees provided that neutral ships which traded with Great Britain or permitted the British to stop and search them would no longer be considered neutral and would be subject to seizure by the French. (See PAPER BLOCKADE) However, few American ships were seized by the French because of Great Britain's superior naval power.

BERLIN BLOCKADE (1948-49). Resulted from a dispute between the U. S. and the Soviet Union over the administration of the city of Berlin. (See POTSDAM AGREEMENT) In 1948, Soviet Russia established a blockade of all road, rail, and water routes to Berlin through Soviet-controlled East Germany. The U. S. organized an air transport system which successfully supplied the Allied sections of Berlin. The Soviet Union lifted the blockade in May, 1949.

BESSEMER PROCESS. New method of manufacturing steel developed by William Kelly, an American, in 1851 and by Henry Bessemer, an Englishman, in 1856. Each man developed the process independently of the other. In 1866 the rival claims were adjusted.

BIBLE COMMONWEALTH. Name given to the MASSACHUSETTS BAY COLONY because its political and social life was dominated for many years by the clergy. Such Puritan clergymen as John Cotton, COTTON MATHER,

Increase Mather and Jonathan Edwards exerted a profound influence on colonial thought and action.

BIDDLE, NICHOLAS (1786-1844). Early American financier. In 1816 President Monroe appointed Biddle president of the Second BANK OF U. S. Because of his conservative money policies, Biddle made many enemies, including ANDREW JACKSON and a number of western congressmen. The Second Bank of U. S. continued in existence until 1836, when its charter expired. (See ELECTION OF 1832)

BIDWELL, JOHN. See PROHIBITION PARTY

BIG FIVE. The five great powers at the PARIS PEACE CONFERENCE (1919) at the end of World War I. They included the U. S., Great Britain, France, Italy and Japan. During World War II (1941-45) the "Big Five" referred to the U. S., Great Britain, France, the Soviet Union and Nationalist China, who were allied in the war against the Axis powers. After World War II the "Big Five" referred to the same group of nations, who were given permanent seats on the SECURITY COUNCIL of the UNITED NATIONS.

BIG FOUR. See PARIS PEACE CONFERENCE (1919)

BIG STICK POLICY. During a boundary dispute between the U. S. and Great Britain over the ALASKA BOUNDARY (1903) President THEODORE ROOSEVELT said he favored the proverb: "Speak softly and carry a big stick." Roosevelt subsequently used this "big stick" policy in connection with the VENEZUELA DEBT DISPUTE (1909) that resulted in the development of the ROOSEVELT COROLLARY.

BIG THREE. The three great powers and their representatives at the PARIS PEACE CONFERENCE (1919) at the end of World War I. The three powers were the U. S., represented by WOODROW WILSON; Great Britain, represented by Lloyd George; and France, represented by Georges Clemenceau. During World War II (1941-45) the "big three" referred to President FRANKLIN D. ROOSEVELT, Winston Churchill, and Josef Stalin, who met frequently during the war to plan strategy. (See YALTA CONFERENCE)

BILL OF RIGHTS, AMERICAN. The first ten amendments to the U. S. Constitution. They were ratified in 1791 to meet the objections of a number of states that the Constitution contained no guarantee of individual liberties and no protection against the powers of the federal government. These amendments listed rights which could not be infringed or denied by Congress or the federal government, such as freedom of speech, press, assembly and religion, the right to a jury trial, and many others.

"BILLY THE KID." See BONNEY, WILLIAM H.

BIMETALLISM. National policy of having currency backed by two metals—gold and silver—instead of by one alone (monometallism). The U. S. followed a bimetallic standard until the DEMONETIZATION ACT (1873) eliminated silver as backing for our currency. The demands of silver mine owners and cheap money advocates for the restoration of bimetallism resulted in the passage of the BLAND-ALLISON ACT (1878) and the SHERMAN SILVER PURCHASE ACT (1890). These acts established limited bimetallism until the PANIC OF 1893 led to a drain of gold from the U. S. Treasury and forced the repeal of the Sherman Silver Purchase Act (1893). The ELECTION OF 1896 was fought mainly on the issue of bimetallism. In 1900 the GOLD STANDARD ACT reestablished monometallism.

BIRNEY, JAMES (1792-1857). Former slaveholder turned ABOLITIONIST, who was outspoken in his appeals for the ending of slavery. He was nominated for the presidency by the LIBERTY PARTY in 1840 and 1844 but received a very small vote.

BLACK CODES. Southern state laws passed during the RECONSTRUCTION ERA (1865-1877) limiting the civil rights of the newly emancipated Negro. For example, these codes provided for the imprisonment of Negroes for vagrancy. The Negro was then farmed out to work—sometimes for his former master.

BLACK FRIDAY (1869). The day a serious stock market panic occurred in New York City, on September 24th, when two financiers, JAY GOULD and JAMES FISK, JR. attempted to "corner" the gold market. Many business firms were forced into bankruptcy by the market manipulations of Gould and Fisk.

BLACK HAWK WAR (1830-1832). After the War of 1812 the U. S. decided to move the Sac and Fox Indians out of Illinois to lands across the Mississippi River. Black Hawk, leader of the Indians, resisted, and most of his tribe were wiped out in the ensuing fighting. ABRAHAM LINCOLN, who was then living in Illinois, served as a captain of volunteers in the Black Hawk War.

"BLACK PRINCE." Famous PRIVATEER commissioned by the U. S. government during the AMERICAN REVOLUTION (1775-83). The *Black Prince* captured more than 30 British ships in less than a year.

BLACK REPUBLICAN. Name applied by Southerners to ABRAHAM LINCOLN, Republican candidate for president in the ELECTION OF 1860, because he opposed further extension of slavery in western territories. During the RECONSTRUCTION ERA, Southerners used the label to refer to Republicans who favored pro-Negro legislation in Congress and in the states.

BLACK TOM EXPLOSION (1916). Explosion at a U. S. munitions depot on Black Tom Island, New Jersey. The explosion occurred one year before the U. S. declaration of war on Germany (1917) and was attributed to German saboteurs.

"BLACK WARRIOR" INCIDENT (1854). The *Black Warrior* was a U.S. merchant ship seized by Spanish authorities in Cuba on a minor pretext. Southern EXPANSIONISTS in the U. S. urged a declaration of war against Spain. However, in 1855 the U. S. accepted Spain's apology and a payment of reparations.

BLAINE, JAMES G. (1830-93). Statesman and political leader, nicknamed the "Plumed Knight" because of his popularity. While Speaker of the House of Representatives (1869-75)

57

he was involved in a political scandal. (See MULLIGAN LETTERS) In the ELECTION OF 1884 he was the Republican Party nominee for president but was defeated by Cleveland in a close election. (See RUM, ROMANISM AND REBELLION) As Secretary of State (1889-92) under President Harrison he was one of the leaders who sponsored the first PAN-AMERICAN CONFERENCE (1889). During the BALTIMORE INCIDENT (1891) he obtained an apology and an indemnity payment from Chile. In 1893 he successfully compromised the BERING SEA DISPUTE with Great Britain.

BLAND-ALLISON ACT (1878). Provided that the U. S. Treasury would buy from $2,000,000 to $4,000,000 of silver each month in the open market. The silver was to be coined into dollars or paper silver certificates were to be issued and used as legal tender. The law was passed over President RUTHERFORD B. HAYES' veto. It remained in force until 1890, when it was superseded by the SHERMAN SILVER PURCHASE ACT of 1890. (See BIMETALLISM and DEMONETIZATION ACT)

BLEEDING KANSAS (1854-60). Civil War in Kansas Territory between pro-slavery and anti-slavery settlers. Under the KANSAS-NEBRASKA ACT (1854) the question of slavery in Kansas was to be determined by POPULAR SOVEREIGNTY, or the vote of the settlers themselves. However, the pro- and anti-slavery settlers set up rival constitutions. Violence and murder broke out between the two groups and more than 200 people were killed before U. S. troops restored order. (See JOHN BROWN, POTTAWATOMIE MASSACRE, BORDER RUFFIANS) Kansas was finally admitted into the Union as a free state in 1861, the year the War Between the States began.

BLOCKADE, SOUTHERN. During the WAR BETWEEN THE STATES (1861-65) the entire Southern and Gulf coasts from Virginia to Texas were blockaded by the North. The blockade became tighter as the war progressed. The failure of the South to get foreign supplies or to export its cotton was part of the reason for the downfall of the CONFEDERATE STATES.

BLOOMER, AMELIA JENKS (1818-94). Women's rights advocate and social reformer. She wrote and spoke eloquently on woman suffrage, temperance and the social rights of women. She designed and wore special trousers for women which were popularly called "bloomers."

BLUE EAGLE. See NATIONAL INDUSTRIAL RECOVERY ACT (NIRA)

BOARD OF EDUCATION V. BARNETTE. See FLAG SALUTE CASES.

BOLIVAR, SIMON (1783-1830). Known as the "George Washington" of South America because of his efforts to gain independence for the people of Latin America. He was the outstanding leader in the revolt of the South American colonies against Spanish rule (1822-29). He became president of Colombia, created Bolivia as an independent nation, and organized the government of Peru.

BOLTING ACT (1678). British colonial law granting New York City a monopoly of the flour export trade.

"BONHOMME RICHARD" AND "SERAPIS." See JONES, JOHN PAUL

BONNEY, WILLIAM H. (1859-81). Better known as "Billy the Kid." At an early age he became involved in violence, cattle rustling and murder. To many he became a symbol of the "lawless" west. At the age of 22 he was killed in a gun battle.

BONUS ARMY (1932). During the GREAT DEPRESSION, more than 10,000 veterans of World War I converged on Washington D.C. to demand immediate cash payment of their soldiers' bonus. (See BONUS BILL of 1924) The government was compelled to use armed force to get the Bonus Army out of the capital.

BONUS BILL (1817). JOHN C. CALHOUN proposed using federal money to pay for the construction of internal improvements such as new roads and canals. President JAMES MADISON vetoed the bill because he believed the federal

59

government did not have the constitutional power to build these projects.

BONUS BILL (1924). Passed over President COOLIDGE'S veto, the act granted veterans of World War I 20-year adjusted service certificates (similar to insurance policies), whose average value was over $1,000. In 1932 a BONUS ARMY staged a huge rally in Washington D.C. to get immediate payment of the certificates. The bill to pay the bonus immediately was defeated in the Senate. In 1936 Congress finally provided for payment of the bonus certificates in bonds of small denominations and in cash.

BOOMERS. Name applied to new settlers in Western territories who staked out homesteads on government land. The name refers to the land "boom" that accompanied the rush of settlers to newly opened land.

BOONE, DANIEL (1734-1820). Early American frontiersman, trapper, and pioneer. In 1767 he led a party of settlers through the CUMBERLAND GAP of the Appalachian Mountains into Kentucky. In 1775 he brought another party of settlers who established a fort at Boonesborough, Kentucky. Because of defects in his Kentucky land titles, Boone lost most of his land holdings there. By this time (1798) Kentucky had become too populated for Boone's frontier tastes and he moved to Missouri.

BOOTH, JOHN WILKES (1838-1865). Well-known actor of the mid-19th century and a fanatical Southern sympathizer. During the presentation of a play at Ford's Theatre in Washington D.C., Booth entered the presidential box and shot LINCOLN (April 14, 1865). After the assassination, Booth jumped to the stage and escaped in spite of a broken leg. Two weeks later he was discovered in a barn near Bowling Green, Virginia. He either shot himself or was shot by one of his pursuers.

BORAH, WILLIAM E. (1865-1940). Republican senator from Idaho from 1907 until his death in 1940. After World War I, Borah was one of the leading opponents of ratification of the VERSAILLES TREATY (1919). He was a leading spokesman for the policy of ISOLATION and opposed U. S. participation in the LEAGUE OF NATIONS or

WORLD COURT. However, he supported U. S. participation in the WASHINGTON DISARMAMENT CONFERENCE (1921-22) and the KELLOGG-BRIAND PACT (1928). In domestic affairs, Borah favored enforcement of the anti-trust laws but opposed most of the NEW DEAL legislative program.

BORDER RUFFIANS. Thugs who at different times during the Civil War in Kansas (see BLEEDING KANSAS, 1854-1856), entered the state from Missouri to vote fraudulently, intimidate Free Soil men by the use of violence, loot and burn the homes of Free Soil leaders. The intervention of federal troops finally halted the lawlessness.

BORDER STATES. Eight states that did not secede from the Union when President LINCOLN was sworn in on March 4, 1861. Of these eight states, Arkansas, Tennessee, North Carolina and Virginia seceded soon after the firing on FORT SUMTER (April 6, 1861). However Missouri, Kentucky, Maryland and Delaware did not secede during the WAR BETWEEN THE STATES (1861-65).

BOSTON MASSACRE (1770). Street incident in Boston before the AMERICAN REVOLUTION (1775-83) during which a squad of British soldiers fired on a heckling crowd of colonists, killing five and wounding a number of others. The funerals of the victims were made the occasion for anti-British demonstrations. The soldiers involved were tried for murder in Boston but were acquitted.

BOSTON POLICE STRIKE (1919). Strike of policemen in Boston which left the city without police protection. The governor of Massachusetts (CALVIN COOLIDGE) called out the state militia to maintain order in the city. Governor Coolidge gained nationwide attention by his stated policy that "there is no right to strike against the public safety by anybody, anywhere, any time."

BOSTON PORT BILL (1774). One of the INTOLERABLE ACTS passed by the British Parliament to punish the colonies for the BOSTON TEA PARTY. The Boston Port Bill provided for the closing of the port of Boston until the destroyed tea was paid for and defiance of British tax laws ended.

61

BOSTON TEA PARTY (1773). A band of colonists disguised as Indians climbed aboard British merchant ships anchored in Boston harbor and dumped their cargo of tea into the bay. The event was designed as a protest against the British tax on tea. The British Parliament retaliated by passing the INTOLERABLE ACTS (1774).

BOUND LABOR. See INDENTURED SERVANTS

BOUNTY. In colonial times, Great Britain gave bounties (payments) to growers of indigo and producers of naval stores in order to encourage export of these articles to England. During the AMERICAN REVOLUTION (1775-83), Congress granted bounties of Western land to those who volunteered to serve in the CONTINENTAL ARMY for the duration of the war. During the WAR BETWEEN THE STATES (1861-65) both the North and the South paid bounties to volunteers for enlisting in the army. (See BOUNTY JUMPERS) The MC KINLEY TARIFF ACT of 1890 provided for a government bounty of 2¢ per pound to American sugar growers to encourage native sugar production.

BOUNTY JUMPERS. During the WAR BETWEEN THE STATES (1861-65) compulsory military service (Conscription Law, 1863) could be avoided by paying $300 or buying a substitute to replace the draftee. The payments to these substitutes were called BOUNTIES. Many states also paid bounties for volunteer enlistments. If a substitute collected the bounty and then deserted, he was known as a "bounty jumper." Some men enlisted and deserted as many as 20 or 30 times before being caught.

BOXER REBELLION (1900). Started by a group of Chinese Nationalists called the "Fists of Righteous Harmony," or "Boxers," who resented foreign exploitation of their country. They began to attack all foreigners living in and around Peking (now Peiping). An international military force, including U. S. troops, came to their rescue. Through the efforts of JOHN HAY, U. S. Secretary of State, the great powers agreed to accept an indemnity from China for losses and damages. Later the U. S. cancelled its share of the payment and China used the money for scholarships to educate Chinese students in the U. S. and in China.

BOYD, BELLE (1843-1900). Confederate woman spy during the WAR BETWEEN THE STATES (1861-65). She was captured and imprisoned during the war but escaped to England.

BOZEMAN TRAIL. Ill-defined wagon trail of the late 19th century that led through Wyoming to Virginia City, Montana. This was a region where the SIOUX INDIANS and the advancing white settlers frequently clashed in bloody conflict.

BRADDOCK, GENERAL EDWARD (1695-1755). English general who, during the FRENCH AND INDIAN WAR, attempted to capture the French stronghold at FORT DUQUESNE. Young GEORGE WASHINGTON was also a member of this expedition. Braddock's forces were almost entirely destroyed (1755) by a surprise attack of the French and their Indian allies. Braddock was killed and Washington returned to Virginia with the remnants of the expedition.

BRADFORD, WILLIAM (1590-1657). One of the PILGRIM leaders who came to the New World on the MAYFLOWER (1620). He was chosen governor of PLYMOUTH COLONY and served with few interruptions for almost 30 years.

BRAGG, GENERAL BRAXTON (1817-76). See CHICKAMAUGA, BATTLE OF

BRAIN TRUST. Advisers of President FRANKLIN D. ROOSEVELT during his first term (1933-37). The Brain Trust suggested policies and planned NEW DEAL legislation. Among the most influential members were Raymond Moley, Rexford Tugwell, Adolph A. Berle and Felix Frankfurter.

BRANDEIS, LOUIS D. (1856-1941). Associate Justice of the U. S. Supreme Court (1916-39). He began his career as an attorney and developed the system of low cost savings bank life insurance in Massachusetts (1907). Over considerable protest, President WOODROW WILSON appointed him to the Supreme Court bench. He wrote

63

frequent dissenting opinions in support of state labor and welfare laws.

BRANDYWINE, BATTLE OF (1777). One of the major military engagements of the AMERICAN REVOLUTION (1775-83). General GEORGE WASHINGTON and his forces attempted to halt the British commander, General Howe, and his army from advancing on Philadelphia. The Americans were defeated and forced to retreat while General Sir William Howe took Philadelphia with little difficulty.

BREAD COLONIES. Middle Colonies (New York, New Jersey, Pennsylvania) that produced enough wheat, corn and foodstuffs so they could export their surplus.

BRICKER AMENDMENT (1954). A proposed Constitutional amendment providing that no provision of a treaty or other international agreement which conflicts with the Constitution shall be binding on the U. S. It was aimed at protecting the U. S. against any decisions of the UNITED NATIONS. The amendment failed to pass Congress.

BRIDGER, JAMES ("JIM") 1804-81. Fur trapper, fur trader and guide. He explored the Spanish southwest, and discovered Great Salt Lake in Utah. He and his partner, Louis Vasquez, established Fort Bridger (1843) on the OREGON TRAIL. He also served as guide to Oregon settlers, to railroad companies and to the U. S. Army.

BROOK FARM. Experimental cooperative community started in 1841 by critic George Ripley and a number of other literary people, including Nathaniel Hawthorne. The aim of the community was to establish an economically self-sufficient group. After a disastrous fire, the community disbanded in 1846.

BROWN, JOHN (1800-1859). Fanatical ABOLITIONIST leader who in 1865 led a band of his followers in the murder of five pro-slavery settlers in Kansas territory. (See POTTAWATOMIE MASSACRE) In 1859 John Brown and his followers seized the U. S. arsenal at Harper's Ferry,

Virginia (see JOHN BROWN'S RAID) in an effort to arm the slaves and thus start a Southern slave rebellion. Brown was quickly captured by a company of U. S. Marines led by ROBERT E. LEE. He was tried as a traitor and hanged.

BROWN V. BOARD OF EDUCATION (1954). See SEGRE-GATION

BRYAN-CHAMORRO TREATY (1914). See NICARAGU-AN CANAL

BRYAN, WILLIAM JENNINGS (1860-1925). Political leader and western spokesman for "free silver." (See BIMETAL-LISM) He was nominated for the Presidency by the DEMOCRATIC and POPULIST PARTIES in the ELEC-TION OF 1896 on a 16-to-1 free silver coinage platform. His "CROSS OF GOLD" SPEECH at the Democratic convention made him nationally famous. However, he lost the election, was renominated by the Democrats again in 1900 and 1908 but was defeated each time. In 1925 he served as attorney in the famous SCOPES TRIAL opposing the teaching of evolution in public schools.

BUCHANAN, JAMES (1791-1868). Fifteenth President of the U. S. In 1856 he was nominated for the Presidency by the DEMOCRATIC PARTY and in a closely contested election (see ELECTION OF 1856) defeated JOHN C. FREMONT, candidate of the newly organized REPUB-LICAN PARTY.

During BUCHANAN's single term (1857-61), Chief Justice ROGER TANEY of the Supreme Court handed down the famous DRED SCOTT DECISION (1857), JOHN BROWN made his famous raid at Harper's Ferry and South Carolina seceded from the Union (ORDI-NANCE OF SECESSION, 1860).

BUDGET AND ACCOUNTING ACT (1921). Established a Bureau of the Budget whose function it is to draw up an estimate of national revenues and expenditures for the coming year. The budget is then submitted by the president to Congress at each regular session.

65

BUENA VISTA, BATTLE OF (1847). Military victory of American forces in northern Mexico during the MEXI-CAN WAR (1846-48). The American army, under General ZACHARY TAYLOR, attacked by a larger Mexican force led by General Santa Anna, nevertheless won a brilliant victory.

BUFFALO BILL. See CODY, WILLIAM F.

BULGE, BATTLE OF THE (1944). One of the last major German counterattacks on the Western Front during WORLD WAR II (1939-45). German forces under General Karl von Rundstedt broke through the line of British and American troops in Belgium and advanced more than 50 miles before being stopped. In the next few weeks the Germans were forced to retreat.

BULL MOOSE PARTY. Another name for the PROGRES-SIVE PARTY organized by THEODORE ROOSEVELT during the presidential election campaign in 1912. It de-rived the name "Bull Moose" from a statement made by Roosevelt about the state of his health. He replied that he felt as strong as a "bull moose."

BULL RUN, BATTLE OF. Also known as the Battle of Manassas. Two battles were fought at Bull Run, Virginia during the WAR BETWEEN THE STATES (1861-65). In the first battle (1861) the Northern army led by General McDowell was completely routed by the Southern forces led by General BEAUREGARD and General JOSEPH E. JOHNSTON. In the second battle of Bull Run (1862) the Union Army led by General Pope was again defeated by the brilliant tactics of General ROBERT E. LEE and THOMAS F. "Stonewall" JACKSON, leaders of the Confederate forces.

BUNCHE, DR. RALPH (1904-   ). U. S. State Department official. He became director of the Trusteeship Division of the United Nations in 1946 and served as U.N. media-tor in the Arab-Israeli War (1947-48). After long nego-tiations he succeeded in having both sides agree to an armistice. For this achievement he received the NOBEL PEACE PRIZE in 1950.

BUNKER HILL, BATTLE OF (1775). One of the early military engagements of the AMERICAN REVOLUTION (1775-83) fought near Boston. The battle was actually fought on a nearby hill called Breed's Hill. The British attempted to dislodge colonial troops entrenched on the hill. After three British charges, during which the British suffered heavy losses, the colonists were forced to retire from the hill for lack of ammunition.

BUNTLINE, NED (1823-86). Pen name of Edward Z. C. Judson, western fur trapper, adventurer and founder of the KNOW-NOTHING PARTY. He met WILLIAM F. CODY, coined the nickname of "Buffalo Bill," and wrote scores of books about the imaginary and real adventures of Buffalo Bill. Judson is credited with originating the type of western adventure story called the "dime novel," of which he wrote more than 400 titles.

BURGOYNE, GENERAL JOHN (1722-92). See SARATOGA, BATTLE OF; TICONDEROGA, FORT and AMERICAN REVOLUTION

BURKE-WADSWORTH ACT (1940). See CONSCRIPTION

BURLINGAME TREATY (1868). Signed by the U. S. and China. Under this treaty, Chinese were permitted to live and travel in the U. S. and American citizens were given special privileges in China. As a result of the signing of this treaty, thousands of Chinese came to the U. S. Many of them worked as laborers on the construction of transcontinental railroads, and as farmers in California.

BURNSIDE, GENERAL AMBROSE E. (1824-81). Union army commander during the WAR BETWEEN THE STATES (1861-65). Burnside commanded the Northern army at the BATTLE OF FREDERICKSBURG (1862) where the Union forces suffered a serious defeat and were forced to retreat.

BURR, AARON (1756-1836). Early New York political leader. The Republican Party victory in the ELECTION OF 1800 resulted in the choice of Jefferson and Burr by the Electoral College. Because of a tie vote in the Electoral College, the choice of president fell to the House of Repre-

sentatives, where the influence of ALEXANDER HAMIL-
TON resulted in Jefferson's becoming president. Thus Burr
became vice-president in 1801. After he was defeated for
the governorship of New York in 1804, a bitter political
feud developed between Burr and Hamilton. Burr challenged
Hamilton to a duel, in which Hamilton was killed. Burr
then became involved in a plan to establish a settlement
in the west (1806). It was rumored, however, that he
planned to establish an independent "Empire of the West"
either by having Western states secede from the Union or by
seizing Spanish territory in Louisiana and Mexico. Burr was
arrested, tried for treason before Chief Justice JOHN
MARSHALL and acquitted.

BUTLER, GENERAL BENJAMIN F. (1818-93). Union general in the WAR BETWEEN THE STATES (1861-65)
and military governor of New Orleans after its capture by
Union forces in 1862. After the war he was elected to
Congress, where he was one of the Radical Republican
leaders that forced the IMPEACHMENT OF JOHNSON,
the president, and enacted a harsh RECONSTRUCTION
program for the defeated South. After 1877 Butler was a
leading figure in the Greenback Movement, and was nominated for the presidency by the GREENBACK PARTY
(1884).

BUTTERNUTS. See COPPERHEADS

CABLE ACT (1922). Prior to the enactment of this law, an alien woman who married a U. S. citizen automatically became a citizen herself. Under the Cable Act, an alien woman married to a U. S. citizen remains an alien until she becomes a naturalized citizen. Similarly, a woman who is an American citizen does not lose her citizenship if she marries an alien.

CABOT, JOHN (1450-98). Italian navigator in the service of King Henry VII of England. In 1497 Cabot crossed the Atlantic Ocean, explored the coast of Labrador and claimed the land for England. In 1498 he commanded another expedition, from which he never returned.

CABRAL, PEDRO (c.1460-c.1526). Portuguese navigator who, in 1500, explored the west coast of Africa. Strong winds and ocean currents drove his ships across the Atlantic Ocean to the east coast of South America. He landed in the area now known as Brazil, and claimed the land for Portugal.

CAIRO CONFERENCE (1943). Held during WORLD WAR II (1941-45) in Cairo, Egypt. Franklin D. Roosevelt of the U. S., Winston Churchill of Great Britain and Chiang Kai-shek of China agreed on military plans to defeat Japan and the terms under which Japan's surrender would be accepted.

CALAMITY JANE (c.1852-1903). Nickname of Martha Jane Burke, who spent much of her life in the frontier mining town of Deadwood, South Dakota. She wore male attire and was a good marksman and a skilled horsewoman. Her skill with a gun led to her nickname of "Calamity Jane."

CALHOUN, JOHN C. (1782-1850). One of the brilliant defenders of the COMPACT THEORY of the Constitution and the Southern STATES RIGHTS DOCTRINE. During his early Congressional career he was leader of the

69

WAR HAWKS who favored war with England in 1812. He was twice elected vice-president (1824 and 1828). While serving as vice-president he wrote the famous South Carolina EXPOSITION AND PROTEST (1828) attacking the protective tariff of 1828 (TARIFF OF ABOMINATIONS) and stating the classic thesis of states rights and NULLIFICATION. He resigned as vice-president in 1832 because of differences with President Jackson and was elected senator from South Carolina for three terms. In his last Senatorial speech, which had to be read for him because of his illness, he criticized but accepted the COMPROMISE OF 1850 as the best possible solution at the time to the slavery problem. (See SLAVERY LEGISLATION)

CALIFORNIA. Originally part of Spanish territory in the New World, it was first explored by Juan Rodriguez Cabrillo (1542) and by SIR FRANCIS DRAKE (1579). It was part of the independent republic of Mexico until 1846, when Americans in California under JOHN C. FREMONT set up an independent nation called the Bear Republic. As a result of the MEXICAN WAR (1846-48) California became part of U. S. territory. The discovery of gold in 1848 led to the GOLD RUSH of 1849. California was admitted to the Union as a free state under the provisions of the COMPROMISE OF 1850.

CALVERT, GEORGE (c.1580-1632). Also called Lord Baltimore. In 1632 he was granted a charter by King Charles I of England to establish a colony in the region of the present state of Maryland. Calvert's aim was to establish a haven in the New World for persecuted Catholics, but he died in the same year that he received the charter. The colony was established by his son, Cecilius Calvert, in 1634 on the shores of Chesapeake Bay.

CAMBRIDGE AGREEMENT (1629). Document drawn up in England by 12 Puritans who were members of the MASSACHUSETTS BAY COMPANY. With this document they agreed to settle in the New World with their families if the charter of the company could be transferred to New England. On the basis of this agreement the MASSACHUSETTS BAY COLONY was established in 1630.

CAMDEN, BATTLE OF (1780). General GATES, commander of the CONTINENTAL ARMY in the southern colonies during the AMERICAN REVOLUTION (1775-83) attacked the British supply base at Camden, South Carolina. The forces of General Cornwallis, the British commander, forced the colonial   y to retreat with heavy losses.

CAMERON, SIMON (1799-1889). One of the leading figures in the REPUBLICAN PARTY after the WAR BETWEEN THE STATES (1861-65), and recognized as the Republican PARTY BOSS of Pennsylvania. He served in President ABRAHAM LINCOLN's war cabinet as Secretary of War and was involved in the negotiation of corrupt army supply contracts.

CANADA. During the WAR OF 1812, the U. S. attempted to invade Canada and the British tried to invade the U. S. from Canada. Soon after the end of the war relations between the U. S. and Canada began to improve. Treaties were signed fixing the boundary between the two countries (see TREATY OF 1818, WEBSTER-ASHBURTON TREATY, 1842; OREGON TREATY, 1846) and providing for an unfortified boundary (RUSH-BAGOT AGREEMENT, 1817). Today there are practically no restrictions on immigration between the two countries. By joint agreement (1954) both countries cooperated in the construction of the St. Lawrence Seaway, which was opened to traffic in 1959. (See WILEY-DONDERO ACT)

CANAL TOLLS CONTROVERSY. By the HAY-PAUNCE-FOTE TREATY (1901) between the U. S. and Great Britain, the U. S. had agreed to permit all nations to use the proposed Panama Canal on an equal basis. In 1912 Congress passed the Tolls Exemption Act, excusing U. S. coastwise shipping from paying tolls when going through the canal. After Great Britain protested, Congress repealed the law.

CANAL ZONE. See HAY BUNAU VARILLA TREATY, 1903

CANNON, JOSEPH G. (1836-1926). Speaker of the House of Representatives from 1903 to 1911 and best known as

71

"Uncle Joe" Cannon. As the result of a "revolt" of members of the House of Representatives in 1910 and 1911 against the high-handed tactics of Cannon, the Speaker was deprived of his membership on the powerful Rules Committee and his right to appoint other committees of the House of Representatives.

CAPITAL OF THE U. S. During the AMERICAN REVOLUTION (1775-83) the capital for brief intervals was in Philadelphia, Baltimore, Lancaster, York, Princeton and New York City. After the Revolution the capital was located in Annapolis, Trenton, New York City and finally WASHINGTON D. C.

CAPPER-VOLSTEAD ACT (1922). Also known as the Co-operative Marketing Act. Under this law farmers' associations and agricultural cooperatives were exempted from the provisions of federal anti-trust laws. This gave agricultural cooperatives the same exemption granted to labor unions under the CLAYTON ANTI-TRUST ACT (1914). (See FARM LEGISLATION)

CAREY ACT (1894). Each state containing federal public lands was eligible to receive up to 1,000,000 acres of land for conservation work and settlement. (See CONSERVATION MOVEMENT)

CARNEGIE, ANDREW (1835-1919). American industrialist and philanthropist. In 1882 he combined with HENRY C. FRICK to buy out competitors in the steel manufacturing business. In 1899 the Carnegie Steel Corporation was formed by the acquisition and consolidation of many smaller steel mills. It thus became one of the largest steel manufacturing companies in the world. In 1901 the company was incorporated into the giant U. S. Steel Corporation. (See MORGAN, JOHN P.) Carnegie used his vast wealth for many philanthropies, including the endowment of more than 2,500 libraries in the U. S. and other countries.

"CAROLINE" AFFAIR (1837). During a brief rebellion in Canada an American ship named the *Caroline* was engaged in carrying supplies to the Canadian rebels. While in American waters the *Caroline* was seized by British authorities and was completely destroyed, and one American was killed. Relations between the U. S. and Great Britain became strained, but the matter was settled by compromise.

CARPETBAGGERS. Northern politicians who came South during the RECONSTRUCTION ERA (1865-77) following the WAR BETWEEN THE STATES to take advantage of the new political power of the emancipated Negro voters. The Carpetbaggers derived their name from the fact that many came South carrying all their belongings in a cheap hand valise called a carpetbag.

CARPETBAG GOVERNMENTS. Name applied to governments of Southern states during the RECONSTRUCTION ERA (1865-77). Many Southern state governments were run by Northern politicians called CARPETBAGGERS, together with the newly emancipated but politically uneducated Negro voters. Most of the Southern carpetbag governments were corrupt, extravagant and wasteful of public funds.

CARRANZA, VENUSTIANO (1859-1920). See WATCHFUL WAITING and TAMPICO INCIDENT

CARSON, CHRISTOPHER ("KIT") 1809-68. American frontiersman, guide and Indian fighter. In 1842 JOHN C. FREMONT hired him as a guide for his Western expedition. During the MEXICAN WAR (1846-48), Carson served as dispatch rider and as guide to General STEPHEN KEARNY and his troops on their way to California. Many of Carson's Western exploits and adventures were breathtaking.

CARTERET, SIR GEORGE (c.1610-1680). See LORD JOHN BERKELEY

CARTIER, JACQUES (1491-1557). French explorer and navigator who, in 1534, discovered the St. Lawrence River and explored it as far as the modern city of Montreal. Cartier made three voyages to the St. Lawrence region between 1534 and 1542, searching for the NORTHWEST PASSAGE to the East. French claims to the St. Lawrence region were based on Cartier's discoveries and explorations.

73

CARTWHEELS. Popular name in the West for the U. S. silver dollar. Many westerners preferred the silver cartwheels to paper dollars, despite the large size and heavy weight of the coins.

CARVER, GEORGE WASHINGTON (c.1864-1943). Negro scientist who was particularly interested in the problems of Southern farmers. His experiments and research resulted in the development of many new uses for peanuts, sweet potatoes, soybeans and cotton waste, as well as such improved methods of farming as artificial fertilization and crop diversification.

"CASH AND CARRY LAW." See NEUTRALITY ACT (1937)

CASS, LEWIS (1782-1866). General, political leader and senator of the early 19th century. The Democratic Party nominated him for the presidency in the ELECTION OF 1848 but he was defeated by ZACHARY TAYLOR, the WHIG PARTY candidate.

CATO CONSPIRACY (1739). Colonial uprisings of Negro slaves. The Cato uprising occurred near Charleston, South Carolina, but was very quickly suppressed with the loss of about 70 lives, both Negro and white.

CATT, CARRIE CHAPMAN (1859-1947). Leader of the WOMEN SUFFRAGE and World Peace Movements in the early 20th century. She led the campaign to get the Woman Suffrage Amendment (see AMENDMENT 19) added to the U. S. Constitution.

CATTLE KINGDOM. Refers to the cattle industry in Texas in the middle decades of the 19th century. Huge ranches with thousands of head of cattle were fed on the "open range" (until the introduction of BARBED WIRE) and were then shipped to large cities in the midwest and the east. (See LONG DRIVE)

CHAMPLAIN, SAMUEL DE (1567-1635). French explorer known as the "Father of New France." He explored the

St. Lawrence River valley in 1603 and established a settlement which is known today as the city of Quebec. This was the first permanent French settlement in the New World. Champlain explored the region north of the Great Lakes and the area that is now New York State. He also discovered Lake Champlain, the body of water which now bears his name.

CHANCELLORSVILLE, BATTLE OF (1863). One of the major military engagements during the WAR BETWEEN THE STATES, fought near Chancellorsville, Virginia. The Union Army under General "Fighting Joe" Hooker was badly defeated by Confederate forces under the command of General ROBERT E. LEE and General "STONEWALL" JACKSON.

CHAPMAN, JOHN (1774-1847). Also known as "Johnny Appleseed." During the westward movement of the early 19th century he sold or gave away apple seeds to families moving west. He also planted apple orchards during his travels through Ohio, Indiana and Illinois. Because of his eccentric behavior and shabby appearance, local legends developed about him after his death.

CHARTER OAK. In 1688 the British Royal Governor SIR EDMUND ANDROS was sent to the colonies to establish and rule a DOMINION OF NEW ENGLAND. When Andros assumed control of Connecticut, the colony refused to surrender its colonial charter, which was hidden in an oak tree since known as the Charter Oak.

CHARTER OF LIBERTIES (1701). Granted by WILLIAM PENN to his Pennsylvania colony. The charter provided for the enactment of laws by the governor with the consent of the colonial assembly. The governor was appointed by the proprietor, William Penn.

CHASE, SALMON P. (1808-73). American statesman and chief justice of the U. S. Supreme Court (1864-73). During the WAR BETWEEN THE STATES (1861-65) he was President Lincoln's Secretary of Treasury and was one of the originators of the NATIONAL BANKING ACT (1863). In the last year of the war (1864) Lincoln appointed him Chief Justice of the Supreme Court. He presided at the trial of JEFFERSON DAVIS and the IM-PEACHMENT OF PRESIDENT JOHNSON.

CHATEAU THIERRY, BATTLE OF (1918). One of the battles of WORLD WAR I in France in which American troops won a notable victory over the Germans.

CHEROKEE INDIANS. Largest single Indian tribe originally living in the western part of the Carolinas, Georgia, Alabama and eastern Tennessee. They were the most important of the so-called FIVE CIVILIZED NATIONS. (See SEQUOYAH) The discovery of gold in Cherokee Territory (1829) led to attempts to remove the tribe across the Mississippi River. Despite a Supreme Court decision against Georgia (Worcester V. Georgia, 1832), the Indians were removed by military force, while President Jackson refused to enforce the decision of the court. The Cherokees were eventually settled in Oklahoma Territory, where they set up civilized communities. In 1892 they sold part of their territory, called the "Cherokee Strip." The discovery of oil on their Oklahoma land in the 20th century brought many of the Indians unexpected wealth.

CHEROKEE STRIP. See CHEROKEE INDIANS

CHERRY VALLEY MASSACRE (1778). In a raid led by the British and Indians, a group of white settlers in Cherry Valley, New York were massacred during the AMERICAN REVOLUTION (1775-83). The town was burned and about 40 people were killed.

"CHESAPEAKE" AFFAIR (1807). During the British war on Napoleon I of France, an English warship, the *Leopard,* opened fire on the American frigate the *Chesapeake,* killing a number of American sailors. The British then seized a number of the *Chesapeake's* crew, maintaining that they were deserters from British naval ships. Some of those seized were American citizens. After the incident Great Britain agreed to pay damages to the American ship but refused to stop her policy of IMPRESSMENT of seamen.

CHEYENNE INDIANS. Originally located in Minnesota, Montana, Oklahoma and the Dakotas. They were friendly to white settlers until 1861, when they went on the warpath because their treaties wth the U. S. were repeatedly violated. War between U. S. forces and the southern tribe of Cheyennes dragged on from 1861 to 1868, during which time there occurred indiscriminate massacres of the Indians by the U. S. Army. One of the bloodiest of these was the Massacre of Sandy Creek (1864). (See PLAINS INDIANS)

CHICKAMAUGA, BATTLE OF (1863). During the WAR BETWEEN THE STATES (1861-65) a Confederate army under General Bragg attacked the Union forces led by General Rosecrans at Chickamauga Creek, Tennessee. The Confederates inflicted a serious defeat on the Union Army and forced it to retreat.

CHICKASAW INDIANS. See FIVE CIVILIZED NATIONS

CHILD LABOR. The use of child labor in factories and on farms was common in the U. S. until World War I (1917). In 1916 Congress passed the Keating-Owen Act, prohibiting the shipment in interstate commerce of products made with child labor. The Supreme Court declared the law unconstitutional (Hammer V. Dagenhart, 1918). A second child labor act in 1919 levied a high tax on interstate goods made with child labor. The Supreme Court also declared this law invalid (Bailey V. Drexel Furniture Co., 1922). In 1924 a Child Labor Amendment was passed by Congress and submitted to the states for ratification, but it never received the necessary three-fourths vote of the states. In 1938 Congress passed the FAIR LABOR STANDARDS ACT which, among other things, set a basic minimum age of 16 for child labor on interstate goods, with a number of exceptions—such as farm workers. The Supreme Court held this law to be constitutional (United States V. Darby Lumber Co., 1941). In addition to this federal statute, all states but two now have their own child labor laws establishing the minimum age at 14, 15, or 16 years for full-time employment in intrastate industries.

CHILD LABOR AMENDMENT. See CHILD LABOR

CHINESE EXCLUSION ACT (1882). Excluded Chinese immigrant laborers for a ten-year period and denied citizenship to all Chinese nationals. The act was renewed for

77

successive ten-year periods until WORLD WAR II (1941-45) when China fought with the U. S. against Japan. Under the MC CARREN-WALTER IMMIGRATION ACT (1952) oriental countries, including China, were included under the same quota system as European countries. Orientals were made eligible for citizenship by naturalization. (See IMMIGRATION LEGISLATION)

CHISHOLM TRAIL. The most famous of the mid-19th century routes along which Texas cattle were driven by cowboys from the open range to railroad shipping points. The Chisholm Trail led from San Antonio, Texas to the rail head at Abilene, Kansas. (See LONG DRIVE and CATTLE KINGDOM)

CHISHOLM V. GEORGIA. See AMENDMENT 11

CHOCTAW INDIANS. See FIVE CIVILIZED NATIONS

CIBOLA, SEVEN CITIES OF. Spanish explorers of the 16th and 17th centuries, including CABEZA DE VACA and Marcos de Niza, were told of these seven cities of fabulous wealth located somewhere north of Mexico. In 1640 FRANCISCO CORONADO organized an expedition to find these fabled places. After two years of wandering in what is now Arizona and New Mexico, Coronado found a few PUEBLO INDIAN villages, cliff dwellings and adobe huts made of sun-dried clay brick. The "cities of gold," he discovered to his regret, were a myth.

CIRCULAR LETTER (1768). Strongly worded protest against the TOWNSHEND ACTS (1767) written by SAMUEL ADAMS and approved by the Massachusetts colonial legislature. The Circular Letter was sent to all the other colonies, with a proposal for some kind of united protest action. A number of colonial legislatures voted approval of the contents of the letter but no united action was taken at the time.

CIVIL AERONAUTICS ACT (1938). Established the Civil Aeronautics Administration (C.A.A.) to regulate civil aviation. In 1940 the C.A.A. was reorganized into a Civil Aeronautics Board (C.A.B.) to encourage the development of civil air transport lines, and a Civil Aeronautics Administration (C.A.A.) to supervise and regulate civilian airlines and to set up standards of air safety.

CIVILIAN CONSERVATION CORPS (C.C.C.). One of the NEW DEAL agencies established in 1933 to relieve unemployment among young men during the GREAT DEPRESSION (see UNEMPLOYMENT LEGISLATION) and at the same time perform useful soil conservation work through planting of trees, construction of small dams and clearing of fire hazards in forests. As many as 300,000 young men were enrolled in the program.

CIVIL LIBERTIES. Basic liberties guaranteed to all under the first ten amendments to the Constitution (see BILL OF RIGHTS, AMERICAN) such as freedom of speech, press, assembly, petition and religion, right to a jury trial, reasonable bail, advice of counsel and others. Many cases involving civil liberties have come before the Supreme Court, including questions of freedom of speech and press (See SCHENCK V. U. S., 1919; ABRAMS V. U. S., 1919), suspension of HABEAS CORPUS, refusals to salute the flag (see FLAG SALUTE CASES), double jeopardy, and freedom of religion.

CIVIL RIGHTS BILLS. Passed by Congress in 1866 as part of its southern RECONSTRUCTION program. The law declared that Negroes were citizens and as such had the same civil rights as white citizens.

In 1875 Congress passed a second Civil Rights Law guaranteeing equal rights to Negroes in public places such as theaters, railroad stations and parks. In many Southern states both laws were evaded or violated. In a series of Civil Rights Cases decided by the Supreme Court in 1883, the judges ruled that while the states could not deny the Negro his civil rights, the court was powerless to stop individuals from discriminating against Negroes. (See SEGREGATION)

CIVIL RIGHTS CASES. See CIVIL RIGHTS BILLS

CIVIL SERVICE COMMISSION. See PENDLETON ACT (1883)

CIVIL SERVICE REFORM. The movement to replace the SPOILS SYSTEM with a Civil Service Merit System began after the WAR BETWEEN THE STATES (1865) and became more vocal after the political scandals of the GRANT administration (see CREDIT MOBILIER, BELKNAP SCANDAL, WHISKEY RING) and the RECONSTRUCTION ERA. (See CARPETBAG GOVERNMENTS) The LIBERAL REPUBLICAN PARTY made Civil Service reform one of its major campaign issues in the ELECTION OF 1872 and GEORGE WILLIAM CURTIS organized the Civil Service Reform League. The climax of the reform movement came in 1881 when President JAMES A. GARFIELD was assassinated by a disappointed office seeker. In 1883 Congress passed the PENDLETON ACT, establishing the Civil Service Commission and a list of classified civil service jobs. Thereafter many presidents have added new federal jobs to the civil service list.

CIVIL SERVICE REFORM LEAGUE. See CURTIS, GEORGE WILLIAM and CIVIL SERVICE REFORM

CIVIL WAR(1861-65). See WAR BETWEEN THE STATES

CIVIL WORKS ADMINISTRATION (C.W.A.). See UNEMPLOYMENT LEGISLATION

CLARK, GEORGE ROGERS (1752-1818). American military leader in the west during the AMERICAN REVOLUTION (1775-83). In 1778 Clark and his men seized British posts at Kaskaskia and Cahokia on the Mississippi River and later captured Vincennes on the Wabash River. Clark's military victories were the basis for American claims to territory between the Ohio and Mississippi Rivers when the TREATY OF PARIS (1783) was signed.

CLARK, J. BEAUCHAMP (1850-1921). Also known as "Champ" Clark. He was a member of the House of Representatives from 1893 to 1895 and from 1897 to 1921. In the House he became one of the leaders who succeeded in curtailing the powers of the Speaker of the House, a position then held by JOSEPH G. CANNON. Clark himself held the position of Speaker of the House from 1911 to 1919.

CLARK, LIEUTENANT WILLIAM. See LEWIS AND CLARK EXPEDITION

CLAY, HENRY (1777-1852). Before the WAR OF 1812, he was a leader of the WAR HAWKS in Congress. In 1820 he took a leading part in framing the MISSOURI COMPROMISE and in the ELECTION OF 1824 he was one of the four presidential candidates, none of whom received a majority of the electoral votes. Clay threw his support to JOHN QUINCY ADAMS, who was chosen president by the House of Representatives. In the following ELECTION OF 1832 Clay, as candidate of the WHIG PARTY, was defeated by ANDREW JACKSON, the Democratic Party candidate. In 1824 Clay originated his so-called AMERICAN SYSTEM, a program of federal aid for internal improvements and a protective tariff. After South Carolina protested against the high tariff of 1828 (TARIFF OF ABOMINATIONS), Clay helped draw up the COMPROMISE TARIFF OF 1833. Clay again received the Whig Party Presidential nomination in 1844 but again he lost. (See ELECTION OF 1844) Despite his failure to win the presidency he continued to serve brilliantly in the Senate. His last major achievement was the preparation and defense of the COMPROMISE OF 1850. Because he was associated with so many congressional compromises, Clay earned the name of the "Great Pacificator." One of his oft-quoted statements was "I had rather be right than be President."

CLAYTON ANTI-TRUST ACT (1914). The purpose of the act was to close some of the loopholes in the SHERMAN ANTI-TRUST ACT of 1890 and more clearly define unfair business practices. The Clayton Act forbade price discrimination and interlocking directorates that tended to create monopolies. It also recognized the legality of strikes and boycotts, limited the use of court injunctions in labor disputes to cases involving irreparable damage to property, and stated that unions were not monopolies under the meaning of the Anti-Trust Laws. Labor was not to be classified as a commodity.

CLAYTON-BULWER TREATY (1850). Signed by the U. S. and Great Britain. It provided that any canal built to connect the Atlantic and Pacific Oceans was to be jointly

81

owned by the two countries. This treaty was set aside by the HAY-PAUNCEFOTE TREATY of 1901.

"CLEAR AND PRESENT DANGER" DOCTRINE. See SCHENCK V. U. S. (1919)

"CLERMONT, THE." See FULTON, ROBERT

CLEVELAND, GROVER (1837-1908). Twenty-second and 24th president of the U. S. In the ELECTION OF 1884, Cleveland, the Democratic Party candidate, won a bitterly contested election, defeating JAMES G. BLAINE, the Republican nominee. During Cleveland's first term (1885-89) Congress passed the PRESIDENTIAL SUCCESSION ACT (1886) and the INTERSTATE COMMERCE ACT (1887). Cleveland made many enemies by favoring a low tariff policy and reform of the veterans' pension system. In the ELECTION OF 1888 Cleveland was defeated by General BENJAMIN HARRISON, the Republican candidate. Nominated for a third time by the Democrats in the ELECTION OF 1892, Cleveland defeated Harrison. In Cleveland's second term (1889-93) Congress repealed the SHERMAN SILVER PURCHASE ACT (1893) and passed the WILSON-GORMAN TARIFF ACT (1894). During this term there also occurred the PANIC OF 1893, the PULLMAN STRIKE (1894) and the VENEZUELA BOUNDARY DISPUTE with England (1895).

CLINTON, DE WITT (1769-1828). Governor of New York State in the early 19th century. During his term of office he was one of the leading supporters of the plan to construct the ERIE CANAL. It was completed and opened by Clinton in 1825.

CLIPPER SHIPS. See MERCHANT MARINE

COAL STRIKE OF 1902. The United Mine Workers Union called the strike against mine owners in order to obtain union recognition, a nine-hour day and a wage increase. After many months of striking, President THEODORE ROOSEVELT forced the mine operators and the union to arbitrate by threatening to operate the mines with federal troops. The union won a wage increase and a shorter work day.

COCHISE (c.1815-1874). Chief of the Apache Indians of Arizona during the late 19th century. He was noted for his courage in warfare and his integrity in obeying treaties. On a number of occasions Cochise led the Apaches against U. S. troops in Arizona. After the death of Cochise, a new Apache leader named GERONIMO began a series of attacks against white settlements. This was known as the Apache War (1871-86).

CODY, WILLIAM F. (1846-1917). Nicknamed "Buffalo Bill." He served as scout and guide for wagon trains moving west in the late 19th century. During the construction of the Kansas Pacific Railroad, Bill Cody killed more than 4,000 buffalo in less than two years to provide food for the railroad construction crews.

COERCIVE ACTS. See INTOLERABLE ACTS

COHENS V. VIRGINIA (1821). In this Supreme Court decision, Chief Justice JOHN MARSHALL stated that the court had the right to review state court decisions involving constitutional questions because the national government and not the states was supreme.

COLD WAR. Refers to the war of propaganda between the U. S. and the Soviet Union after WORLD WAR II (1945). The Cold War developed because of inability of the two nations to agree on a peace treaty for Germany or the control of nuclear weapons. (See ATOM BOMB) In addition, differences of opinion in the UNITED NATIONS on many world problems divided the two nations.

COLFAX, SCHUYLER (1823-85). Vice-president of the U. S. during President GRANT'S first administration (1869-73). Colfax was involved in the CREDIT MOBILIER scandal, which ruined his political career.

COLLECTIVE BARGAINING. See LABOR UNIONS and LABOR UNION LEGISLATION

COLONIAL GOVERNMENT. See ROYAL COLONIES, PROPRIETARY COLONIES, and SELF-GOVERNING COLONIES

83

"COLOSSUS OF THE NORTH." Name applied to U. S. by people of Latin America because of our size, wealth, extensive commerce, military power and frequent interference with the internal and foreign affairs of Latin American countries before 1933. (See ROOSEVELT COROLLARY)

COLT, SAMUEL (1814-62). Patented the first practical revolver (1835) for rapid firing of bullets. Colt manufactured a large number of his guns for the U. S. Army during the MEXICAN WAR (1846-48).

COLUMBIA TREATY (1903). See PANAMA REVOLUTION, 1903

COLUMBUS, CHRISTOPHER (c.1451-1506). Italian navigator sailing under the Spanish flag who accidentally discovered America (1492) while searching for a westward water route to the East. His first landing was on an island in the Bahamas. He made four voyages across the Atlantic Ocean but died a poor and disappointed man.

COMMITTEE OF PUBLIC INFORMATION (1917). See WARTIME AGENCIES, WORLD WAR I

COMMITTEES OF CORRESPONDENCE (1772). Groups of colonists organized at the suggestion of SAMUEL ADAMS in Massachusetts and in most other colonies for the purpose of keeping people informed of new developments in the war of nerves between Great Britain and the colonies.

COMMON LAW, ENGLISH. The law and judicial decisions of English courts extending back to the Middle Ages. Many of our rules of legal procedure are based on the English Common Law and it is often cited as historical precedent to justify decisions in American law courts. The law courts of the federal government and of all states except Louisiana follow the Common Law.

"COMMON SENSE." See PAINE, THOMAS

COMMONWEALTH V. HUNT (1842). Decision of the Massachusetts Supreme Court holding that labor unions were not unlawful conspiracies and that strikes called to establish closed shops were legal. This landmark decision was followed by similar decisions in other state courts.

COMMUNISM. A political and economic system based on the philosophy of Karl Marx and practiced in the Soviet Union since 1917. Politically, Communism refers to government by one party and a dictator. Economically, it refers to government ownership and operation of all means of production, from raw materials to finished product. Under Communism almost every right guaranteed to citizens in a democracy is denied.

COMMUNIST PARTY. Minor party, originally called the Workers Party, organized in 1919. The party platform was based on Marxian principles. (See COMMUNISM) Its goal was the overthrow of capitalism and the establishment of a "dictatorship of the proletariat" in the U. S., by force and violence if necessary. The party nominated presidential and other candidates in most elections but rarely polled more than 1,000 votes in a national election. During WORLD WAR II (1941-45) evidence of Communist espionage in the U. S. led to the prosecution under the SMITH ACT (1940) of the American Communist Party leaders on charges of conspiracy to overthrow the government by force.

COMPACT THEORY. States rights theory of government which held that the Constitution was an agreement or compact between the national government of limited powers and the sovereign states possessing all other government powers. The Compact Theory, first enunciated in the VIRGINIA AND KENTUCKY RESOLUTIONS (1798), is the basis of the STATES RIGHTS DOCTRINE, which in turn is the basis for the NULLIFICATION doctrine and the right to secede. The leading exponent of the Compact Theory was JOHN C. CALHOUN.

COMPANY OF NEW FRANCE (1627). Also called "The Hundred Associates." It was a joint stock company chartered by the King of France to establish settlements in NEW FRANCE. The company was also given a monopoly of the fur trade in the region.

COMPROMISE OF 1850. Also known as the "Omnibus Bill." It consisted of a series of five measures sponsored in

Congress by HENRY CLAY and STEPHEN A. DOUGLAS in an effort to solve the dispute between the North and South over the question of slavery in newly acquired territories. The Compromise provided that California was to be admitted as a free state. The remainder of the Mexican Cession was to be divided into Utah and New Mexico Territories without any specific slavery regulations. Part of the Texas territory was to be added to New Mexico, for which Texas was to receive a payment of $10,000,000 from the U. S. The slave trade, but not slavery, was prohibited in the District of Columbia, and Congress was not to interfere with the slave trade in the Southern states. A stricter FUGITIVE SLAVE LAW was also enacted as part of the Compromise.

COMPROMISE TARIFF (1833). Passed after South Carolina nullified the TARIFF OF 1832 and threatened to secede from the Union. The Compromise Tariff, devised by HENRY CLAY, provided for a gradual reduction of the tariff rates until 1842, at which time no rates were to be over 20%. (See TARIFF LEGISLATION)

COMSTOCK LODE. A fabulously rich gold and silver mining region discovered near Virginia City, Nevada in 1859. News of the discovery brought a horde of adventurers and miners, called "Fifty-niners," to Nevada. The Comstock Lode yielded more than three-quarter billion dollars in gold and silver.

CONCORD, BATTLE OF (1775). One of the first military clashes of the AMERICAN REVOLUTION (1775-83). British troops sent to destroy military supplies at Concord, Massachusetts, were met by colonial MINUTEMEN and a brief skirmish ensued. On the return march to Boston, the British were harassed by the fire of colonial farmers. Ralph Waldo Emerson, the American poet and philosopher, called the battle "the shot heard round the world."

CONESTOGA MASSACRE (1763). See PAXTON BOYS

CONESTOGA WAGON. Also called "covered wagon" and "prairie schooner." It was developed about 1750 and was used by many pioneers who moved west. The sturdily built wagon, pulled by teams of horses, carried all the possessions of the migratory families. The black cigars smoked by the Conestoga wagon drivers is the derivation of the word "stogie," meaning a cheap cigar.

CONFEDERATE CONSTITUTION (1861-65). Drawn up at Montgomery, Alabama, under which the CONFEDER-ATE STATES OF AMERICA was established after the secession of the South. The constitution was modeled after the U. S. document, but it had a number of significant variations. The Confederate president could hold office for six years but was ineligible for re-election. The powers of the central government were strictly limited. Protective tariffs were prohibited. Cabinet members could sit in Congress, but the importation of new slaves was prohibited.

CONFEDERATE STATES OF AMERICA (1861-65). New nation organized by eleven states that seceded from the Union. JEFFERSON DAVIS was chosen president and ALEXANDER H. STEPHENS vice-president. The CON-FEDERATE CONSTITUTION was modeled on the U. S. Constitution but included a number of significant differences. The Confederacy came to an end with the conclusion of the WAR BETWEEN THE STATES (1865).

CONGRESS OF INDUSTRIAL ORGANIZATIONS (C.I.O.). Originally organized by JOHN L. LEWIS as the Committee for Industrial Organization (part of the AMERICAN FEDERATION OF LABOR) to unionize skilled and un-skilled workers. The C.I.O. grew rapidly and in 1938 split from the A.F.L. to become the independent Congress of Industrial Organizations. In 1955 it was reunited with the A.F.L. to form the AFL-CIO.

CONKLING, ROSCOE (1829-88). Senator from New York and one of the leaders of the STALWART or conservative wing of the REPUBLICAN PARTY in the last quarter of the 19th century. He opposed President RUTHERFORD B. HAYES, who in 1878 removed CHESTER A. ARTHUR and Alonzo B. Cornell, two of Conkling's friends, from posts in the New York Custom House. This was a violation of "Senatorial Courtesy."

CONNALLY ACT (1935). Passed by Congress to regulate the production of petroleum in the U. S. The law forbad

87

the shipment in interstate or foreign commerce of petroleum produced in excess of state petroleum quota production laws. The purpose of the law was to conserve our oil resources and at the same time avoid an overproduction of oil that would reduce prices to an unprofitable level.

CONNALLY-FULBRIGHT RESOLUTION. See FULBRIGHT RESOLUTION

CONNECTICUT. One of the thirteen original colonies. (See THIRTEEN COLONIES) The first settlement in the Connecticut colony was founded by THOMAS HOOKER in 1636 and was motivated primarily by a desire for more and better farm land. In 1639 the Connecticut settlers adopted the FUNDAMENTAL ORDERS, considered the first written constitution in America. Connecticut was one of the thirteen original states under the ARTICLES of CONFEDERATION and one of the first states to ratify the U. S. CONSTITUTION.

CONQUERED PROVINCE THEORY. Theory proposed after the War Between the States (1861-65) by THADDEUS STEVENS as the basis for readmission of the seceded states into the Union. Under this theory the Southern states were conquered provinces and should be put under military rule. This theory was incorporated in the RECONSTRUCTION ACT (1867) passed by Congress.

CONQUISTADORES. Spanish adventurers who came to the New World in the 16th and 17th centuries, during the age of exploration, in search of riches and a water route to the East. They explored vast regions, conquered territories from the Indians and claimed them for the rulers of Spain. Among the most famous of the Spanish Conquistadores were CORTEZ and PIZARRO.

CONSCIENCE WHIGS. Anti-slavery Whigs of New England who joined the FREE SOIL PARTY in the ELECTION OF 1849. The Conscience Whigs left the Whig Party because it was said their consciences troubled them over the party failure to take a definite stand on the slavery issue.

CONSCRIPTION. Also called a "draft." It is a method of raising an army by requiring military service of all able-bodied men. The draft was first used by both North and South during the WAR BETWEEN THE STATES (1861-65). (See DRAFT RIOTS) It was used again during WORLD WAR I (1917-18) under the SELECTIVE SERVICE ACT (1917). Prior to WORLD WAR II Congress passed the Burke-Wadsworth Act (1940), establishing the first peacetime draft in our nation's history. The draft was continued during the war and in 1948 a new peacetime SELECTIVE SERVICE ACT was passed.

CONSERVATION MOVEMENT. The policy by which government and industry seek to save natural resources from exhaustion. These resources include coal, oil, gas, minerals, forests, soil, water and wildlife. The conservation movement started in the late 19th century with the enactment of such laws as the FOREST RESERVE ACT (1891) and the CAREY ACT (1894). It became popular in the 20th century through the work of such conservation leaders as GIFFORD PINCHOT and President THEODORE ROOSEVELT. (See NATIONAL CONSERVATION COMMISSION, 1908; NEWLANDS RECLAMATION ACT, 1902). With each succeeding decade the conservation movement grew stronger. The NEW DEAL administration of FRANKLIN D. ROOSEVELT, in particular, took many forward steps to strengthen the American conservation program through such legislation as the TENNESSEE VALLEY AUTHORITY ACT, 1933; the CIVILIAN CONSERVATION CORPS, 1933; and the AGRICULTURAL ADJUSTMENT ACT, 1938.

CONSPIRACY OF PONTIAC (1763-66). See PONTIAC

CONSTITUTIONAL CONVENTION (1787). Called by Congress to revise and amend the ARTICLES OF CONFEDERATION. Thirteen states were represented by 55 delegates at Philadelphia. The delegates unanimously chose GEORGE WASHINGTON president of the Convention. Other leading delegates at the Convention included ALEXANDER HAMILTON, JAMES MADISON, ROBERT MORRIS and BENJAMIN FRANKLIN. Because of economic and political differences, the convention agreed to a number of compromises. These included the GREAT COMPROMISE, establishing a Congress of two houses, and the SLAVERY COMPROMISE. When the convention completed its work it presented the new Constitution to the states for ratification. (See FEDERALIST, THE)

CONSTITUTIONAL UNION PARTY. Minor political party that appeared in local Southern elections as early as 1852 and in the national presidential ELECTION OF 1860. The party nominated John Bell of Tennessee for president on a platform calling for obedience to the Constitution and the laws of the U. S. but taking no stand on the burning issue of slavery. Bell received the electoral votes of only three states—Kentucky, Tennessee and Virginia—and the party disappeared as the War Between the States started (1861).

"CONSTITUTION" AND "GUERRIERE" (1812). Famous naval battle during the WAR OF 1812 between the U. S. frigate *Constitution*, commanded by Captain Isaac Hull, and the British frigate *Guerriere*. The *Constitution* won a brilliant victory and subsequently continued its victorious record during the war. The ship, affectionately called *Old Ironsides*, was subsequently preserved as a national memorial.

CONSTITUTION, U. S. Document written at the CONSTITUTIONAL CONVENTION (1787) in Philadelphia and put into effect in 1789 after it was ratified by nine states. The Constitution is the oldest written document of its kind in existence. Unique features of the Constitution are its system of checks and balances, its separation of executive, legislative and judicial powers, and its division of powers between state and federal governments. Since its adoption, 23 amendments have been added to the Constitution, and its contents have been interpreted by thousands of Supreme Court decisions. (See JUDICIAL REVIEW)

CONTINENTAL ARMY. Military force organized by the Second CONTINENTAL CONGRESS in 1775 with GEORGE WASHINGTON as commander - in - chief. Throughout the AMERICAN REVOLUTION the army was beset by problems of inadequate food, limited supplies, scarcity of equipment, lack of money, shortages of transport, brief enlistment periods and outbreaks of typhus and smallpox. Despite these staggering handicaps, the army succeeded in bringing the war to a victorious conclusion. (See YORKTOWN, BATTLE OF)

CONTINENTAL ASSOCIATION (1774). Organization set up by the First CONTINENTAL CONGRESS to boycott all British merchandise and stop all trade with England in protest against British tax laws and repressive measures.

CONTINENTAL CONGRESS. Two organizations were called Continental Congresses. The First Continental Congress met in Philadelphia (1774) and included representatives of all colonies except Georgia. It drew up a Declaration of Rights and Grievances, which it sent to the English Parliament, and organized the CONTINENTAL ASSOCIATION to effect an economic boycott of England. The SECOND CONTINENTAL CONGRESS met in 1775 and served as the provisional government of the colonies during the AMERICAN REVOLUTION.

CONTINENTAL CURRENCY. Paper money issued by order of the Second CONTINENTAL CONGRESS during the first year of the American Revolution (1775). Congress issued about $250 million and the states about $200 million more. This currency rapidly depreciated in value until about $80 of it was worth $1 in gold or silver. This was the origin of the phrase "not worth a continental."

CONTINENTALS. Colonial soldiers who fought in the AMERICAN REVOLUTION (1775-83). The name was derived from the SECOND CONTINENTAL CONGRESS, under whose authority they were fighting.

CONTINUOUS VOYAGE DOCTRINE. During the Napoleonic Wars (1804-15) between Great Britain and Napoleon I of France, American shippers took cargoes from French West Indies colonies to U. S. ports and then reshipped them to French ports. The purpose of this "broken voyage" was to establish the goods as American and neutral—therefore not subject to British seizure. The British courts, however, established the doctrine of "continuous voyage," holding that the stopover in a U. S. port was only a subterfuge and American ships were really carrying enemy (French) goods to and from enemy ports. As a result, such U. S. ships were seized by the British. During the War

91

Between the States (1861-65) British ships used the same device to carry Confederate goods. The U. S. therefore used the British doctrine of "continuous voyage" to seize British ships carrying Confederate goods.

CONTRACT LABOR LAW (1885). Prohibited the further immigration of contract laborers to the U. S. Contract laborers were persons whose passage to the U. S. was paid by American businessmen in return for an agreement to work for a specified number of years.

CONVENTION OF 1800. Also known as the Treaty of Morfontaine. It officially put an end to the U. S.-French TREATY OF ALLIANCE of 1778 under which the French had aided the colonies during the American Revolution (1775-83).

CONVOY SYSTEM. During World War I and World War II a large number of Allied merchant ships was sunk by enemy submarines. To reduce the number of sinkings the U. S. copied the British system of having a large number of merchant ships sail as a group, under the protection of warships. This convoy system proved to be successful in both wars. (See ATLANTIC, BATTLE OF THE)

CONWAY CABAL (1777). So-called plot to remove General WASHINGTON from command of the CONTINENTAL ARMY after his defeats at the BATTLE OF BRANDYWINE and BATTLE OF GERMANTOWN. General Thomas Conway, an army officer, wrote to Congress and to General Gates criticizing the conduct of the war and General Washington's leadership. Actually there was no plot, and Conway subsequently expressed his regrets to Washington for the incident.

COOKE, JAY (1821-1905). American financier. He was the founder and owner of the famous banking house of Jay Cooke and Co., which floated federal loans to supply the government with money during the WAR BETWEEN THE STATES (1861-65). The attempt of his firm to raise funds for further expansion of the Northern Pacific Railroad resulted in financial disaster. Jay Cooke and Co. went bankrupt and precipitated the PANIC OF 1873.

COOLIDGE, CALVIN (1872-1933). Thirtieth president of the U. S. In 1919 he was elected governor of Massachusetts and won national prominence by his vigorous action in ending the BOSTON POLICE STRIKE. The REPUBLICAN PARTY nominated him for the vice-presidency in the ELECTION OF 1920, with WARREN G. HARDING as the presidential candidate. On the death of Harding in 1923 Coolidge became president. In the ELECTION OF 1924 Coolidge was elected for a full presidential term but he refused to run again in 1928, stating: "I do not choose to run."

During Coolidge's presidency (1923-29), Congress passed the JOHNSON-REED IMMIGRATION ACT (1924). Coolidge vetoed the McNary Haugen Bill for farm relief in 1927 and again in 1928. The KELLOGG-BRIAND PACT (1928) was signed before Coolidge left the presidency.

COOPERATIVE MARKETING ACT. See CAPPER-VOLSTEAD ACT

COOPER, PETER (1791-1883). American businessman, inventor and philanthropist. He built the first American steam locomotive, called the "Tom Thumb," in 1830 and thereafter gained financial success in iron and steel manufacturing. In 1866 Cooper provided most of the financial support for laying CYRUS FIELD's first Atlantic cable. Cooper was nominated for president by the GREENBACK PARTY in the ELECTION OF 1876.

COOPER UNION SPEECH (1860). Important speech made by ABRAHAM LINCOLN before the ELECTION OF 1860. In it, he exposed the weaknesses of STEPHEN A. DOUGLAS' doctrine of POPULAR SOVEREIGNTY and expressed his belief that slavery must not be extended into Western territories. The speech made Lincoln a nationally known figure and paved the way for his nomination for the presidency.

COPPERHEADS. Also called "Butternuts." They were Northern Democrats during the WAR BETWEEN THE STATES (1861-65) who favored an immediate end to the war and

93

peaceful secession of the South. During the war, Copperheads formed various organizations, such as the "Knights of the Golden Circle," "Order of American Knights," and "Sons of Liberty." A number of Copperheads were tried for treason and convicted before the end of the war.

CORAL SEA, BATTLE OF THE (1942). One of the major naval engagements in the Pacific during World War II, between U. S. and Japanese fleets off the northeast coast of Australia. At no time during the battle were warships engaged in actual fighting with each other; all of the fighting was done by airplanes launched from aircraft carriers. Although the U. S. lost the aircraft carrier *Lexington,* the battle stopped the further advance of the Japanese toward Australia.

CORDUROY ROAD. In colonial times and in the early 19th century dirt roads often became impassable because of mud. To provide a solid surface, logs were laid side by side across the dirt roads, forming a corduroy effect. It made the roads passable but bumpy.

CORONADO, FRANCISCO (c.1510-1554). Spanish explorer and adventurer who went in search of the fabled SEVEN CITIES OF CIBOLA. He explored the area that is now the southwest quarter of the U. S., reaching a point as far north as present-day Kansas (1640-42).

CORREGIDOR. Island fortress in Manila Bay. In the early months of WORLD WAR II (1941-45) Japan invaded the Philippine Islands and eventually forced the American garrison to surrender. A small force of American troops held Corregidor as long as possible, but finally surrendered in 1942. This put an end to organized U. S. military resistance in the Philippine Islands until U. S. forces returned in 1944 and reconquered the islands.

CORTEZ, HERNANDO (1485-1547). One of the great Spanish CONQUISTADORES who in 1519 landed in Mexico with about 500 men. With this small force he conquered and destroyed the civilization of the AZTEC Indians in less than two years. Cortez then claimed Mexico for the King of Spain.

COTTON GIN. Earliest model of the cotton gin was invented by ELI WHITNEY in 1793. It put an end to the slow hand picking method of separating seeds and fibers, encouraged the growth of the PLANTATION SYSTEM, made slavery an important element in the South's economic system and tremendously increased the output of cotton.

COTTON, JOHN (1584-1652). Puritan clergyman who came to the Massachusetts Colony in 1633. The banishment of ANNE HUTCHINSON and ROGER WILLIAMS from the colony was due in large part to Cotton's opposition to their liberal religious ideas. Williams and his followers founded the RHODE ISLAND COLONY.

COTTON PICKER. A device for picking cotton from cotton plants by means of a vacuum machine. The cotton picker was perfected by the Rust Brothers in 1927.

COUNCIL OF ECONOMIC ADVISERS. See EMPLOYMENT ACT of 1946

COURT PACKING PLAN. See JUDICIARY REORGANIZATION BILL (1937)

COVENANT OF THE LEAGUE OF NATIONS. Charter or constitution of the LEAGUE OF NATIONS. It was part of the TREATY OF VERSAILLES (1919) at the end of WORLD WAR I.

COVERED WAGON. See CONESTOGA WAGON

COVODE RESOLUTION (1868). Resolution of the House of Representatives impeaching President Andrew Johnson. (See IMPEACHMENT OF JOHNSON)

COWPENS, BATTLE OF (1781). During the AMERICAN REVOLUTION (1775-83) Daniel Morgan, leader of an American force, practically destroyed a British force at Cowpens, near the North-South Carolina border.

COX, JAMES M. (1870-1957). Nominated for the presidency by the Democratic Party in 1920 because of his strong

95

support of President WOODROW WILSON and U. S. participation in the League of Nations. Cox was decisively defeated by WARREN G. HARDING, the Republican candidate, in the ELECTION OF 1920.

COXEY, JACOB (1854-1951). During the PANIC OF 1893 and the depression that followed, Coxey led a group of about 500 unemployed workers from Ohio to Washington, D. C. to dramatize the plight of jobless workers and to ask for government relief. The group became known as "Coxey's Army." When they reached Washington they were dispersed by the police and Coxey was arrested for trespassing on the Capitol lawn.

COXEY'S ARMY. See COXEY, JACOB

CRAWFORD, WILLIAM H. (1772-1834). See ELECTION OF 1824

CRAZY HORSE, CHIEF (c.1849-1877). One of the chiefs of the Sioux Indians. He participated in the BATTLE OF LITTLE BIG HORN (1876) at which GENERAL GEORGE CUSTER's force was wiped out. Crazy Horse was subsequently captured by General Miles.

CREDIT MOBILIER (1872). One of the major scandals uncovered during President ULYSSES S. GRANT's administration. Credit Mobilier was a business corporation organized in 1864 by a few important stockholders of the Union Pacific Railroad. They gave very profitable construction contracts to the Credit Mobilier, thus deriving enormous profits from the transactions. To prevent Congressional interference with the Credit Mobilier, a Massachusetts congressman named Oakes Ames distributed company stock to other congressmen. Vice-President SCHUYLER COLFAX was also involved in the scandal.

CREEK CONFEDERACY. Organization formed by a group of Creek Indian tribes for defense against white settlers and other Indians. The confederacy was in existence during the CREEK WAR (1813-14).

CREEK INDIANS. Originally inhabited Georgia, Alabama and part of the Mississippi Territory. After their defeat in the CREEK WAR, they moved to new lands west of the Mississippi River, where they became one of the FIVE CIVILIZED NATIONS.

CREEK WAR (1813-14). As a result of encroachment of white settlers on their lands in Alabama, Georgia and Mississippi, the CREEK INDIANS launched a war against the white settlers. At Fort Mims they massacred a large number of settlers and Negro slaves. However, ANDREW JACKSON, at the head of a force of frontiersmen, thoroughly defeated them. The Creeks were forced to evacuate a large area of their former lands.

CREOLE. People of French or Spanish descent who were born in the New World. In colonial times creoles constituted a class separate and distinct from the French and Spanish settlers who came from Europe.

CREOLE CASE. (1842). An American merchant ship, the *Creole*, carrying Negro slaves from Virginia to New Orleans, was seized by the slaves during the voyage. The ship was then sailed to the British island of Nassau, where the British freed all the slaves except those involved in the mutiny. DANIEL WEBSTER, U. S. Secretary of State, protested and demanded the return of the slaves because they were the property of U. S. citizens. The British took no immediate action, but in 1855 they paid the U. S. an indemnity of about $100,000.

CREVECOEUR, ST. JOHN DE (1735-1813). French adventurer and author. He settled in the Ohio Valley in 1769 and later published his views of life in the New World in *Letters From An American Farmer,* which were widely read both in Europe and America.

CRIME OF RECONSTRUCTION. Name applied by Southerners and some Northerners to the harsh Reconstruction laws passed by Congress after the WAR BETWEEN THE STATES (1861-65). It also referred to the wasteful CARPETBAG GOVERNMENTS that controlled Southern state governments during the RECONSTRUCTION ERA (1865-77).

CRIME OF '73. See DEMONETIZATION ACT

"CRISIS, THE." See PAINE, THOMAS

CRITICAL PERIOD. Applied by past historians to the era from 1783 to 1789, when the U. S. was governed under the ARTICLES OF CONFEDERATION and experienced an economic depression. Recent historical research has indicated that the era was not so "critical" as originally supposed.

CRITTENDEN AMENDMENTS (1860). After the secession of the Southern States (1861) Senator John Crittenden of Kentucky proposed a number of constitutional amendments as a compromise between the North and South and as a means of bringing the South back into the Union without the use of force. The most important provision of the Crittenden Amendments was a plan to restore the line established by the MISSOURI COMPROMISE (1820). Congress rejected these amendments.

CROATOAN. See LOST COLONY

CROCKETT, DAVID ("DAVY") (1786-1836). Frontiersman and Western trail blazer. He served in the CREEK WAR (1813-14) under ANDREW JACKSON and later was elected to Congress as representative from Tennessee for six years. After his defeat in the election of 1834, Crockett left Tennessee for Texas. He was one of the defenders of the ALAMO during the TEXAS WAR FOR INDEPENDENCE and died during the siege.

CROKER, RICHARD (1841-1922). Also known as "Boss" Croker. He was leader of TAMMANY HALL, the Democratic Party machine in New York City from 1886 to 1902. The "Croker Era" was marked by flagrant corruption in the city's financial affairs. The election of Seth Low, a reform mayor, in 1901, ended Croker's leadership of Tammany Hall. (See PARTY BOSS)

"CROSS OF GOLD" SPEECH (1896). Address at the DEMOCRATIC PARTY convention by WILLIAM JENNINGS

BRYAN, their presidential candidate in the ELECTION OF 1896. In his speech to the convention Bryan called for free and unlimited coinage of silver. (See BIMETALLISM) He ended with the words: "You shall not press down upon the brow of labor this crown of thorns; you shall not crucify mankind upon a cross of gold."

CUBA. Caribbean island possession of Spain until 1898. The U. S. declared war on Spain in 1898 (see SPANISH-AMERICAN WAR) in part because of our economic interests in Cuba. After the war Cuba became independent but was limited in certain powers by the PLATT AMENDMENT (1901) which established a U. S. protectorate. On the basis of this amendment the U. S. intervened in Cuban affairs on a number of occasions. In 1934 the U. S., following a GOOD NEIGHBOR POLICY, rescinded the Platt Amendment. Cuba's history since 1934 has been marred by dictatorships, civil wars and revolutions. In 1959 Fidel Castro, a revolutionary leader, established a dictatorship.

CUBAN QUARANTINE (1962). Two years after Fidel Castro established his government in Cuba, the new regime became avowedly Communist in its domestic policies and pro-Soviet in its foreign policies. The Castro government of Cuba entered into close economic and military relations with the Soviet Union. The shipment of military equipment to Cuba by the Soviet Union and the arrival of hundreds of Soviet technicians on the island posed a serious threat to the security of the Western Hemisphere. In October, 1962 President John F. Kennedy, by proclamation, ordered a naval and air quarantine of Cuba in order to stop the further shipment of missiles, rockets, bomber aircraft or related military equipment to the Cubans. This limited blockade by the U. S. created an international crisis that threatened to erupt into a third world war.

CULLOM ACT (1887). See INTERSTATE COMMERCE ACT

CULPEPER'S REBELLION (1677). A brief rebellion in the Carolina colony against the arbitrary rule of the proprietary

99

governor. John Culpeper, one of the rebel leaders, was tried for treason but was acquitted.

CUMBERLAND GAP. Important pass in the Appalachian Mountains between Virginia and Kentucky, used in colonial times and the early 19th century by settlers moving west. The old WILDERNESS ROAD led through this pass into Kentucky.

CUMBERLAND ROAD. Also called the "National Road." It was one of the first interstate roads built with money from the federal treasury. It began at Cumberland in western Maryland and extended west through Ohio and Indiana to Vandalia, Illinois. Thousands of settlers moving west used this road on the first leg of their journey. Construction of the Cumberland Road began in 1811 and was completed a few years later.

CURRENCY ACT (1764). Passed by British Parliament as part of Prime Minister GEORGE GRENVILLE'S colonial program. The act forbad the issue of paper money by colonial governments or the use of colonial currency in payment for merchandise imported from England.

CURRENCY ACT (1834). Provided for coinage of gold and silver at a ratio of approximately 16 ounces of silver to 1 ounce of gold. In 1873 Congress replaced this law with the DEMONETIZATION ACT. (See BIMETALLISM)

CURTIS, GEORGE WILLIAM (1824-92). In 1863 he became editor of HARPER'S WEEKLY, an influential periodical. After the War Between the States (1865) he became leader of the Civil Service Reform League and urged enactment of CIVIL SERVICE REFORM legislation.

CUSHING, CALEB (1800-79). First American commissioner to China (1844). In this capacity he negotiated the first treaty opening Chinese ports to American trade. He was one of the U. S. representatives who settled the ALABAMA CLAIMS dispute (1871).

CUSTER, GENERAL GEORGE A. (1839-76). See SIOUX WAR

CUTLER, MANASSEH (1742-1823). American scientist and land company organizer. In 1786 he helped organize the Scioto Company and the OHIO COMPANY. He succeeded in buying 1,500,000 acres of land in Ohio and helped to establish a settlement at Marietta.

DAKOTA INDIANS. See SIOUX INDIANS

"DAMN THE TORPEDOES; FULL SPEED AHEAD." See FARRAGUT, DAVID G.

DANA, CHARLES A. (1819-97). He became editor and part owner of the New York *Sun* in 1868. During his many years as editor, Dana's brilliant writing and the *Sun's* editorials had a profound influence on the thinking of Americans and the policies of the national government.

DANBURY HATTERS CASE (1908). Also known as Loewe v. Lawler. This Supreme Court decision held that a union-sponsored boycott of hats made by Danbury (Conn.) man-ufacturers was a combination in restraint of trade and there-fore a violation of the SHERMAN ANTI-TRUST ACT. The union was compelled to pay triple damages. (See LABOR UNION LEGISLATION)

DARE, VIRGINIA. First white child of English parents born in the New World (1587). She and her parents were mem-bers of the ROANOKE COLONY established by SIR WALTER RALEIGH.

DARK HORSE. A candidate who is relatively unknown yet is nominated for a high political office as a compromise candidate when a political party is split over two leading candidates. JAMES K. POLK (see ELECTION OF 1844), JAMES A. GARFIELD (see ELECTION OF 1880), and John W. Davis (see ELECTION of 1924) were all "dark horse" candidates.

DARTMOUTH COLLEGE CASE (1819). Also known as Dartmouth v. Woodward. In this Supreme Court decision, Chief Justice JOHN MARSHALL held that the state of New Hampshire acted illegally when it changed the provi-sions of the Dartmouth College charter without the consent

102

of the college. A charter was held to be a contract guaranteed under the Constitution.

DAVENPORT, JOHN (1597-1670). Puritan clergyman who, together with his followers from England, established a settlement at New Haven (1638). This settlement later joined the Connecticut colony (1664).

DAVIS, JEFFERSON (1808-89). President of the CONFEDERATE STATES OF AMERICA (1861-65). Davis was a strong supporter and leading spokesman of the principle of STATES RIGHTS and the expansion of slavery in Western territories. After the secession of the South, he was elected president of the Confederacy. After the surrender of General ROBERT E. LEE and the collapse of the Confederate Armies, Davis was captured, imprisoned for two years and then released. (See WAR BETWEEN THE STATES)

DAWES ACT (1887). Offered American citizenship and 160 acres of land to all Indian families and 80 acres to unmarried Indian adults who were willing to leave their tribal reservations. In 1924 all Indians were granted American citizenship.

DAWES, CHARLES G. (1865-1951). See DAWES PLAN

DAWES PLAN (1924). After Germany defaulted on its REPARATIONS payments (1923) following World War I, a plan was drawn up under the direction of Charles G. Dawes for a reduction and resumption of payments to the Allied Powers. These payments were again revised and reduced by the YOUNG PLAN (1929).

DAWES, WILLIAM (1745-99). See REVERE, PAUL

"DAY WHICH WILL LIVE IN INFAMY." See PEARL HARBOR ATTACK

D DAY. June 6, 1944. The day on which American and British forces, under the command of General DWIGHT D. EISENHOWER, landed on the coast of Normandy, France to reopen a long-awaited second front in WORLD WAR II (1941-45).

DEANE, SILAS (1737-89). American diplomat who represented the U.S. in France during the American Revolution. He obtained military and financial aid from France and also enlisted the services of such European military men as DE KALB, LAFAYETTE, PULASKI and STEUBEN to fight in the American Revolution. Together with BENJAMIN FRANKLIN and Arthur Lee, Silas Deane arranged the French TREATY OF ALLIANCE (1778).

"DEATH SENTENCE." See WHEELER-RAYBURN ACT (1935)

DEBS, EUGENE V. (1855-1926). Labor leader in the late 19th and early 20th century. In 1893 he organized the American Railway Union and in the following year this union started the famous PULLMAN STRIKE (1894). Debs was jailed briefly for violation of a court injunction. After his release he became leader of the Social Democratic Party, which changed its name in 1900 to SOCIALIST PARTY. Debs was its presidential candidate five times. During World War I (1917-18) Debs was a leading pacifist. As a result of his public speeches against the war he was convicted under the wartime ESPIONAGE ACT (1917). Although in prison in 1920, he was nominated for the presidency by the Socialist Party and polled a million votes. Debs was released from prison after the war by order of President HARDING.

DEBTOR-CREDITOR NATION. Before 1914 the U. S. was a debtor nation. The total value of American exports and payments to foreign countries was generally more than the total value of American imports and payments to the U.S. During and after World War I, the U.S. for the first time changed from a debtor to a creditor nation, and has remained a creditor nation since then.

DEBTOR LAWS. Under English COMMON LAW a debtor who could not pay his debts could be imprisoned. In the early 19th century individual states passed laws restricting imprisonment for debt. In 1821 Kentucky became the first state to abolish imprisonment for unpaid debts.

DECATUR, STEPHEN (1779-1820). Served in the undeclared naval war with France (1798) and in the war with the

104

BARBARY PIRATES (1804). During the WAR OF 1812 he was captain of the warship *United States* and won many notable victories over larger and more powerful British vessels. In 1815 he put an end to the tribute exacted by the Barbary pirates on foreign ships. A famous quotation is attributed to Decatur: "Our country, in her intercourse with foreign nations, may she always be in the right; but our country, right or wrong."

DECLARATION OF INDEPENDENCE (1776). Planned by a committee of the SECOND CONTINENTAL CONGRESS consisting of THOMAS JEFFERSON, JOHN ADAMS, BENJAMIN FRANKLIN, Roger Sherman and Robrt R. Livingston. Most of the wording of the Declaration was the work of Jefferson. The Declaration was finally adopted on July 4, 1776. It consists of three distinct sections. The first section lists the unalienable rights of man, such as "life, liberty, and the pursuit of happiness." The second section contains a long list of grievances against the British king. The last section contains the final declaration that these colonies are free and independent states. This is followed by the signature of JOHN HANCOCK and 55 other names.

DECLARATION OF WOMEN'S RIGHTS (1848). See FEMINIST MOVEMENT

DECLARATORY ACT (1766). Passed by the British Parliament after the repeal of the *Stamp Act* (1765). The Declaratory Act stated that the king and Parliament had the right to make laws that were binding on the colonies in America despite the lack of colonial representation in Parliament.

DEGRASSE, ADMIRAL FRANCOIS (1723-88). See BATTLE OF YORKTOWN (1781)

DE KALB, JOHANN (1721-80). German soldier of fortune who joined the Continental Army during the American Revolution to fight for American independence. He was with Washington at VALLEY FORGE and fought in many of the southern battles of the war. He was wounded at the BATTLE OF CAMDEN and died in 1780.

DELAWARE COLONY. Originally settled by the Dutch (1631) and later by Swedish colonists (1637). The English seized control of the region (1664) at the same time that they captured NEW AMSTERDAM. Delaware was put under the authority of WILLIAM PENN, the proprietor of the PENNSYLVANIA COLONY. In 1704 Delaware was organized as a separate colony but remained under the control of the Penn family until the beginning of the AMERICAN REVOLUTION (1775).

DE LEON, PONCE (c.1460-1521). Spanish explorer who in 1513 reached the shores of America in his search for a fabled "fountain of youth." He gave the name of Florida to the place where he landed, the southeast peninsula of what is now the U.S., and laid the basis for Spain's claim to the territory.

DELIMA V. BIDWELL (1901). See INSULAR CASES

DELOME LETTER (1898). The Spanish minister to the U. S. wrote a confidential letter to a Cuban friend describing President MC KINLEY as "weak," "a cheap politician" and "caterer to the rabble." The letter was stolen from the Havana Post Office and was published in the New York *Journal.* (See HEARST, WILLIAM RANDOLPH) The letter was one of the factors that turned American public opinion against Spain. (See SPANISH-AMERICAN WAR, 1898)

DEMOCRATIC PARTY. Developed after the ELECTION of 1828. In that election, the DEMOCRATIC-REPUBLICAN PARTY, led by their presidential candidate ANDREW JACKSON, shortened their name to Democratic Party. It included among its supporters the small farmers, frontiersmen, mechanics and debtors. After Jackson's victories in the ELECTION OF 1828 and the ELECTION OF 1832 the Democratic party elected VAN BUREN in 1836, POLK in 1844, PIERCE in 1852 and BUCHANAN in 1856. From the end of the WAR BETWEEN THE STATES (1865) to 1933 the Democrats won only four presidential elections—in 1884 and 1892, with GROVER CLEVELAND as candidate, and in 1912 and 1916, with WOODROW WILSON as candidate. Beginning in 1932 the Democratic Party elected FRANKLIN D. ROOSEVELT for four terms and in the ELECTION OF 1948 won a victory with HARRY S. TRUMAN as their candidate. One of the outstanding leaders of the party, WILLIAM JENNINGS BRYAN, was nominated for the presidency three times (1896, 1900, 1908) but was never elected. Since 1865 the Democratic Party platform has included such planks as low tariffs, anti-imperialism, a bimetallic money standard (see BIMETALLISM), participation in world affairs, repeal of the Prohibition Amendment and government regulation and control of industry.

DEMOCRATIC-REPUBLICAN PARTY. Political groups have used this name on two occasions. It was first used by the supporters of THOMAS JEFFERSON. After the Constitution and the new government went into operation the ANTI-FEDERALISTS called themselves Democratic-Republicans. They favored a strict construction of the Constitution and strong state, rather than national, government. When Jefferson became president after the ELECTION OF 1800, the Democratic-Republicans shortened their name to Republicans.

The second use of the name Democratic-Republican resulted from a split in Jefferson's old Republican Party after JOHN QUINCY ADAMS won the presidency in the ELECTION OF 1824. The supporters of ANDREW JACKSON, JOHN C. CALHOUN and the doctrine of STATES RIGHTS formed a party which was called Democratic-Republican. By 1828 this name was changed to DEMOCRATIC PARTY.

DEMONETIZATION ACT (1873). Provided that silver dollars were no longer to be considered standard coins and would no longer be coined into dollars. Silver mine owners and debtors called the Demonetization Act the "Crime of '73." Their demands led to the subsequent passing of the BLAND-ALLISON SILVER PURCHASE ACT (1878).

DEPOSIT ACT (1836). After the charter of the Second BANK OF U. S. expired (1836) Congress passed the Deposit Act, providing for the deposit of federal funds in state banks. The law also stated that federal surplus funds were to be distributed to the states as loans subject to recall. The federal government never asked the states for the return of these loaned funds.

107

DESERET. When the MORMONS moved west to Utah in 1847 they settled in Mexican Territory. After the U.S. obtained this territory by the treaty ending the MEXICAN WAR (1848), the Mormons asked to be admitted to the Union as the state of Deseret. The request was rejected by Congress, mainly because polygamy had not been outlawed in the proposed state. Utah was not admitted to the Union as a state until 1896.

DESERT LAND ACT (1877). One of many acts of Congress providing for the distribution of public land. Under this law an individual could acquire one square mile of public desert land for $160 (640 acres at 25¢ per acre) provided the owner irrigated the land within a three-year period after taking possession.

DE SOTO, HERNANDO (c.1500-1542). Spanish explorer and adventurer who discovered the Mississippi River. He explored the region on either side of the river (1539-42) but died during the expedition. He was buried by his followers in the great river he had found.

DESTROYER-MILITARY BASE EXCHANGE (1940). One year before the U. S. entered World War II the U. S. and Great Britain arranged for an exchange of 50 overage U. S. destroyers in return for British 99-year leases on naval and air bases in Newfoundland, Bermuda, the Bahamas, Jamaica, British Guiana and other British islands in the Caribbean Sea. The exchange aided the badly weakened British Navy and helped the U. S. prepare bases in anticipation of our involvement in the war.

DE VACA, CABEZA (c.1490-1557). Spanish explorer and adventurer who was a member of the expedition to Florida with NARVAEZ in 1528. De Vaca was one of the few survivors of the expedition, shipwrecked off the coast of Texas. He and a few comrades traveled overland through Texas, New Mexico and Arizona. Their stories were probably the origin of the famed legend of the SEVEN CITIES OF CIBOLA.

DEWEY, GEORGE (1837-1917). Commander of the American Asiatic Fleet at the outbreak of the SPANISH-

AMERICAN WAR (1898). As a result of Dewey's brilliant victory at the BATTLE OF MANILA BAY, the Philippine Islands easily and quickly came under U.S. control.

DEWEY, THOMAS E. (1902-   ). See ELECTION OF 1944 and ELECTION OF 1948

DIAZ, BARTHOLOMEW (c.1450-1500). Portuguese navigator who in 1486 became the first European to sail down the entire west coast of Africa to the Cape of Good Hope. His voyage blazed the way for future voyages around Africa to the Far East, such as the voyages of VASCO DA GAMA.

DICKINSON, JOHN (1732-1808). Colonial patriot, author of *Letters from a Farmer in Pennsylvania,* in which he presented colonial arguments against the levy of colonial taxes by the British Parliament. Dickinson was also the author of the OLIVE BRANCH PETITION (1775).

DILLINGHAM IMMIGRATION ACT (1921). Also called the Emergency Quota Law. It established the quota system of restricting immigration. Under this law each European country could send a quota of immigrants equal to 3% of the number of foreign-born persons of that nationality living in the U.S. according to the census of 1910. (See IMMIGRATION LEGISLATION)

DINGLEY TARIFF (1897). Removed many import items from the free list and raised the tariff on most other items. Thus the reduced rates of the WILSON-GORMAN TARIFF of 1894 were almost entirely eliminated. (See TARIFF LEGISLATION)

DINWIDDIE, ROBERT (1693-1770). Royal colonial governor of Virginia (1751-58) during the early years of the FRENCH AND INDIAN WAR (1754-63). In 1754 he sent GEORGE WASHINGTON and the colonial militia to protect a newly established British outpost called FORT NECESSITY.

DISARMAMENT, NAVAL. See WASHINGTON DISARMAMENT CONFERENCE (1922) and LONDON NAVAL CONFERENCE (1930)

DISPLACED PERSONS ACT (1948). Provided that 205,000 Europeans who were in displaced persons camps before December 31, 1945 were to be admitted to the U.S. in two years. This number was in addition to the national quotas established by the NATIONAL ORIGINS ACT of 1929.

DISSENTERS. English Protestants who refused to adhere to Anglicanism, the established religion of England. During the colonial period many dissenters came to the New World to escape religious persecution.

DIX, DOROTHEA L. (1802-87). Nineteenth century social reformer. She started campaigns for civilized treatment and housing of prison inmates and more humane treatment of the insane and poor. Because of her work many states established publicly supported asylums for the insane and abolished the practice of chaining prisoners.

DIXIE. Popular term applied to the South, particularly the South of slaves and plantations before the WAR BETWEEN THE STATES (1861-65). The popular song "Dixie" was composed in 1859 by Daniel D. Emmett, an entertainer, and became one of the most popular marching songs of the Confederate Army during the War Between the States.

DIXIECRATS. Third party, also called "States Rights Party," formed by Southern Democrats during the presidential election campaign of 1948 to oppose the regular Democratic Party civil rights program. In the election, Strom Thurmond, the Dixiecrat presidential candidate, received 39 electoral votes of Southern states. (See ELECTION OF 1948)

DOLLAR DIPLOMACY. U. S. policy in the early 20th century of using American diplomatic influence to encourage and protect American investments in Latin America. With the beginning of the GOOD NEIGHBOR POLICY in 1933 the U. S. abandoned its dollar diplomacy policy.

DOMESTIC SYSTEM. System of production by craftsmen working at home and doing most of the work by hand. The Domestic System was the usual method of producing goods in England before 1750 and in the U. S. before 1800. The INDUSTRIAL REVOLUTION, which began in England about 1750 and in the U. S. after the War of 1812, replaced the Domestic System with the FACTORY SYSTEM.

DOMINION OF NEW ENGLAND (1686-89). Established by King James II of England in 1684 in an effort to get better control over some of the English colonies in the New World. The Dominion included the New England colonies as well as New York, New Jersey and Pennsylvania. The first and only royal governor was SIR EDMOND ANDROS.

DONNER PARTY (1846-47). One of the many groups of pioneers which met disaster on the way west. The Donner Party, consisting of about 100 people, was trapped by early blizzards while trying to cross the Sierra Nevada Mountains. About half of the party was rescued and finally reached California.

DONGAN CHARTER (1686). Thomas Dongan, British colonial governor of New York, granted a charter of liberties to the people of the colony establishing a form of city government that was liberal for those times.

"DON'T GIVE UP THE SHIP." See LAWRENCE, CAPTAIN JAMES

DOOLITTLE, JAMES (1896-   ). U. S. Air Force general. During World War II he led a famous bombing raid (1942) over Tokyo, Yokohama and other Japanese cities from a U. S. aircraft carrier in the Pacific Ocean. The attack revealed the vulnerability of Japan to eventual concentrated air attack by the U. S.

DORR'S REBELLION (1842). A movement to revise the Rhode Island constitution and widen the suffrage, led by Thomas W. Dorr, resulted in the election of two governors and two legislatures in Rhode Island. The conservative government of Governor Samuel King declared Dorr's government to be an illegal insurrection and called out the state militia to suppress it. Dorr fled from Rhode Island and the so-called rebellion collapsed.

DOUGHBOYS. Nickname for American soldiers during WORLD WAR I (1917-18).

111

DOUGHFACES. Name applied to Northerners who supported the Southern program of extending slavery in Western territories before the WAR BETWEEN THE STATES (1861).

DOUGLAS, STEPHEN A. (1813-61). Nicknamed the "little giant" because of his short stature and his oratorical ability. He was senator from Illinois (1847-61), author of the controversial KANSAS-NEBRASKA ACT (1854)—which incorporated the principle of POPULAR SOVEREIGNTY—and a participant in the famous LINCOLN-DOUGLAS DEBATES (1856) over the extension of slavery in the Western territories. In the ELECTION OF 1860 he was the presidential candidate of the Northern Democrats.

DOW, NEAL (1804-97). See PROHIBITION PARTY

DOWNES V. BIDWELL (1901). See INSULAR CASES

DRAFT. See CONSCRIPTION

DRAFT RIOTS (1863). Occurred in New York City during the WAR BETWEEN THE STATES (1861-65) in protest against the military service laws. (See CONSCRIPTION) Northern draft laws for military service permitted those who could afford it to hire a substitute or be exempted from service by paying $300. The New York riots lasted for several days and resulted in the killing and wounding of hundreds of people.

DRAGO DOCTRINE (1907). Policy suggested by Louis Drago of Argentina at the Second Hague Conference and adopted by the nations present. The doctrine provided that unpaid international debts should not be collected by force unless the debtor nation refused to arbitrate or to accept the decision of an arbitration commission. The doctrine was an outgrowth of the VENEZUELA DEBT DISPUTE (1902), the SANTO DOMINGO DEBT DISPUTE (1905) and the announcement of the ROOSEVELT COROLLARY (1904).

DRAKE, EDWIN L. (1819-80). Known as the "father of the

112

American oil industry." In 1859 he drilled the first successful oil well in the U.S. near Titusville, Pennsylvania.

DRAKE, SIR FRANCIS (c.1540-96). English adventurer (see SEA DOGS) and ship captain who raided Spanish treasure ships sailing from the New World to Spain. During one of these raiding expeditions Drake sailed around the world (1577-80), thus duplicating the voyage of one of MAGELLAN's ships. During the war with Spain, Drake was vice-admiral of the British fleet that defeated the SPANISH ARMADA (1588).

DRED SCOTT DECISION (1857). Also known as Dred Scott v. Sanford. Dred Scott, a slave, was taken by his master from Missouri, a slave state, to Illinois, a free state, and then back to Missouri. Scott claimed his stay in Illinois made him a free man. Chief Justice ROGER TANEY, in his decision, stated that Negroes were property, that they did not become free when taken to a free state, and that the MISSOURI COMPROMISE, which had prohibited slavery in part of the Louisiana Territory, was therefore unconstitutional. By this decision, slavery became legal in all U.S. territories. The decision was denounced by anti-slavery groups in the North and in Congress.

DUE PROCESS OF LAW. The phrase appears in AMENDMENT 5 as a restriction on the federal government and in AMENDMENT 14 as a restriction on state powers. Both clauses were subject to numerous Supreme Court decisions relating to the rights of Negroes and to state laws restricting the functions of private corporations during the past century. In its early decisions the Court interpreted "due process" to mean legal procedures. In its later decisions the Court expanded the meaning to include unjust results arising from discriminatory legislation.

DUKE, JAMES B. (1856-1925). Made a fortune in the tobacco industry after merging a number of companies to form the American Tobacco Corporation, of which he became president. In 1911 the Supreme Court ordered the dissolution of the company because it violated the SHERMAN ANTI-TRUST ACT (1890).

DULLES, JOHN FOSTER (1888-1959). American statesman. As Secretary of State under President DWIGHT EISENHOWER he developed and executed the plan to establish the NORTH ATLANTIC TREATY ORGANIZATION (1949) and the SOUTHEAST ASIA TREATY ORGANIZATION (1954).

DULUTH, DANIEL (1636-1710). French explorer and Indian fighter. After exploring the Great Lakes region of Canada and the Lake Superior area he claimed the upper Mississippi Valley for France.

DUMBARTON OAKS CONFERENCE (1944). Held in Washington D.C., where representatives of the U.S., Great Britain, the Soviet Union and China met to draft a charter for a new world organization to be called the UNITED NATIONS. The work of this conference was completed at the SAN FRANCISCO CONFERENCE (1945).

DU PONT, ELEUTHERE IRENEE (1771-1834). American manufacturer of gunpowder and founder of the DuPont industrial empire. DuPont's descendants continued to expand the business until it became one of the largest chemical corporations in the world.

DUQUESNE, FORT. During the FRENCH AND INDIAN WAR (1754-63) it was the objective of the British General BRADDOCK. Although Braddock's expedition failed, the English captured the fort before the end of the war. After the war Fort Duquesne was renamed Fort Pitt. Today it is the site of the city of Pittsburgh.

DUST BOWL. Part of the Great Plains region including the states of Kansas, Nebraska, Texas, Oklahoma and New Mexico. Frequent dust storms, resulting from drought and unwise farming methods, developed in this region, particularly during the 1930's.

DUTCH EAST INDIA COMPANY. A private stock company in Holland that financed HENRY HUDSON's first voyage of exploration (1609) in the New World. Hudson was directed to search for a water passage to the Far East.

DUTCH WEST INDIA COMPANY. Private stock company in Holland that received a charter (1621) to establish settlements in the region of New York for the purpose of developing trade. Dutch settlements were established on Manhattan Island, at Fort Orange (present site of Albany), in Delaware and in New Jersey.

EATON, PEGGY (c. 1796-1879). Wife of John Eaton, Secretary of State in President ANDREW JACKSON's cabinet. Because of Mrs. Eaton's shady past as a barmaid she was snubbed by Washington society, although Jackson insisted that she be accepted. MARTIN VAN BUREN, the only member of the cabinet to support Jackson in the Eaton affair, became one of Jackson's closest advisers and received his support for the presidential nomination in the ELECTION OF 1836.

ECONOMIC AND SOCIAL COUNCIL (ECOSOC). See UNITED NATIONS

EDISON, THOMAS A. (1847-1931). One of our greatest scientific geniuses in the application of electricity to practical uses. He invented the phonograph (1877), the electric light (1879), and moving pictures (1894). In all, he obtained more than 1,300 patents in his lifetime.

EDWARDS, JONATHAN (1703-1758). See BIBLE COMMONWEALTH

EISENHOWER DOCTRINE (1957). Policy to help countries of the Middle East defend themselves against Communist infiltration, subversion or attack. In line with this policy, U. S. Marines landed in Lebanon in 1958 at the request of the Lebanese government. After the Communist threat passed the marines were withdrawn.

EISENHOWER, DWIGHT D. (1890-   ). Thirty-fifth president of the U.S. In WORLD WAR II (1941-45) he led the U. S. invasion of North Africa (1942) and the invasion of Western Europe (1944), establishing a second front. In 1952 he was nominated for the presidency by the Republican Party and was elected. (See ELECTION OF 1952) He was returned to the presidency again in the ELECTION OF 1956. In domestic affairs Eisenhower's presidency was featured by efforts to balance the budget, stop inflation and

116

enforce Supreme Court decisions against Negro SEGRE-GATION in the South. In foreign affairs Eisenhower concluded the KOREAN WAR (1950-53) with an armistice, announced the EISENHOWER DOCTRINE (1957) for the Middle East, continued former President HARRY S. TRUMAN's foreign aid program, resisted Soviet efforts to force the Western Allies out of Berlin and tried to reduce the tensions created by the COLD WAR with the Soviet Union.

EL DORADO. Mythical land of gold whose location shifted as different stories were told by the Indians and Spanish explorers of the New World. The tales of CABEZA DE VACA and MARCOS DE NIZA about the SEVEN CITIES OF CIBOLA induced PIZARRO and Orellanna to explore parts of South America and lured CORONADO to go north from Mexico in search of El Dorado.

ELECTION OF 1788. In this first national election under the new U.S. Constitution, GEORGE WASHINGTON was unanimously elected to the presidency by the Electoral College. JOHN ADAMS became the first vice-president.

ELECTION OF 1792. WASHINGTON ran for a second term as president and was again elected unanimously by the Electoral College. JOHN ADAMS, the choice of the FEDERALIST PARTY, was elected vice-president after a spirited contest.

ELECTION OF 1796. The FEDERALIST PARTY nominated JOHN ADAMS for president and the REPUBLICAN PARTY named THOMAS JEFFERSON as their candidate. During the voting by the Electoral College, the ballots were not marked to indicate which votes were for the presidency and which for vice-presidency. When the votes were counted it was found that John Adams had the largest number of votes and Thomas Jefferson was second. Thus John Adams, a Federalist, became the new president, and Thomas Jefferson, a Republican, became vice-president. (See AMENDMENT 12)

ELECTION OF 1800. The REPUBLICAN PARTY candidates were THOMAS JEFFERSON for president and AARON BURR for vice-president. The FEDERALIST

117

PARTY chose JOHN ADAMS as their presidential candidate and Charles C. Pinckney for vice-president. The Electoral College gave Jefferson 73 votes, Burr 73, Adams 65 and Pinckney 64. Since Burr and Jefferson were tied, the choice of president devolved upon the House of Representatives. Through HAMILTON's influence over Federalist votes, Jefferson was elected president by the House of Representatives after 36 ballots. To avoid future tie votes by the Electoral College, AMENDMENT 12 was added to the U. S. Constitution (1804).

ELECTION OF 1804. The Republican Party nominated THOMAS JEFFERSON and the FEDERALIST PARTY chose CHARLES C. PINCKNEY as presidential candidates. Jefferson was easily elected with a large majority of popular votes.

ELECTION OF 1808. A Republican Congressional Caucus nominated JAMES MADISON for president while another group of Eastern Republicans nominated George Clinton for the same office. The FEDERALIST PARTY nominated CHARLES COTESWORTH PINCKNEY for president. Although the Northeast voted against the Republican candidates because of the damage to its shipping industry resulting from the EMBARGO ACT (1808), Madison won an easy victory, while George Clinton was elected vice-president.

ELECTION OF 1812. The REPUBLICAN PARTY congressional caucus renominated JAMES MADISON for president on a "war with England" platform. The FEDERALIST PARTY nominated DE WITT CLINTON of New York for president on a peace policy platform. The votes of Southern and Western states who favored war with England gave Madison a solid victory in the election.

ELECTION OF 1816. JAMES MONROE, the Republican candidate, was easily elected over the FEDERALIST PARTY candidate RUFUS KING. This was the last election in which the Federalist Party nominated a candidate for the presidency.

ELECTION OF 1820. JAMES MONROE was unopposed by any candidate in the election. He received all but one of the electoral votes, with three electors abstaining from voting. The single vote not cast for Madison was given to JOHN QUINCY ADAMS.

ELECTION OF 1824. Four candidates were nominated for the presidency as "favorite sons" of their states—JOHN QUINCY ADAMS, William H. Crawford, HENRY CLAY and ANDREW JACKSON. None of the candidates received a majority of the electoral votes, although Jackson, with 94, was first and John Quincy Adams, with 84, was second. In such a situation the Constitution provides that the House of Representatives chooses the president. Clay threw his influence to John Quincy Adams who, as a result, was elected president.

ELECTION OF 1828. ANDREW JACKSON, the Democratic-Republican Party candidate, and JOHN QUINCY ADAMS, the National-Republican Party candidate, ran in this election. Jackson won an overwhelming victory, carrying all Southern and Western states as well as the state of Pennsylvania.

ELECTION OF 1832. The NATIONAL REPUBLICAN PARTY nominated HENRY CLAY for president and the DEMOCRATIC PARTY renominated ANDREW JACKSON. This was the first election campaign in which the presidential candidates were nominated by national party conventions instead of by party caucuses. The major issue of the campaign was President Jackson's veto (1832) of the bill to recharter the Second BANK OF U. S. Jackson won an overwhelming victory, receiving 219 electoral votes to 49 for Clay.

ELECTION OF 1836. Outgoing President Jackson threw his support to MARTIN VAN BUREN, who became the Democratic Party nominee for president. WILLIAM HENRY HARRISON was nominated by the ANTI-MASON PARTY of Pennsylvania, DANIEL WEBSTER by the Massachusetts WHIG PARTY and Hugh Lawson White by the anti-Jackson faction in Tennessee. The major issues of the campaign were Jackson's policies on the tariff and internal improvements, and his veto of the bill to recharter the second BANK OF U. S. Van Buren was elected with a bare majority of popular votes.

ELECTION OF 1840. The WHIG PARTY passed over their acknowledged leader HENRY CLAY to nominate WILLIAM HENRY HARRISON, a popular military leader. JOHN TYLER was the Whig nominee for vice-president. The Democratic Party convention renominated President MARTIN VAN BUREN. The campaign was not fought on any basic issues but there were many parades, mass meetings and campaign songs such as "Tippecanoe and Tyler too" and "Van, Van is a used-up man." Harrison and the Whig Party won a landslide victory. When Harrison died one month after his inauguration John Tyler became president.

ELECTION OF 1844. The WHIG PARTY nominated HENRY CLAY for the presidency while the DEMOCRATIC PARTY named JAMES K. POLK. The major issue in the election was the question of the annexation of Texas and Oregon. The Democrats favored "reannexation of Texas and reoccupation of Oregon." Clay, on the other hand, tried to evade the issue of territorial expansion. Polk won the election in a close popular vote, although he received 65 electoral votes more than Clay.

ELECTION OF 1848. The Democrats nominated LEWIS CASS while the Whigs nominated ZACHARY TAYLOR, hero of the MEXICAN WAR. Neither major party took a definite stand on the issue of prohibiting slavery in the newly acquired MEXICAN CESSION. The FREE SOIL PARTY, newly organized, nominated MARTIN VAN BUREN and took a firm stand against the further extension of slavery. Taylor and the Whigs won, mainly because many anti-slavery Democrats voted for Van Buren. When Taylor died in 1850 Vice-President MILLARD FILLMORE succeeded to the presidency.

ELECTION OF 1852. The Democrats nominated FRANKLIN PIERCE for president while the Whigs named another MEXICAN WAR hero, GENERAL WINFIELD SCOTT, hoping to repeat their former success with GENERAL ZACHARY TAYLOR in the ELECTION OF 1848. Both parties endorsed the COMPROMISE OF 1850. Pierce won an overwhelming victory.

ELECTION OF 1856. The newly organized REPUBLICAN PARTY nominated JOHN C. FREMONT for the presi-

120

dency and fought the campaign on the slogan "Free Soil, Free Speech, Fremont." The Democrats chose JAMES BUCHANAN as their candidate. Buchanan won the election by getting 174 electoral votes to Fremont's 114.

ELECTION OF 1860. In this momentous election the DEMO-CRATIC PARTY split over the question of slavery in the territories. The Northern Democrats nominated STEPHEN A. DOUGLAS for president but the Southern Democrats named John C. Breckenridge. The REPUBLICAN PARTY nominated ABRAHAM LINCOLN on a platform opposing the extension of slavery in territories, favoring free land to Western homesteaders and federal aid to build transcontinental railroads. A third group, the CONSTITUTIONAL UNION PARTY, named John Bell as presidential candidate. Lincoln won the election, with 180 electoral votes as against 123 for all other candidates combined. However, he did not get a majority of the popular votes.

ELECTION OF 1864. The REPUBLICAN PARTY, calling itself the Union Party, renominated ABRAHAM LIN-COLN for the presidency and ANDREW JOHNSON for the vice-presidency. The Northern DEMOCRATIC PAR-TY chose General GEORGE B. MC CLELLAN as their candidate and campaigned on the issue of ending the war immediately. News of General WILLIAM T. SHERMAN's victories in Georgia assured Lincoln of re-election. He won a landslide victory with 212 electoral votes to 21 for Mc-Clellan. After Lincoln's assassination (1865), Vice-President Johnson succeeded to the presidency.

ELECTION OF 1868. The REPUBLICAN PARTY nominated GENERAL ULYSSES S. GRANT for president on a platform endorsing the radical RECONSTRUCTION program. The DEMOCRATIC PARTY named Horatio Seymour on a platform condemning the radical Reconstruction plan and advocating the payment of the national debt in GREENBACKS. During the campaign the Republicans made the most of "WAVING THE BLOODY SHIRT." Grant won most of the electoral votes but only a small majority of the popular votes.

ELECTION OF 1872. In spite of scandals exposed during GRANT's first presidential administration, the Republican

Party renominated him for the presidency. The Democrats named HORACE GREELEY, editor of the New York *Tribune,* as their candidate. Greeley was also supported by the newly organized LIBERAL-REPUBLICAN PARTY. In the election campaign the Democrats and Liberal Republicans called for an end to Reconstruction in the South, Civil Service Reform and the elimination of corruption in government. Grant was reelected by an electoral vote of 286 to 66 for Greeley.

ELECTION OF 1876. One of the most critical elections in our history. The Republicans nominated RUTHERFORD B. HAYES on the basis of his war record and his support of political reforms. The Democrats chose SAMUEL J. TILDEN, the man who helped to smash the TWEED RING in New York City. The major issues in the election were CIVIL SERVICE REFORM, the tariff and the currency system. The electoral count gave Tilden 184 undisputed votes and Hayes 165. However, 19 votes from Florida, Louisiana and South Carolina and one vote from Oregon were in dispute. A special Electoral Commission was set up by an act of Congress (ELECTORAL COMMISSION ACT) to determine which electoral votes were valid. The commission awarded all the disputed electoral votes to Hayes, who thus was chosen president by an electoral vote of 185 to 184 for Tilden.

ELECTION OF 1880. As a result of a deadlock between the STALWART supporters of ULYSSES S. GRANT and the HALF BREED supporters of JAMES G. BLAINE, the REPUBLICAN PARTY nominated JAMES A. GARFIELD, a so-called "dark horse." The Democrats nominated General Winfield S. Hancock. Garfield won the election, although he received a bare majority of the popular vote. When Garfield was assassinated in 1881 Vice-President CHESTER A. ARTHUR succeeded to the presidency.

ELECTION OF 1884. The REPUBLICAN PARTY nominated JAMES G. BLAINE as their presidential candidate. The Democrats named GROVER CLEVELAND, reform governor of New York State. The campaign featured "mudslinging" and name-calling on both sides. During the campaign one of Blaine's supporters labeled the Democrats as the party of "Rum, Romanism and Rebellion." This seriously damaged Blaine's chances in New York State. A close victory of only 1149 popular votes in New York State gave Cleveland the presidency and provided the Democratic Party with its first presidential victory since 1856.

ELECTION OF 1888. President GROVER CLEVELAND was renominated by the DEMOCRATIC PARTY and General BENJAMIN HARRISON, grandson of WILLIAM HENRY HARRISON, was nominated by the Republicans. The major election issue was the protective tariff, which the Republicans favored and the Democrats opposed. Harrison won the election on the basis of electoral votes although Cleveland received 100,000 more popular votes than he did. (See MINORITY PRESIDENTS)

ELECTION OF 1892. The REPUBLICAN PARTY renominated BENJAMIN HARRISON and the DEMOCRATIC PARTY renamed GROVER CLEVELAND. The high MC KINLEY TARIFF (1890) was one of the major issues in the election. A third political group, the POPULIST PARTY, nominated JAMES B. WEAVER and made "free silver" a major campaign issue. The election results gave Cleveland a clear-cut victory. The Populist Party showed surprising strength by polling more than 1,000,000 popular votes, mainly in the West.

ELECTION OF 1896. In this bitterly contested election, the DEMOCRATIC PARTY nominated WILLIAM JENNINGS BRYAN for the presidency on a platform calling for free and unlimited coinage of silver at a 16-to-1 ratio. (See BIMETALLISM) In accepting the nomination Bryan made his famous "CROSS OF GOLD" SPEECH. The POPULIST PARTY also nominated Bryan and then merged with the Democratic Party. The REPUBLICAN PARTY named WILLIAM MC KINLEY on the first ballot, with a gold standard platform. Bryan's radical speeches alarmed "big business" interests who brought pressure to bear to get McKinley elected. The electoral results gave McKinley a clear-cut victory, although only 600,000 popular votes separated the two candidates.

ELECTION OF 1900. The REPUBLICAN PARTY renominated President WILLIAM MC KINLEY as their presiden-

123

tial candidate and THEODORE ROOSEVELT as vice-presidential candidate. The DEMOCRATIC PARTY renominated WILLIAM JENNINGS BRYAN. The election was fought on the old issue of "free silver" and the newer issue of imperialism resulting from colonial acquisitions after the SPANISH-AMERICAN WAR (1898). McKinley won an easy victory. After McKinley's assassination in 1901, Vice-President Theodore Roosevelt became president.

ELECTION OF 1904. The REPUBLICAN PARTY nominated THEODORE ROOSEVELT, who had succeeded to the presidency on the death of President MC KINLEY (1901). The DEMOCRATIC PARTY nominated Alton B. Parker, a conservative New Yorker. The SOCIALIST PARTY nominated EUGENE V. DEBS. In the election, Roosevelt won an easy victory, carrying every state outside of the SOLID SOUTH.

ELECTION OF 1908. At the REPUBLICAN PARTY convention, President THEODORE ROOSEVELT supported WILLIAM HOWARD TAFT, his Secretary of War, for the presidential nomination. Taft was named on the first ballot. The DEMOCRATIC PARTY nominated WILLIAM JENNINGS BRYAN for the third and last time. Taft was elected with a majority of more than 1,000,000 popular votes.

ELECTION OF 1912. Despite THEODORE ROOSEVELT's opposition, the REPUBLICAN PARTY renominated WILLIAM HOWARD TAFT for the presidency. The Progressive Republicans held their own convention and nominated Theodore Roosevelt, thus splitting the party. The DEMOCRATIC PARTY convention was also split but finally united on WOODROW WILSON as the party nominee. The SOCIALIST PARTY named EUGENE V. DEBS as presidential candidate. The Republican Party split threw the election to Wilson, who received an overwhelming total of 435 electoral votes.

ELECTION OF 1916. President WOODROW WILSON was renominated by the DEMOCRATIC PARTY, while the REPUBLICAN PARTY convention chose CHARLES EVANS HUGHES, an associate justice of the Supreme Court, as their presidential candidate. The PROGRESSIVE

PARTY gave its support to Hughes. The campaign was based on Republican criticism of Wilson's foreign policies. Wilson and the Democratic Party based their campaign on the slogan: "He kept us out of war" (meaning WORLD WAR I). The election results were very close but late returns from California gave the election to Wilson.

ELECTION OF 1920. The REPUBLICAN PARTY nominated Senator WARREN G. HARDING as their presidential candidate and CALVIN COOLIDGE for the vice-presidency. The DEMOCRATIC PARTY convention named Governor JAMES M. COX of Ohio for president and FRANKLIN D. ROOSEVELT for vice-president. The SOCIALIST PARTY nominated EUGENE V. DEBS, their perennial candidate, who at the time of nomination was in prison for violation of the wartime ESPIONAGE ACT. The campaign was based mainly on the question of U.S. membership in the LEAGUE OF NATIONS. Harding won an overwhelming victory. When he died in 1923 during his term of office, Vice-President Coolidge became president.

ELECTION OF 1924. CALVIN COOLIDGE was nominated by the REPUBLICAN PARTY as presidential candidate. At the convention of the DEMOCRATIC PARTY, the two leading candidates, William G. McAdoo and ALFRED E. SMITH of New York, were deadlocked after more than 100 ballots. The convention finally chose John W. Davis, a "dark horse," as presidential candidate. Election issues included the plight of the farmer as well as political and social reform. Coolidge and the Republicans won an easy victory.

ELECTION OF 1928. Because CALVIN COOLIDGE did not "choose to run," the REPUBLICAN PARTY nominated HERBERT HOOVER, Secretary of Commerce, for the presidency. The DEMOCRATIC PARTY nominated Governor ALFRED E. SMITH of New York. Hoover won an overwhelming victory, mainly because Smith, a strong anti-prohibitionist, had been associated with the New York TAMMANY political machine and was of the Roman Catholic faith. It was the first election since the WAR BETWEEN THE STATES (1865) in which the Republicans won any states in the SOLID SOUTH.

ELECTION OF 1932. The REPUBLICAN PARTY renominated HERBERT HOOVER for the presidency, while the DEMOCRATIC PARTY named FRANKLIN D. ROOSEVELT, governor of New York State. The major issues were the methods to be used to cope with depression problems and the repeal of the PROHIBITION amendment. During the campaign, Roosevelt announced his proposed NEW DEAL for the American people. Roosevelt and the Democrats won a landslide victory, carrying the electoral votes of **all but six states.**

ELECTION OF 1936. The REPUBLICAN PARTY nominated Alfred M. Landon, governor of Kansas, and the DEMOCRATIC PARTY renominated FRANKLIN D. ROOSEVELT for a second presidential term. The major issues of the campaign were Roosevelt's NEW DEAL legislative program and his plan to "pack" the Supreme Court. (See JUDICIARY REORGANIZATION BILL) Roosevelt won the electoral votes of every state except Maine and Vermont.

ELECTION OF 1940. The REPUBLICAN PARTY nominated Wendell L. Willkie, a well-known businessman, while the DEMOCRATIC PARTY broke the two-term precedent by renominating FRANKLIN D. ROOSEVELT for a third presidential term. The major campaign issues included our neutrality policies, our national defense program, and the precedent-breaking third-term issue. Roosevelt won the election, although the margin of victory was much smaller than it had been in 1932 and 1936.

ELECTION OF 1944. The Republicans nominated Thomas E. Dewey, governor of New York, for president. The Democratic convention renominated FRANKLIN D. ROOSEVELT for president for the fourth time and Senator HARRY S. TRUMAN of Missouri for vice-president. The major issues of the campaign were Roosevelt's opposition to further farm aid and his "tax the rich" program. Roosevelt won his fourth presidential election, carrying 53% of the popular vote. On Roosevelt's death in 1945, Harry Truman succeeded to the presidency.

ELECTION OF 1948. The Democratic Party nominated HARRY S. TRUMAN despite the opposition of Southern and left-wing Democrats. The left-wing Democrats formed a third party, called PROGRESSIVES, and nominated HENRY WALLACE for president. The Southern Democrats also formed a new party, called the DIXIECRATS, and nominated Governor J. Strom Thurmond of South Carolina. The Republicans again nominated Governor Thomas E. Dewey of New York for president. Despite the Democratic Party splits, Truman won a very close but surprising personal victory.

ELECTION OF 1952. The REPUBLICAN PARTY nominated General DWIGHT D. EISENHOWER for president. Because President HARRY S. TRUMAN declined to run for another term, the DEMOCRATIC PARTY nominated Adlai E. Stevenson, governor of Illinois. The election issues were based on Republican opposition to Truman's conduct of the KOREAN WAR (1950-53), the unbalanced budget, the growing national debt and Truman's opposition to the TAFT-HARTLEY ACT. Eisenhower and the Republicans won a decisive victory, getting 442 electoral votes to Stevenson's 89.

ELECTION OF 1956. The REPUBLICAN PARTY renominated DWIGHT D. EISENHOWER and the DEMOCRATIC PARTY renominated Adlai Stevenson for the presidency. The major issues were Eisenhower's conduct of the presidential office, and McCarthyism. (See JOSEPH MC CARTHY) In the election, Eisenhower won an even more decisive victory than in 1952.

ELECTION OF 1960. The REPUBLICAN PARTY nominated Richard Nixon for the presidency and the DEMOCRATIC PARTY named JOHN F. KENNEDY. The major issues of the campaign were the loss of national prestige, the danger of inflation and the Catholic faith of the Democratic candidate. Kennedy won the election by a very narrow margin.

ELECTORAL COMMISSION ACT (1876). To settle the problem of 20 disputed electoral votes in the ELECTION OF 1876, Congress established an Electoral Commission. This commission, consisting of eight Republicans and seven Democrats, awarded all of the disputed votes to RUTHER-

FORD B. HAYES, the Republican candidate, who thereby became president. (See TILDEN, SAMUEL J.)

ELECTORAL COUNT ACT (1887). Enacted to prevent a repetition of the dispute in the Hayes-Tilden ELECTION OF 1876. The law provided that if a state sent two sets of electoral votes to Congress, the votes approved by the state governor were to be considered official.

ELKINS ACT (1903). Provided for regulation of interstate railroads. The law specifically forbad companies to accept railroad rebates or other privileged rate reductions. (See RAILROAD LEGISLATION)

EMANCIPATION PROCLAMATION (1863). Military order by President ABRAHAM LINCOLN issued during the WAR BETWEEN THE STATES (1861-65) declaring that all slaves in states fighting against the Union were free. The proclamation did not apply to slaves in the BORDER STATES. (See AMENDMENT 13)

EMBARGO ACT (1807). Passed in an effort to stop the British and French seizure of neutral American ships during the Napoleonic Wars in Europe. The act stopped all American ships from going to any foreign port and thereby proved to be far more damaging to U. S. shipping interests than it was to the English or French. The Embargo Act was repealed in 1809.

EMERGENCY BANKING ACT (1933). See BANK HOLIDAY

EMERGENCY RAILROAD TRANSPORTATION ACT (1933). See RAILROAD LEGISLATION

EMERGENCY TARIFF ACT (1921). Passed specifically to help farmers. It was replaced the following year by the comprehensive FORDNEY-MC CUMBER TARIFF ACT (1922). (See TARIFF LEGISLATION)

"EMPIRE BUILDER." See HILL, JAMES J.

128

EMPLOYMENT ACT (1946). Committed the national government to a policy of maintaining full employment by all the means at its disposal. The act also established a Council of Economic Advisors to provide the president with accurate information and expert advice on the economic problems of the nation.

"EMPRESS OF CHINA." The first U. S. merchant ship to reach China (1784) and open the China trade. This trade with the Orient brought immense wealth to American shipowners and traders in the 19th century.

ENTAIL. System of land ownership in England and the early English colonies. A person who owned land in "entail" could never sell it. This system thus tended to increase the land holdings of a few wealthy colonists by inheritance, and to make it difficult for other settlers to buy land. By 1800 the right of entail was abolished in almost all states.

E PLURIBUS UNUM. Official motto of the Great Seal of the U.S. It means "One (nation) from many (states)," and is derived from an ancient Latin poem.

ERA OF GOOD FEELINGS. The period from 1817 to 1825, during which JAMES MONROE was president. Sharp party rivalries diminished and a spirit of nationalism developed. (See NATIONALIST ERA)

ERDMAN ACT (1898). See YELLOW DOG CONTRACTS

ERICSON, LEIF (c.1000). According to early Norse legends, Leif Ericson sailed from Greenland about 1000 A.D. and reached North America about 500 years before Columbus. However, no permanent settlements were established and the voyage had no tangible results.

ERICSSON, JOHN (1803-89). Invented and patented the screw propeller for moving ships through water (1836). During the WAR BETWEEN THE STATES (1861-65) he designed the *Monitor,* an ironclad ship which fought an indecisive naval battle with the Southern ironclad ship, the *Merrimac,* thus introducing the era of iron and steel ships. (See MONITOR AND MERRIMAC)

ERIE CANAL. Built by New York State through the efforts of Governor DE WITT CLINTON and opened for traffic in 1825. The canal provided a shallow-water route stretching for 360 miles across New York State from the Hudson River to Lake Erie, and reduced tenfold the cost of transporting freight across the state.

ERIE RAILROAD. Built before the WAR BETWEEN THE STATES (1861) across New York State. From 1866 to 1868 a struggle for financial control of the line began between Daniel Drew, JAY GOULD and JAMES FISK on one hand and CORNELIUS VANDERBILT on the other. The financial struggle was marked by political trickery, issue of illegal stock and outright violence. Eventually the Erie Railroad went into bankruptcy and was reorganized in 1878.

ESCH-CUMMINS TRANSPORTATION ACT (1920). Enacted to help financially weak railroads. THE INTERSTATE COMMERCE COMMISSION was empowered to establish rates that would give railroads a fair return, to permit roads to consolidate if economically desirable, and to establish a fund to help weak railroads financially. A Railroad Labor Board was also established to settle railroad labor disputes.

ESPIONAGE ACT (1917). Provided severe penalties for anyone giving aid or information to the enemy or interfering with the national war effort or the CONSCRIPTION laws during WORLD WAR I (1917-18). A few hundred pacifists, including EUGENE V. DEBS, the Socialist leader, were imprisoned.

ESSEX JUNTO. The faction of the FEDERALIST PARTY in New England which firmly believed that government should be run only by the rich and well-born. They favored HAMILTON'S FINANCIAL PLAN, opposed the WAR of 1812 and were the dominant group at the HARTFORD CONVENTION (1814).

EUROPEAN DEFENSE COMMUNITY (E.D.C.). By an agreement signed in 1952 by the U. S. and seven European nations (Great Britain, West Germany, France, Belgium, Holland, Luxembourg and Italy), a single army was estabtablished for the defense of Western Europe against possible military aggression by the Soviet Union. The E.D.C. was to be the military arm to implement the NORTH ATLANTIC TREATY ORGANIZATION.

EUROPEAN RECOVERY PROGRAM. See FOREIGN AID PROGRAM

EVER NORMAL GRANARY PLAN. See AGRICULTURAL ADJUSTMENT ACT (1938)

EXPANSIONISTS. American political leaders who believed that the U. S. was destined to grow in size. Prior to the War of 1812 such Expansionists were called WAR HAWKS. After the war, Expansionists expressed their idea of territorial expansion in terms of MANIFEST DESTINY. During and after the SPANISH-AMERICAN WAR (1898) advocates of territorial expansion overseas were called supporters of a policy of IMPERIALISM.

EX PARTE MERRYMAN (1861). See HABEAS CORPUS

EXPORT-IMPORT BANK (1934). Established by Congress to provide financial help to American businesses engaged in foreign trade.

EXPOSITION AND PROTEST (1828). Document prepared by Vice-President JOHN C. CALHOUN as a protest against the high protective tariff of 1828 (TARIFF OF ABOMINATIONS). The Exposition and Protest stated that protective tariffs were unconstitutional. Furthermore, under the COMPACT THEORY of Union, any state that decided a law of Congress was unconstitutional could declare it null and void and refuse to enforce it.

131

"FABULOUS FIFTIES." Era from 1950 to 1960 during which the U. S. enjoyed economic prosperity, and revolutionary changes took place in many fields. AUTOMATION was introduced in industry; installment buying made possible the purchase of mass-produced articles by practically everyone. On farms the application of scientific methods produced record crops. The development of penicillin, polio vaccine, and antibiotics resulted in vast forward strides in medicine. Nuclear power was harnessed to drive ships and generate electricity. Man-made satellites were rocketed into space to circle the earth.

FACTORY SYSTEM. The method of manufacturing in factories with the use of machines. The factory replaced the DOMESTIC SYSTEM in which manufactured goods were made at home by hand. Both the INDUSTRIAL REVOLUTION and the Factory System began in England in the middle of the 18th century. The first textile factory in the U. S. was built in 1790 in Pawtucket, Rhode Island. The WAR OF 1812 stimulated the opening of many factory industries and since then the building of factories in the U. S. has never ceased.

FAIR DEAL (1948). See TRUMAN, HARRY S.

FAIR EMPLOYMENT PRACTICES ACTS. In 1946 Congress attempted to pass a Fair Employment Practices Act forbidding employment discrimination because of color, race or religion in all industries working on federal contracts. The bill was defeated as a result of a FILIBUSTER of Southern senators. However, a number of states, including New York, New Jersey, Massachusetts, Connecticut and Washington, have passed state Fair Employment Practices Acts.

FAIR LABOR STANDARDS ACT (1938). Known also as the Wages and Hours Act. This law established a 40-cent minimum wage and a 40-hour maximum work week for

132

employees engaged in interstate industries. The law also established "time and a half" rates for overtime work and abolished child labor in interstate industries. In subsequent years Congress raised the minimum wage gradually to $1.25 per hour. The constitutionality of the law was upheld by the Supreme Court in United States v. Darby (1941).

FALL, ALBERT (1861-1944). See TEAPOT DOME SCANDAL

FALLEN TIMBERS, BATTLE OF (1794). Decisive victory of American forces under ANTHONY WAYNE against Indians on the frontier. This battle was one of many similar skirmishes with hostile Indians on the frontier during the 18th and 19th centuries.

FAREWELL ADDRESS (1796). Famous speech made by GEORGE WASHINGTON just before he retired from the presidency. In the address Washington warned against the dangers of sectional rivalries, the evils of party strife and the importance of avoiding entangling alliances with foreign nations. This last bit of advice was the start of the American policy of ISOLATION, which lasted until 1945.

FARM BLOC. A group of Midwestern senators and representatives in Congress, both Republicans and Democrats, who seek to help the farmer by means of Congressional legislation. This Farm Bloc is an informal grouping and not a definite organization. The bloc has been active in Congress since the end of World War I and has been responsible for much of the favorable FARM LEGISLATION in the last three decades.

FARM CREDIT ADMINISTRATION (F.C.A.). A federal NEW DEAL agency established by Congress in 1933 to centralize and coordinate the work of providing loans to farmers during the GREAT DEPRESSION. The Federal Land Banks (see FEDERAL FARM LOAN ACT) and the Federal Farm Board (see AGRICULTURAL MARKETING ACT) were put under the Farm Credit Administration and regulations for farm loans were liberalized.

FARMER-LABOR PARTY. Organized about 1920 by some former members of the PROGRESSIVE PARTY, together

133

with a number of Midwestern farmer and labor organizations. The party platform called for government ownership of public utilities, aid to farmers and legislation to improve labor conditions. In the presidential ELECTION OF 1920 the Farmer-Labor Party polled less than 300,000 votes. However, in subsequent elections it elected a number of U. S. senators, including Henrik Shipstead and Ernest Lundeen, and won many local elections in North Dakota, South Dakota and Minnesota. During the presidential ELECTION OF 1924 the party was dissolved and the former members supported ROBERT LA FOLLETTE, the Progressive Party candidate. Thereafter the Farmer-Labor Party was revived briefly until 1933, when it came to an end with the election of FRANKLIN D. ROOSEVELT and the beginning of the NEW DEAL.

FARMERS' ALLIANCE. Associations of farmers organized in the 1870's and 1880's for the purpose of getting government regulation of railroad rates and obtaining other legislative aid for farmers. At the height of its power (1890) the Farmers' Alliance had more than a million farmer members. In 1892 the Farmers' Alliance merged with the newly organized POPULIST PARTY and gradually the Alliance disappeared as a separate organization.

"FARMERS LETTERS." See DICKINSON, JOHN

FARM LEGISLATION. After the WAR BETWEEN THE STATES (1861-65), efforts to help the farmer took the form of legislation to regulate railroads (see RAILROAD LEGISLATION) and to inflate the currency (see GREENBACKS and BIMETALLISM). In 1889 Congress established the Department of Agriculture. After WORLD WAR I (1917-18) efforts of the Congressional FARM BLOC to provide help to farmers through legislation did not succeed, despite the enactment of the CAPPER-VOLSTEAD ACT (1922) and the AGRICULTURAL MARKETING ACT (1929). With the beginning of the NEW DEAL (1933) program, however, Congress passed a number of laws to provide direct agricultural relief. These included the AGRICULTURAL ADJUSTMENT ACT of 1933 (declared unconstitutional), the SOIL CONSERVATION AND DOMESTIC ALLOTMENT ACT (1936) and the AGRICULTURAL ADJUSTMENT ACT OF 1938.

To help farmers with mortgage problems, and tenant farmers, Congress also passed the FARM MORTGAGE MORATORIUM ACT (1935) and the BANKHEAD-JONES FARM TENANT ACT (1937).

FARM MORTGAGE MORATORIUM ACT. Also known as the Frazier-Lemke Farm Mortgage Moratorium Act. The first law under this name (1934) sought to prevent further farm mortgage foreclosures by providing that foreclosed farms could be repurchased by former owners at lower values and with lower interest payments. The Supreme Court (Louisville Bank v. Radford, 1935) held this law to be unconstitutional. Congress immediately passed a second Farm Mortgage Moratorium Act (1935) known as the Second Frazier-Lemke Act. It provided that farmers who defaulted on mortgage payments could ask for a three-year moratorium on payments and pay a fair rental during the period of nonmortgage payment. The Supreme Court upheld the constitutionality of this law in 1937.

FARM SECURITY ADMINISTRATION. See BANK-HEAD-JONES FARM TENANT ACT (1937)

FARRAGUT DAVID G. (1801-70). Commander of a naval force during the WAR BETWEEN THE STATES (1861-65). In 1862 Farragut led a flotilla of gunboats from the Gulf of Mexico up the Mississippi River to New Orleans. In this maneuver he destroyed the Confederate fleet guarding the city and opened the way for the capture of New Orleans by Union forces. In 1864 he defeated a Confederate flotilla in Mobile Bay, Alabama. At this battle Farragut is supposed to have replied to a warning about enemy torpedoes with the words: "Damn the torpedoes; full speed ahead."

"FATHER OF THE CONSTITUTION." See MADISON, JAMES

FAVORITE SONS. A term applied to persons who are nominated for the presidency by their own state delegations at national conventions.

FEDERAL COMMUNICATIONS ACT (1934). Established the Federal Communications Commission (F.C.C.) with power to license and regulate radio and television broadcasting in the U. S. The regulation of telegraph, telephone and cable lines, formerly under the control of the INTER-STATE COMMERCE COMMISSION (see MANN-ELKINS ACT, 1910) was also transferred to the jurisdiction of the F.C.C.

FEDERAL DEPOSIT INSURANCE CORPORATION. See BANKING ACT of June 1933

FEDERAL EMERGENCY RELIEF ADMINISTRATION (F.E.R.A.). See UNEMPLOYMENT LEGISLATION

FEDERAL FARM BOARD. See AGRICULTURAL MAR-KETING ACT (1929)

FEDERAL FARM LOAN ACT (1916). Established 12 Federal Land Banks that were to make money available to local banks for loans to farmers at interest rates not higher than 6% and for periods of time up to 33 years.

FEDERALIST, THE (1787-1788). A series of 85 letters or essays written by ALEXANDER HAMILTON, JAMES MADISON and JOHN JAY. They were first published in New York and later collected in book form and called *The Federalist*. The essays explained the contents of the Constitution so skillfully that it won over many New Yorkers who had opposed its ratification.

FEDERALIST PARTY. Originally the name "Federalist" referred to those who favored a strong union of states and ratification of the Constitution (1789). (See FEDERALIST, THE) These Federalist supporters included conservative businessmen, merchants, planters, lawyers, the clergy and large landowners. After the adoption of the Constitution, the Federalists became an organized political party that favored a loose interpretation of the Constitution, a strong national government and a sound financial policy for the nation. ALEXANDER HAMILTON was leader of the party. Although Washington refused to ally himself with any political faction, JOHN ADAMS, who followed him as president, was a Federalist. The Federalist Party continued as an important force in state and national politics after 1801 although it did not succeed in electing another

136

president after John Adams. In 1814 the Federalists sponsored the HARTFORD CONVENTION, which met to oppose the continuance of the WAR OF 1812. This made the party so unpopular that it soon disappeared entirely from state and national politics.

FEDERAL RESERVE ACT (1913). Also known as the Glass-Owen Act. Main objective of the law was to provide an elastic currency that would expand and contract with the needs of business. The Act divided the U. S. into 12 Federal Reserve Districts, each with a Federal Reserve Bank. All National Banks (see NATIONAL BANKING ACT, 1863) were required, and State Banks were invited, to join the Federal Reserve System. The Federal Reserve Banks were to rediscount notes on which member banks of the Federal Reserve System had loaned money, thus making more money available. By increasing or decreasing its rediscount rate the Federal Reserve Board could encourage or discourage lending by member banks. A Federal Reserve Board was established to administer this act. By the BANKING ACT OF 1935 the name of the Board was changed to the Board of Governors of the Federal Reserve System and the powers of the Federal Reserve System were expanded.

FEDERAL SYSTEM. A system of government which consists of a national government for the whole country and many state governments to provide home rule on local matters. This division of powers between national and state governments was established by the U. S. Constitution.

FEDERAL TRADE COMMISSION ACT (1914). Enacted during President WOODROW WILSON's administration. The law established an agency called the Federal Trade Commission (F.T.C.) with power to investigate and stop unethical business practices, such as false or misleading advertising, of interstate corporations.

FEMINIST MOVEMENT. The movement to give women equal rights with men began in the early 19th century through the work of LUCRETIA MOTT, ELIZABETH CADY STANTON, SUSAN B. ANTHONY, the GRIMKÉ SISTERS and other feminist leaders. Numerous women suffrage societies were organized to agitate for equal rights

137

for women. In 1848 a Women's Rights Convention was held at Seneca Falls, N. Y. at which a Declaration of Women's Rights was drawn up. Before the War Between the States began (1861), women's colleges or seminaries were established. Mount Holyoke College was opened in 1837, Elmira College in 1855 and Vassar College in 1861. Oberlin College was the first men's institution that opened its doors to women students (1834). After the War Between the States (1865), the Feminist Movement grew stronger and by 1900 a number of states and territories had granted women the right to vote (see WOMEN SUFFRAGE) and to own property in their own names. Women suffrage leaders of the early 20th century included CARRIE CHAPMAN CATT and Anna Howard Shaw. After World War I (1918), the presence of women in industry and in the professions became an accepted fact. In 1920 AMENDMENT 19 gave all women the right to vote. During WORLD WAR II (1941-45) women for the first time served in branches of the armed forces.

FENIAN MOVEMENT. During the 1850's Americans of Irish ancestry organized a Fenian movement to help Ireland gain its independence from Great Britain. The American Fenians sent arms, men and money to Ireland but their contribution did little to help the Irish rebels. In 1866 one group of American Fenians crossed the border into Canada with a few hundred men in an unsuccessful raid.

FIELD, CYRUS W. (1819-1892). American financier who planned and built the first transatlantic cable between the U. S. and Great Britain. After a number of preliminary failures a successful trans-Atlantic cable was laid on the ocean floor in 1866.

"FIFTY-FOUR FORTY OR FIGHT." See OREGON TREATY

"FIFTY-NINERS." See COMSTOCK LODE and GOLD RUSH

FILIBUSTER, CONGRESSIONAL. A parliamentary device by which a speaker holds the floor by continuous speaking, thus making it impossible for the legislature to continue with its regular business. Filibusters are common in the

U. S. Senate, where senators have the right to unlimited speaking time unless the Cloture Rule is invoked. The individual filibustering record was set by Senator J. Strom Thurmond of North Carolina, who spoke for more than 24 hours against a proposed CIVIL RIGHTS BILL (1957).

FILIBUSTERING EXPEDITIONS. In the 16th, 17th and 18th centuries a filibuster referred to a private military expedition organized by one or a group of buccaneers to capture ships, towns or even countries. In the 19th century a number of filibustering expeditions were organized by American adventurers for the purpose of seizing control of countries in the Caribbean area. These expeditions were not authorized by the U. S. and frequently caused much embarrassment to the U. S. government. Among the noted leaders of such expeditions was WILLIAM WALKER, who led an expedition to Nicaragua, and Narciso Lopez, who led an expedition to Cuba in the 1850's.

FILLMORE, MILLARD (1800-1874). Thirteenth president of the U. S. He served in Congress as a member of the WHIG PARTY and in 1848 was nominated by the Whigs for the vice-presidency, with ZACHARY TAYLOR as the presidential candidate. Both were elected. On Taylor's death in 1850, Fillmore succeeded to the presidency and finished Taylor's unexpired term. Fillmore was not renominated by the Whigs, although he was subsequently nominated for president by the KNOW-NOTHING PARTY in 1856.

During Fillmore's presidential term Congress passed the COMPROMISE OF 1850, under which California was admitted into the Union as a free state. A stricter FUGITIVE SLAVE LAW was enacted and the slave trade was prohibited in the District of Columbia.

"FIRST CIVILIZED AMERICAN." See FRANKLIN, BENJAMIN

"FIRST IN WAR, FIRST IN PEACE." See LEE, RICHARD HENRY

FISH, HAMILTON (1808-93). Governor of New York State, U. S. senator and Secretary of State (1867-77) under President ULYSSES S. GRANT. As Secretary of State, Fish negotiated the Treaty of Washington (1871) settling the ALABAMA CLAIMS dispute. He also settled the VIRGINIUS AFFAIR (1873) with Spain and arranged a trade treaty with Hawaii.

FISHING RIGHTS. A long-standing disagreement existed between the U. S. and Canada over American fishing rights in Canadian waters and Canadian fishing rights in the waters off Alaska. An attempt in 1872 to arbitrate the fishing rights of the U. S. in Canadian waters failed, but in 1910 the fishing rights dispute was finally settled. The disagreement about Alaskan fishing rights was also settled by arbitration.

FISK, JAMES, JR. (1834-72). American businessman and financier. During a financial struggle for the control of the ERIE RAILROAD he joined with JAY GOULD and Daniel Drew against CORNELIUS VANDERBILT. As a result of this struggle for control the Erie Railroad was ruined. In 1869 Fisk and Gould also attempted to corner the market in gold. Their manipulations resulted in the stock market crash in 1869 known as BLACK FRIDAY. Fisk also engaged in stock manipulations to control steamship and ferry lines.

FITCH, JOHN (1743-98). American inventor who experimented with steam-driven boats in 1787. His boat consisted of a steam engine that moved a series of oars attached to bars. The method proved impractical, although the boat moved. In spite of this failure, Fitch is sometimes credited with the invention of the steamboat.

FIVE CIVILIZED NATIONS. Name applied to five Indian tribes whose social, cultural and economic development was far above that of other Indian tribes. The five civilized tribes included the Cherokees, Choctaws, Chickasaws, Creeks and Seminoles. All of them were originally located in southeast U. S. but were moved to Indian territory west of the Mississippi River by 1840. It was after their removal here that they became known as the Five Civilized Nations. The CHEROKEES, for example, developed a written alphabet and published newspapers and books.

FIVE NATIONS. See IROQUOIS INDIANS

FIVE POWER NAVAL PACT (1922). One of the treaties signed at the WASHINGTON DISARMAMENT CONFERENCE. The pact, signed by the U. S., Great Britain, Japan, France and Italy, provided that the signatory nations would maintain a capital ship tonnage ratio of 5:5:3:1⅔: 1⅔ respectively in their naval armaments. Battleships over 10,000 tons were not to be built for the next ten years. This was known as the Naval Holiday. No agreement, however, could be reached on submarines. (See LONDON NAVAL CONFERENCE, 1930)

FLAG, AMERICAN. The first U. S. flag, used by George Washington for the CONTINENTAL ARMY, consisted of 13 stripes and a blue corner containing the crosses of St. George and St. Andrew. In 1777 Congress passed a resolution establishing the official U. S. flag of 13 stars and 13 stripes. In 1794 Congress added 2 stars and 2 stripes to indicate the admission of VERMONT and Kentucky as new states. In 1818 Congress decided to make permanent the 13 stripes representing the 13 original states and to add one new star for each newly admitted state. Although the origin of the U. S. flag has been attributed to BETSY ROSS, the historical evidence does not justify this claim.

FLAG SALUTE CASES. Because of religious principles, members of a minor religious sect (Jehovah's Witnesses) violated a state law by refusing to salute the American flag. This refusal was not based on disloyalty to the U. S. but on the grounds that their religious principles forbad it and AMENDMENT 1 of the U. S. Constitution guaranteed them freedom of religion. In 1940 the Supreme Court (Gobitis Case) held that the state law was not a violation of the U. S. Constitution. However, in 1943 the court reversed itself (Board of Education v. Barnette) and held that such laws violated the First Amendment.

FLATBOATS. Large flat-bottomed raftlike boats that could float in shallow river water. These boats were used on inland rivers and canals in the 17th and 18th centuries in the U. S. Flatboats moved with the river current, were pushed by long poles or were pulled by horses and mules that walked along the banks of the waterway.

FLETCHER V. PECK (1810). The Georgia legislature had given large land grants along the Yazoo River to private land speculators in 1795. Because of fraud surrounding the grants, the next Georgia legislature rescinded them. The original grantees sued for the land and the case was brought to the Supreme Court. In his decision, Chief Justice JOHN MARSHALL held that the original grants were valid contracts which could not be rescinded since all contracts were guaranteed under the Constitution (Art. 1, Sec. 10, Cl. 1). The second Georgia law rescinding the land grants was therefore unconstitutional. This was the first instance in which the Supreme Court assumed the right to declare a *state* law unconstitutional.

FLORIDA. Florida was first discovered by the Spanish explorer PONCE DE LEON in 1513. Although he thought it was an island, later explorations by NARVAEZ and DE SOTO indicated that it was a peninsula of the mainland. In 1562 French explorers began establishing settlements on the Florida coast. The Spanish ruthlessly wiped out these settlements and in 1565 MENENDEZ established a Spanish colony at St. Augustine. Thereafter there were frequent bloody clashes between the English settlements in Georgia and the Spanish in Florida. During the FRENCH AND INDIAN WAR (1754-63), Spain joined France against Great Britain. After the British victory in the war, Great Britain took Florida from Spain and held it for 20 years (1763-83). During the American Revolution Florida became a refuge for TORIES fleeing from the THIRTEEN COLONIES. By the TREATY OF PARIS (1783) ending the American Revolution, Great Britain receded Florida to Spain. After the U. S. purchase of the Louisiana Territory (see LOUISIANA PURCHASE, 1803) the U. S. claimed West Florida was part of the Louisiana Purchase. (See WEST FLORIDA DISPUTE) The U. S. took possession of West Florida in 1812. After the WAR OF 1812 General ANDREW JACKSON invaded Florida (1817-18) to stop raids of the SEMINOLE INDIANS across the border. (See SEMINOLE WARS) In 1819 Spain sold Florida to the U. S. (Adams-Onis Treaty). In 1845 Florida became the 27th state in the Union.

FLORIDA PURCHASE (1819). Florida was purchased (Adams-Onis Treaty) from Spain by the U. S. for $5,000,-
142

000. The U. S. bought it primarily to stop Indian raids from Florida which the Spanish authorities were unable to control. By the treaty of purchase the U. S. relinquished all claims to Texas as part of the original Louisiana Territory. The southern boundary between Spanish Mexico and the Louisiana Territory was fixed at the Sabine River, then north and west to the 42nd parallel of latitude. The purchase also settled the WEST FLORIDA DISPUTE.

"FLYING CLOUD." One of the famous clipper ships built in the U. S. and used in the 1840's and 1850's for long ocean voyages. The *Flying Cloud* was designed by the famous naval architect Donald McKay, and used sails only as a source of power. The *Flying Cloud* set a speed record (1854) for sailing ships by going from Boston around the southern tip of South America to San Francisco in 89 days. (See MERCHANT MARINE)

FORAKER ACT (1900). Established a form of government for the newly acquired island of PUERTO RICO (TREATY OF PARIS, 1898). Under the act, Puerto Rico was set up as an unorganized U. S. territory. The islanders were to be considered citizens of Puerto Rico, not of the U. S., but were to be under U. S. protection. The governor of the island and an executive council were to be appointed by the President with the consent of the U. S. Senate. The Foraker Act was superseded in 1917 by the JONES ACT.

FORBES EXPEDITION. One of a number of military expeditions (1758) organized by the British during the FRENCH AND INDIAN WAR (1754-63) to seize FORT DUQUESNE from the French. Before starting the campaign, the FORBES ROAD was cut out of the wilderness to make possible the movement of soldiers and artillery. When the Forbes Expedition finally reached Fort Duquesne they found that the French had already burned and abandoned it.

FORBES ROAD. A colonial wagon road about 80 miles long, built in 1758 for the FORBES EXPEDITION organized by the British to seize FORT DUQUESNE from the French. The road ran west through Pennsylvania from Fort Loudon (near Bedford) to Fort Pitt (now Pittsburgh). After the French and Indian War (1763) the Forbes Road was the principal highway used by settlers of the Middle Atlantic colonies moving across the Allegheny Mountains into the Ohio Valley.

FORCE ACT (1833). After South Carolina passed its ORDINANCE OF NULLIFICATION in 1832, declaring the TARIFF OF 1828 (see TARIFF OF ABOMINATIONS) and of 1832 null and void, Congress passed the Force Act giving President ANDREW JACKSON power to use the armed forces if necessary to enforce the collection of the tariff in South Carolina or any other state. However, armed force was not used because South Carolina accepted the COMPROMISE TARIFF of 1833.

FORCE ACTS (1870-75). A number of laws passed by Congress after the War Between the States as part of the southern RECONSTRUCTION program. The Force Acts authorized the president to use the army to enforce the CIVIL RIGHTS BILLS (1866) and the rights of Southern Negroes under AMENDMENT 14 and AMENDMENT 15. These Acts were aimed specifically at such organizations as the KU KLUX KLAN, which sought to frighten Negroes from voting during Congressional elections, running for political office or serving on juries.

FORD, HENRY (1863-1947). American automobile manufacturer. He built his first car in 1893 and formed the Ford Motor Company in 1903. By the year 1909 he had developed a system of manufacturing automobiles at low cost. Ford did not invent the automobile but he perfected a mass production system based on standardized parts and an assembly line. Fifteen million "Model T" Ford cars, known as "flivvers," were manufactured between 1910 and 1929 and sold at low prices. Today the Ford Motor Company is one of the largest manufacturing organizations in the world.

FORDNEY-MC CUMBER TARIFF ACT (1922). Passed by Congress during the Republican administration of President WARREN G. HARDING. General tariff rates were raised to their highest level in our history. The Act also established a Tariff Commission which was to make a continuing study of the need for tariff rate changes. The President was empowered to raise or lower rates as much as 50% if the studies of the Tariff Commission revealed the need for changes. This provision of the law was called the "flexible clause." (See TARIFF LEGISLATION)

FOREIGN AID PROGRAM. At the end of World War II (1945) the U. S. feared that many nations in Europe and Asia would turn to Communism because of shortages of food and housing, the destruction of farms and factories, the general disruption of economic and social life, and the spread of Communist propaganda. To offset this danger and at the same time restore the economies of war-torn nations, the U. S. began a program of foreign economic aid under the MARSHALL PLAN (1947). This aid was in the form of low-interest loans as well as outright gifts of money and equipment. In 1949 President HARRY S. TRUMAN also announced his Point Four Program to provide economic aid to backward and economically under-developed areas of the world to raise their standards of living and thus avert the spread of Communism. In 1961 President JOHN F. KENNEDY announced a similar program, called Alliance for Progress, for Latin American nations. These economic aid programs were administered at various times by agencies of different names including Economic Cooperation Administration, Foreign Operations Administration and the International Cooperation Administration (I.C.A.).

FOREST RESERVE ACT (1891). One of the early Congressional laws passed as part of the CONSERVATION MOVEMENT. The act authorized the President to set aside tracts of forest lands as reserves on any public lands owned by the government.

FORREST, NATHAN BEDFORD (1821-77). Confederate general in the WAR BETWEEN THE STATES (1861-65). He was noted for his legendary exploits as leader of cavalry raiders. He won many brilliant victories during the war but surrendered after his defeat at Selma, Alabama. When asked how he won so many victories he is said to have replied: "Git thar fustest with the mostest." After the war, Forrest was a leading organizer of the KU KLUX KLAN and was its first Grand Wizard.

FORT. . . . See under name of fort

145

FORT DONELSON, BATTLE OF (1862). Military engagement fought early in the WAR BETWEEN THE STATES (1861-65). Fort Donelson, a military fortification in Tennessee, was held by the Southern Confederacy. In 1862 General ULYSSES S. GRANT, leading a Union army, besieged the fort and forced its unconditional surrender. Thereafter he became known as "unconditional surrender Grant."

FORTY-NINERS. Adventurers who went to California in 1849 after hearing news of the discovery of gold. The forty-niners came mainly from Eastern U. S. but also from Europe, South America and remote parts of the world. Some of the forty-niners traveled overland across the plains and mountains to California. Others took the longer but safer water routes. The voyage around Cape Horn took six months by sailing vessel. A shorter water route was one which went to Panama. From there passengers went overland to the Pacific coast, where they took another sailing vessel north to California.

FOUR FREEDOMS. In 1941, while World War II was raging in Europe but while the U. S. was still neutral, President FRANKLIN D. ROOSEVELT delivered a famous address in which he listed the four freedoms that he considered essential for world peace: freedom of speech and expression, freedom of religion, freedom from want, and freedom from fear.

FOUR POWER PACT (1922). See WASHINGTON DISARMAMENT CONFERENCE

FOURTEEN POINTS (1918). War aims of the U. S. in World War I (1917-18) as announced by President WOODROW WILSON to Congress. The Fourteen Points contained five general aims, eight specific aims and a fourteenth aim providing for the establishment of a LEAGUE OF NATIONS. The five general aims included the ending of secret treaties, guarantee of freedom of the seas, reduction of world tariffs, reduction of world armaments, and adjustment of colonial claims in the interests of colonial people. The eight specific aims related to territorial changes in Germany, Austria-Hungary, Bulgaria and Turkey and included the re-establishment of Poland as an independent nation.

FRAME OF GOVERNMENT (1682). Document under which WILLIAM PENN organized the government of the PENNSYLVANIA COLONY. The Frame of Government provided for a proprietary governor, a council and an assembly elected by the colonial freeholders. In 1701 Penn granted the colony a CHARTER OF LIBERTIES.

FRANCE, U. S. RELATIONS WITH. In 1778 France signed a TREATY OF ALLIANCE with the U. S. and thereafter provided direct military assistance during the AMERICAN REVOLUTION (1775-83). In 1793 the U. S. refused to help France (see GENET AFFAIR) in her war with Great Britain and subsequently the U. S. revoked the Treaty of Alliance (1800). During the Napoleonic Wars in Europe (1804-14) the French government issued the BERLIN AND MILAN DECREES (1806-7) which affected U. S. neutral shipping. The MAXIMILIAN AFFAIR (1864-67) in Mexico resulted in a brief flurry of U. S. hostility to the French government but the gift of the Statue of Liberty (1884) to the U. S. ushered in an era of cordial U. S.-French relations. The U. S. helped France with loans and supplies in the early years of WORLD WAR I (1914-18) and eventually entered the war on the side of the Allied Powers. Similarly, in WORLD WAR II (1939-45) the U. S. aided France and eventually entered the war (1941), liberated France from the yoke of Nazi German rule and helped defeat the Axis Powers. After World War II France joined the NORTH ATLANTIC TREATY ORGANIZATION (1949) sponsored by the U. S.

FRANCISCAN MISSIONARIES. The Franciscans were a European Catholic missionary organization many of whose members accompanied French and Spanish explorers to the New World. The Franciscans also conducted their own explorations and established Christian missions among the Indians in Florida, Mexico, Texas and what is now Southwest U. S. In French territory the Franciscans established missions along the Ohio, upper Mississippi and St. Lawrence Rivers as well as along the Great Lakes.

FRANKLIN, BENJAMIN (1706-90). As a Philadelphia printer before the American Revolution, Franklin published the Pennsylvania *Gazette* and *Poor Richard's Almanac*. He helped found the University of Pennsylvania (then known

147

as the Philadelphia Academy) and organized the first circulating library in America. As a man of science he invented the Franklin stove, bifocal spectacles, the lightning rod and many other devices. He drew up the ALBANY PLAN OF UNION (1754) and in 1766, while in England, convinced the British to repeal the STAMP ACT. In 1776 he was a member of the committee that framed the DECLARATION OF INDEPENDENCE. As ambassador to France during the American Revolution he secured French aid for the American cause. At the CONSTITUTIONAL CONVENTION (1787) he served as a moderating influence between the rival factions. Because of his wide interests, his scientific curiosity, his great talents as a writer and statesman and his contributions to the establishment of the new nation he is sometimes known as the "first civilized American."

FRANKLIN, STATE OF (1784). When the U. S. was governed by the ARTICLES OF CONFEDERATION (1781-89) the inhabitants of eastern Tennessee established a new state which they named "Franklin." A state constitution was written, John Sevier was elected governor, laws were passed and taxes collected. When Congress failed to recognize the new state, it went out of existence (1788) and the area reverted to North Carolina. Because of the brief career of the state of Franklin it is often referred to as the "lost state."

FREDERICKSBURG, BATTLE OF (1862). One of the major military engagements of the WAR BETWEEN THE STATES (1861-65), fought at Fredericksburg, Va. The Union Army, led by General Burnside, boldly attacked Fredericksburg only to be repulsed with serious losses by the Confederate Army.

FREEDMEN'S BUREAU (1865). An agency established by Congress after the WAR BETWEEN THE STATES (1861-65), to provide food, clothing and other necessities to the newly emancipated Negro. President ANDREW JOHNSON vetoed the bill but Congress passed a Freedmen's Bureau Bill over the president's veto.

FREEDOM OF SPEECH. See ABRAMS V. U. S. and SCHENCK V. U. S.

FREEDOM OF THE PRESS. The trial of JOHN PETER ZENGER (1734) at which the defendant was acquitted was a landmark in establishing the principle of freedom of the press in colonial times. One of the colonial objections to the STAMP ACT (1765) was that stamps on newspapers were a restriction on freedom of the press. The Virginia Bill of Rights (1776) included freedom of the press as one of its basic principles and AMENDMENT 1 to the U. S. Constitution made it one of the keystones of the American BILL OF RIGHTS. The ALIEN AND SEDITION ACTS (1798) which restricted newspaper criticism of the President and Congress were attacked as violating the First Amendment. Similarly the ESPIONAGE ACT (1917) passed during WORLD WAR I (1917-18) was criticized for the same reason.

FREEDOM OF THE SEAS. Principle of international law that guarantees to all nations the right to use the high seas (outside territorial waters) in peace and war. Prior to the WAR OF 1812 (1812-14) the U. S. maintained that both Great Britain and France violated "freedom of the seas" when they seized and searched U. S. merchant ships on the high seas. The issue was again raised during WORLD WAR I (1914-18). The U. S. asserted that unrestricted German SUBMARINE WARFARE (see "LUSITANIA") was a violation of the principle of freedom of the seas. During World War I President WOODROW WILSON included "freedom of the seas" in his "FOURTEEN POINTS" (1918) as one of the reasons why the U. S. was fighting. During WORLD WAR II (1939-45), the war aims of the U. S. and Great Britain, as embodied in the ATLANTIC CHARTER (1941), also asserted the principle of "freedom of the seas."

FREEPORT DOCTRINE (1858). So named after the town of Freeport, Illinois where Lincoln and STEPHEN A. DOUGLAS met in one of their famous debates. (See LINCOLN-DOUGLAS DEBATES) In the Freeport Doctrine, Douglas stated that the people of a territory ultimately decided whether or not they wanted slavery because the decision had to be enforced by local police regulations. However, this doctrine contradicted Douglas' support of the DRED SCOTT DECISION (1857) which held that slavery

149

was legal in all territories whether the people of the territory wanted it or not.

FREE SILVER. See BIMETALLISM, ELECTION OF 1896 and BRYAN, WILLIAM JENNINGS

"FREE SOIL, FREE SPEECH, FREE LABOR AND FREE MEN." See FREE SOIL PARTY

FREE SOIL PARTY (1848-1854). Political group organized for the single purpose of fighting the extension of slavery in the newly acquired Western territories. The Free Soil Party included former LIBERTY PARTY members as well as anti-slavery WHIGS and DEMOCRATS. In the ELECTION OF 1848 the Free Soilers nominated MARTIN VAN BUREN for president on a platform calling for "free soil, free speech, free labor and free men." In 1854 the Free Soil Party disbanded and many of its members joined the newly organized REPUBLICAN PARTY.

FREMONT, JOHN C. (1813-90). Led a number of Western exploring expeditions across the Rocky Mountains which earned him the name of "Pathfinder." Just before the MEXICAN WAR (1846) he participated in the California revolt that established the "Bear Republic." While in California, Fremont became involved in a quarrel with General STEPHEN W. KEARNY that led to Fremont's court martial. In 1852 he was elected senator from California and in 1856 was the first presidential candidate of the newly organized REPUBLICAN PARTY. During the ELECTION OF 1856 he adopted the slogan "Free soil, Free speech, Fremont," but he was defeated by JAMES BUCHANAN. During the WAR BETWEEN THE STATES (1861-65) he served as a general in the west.

FRENCH AND INDIAN WAR (1754-63). Last of the colonial wars between Great Britain and France in America over rival territorial claims. Highlights of the war included the defeat of GENERAL BRADDOCK in his effort to capture FORT DUQUESNE (1755), the capture of Louisburg by LORD JEFFREY AMHERST (1758), and the Battle of Quebec where the British under GENERAL

WOLFE defeated the French under GENERAL MONT-CALM. Both generals were killed in the battle. Under the TREATY OF PARIS (1763), ending the war, France lost almost all of her colonial possessions in the New World.

FRENCH AND INDIAN WARS (1689-1763). Century-long series of colonial wars between France and Great Britain in America. These wars included King William's War (1689-97), Queen Anne's War (1701-13), King George's War (1744-48), and the FRENCH AND INDIAN WAR (1754-63). Fought over rival territorial claims, fishing rights and fur trade in the New World, these wars were the American counterpart of the European "Second Hundred Years War." None of the colonial wars was decisive except the last, which resulted in the loss of almost all of France's colonies in the New World.

FRICK, HENRY C. (1849-1919). American steel manufacturer of the late 19th century. He played a leading role in the organization of the Carnegie Steel Corporation (1892). Frick frequently differed with ANDREW CARNEGIE over labor policies and it was Frick's policies that in large measure resulted in the famous HOMESTEAD STRIKE (1892). The Frick Museum in New York City was established through his philanthropy.

FROBISHER, MARTIN (1535-94). English navigator and explorer who made a number of voyages to the Arctic region in search of a NORTHWEST PASSAGE (1576-78). Although he never found the passage, Frobisher Bay is named after him. Frobisher was knighted by Queen Elizabeth I because of his bravery during the defeat of the SPANISH ARMADA (1588).

FRONTENAC, COMTE DE (1620-98). Appointed governor of New France in the New World in 1672, a position which he filled with great skill for many years. His wise and just administration resulted in good French relations with the Indians, the development of the fur trade, and the exploration of the Great Lakes and Mississippi Valley. During King William's War (1689-97) between France and England, Frontenac conducted a number of successful military campaigns against the English colonies and the Iroquois Indians.

151

FRONTIER. Name given to the western boundary where civilized settlements ended and the wilderness began. As Americans moved away from the Atlantic seaboard, the frontier naturally was pushed farther and farther west. For almost four centuries the frontier influenced the life and thinking of Americans. People who lived on the frontier were generally self-reliant, democratic, cooperative, hospitable, and skillful with ax and rifle. By the year 1890, when the last open regions in the west were settled, the frontier came to an end.

FUGITIVE SLAVE LAWS. A law for the return of runaway slaves had been enacted by Congress as early as 1793, but Southern slaveholders found it to be unsatisfactory. In order to get Southern support for the COMPROMISE OF 1850, a stricter Fugitive Slave Law was included as one of the five parts of the Compromise. Under the law of 1850, federal agents were given power to arrest fugitives anywhere in the country and arrange for their return to Southern slave masters. The law was denounced by Northern ABOLITIONISTS because Northern officials who refused to aid in seizing runaway slaves and any person who aided Negro fugitives could be heavily fined or imprisoned. (See UNDERGROUND RAILROAD)

FULBRIGHT RESOLUTION (1943). Also known as the Connally-Fulbright Resolution. It was passed by Congress during World War II and authorized American participation in the establishment of a postwar peace organization. On the basis of this resolution the DUMBARTON OAKS CONFERENCE (1944) and the SAN FRANCISCO CONFERENCE (1945) were held to draw up the UNITED NATIONS charter.

"FULL DINNER PAIL." During the election campaign of 1900 the REPUBLICAN PARTY that had renominated WILLIAM MC KINLEY for president took as one of its major campaign slogans the "full dinner pail." This slogan, representing the era of prosperity of the first McKinley administration (1897-1901), was highly effective during the campaign and helped to reelect McKinley.

FULTON, ROBERT (1765-1815). American inventor of the first successful steamboat, named the *Clermont* (1807).

The ship, called "Fulton's Folly" by doubters, made the 150-mile trip from New York City to Albany and back in less than three days. After Fulton's successful demonstration of the *Clermont,* steamboats were built and used on all large U. S. rivers and eventually were used to cross the Atlantic Ocean. (See SAVANNAH) Before he built his steamboat Fulton also experimented with the construction of submarines and torpedoes for the British and French governments.

FUNDAMENTAL ORDERS OF CONNECTICUT (1639). The first written constitution in America. It was drawn up by representatives of the Connecticut settlers as a plan for the government of the colony.

FUNSTON, GENERAL FREDERICK (1865-1917). American commander in the PHILIPPINE ISLANDS after the U. S. acquired the islands at the end of the SPANISH-AMERICAN WAR (1898). For three years after the U. S. took possession of the islands guerillas fought a jungle campaign against American rule. The capture of the rebel leader AGUINALDO by General Funston brought the insurrection to an end.

FUR TRADING. One of the major reasons for the establishment of French and Dutch settlements in the New World. In the English colonies fur trading was, next to farming, the most important economic activity of the settlers, particularly along the frontier. In the French colonies in Canada, along the Great Lakes and in the Mississippi Valley, fur trading was even more important than farming.

GADSDEN PURCHASE (1853). Strip of territory on Southwest border between Mexico and the U. S. The United States made the purchase from Mexico for $10,000,000 in order to have a direct route for a railroad to southern California. The American agent who arranged the treaty of purchase was James Gadsden (1788-1858), U. S. minister to Mexico during President FRANKLIN PIERCE's administration.

GAGE, GENERAL THOMAS (1721-87). British general appointed governor of Massachusetts Colony after the BOSTON TEA PARTY (1773) to enforce the INTOLERABLE ACTS (1774). He was commander of British troops in Boston in 1775 and ordered the arrest of SAMUEL ADAMS and JOHN HANCOCK. When he sent the colonial militia to Lexington and Concord, it led to the first bloodshed of the AMERICAN REVOLUTION. (See LEXINGTON, BATTLE OF)

GAG RULE (1836). Refers to a resolution passed by the House of Representatives forbidding the reading of antislavery petitions in that House of Congress. JOHN QUINCY ADAMS, a member of the House at that time, made repeated speeches of protest against this Gag Resolution on the ground that it denied the people the constitutional right of petition. The Gag Resolution was finally repealed in 1844.

GALLATIN, ALBERT (1761-1849). Secretary of the Treasury (1801-14) under President THOMAS JEFFERSON and President JAMES MADISON. Except for ALEXANDER HAMILTON, Gallatin is considered the greatest Secretary of the Treasury in our history. To effect economies in government Gallatin cut government spending, reduced the number of government jobs and cut down the size of the nation's military force. This proved to be financially sound but left the country relatively unprepared for the WAR OF 1812. Gallatin was one of the U. S. delegates who

154

arranged the TREATY OF GHENT ending the War of 1812.

GAMA, VASCO DA (c.1460-1524). Portuguese navigator. He was the first European to reach India by sailing around the southern tip of Africa (1498). This voyage established a new all-water route to the East and broke the monopoly of the Eastern trade held by Italian merchants up to that time.

GARFIELD, JAMES ABRAM (1831-1881). Twentieth president of the U. S. After serving with distinction in the War Between the States (1861-65) Garfield entered politics and was elected to Congress as representative from Ohio for 17 years and as senator (1880) for one year. In the Republican National Convention of 1880 a deadlock over the choice of candidate resulted in Garfield's nomination as a DARK HORSE or compromise nominee. In the ELECTION OF 1880 Garfield defeated General Hancock, the Democratic Party candidate, by an electoral vote of 214 to 155. On July 2, 1881, after only four months in the presidential office, Garfield was shot by Charles Guiteau, a half-mad political office seeker. Garfield died a few weeks later and was succeeded by Vice-President CHESTER A. ARTHUR. During his brief term as president Garfield tried to reunite the two rival factions of his party, known as the STALWARTS and the HALF BREEDS.

GARRISON, WILLIAM LLOYD (1805-79). One of the Northern ABOLITIONIST leaders before the War Between the States (1861). His violently anti-slavery newspaper *The Liberator* aroused hostility both in the North and the South. At one time Garrison was almost lynched in Boston and his printing presses were destroyed. He publicly burned the U. S. Constitution because it recognized slavery, urged Northern secession from the Union and opposed the War Between the States until President Lincoln issued the EMANCIPATION PROCLAMATION (1863). Because of his extreme views he had relatively few followers even among those who opposed slavery.

"GASPEE," BURNING OF THE (1772). One of the incidents of violence preceding the AMERICAN REVOLUTION (1775-1783). A British customs ship, the *Gaspee*, patrolling

155

the waters near Providence, Rhode Island, was set afire by American colonists in protest against the British anti-smuggling policy. The incident tended to harden further the NEW COLONIAL POLICY of the British to enforce the NAVIGATION ACTS.

GATES, GENERAL HORATIO (1727-1806). American commander during the AMERICAN REVOLUTION and leader of the victorious American forces at the BATTLE OF SARATOGA (1777). In the BATTLE OF CAMDEN (South Carolina, 1780) General Gates suffered a major defeat at the hands of the British, after which he was succeeded by General NATHANAEL GREENE.

GENERAL COURT. Assembly of the MASSACHUSETTS BAY COLONY that met in Boston four times a year to conduct the business of the colony. It included the governor, his assistants and representatives of the settlers. The General Court levied taxes and fines, passed regulations for the government of Massachusetts Bay and ordered undesirable immigrants to return to England.

GENESEE ROAD. Early 19th century road in New York State extending from Albany on the Hudson River to Buffalo on Lake Erie. In general it followed the old Mohawk Trail.

GENET AFFAIR (1793). The new French Republic sent a minister named Citizen Edmond Genet to the U. S. to obtain American aid in the French war against Great Britain. By the TREATY OF ALLIANCE (1778) and other treaties with France, the U. S. had promised to help France protect its West Indies colonies. However, President Washington announced the PROCLAMATION OF NEUTRALITY (1793) in which he stated that the U. S. would not take sides in the European war. When Genet appealed for support directly to the American people, Washington prepared to ask for Genet's recall. Genet, however, asked for permission to remain in the U. S. as a private individual because a new and violent change in the French government made him fear for his life if he returned. Permission was granted.

GENEVA CONVENTION. A number of international agreements signed by various nations establishing humane rules of war relating to care of the wounded and sick, identification of the dead, treatment of prisoners of war and the neutrality of medical personnel in time of war. The first Geneva Convention was signed by 12 nations at the first conference of the International Red Cross in 1864 in Geneva, Switzerland. Today almost every nation in the world, including the U. S., is a signatory of the Geneva Convention.

GENTLEMEN'S AGREEMENT (1907). Informal agreement between Japan and the U. S. by which Japan agreed to deny passports to Japanese who intended to migrate to the U. S. The U. S. in turn arranged for the ending of segregation of Japanese and other Oriental children in the schools of San Francisco. This agreement stopped Japanese immigration to the U. S. until 1952. (See MC CARRAN-WALTER IMMIGRATION ACT, IMMIGRATION LEGISLATION, and JAPAN, U. S. RELATIONS WITH)

GEORGE III (1738-1820). King of Great Britain (1760-1820) during the critical era when the American colonies protested against autocratic British rule, started the AMERICAN REVOLUTION and eventually established an independent republic (1783). George III encouraged his followers in the British Parliament to pass many of the restrictive laws (SUGAR ACT, 1764; STAMP ACT, 1765; INTOLERABLE ACTS, 1774) that led to the American Revolution. George III was still on the British throne during our WAR OF 1812.

GEORGIA COLONY (1733). Last of the Thirteen English Colonies to be established in America. Its founder was JAMES OGLETHORPE, who established the settlement under a charter from King George II. Oglethorpe set up the colony as a refuge for debtors and other poor Englishmen. Many German Protestants also settled there. The colony was named Georgia in honor of King George II.

GEORGIA PLATFORM (1850). Statement of principles by conservative Southerners opposing drastic action over the slavery issue before the War Between the States (1861). The Georgia Platform, announced immediately after the COMPROMISE OF 1850, stated that the solution to the

157

slavery issue as fixed in the Compromise should be accepted as permanent by North and South.

GERMANTOWN, BATTLE OF (1777). One of the major military engagements during the AMERICAN REVOLUTION (1775-83). General WASHINGTON and his forces attempted a surprise attack on the British army under Sir William Howe at Germantown, Pennsylvania. The Americans were defeated and forced to retreat.

GERONIMO (c.1829-1909). Leader of the APACHE Indian tribe in the late 19th century. He was one of the important Apache leaders during the Apache War (1871-76) against white settlers in Arizona. Geronimo was notorious not only for his fierceness and bravery but also for his brutality. In 1886 he surrendered to General NELSON A. MILES.

GERRY, ELBRIDGE (1744-1814). One of the Massachusetts leaders in the movement for colonial independence. He was a member of the Second CONTINENTAL CONGRESS, a signer of the DECLARATION OF INDEPENDENCE and a member of the Philadelphia CONSTITUTIONAL CONVENTION (1787). However, Gerry refused to approve the Constitution because of the many powers granted to the national government and because of the omission of a BILL OF RIGHTS. Gerry served in Congress (1789-93), was a member of the U. S. delegation in the XYZ AFFAIR, served as governor of Massachusetts (1810-12) and as vice-president (1813-14) under President Madison. The GERRYMANDER system was named after him.

GERRYMANDER. Political device for drawing irregular election district lines so that they favor one political party over another. The device derived its name from Governor ELBRIDGE GERRY of Massachusetts who made extreme use of the method for his own party advantage. One of the election districts in Massachusetts was so grotesque that it looked like a salamander. Hence the word was combined with Gerry's name to form the word "gerrymander."

GETTYSBURG ADDRESS (1863). Speech delivered by President ABRAHAM LINCOLN on November 19th during the WAR BETWEEN THE STATES (1861-65). The address was part of the dedication ceremonies for the establishment of a national cemetery on the battlefield at Gettysburg. One of the most famous speeches in our history, it began with the words: "Fourscore and seven years ago . . ." and ended with Lincoln's definition of democracy as a government ". . . of the people, by the people, for the people."

GETTYSBURG, BATTLE OF (1863). Most important military engagement during the WAR BETWEEN THE STATES (1861-65) and considered to be the turning point of the war. General ROBERT E. LEE and his Confederate Army had invaded southern Pennsylvania in an effort to create panic in the North. His army was met by General GEORGE G. MEADE, a commander of a large Union force at Gettysburg. After four days of terrible bloodshed on both sides, General Lee retreated to Virginia. (See PICKETT'S CHARGE)

GHENT, TREATY OF (1814). Treaty between U. S. and Great Britain ending the War of 1812. It was signed in Ghent, Belgium. Neither side obtained any advantages as a result of the treaty. The defeat of Napoleon in Europe, however, put an end to the need for the British seizure of neutral ships or IMPRESSMENT of seamen.

GIBBONS V. OGDEN (1824). The state of New York had given Robert R. Livingston and ROBERT FULTON a monopoly to run steamboats on the Hudson River (1808). In this case, Chief Justice JOHN MARSHALL held that the Hudson River, since it touches two states, affected interstate commerce, which, broadly interpreted, included every kind of intercourse between states. Under the U. S. Constitution, only Congress had the power to regulate interstate commerce (Art. 1, Sec. 8, Cl. 3).

G.I. BILL OF RIGHTS (1944). Passed by Congress while World War II (1941-45) was still in progress. The law provided that veterans of the war were to receive free tuition and maintenance pay if they wished to continue their education; pensions, hospitalization and other benefits. Similar benefits were granted to veterans of the KOREAN WAR in 1952.

GILA TRAIL. One of the routes used by American pioneers in the early 19th century to reach the Pacific coast. The

159

Gila Trail led from Santa Fe, New Mexico, west to California. (See SANTA FE TRAIL)

GILBERT, SIR HUMPHREY (1539-83). English navigator and explorer during the 16th century. In 1578 he was commissioned by Queen Elizabeth of England to search for the NORTHWEST PASSAGE and if possible establish a colony in the New World to be used as a base of operations against Spain. In 1583 he reached Newfoundland and claimed the region for England. He was lost when his vessel was shipwrecked on his way back to England.

"GILDED AGE." Name of a novel by Mark Twain and Charles Dudley Warner. They used the title to characterize the era of our history during the second half of the 19th century. During this time many great fortunes were made as a result of American industrial expansion and the showy display of wealth became fashionable. (See LITERATURE, AMERICAN)

G.I.'S. Nickname for American soldiers during WORLD WAR II (1941-45).

"GIT THAR FUSTEST WITH THE MOSTEST." See FORREST, NATHAN BEDFORD

"GIVE ME LIBERTY." See HENRY, PATRICK

GLASS-STEAGALL ACT (1932). Passed by Congress during President HERBERT HOOVER's administration. The law gave the Federal Reserve Banks power to rediscount commercial paper which formerly had been ineligible for discount under the FEDERAL RESERVE ACT of 1913. Congress hoped that this more liberal policy would help many banks with "frozen assets." The BANKING ACT of 1933 and the BANKING ACT of 1935 are also known as Glass-Steagall Acts because they were sponsored by the same legislators.

GODKIN, EDWIN L. (1831-1902). Famous editor (1883-1900) of the New York *Evening Post,* who waged a vigorous campaign for CIVIL SERVICE REFORM in the 1880's. His outspoken criticism of the SPOILS SYSTEM helped arouse public opinion in favor of the PENDLETON ACT (1883) establishing the federal civil service system.

GOETHALS, COLONEL G. W. (1858-1928). See PANAMA CANAL

GOLD CLAUSE CASES (1935). After Congress and President FRANKLIN D. ROOSEVELT devalued the gold dollar (GOLD REPEAL RESOLUTION, 1933, and GOLD RESERVE ACT, 1934), the Supreme Court was asked to determine the constitutionality of the measures as they applied to government and private bonds payable in gold. In 1935 the Supreme Court held (Norman v. B. and O. Railroad; Norty v. U. S.) in substance that bondholders must accept payment based on the devalued gold dollar.

GOLDEN HILL RIOT (1771). One of many clashes between British troops stationed in the colonies and the protesting colonists. The Golden Hill Riot occurred in New York City as the result of colonial protests against the British QUARTERING ACT (1765). Unlike the BOSTON MASSACRE (1770), there were no casualties on either side in the Golden Hill Riot.

"GOLDEN TWENTIES." Name given to the era of great prosperity between 1921 and 1929 and particularly during the presidency of CALVIN COOLIDGE (1923-29). During the "Golden Twenties" the U. S. experienced an era of unusual business prosperity. However, the era was featured by stock market speculation, free public spending, and critical agricultural conditions because of low crop prices. Because the decade also coincided with the PROHIBITION ERA and its attendant bootlegging and crime, it was also known as the "Roaring Twenties."

GOLD REPEAL RESOLUTION (1933). At the height of the GREAT DEPRESSION Congress, by joint resolution, cancelled the gold repayment clause in all federal and private securities and validated payment in any money that was legal tender. The validity of this action was upheld in the GOLD CLAUSE CASES (1935) by the Supreme Court.

GOLD RESERVE ACT (1934). One year after FRANKLIN D. ROOSEVELT became president during the GREAT DEPRESSION, Congress passed this act giving the president power to fix the gold content of the dollar at 50% to

161

60% of its former weight. The president fixed the price of gold at $35 per ounce, replacing the old price of $20.67. Thus the value of the gold dollar was fixed at 59.06 cents of its former value. All gold used for currency was taken out of circulation to be held by the government only. This law established a modified gold bullion standard in place of the former gold money standard. The validity of this law was upheld by the U. S. Supreme Court in the GOLD CLAUSE CASES (1935).

GOLD RUSH. News of the discovery of gold in California in 1848 led to a gold rush the following year. (See FORTY-NINERS) A rush of adventurers (called "FIFTY-NINERS") to Nevada occurred in 1859 when news of the discovery of silver reached the East. (See COMSTOCK LODE) In 1896 the discovery of gold in the Klondike region of Canada led to another gold rush the following year. (See KLONDIKE GOLD RUSH) In these gold rushes, a few prospectors became fabulously wealthy but most of the people suffered severe hardships and gained nothing.

GOLD STANDARD ACT (1900). After the failure of the free silver advocates led by **WILLIAM JENNINGS BRYAN** in the ELECTION OF 1896 to establish BI-METALLISM as a national policy, Congress passed the Gold Standard Act establishing a single gold standard and providing that all currency in circulation be redeemable in gold. The law also gave National Banks the right to increase the amount of paper money they could issue from 90% to 100% of the value of U. S. bonds they owned and deposited with the U. S. Treasury. (See NATIONAL BANKING ACT, 1863) The U. S. remained on the gold standard until 1933. (See GOLD REPEAL RESOLUTION, 1933 and GOLD RESERVE ACT, 1934)

GOMPERS, SAMUEL (1850-1924). Leading figure in the organization of the AMERICAN FEDERATION OF LABOR in 1886. He became president of the A.F.L. in 1886 and was its president, with the exception of one year, until his death in 1924. Gompers' labor union principles included the organization of skilled craft unions rather than industrial unions, the use of arbitration rather than violence to settle labor disputes, the use of democratic procedures in labor union organizations, the avoidance of permanent alliances with any political party, and emphasis on immediate labor objectives such as higher wages, shorter hours and better working conditions.

GOOD NEIGHBOR POLICY. Policy for Latin America announced at the Montevideo PAN AMERICAN CONFERENCE (1933) by CORDELL HULL, Secretary of State under President FRANKLIN D. ROOSEVELT. The U. S. renounced its policy of interfering in Cuba under the PLATT AMENDMENT, or anywhere else in Latin America under the ROOSEVELT COROLLARY.

GOODYEAR, CHARLES (1800-60). Inventor of the process of vulcanizing rubber (1839) so that it could be used to make household articles. It is reported that he discovered the process by accidentally mixing hot sulphur and raw rubber. After patenting his invention (1844) he sold the rights and thereafter received only a small return from it.

G. O. P. Title of the REPUBLICAN PARTY. The initials stand for "Grand Old Party," although the DEMOCRATIC PARTY is 30 years older.

GORGAS, DR. WILLIAM C. (1854-1920). See PANAMA CANAL

GORGES, SIR FERDINANDO (c.1566-1647). One of the leading figures in the PLYMOUTH COMPANY (1606) and organizer of an expedition to establish a settlement in the region of Maine (1607). Captain JOHN MASON was also one of the leaders of the Maine settlement. However, the colony failed in 1608. Gorges was never able to establish a permanent settlement in Maine. In 1677 his heirs finally sold the Maine province to the Massachusetts colony.

GOULD, JAY (1836-92). Involved in 1869 with JAMES FISK, JR. in a plan to "corner" the gold supply of the nation and force up the price of gold. Both men succeeded in raising the price of gold. Jay Gould was warned by President Grant's brother-in-law that the U. S. Treasury was about to sell gold in the open market. Gould therefore began to sell his gold. When the U. S. Treasury finally began to sell government gold, the "corner" in gold was broken. A serious

163

stock market panic, known as BLACK FRIDAY (1869), followed. Gould was also associated with James Fisk, Jr. and Daniel Drew in the struggle with COMMODORE CORNELIUS VANDERBILT to control the ERIE RAILROAD.

"GO WEST, YOUNG MAN." Phrase first used by an Indiana newspaperman named J. L. B. Soule in 1851 but generally attributed to HORACE GREELEY, who used it in 1865 in a New York *Tribune* editorial.

GRAND ARMY OF THE REPUBLIC. Also known as the G. A. R. It was a veterans' organization made up of soldiers who had served in the Union Armies during the WAR BETWEEN THE STATES (1861-65). The organization was active and successful in lobbying for veterans' pensions in the late 19th century.

GRANDFATHER CLAUSES. Restrictions established by Southern states after the WAR BETWEEN THE STATES (1865) to keep Negroes from voting. The clauses exempted from poll taxes and from property and educational voting requirements all persons who had the right to vote or whose ancestors had the right to vote before January 1, 1867. This gave poor Southern whites suffrage but deprived Negroes of it. In 1915 the Supreme Court held these "grandfather" clauses to be unconstitutional.

GRAND MODEL (1669). Complicated system of government prepared by the English philosopher John Locke for the government of the Carolina colonies. It was so cumbersome that it failed to work and was finally replaced by a simpler system of colonial government.

GRANGER CASES (1877-86). A number of U. S. Supreme Court decisions involving the rights of states to regulate grain elevators and railroads. In the first group of cases the Court upheld the power of the states. In Munn v. Illinois (1877), for example, the Court held that an Illinois statute fixing maximum storage rates for grain elevators was constitutional. A few years later another series of cases involving state laws regulating railroad rates were declared unconstitutional. In Wabash v. Illinois (1886), for example, the Court held that an Illinois law prohibiting rate discrimination by railroads for long and short hauls was unconstitutional because it infringed on the exclusive right of Congress to regulate interstate commerce.

GRANGER LAWS. Western state laws passed in the 1870's regulating grain elevators and railroad freight rates, long and short haul railroad discrimination, rebates and other railroad abuses. A number of cases (See GRANGER CASES) were brought to the U. S. Supreme Court which held most of the Granger Laws to be unconstitutional. Failure of the laws led to the enactment of the federal INTERSTATE COMMERCE ACT (1887). (See also RAILROAD LEGISLATION)

GRANGER MOVEMENT. See PATRONS OF HUSBANDRY

GRANT, ULYSSES S. (1822-85). Eighteenth president of the U. S. At the outbreak of the WAR BETWEEN THE STATES (1861) he rejoined the army and soon became commander of the Union forces in the West. During the war he led his men in the capture of FORT HENRY (1862) and FORT DONELSON (1862) (see UNCONDITIONAL SURRENDER GRANT), the victory at the BATTLE OF SHILOH (1862), the capture of Vicksburg (see BATTLE OF VICKSBURG, 1863) and the victory at the Battle of Chattanooga (1863). In 1864 he was made supreme commander of the Union Armies and started the WILDERNESS CAMPAIGN to capture Richmond, the capital of the Confederacy. On April 9, 1865, General ROBERT E. LEE surrendered to Grant at APPOMATTOX COURTHOUSE, thus ending the war.

In 1868 the REPUBLICAN PARTY nominated Grant for the presidency. He won an overwhelming victory in the ELECTION OF 1868 and again in the ELECTION OF 1872. During his two terms as president (1869-77) the first transcontinental railroad was completed, the BLACK FRIDAY stock market crash occurred (1869), AMENDMENT 15 was ratified (1870), the TREATY OF WASHINGTON (1871) was signed with England, the silver DEMONETIZATION ACT (1873) was passed and the financial PANIC OF 1873 occurred. A number of political scandals marred his presidency, including the

165

WHISKEY RING scandal, the CREDIT MOBILIER and the BELKNAP SCANDAL.

GRAY, CAPTAIN ROBERT (1755-1806). American sea captain and the first American to circumnavigate the globe (1789-90). During one of his voyages to the west coast he discovered the Columbia River (1792). His discovery was one of the bases for subsequent U. S. claims to the OREGON TERRITORY.

GREAT BRITAIN, U. S. RELATIONS WITH. After the AMERICAN REVOLUTION (1775-83) relations between the U. S. and Great Britain were bitter and continued to grow worse until the outbreak of renewed hostilities in the WAR OF 1812. After the TREATY OF GHENT (1814), however, relations between the two countries improved. Early evidence of Britain's changing attitude to the U. S. is found in the RUSH-BAGOT AGREEMENT (1817) providing for an unfortified boundary between Canada and the U. S., in the TREATY OF 1818 and the WEBSTER-ASHBURTON TREATY (1842) settling the boundary between the U. S. and Canada. During our WAR BETWEEN THE STATES (1861-65) Great Britain remained neutral, although the South had expected help from Britain. After the war relations with Great Britain continued to improve because of our growing naval power, Britain's desire to keep Latin American countries independent for trading purposes, and our own growing trade with Great Britain and members of the British Empire. In 1871 the two countries settled the ALABAMA CLAIMS dispute by signing the TREATY OF WASHINGTON (1872). In 1897 they settled the VENEZUELA BOUNDARY DISPUTE. In the 20th century Great Britain and the U. S. were drawn together by common interests in WORLD WAR I (1914-18), the WASHINGTON DISARMAMENT CONFERENCE (1922), WORLD WAR II (1941-45), the UNITED NATIONS, the NORTH ATLANTIC TREATY ORGANIZATION (1949) and the SOUTHEAST ASIA TREATY ORGANIZATION (1954), among others.

GREAT COMPROMISE. An agreement reached at the CONSTITUTIONAL CONVENTION (1787) by which the

VIRGINIA PLAN and the NEW JERSEY PLAN for a new government were combined and modified to yield a compromise that delegates from both large and small states were willing to accept. Under the Great Compromise, a Congress of two houses was established. In the Senate each state was to be represented by two delegates. This aimed to maintain the equality of the states. In the House of Representatives each state was to have a number of delegates based on the size of its population. In each house the senators and representatives were to vote as individuals and not as part of a state delegation. No law could be passed except with the majority approval of both houses of Congress.

GREAT DEPRESSION (1929-1935). The period of economic stagnation that followed the PANIC OF 1929. During the height of the depression more than 10,000,000 persons were unemployed, thousands of farms were foreclosed for failure to pay mortgages and thousands of banks closed their doors because of temporary insolvency. The depression reached its lowest point in 1933 when President FRANKLIN D. ROOSEVELT ordered all banks in the country closed. (See BANK HOLIDAY)

GREAT PLAINS. See INTERIOR PLAINS

GREELEY, HORACE (1811-72). Founder and editor of the New York *Tribune*. In 1841 Greeley began publication of the paper, which soon became one of the most influential dailies in the U. S. in molding public opinion. As editor, Greeley was a strong supporter of the WHIG PARTY and one of the founders of the REPUBLICAN PARTY (1854). He favored a high protective tariff and opposed women suffrage, the Mexican War and slavery. He helped Lincoln get the presidential nomination in 1860 and supported the Northern viewpoint in the War Between the States (1861-65). Although Greeley ran as a candidate for public office a number of times he was never elected. He was appointed to the House of Representatives for three months to fill a vacancy but was defeated in elections for the Senate in 1861 and 1867. He was nominated for the presidency by the LIBERAL REPUBLICAN PARTY and the DEMOCRATIC PARTY but he was defeated in the ELECTION OF 1872. (See "GO WEST, YOUNG MAN")

167

GREENBACK LABOR PARTY. See GREENBACK PARTY

GREENBACK PARTY. Organized about 1874 by debtor groups who favored inflation of the currency by the printing of more greenback paper money. The Greenback Party nominated presidential candidates in 1876, 1880 and 1884 but never polled a large vote. Its greatest success was in the Congressional election of 1878 when the party polled more than 1,000,000 votes. In that year the support of labor groups resulted in a change of name to Greenback Labor Party. The most important Greenback Party leaders were PETER COOPER, their presidential candidate in 1876, JAMES B. WEAVER, their candidate in 1880, and BENJAMIN F. BUTLER, their candidate in 1884. Most of the Greenback Party supporters merged with the POPULIST PARTY after 1888.

GREENBACKS. Paper money issued by the national government during the WAR BETWEEN THE STATES under the Legal Tender Act (1862). At the end of the war $432,000,-000 in greenbacks was in circulation. The legality of paying debts in Greenbacks instead of in gold became an important issue before the U. S. Supreme Court. (See LEGAL TENDER CASES) In the ELECTION OF 1868 the Democratic Party endorsed the OHIO IDEA of issuing greenbacks to pay the national debt. The movement to get more greenbacks printed and thus inflate the currency resulted in the formation of the GREENBACK PARTY. President ULYSSES S. GRANT and the Republican Party rejected the Ohio Idea. In 1879 Congress passed the RESUMPTION ACT, which provided for the redemption of greenbacks in gold. Since few greenbacks were presented for redemption, Congress agreed to keep $346,000,000 of them in circulation permanently.

GREENE, GENERAL NATHANIEL (1742-86). American commander in the American Revolution (1775-83). After the defeat of General HORATIO GATES by the British at the BATTLE OF CAMDEN (South Carolina), General Greene was sent to replace Gates in the South. At the BATTLE OF GUILFORD COURTHOUSE (North Carolina) in 1781 General Greene inflicted heavy losses on

168

the British. He continued to harass the British forces in the South till the end of the war.

GREEN MOUNTAIN BOYS. See ALLEN, ETHAN, and FORT TICONDEROGA

GREENVILLE, TREATY OF (1795). Signed after the defeat of the Indians in the old NORTHWEST TERRITORY by ANTHONY WAYNE. The treaty opened the territory to settlement with a reasonable degree of safety for settlers from Indian attacks. However, both settlers and Indians violated the boundary line established by the treaty to divide white settlements from Indian territory.

GRENVILLE, GEORGE (1712-70). Prime minister of Great Britain (1763-65) who attempted to enforce the Trade and NAVIGATION ACTS in the American colonies. He was also instrumental in getting KING GEORGE III to issue the PROCLAMATION OF NEUTRALITY (1763) and getting the British Parliament to pass the SUGAR ACT (1764), the CURRENCY ACT (1764) and the STAMP ACT (1765).

GRIMKÉ SISTERS (Sarah Grimké 1792-1873; Angelina Grimké 1805-79). Although they were members of a distinguished and aristocratic Southern family, both became anti-slavery crusaders. By their speeches and writings they furthered the Abolition Movement. (See ABOLITION-ISTS) In addition to their anti-slavery work they also crusaded for equal rights for women.

GUADALCANAL, BATTLE OF (1942). One of the turning points in the Pacific Ocean fighting during World War II (1941-45). The U. S. won a costly victory over the Japanese on land and sea which resulted in the capture of a small island called Guadalcanal, in the Solomon Islands group in the South Pacific. However Guadalcanal was strategically important because it was the first major offensive step taken by the U. S. in the campaign to drive the Japanese out of their conquered territories and back to their home islands.

GUADALUPE HIDALGO, TREATY OF (1848). Treaty of peace ending the MEXICAN WAR (1846-48). Under the

169

terms of the treaty, Mexico recognized the Rio Grande River as the southern boundary of Texas and ceded to the U. S. the entire upper California and New Mexico Territories, an area of a half-million square miles. In return for this cession of land the U. S. agreed to pay Mexico $15,000,-000 as well as to pay all claims of American citizens against the Mexican government.

GUAM. Small island in the west Pacific Ocean acquired by the U. S. from Spain at the end of the SPANISH-AMERICAN WAR (1898). (See TREATY OF PARIS, 1898) The island was captured (1941) by the Japanese during WORLD WAR II (1941-45) and was retaken by American forces in 1944.

GUILFORD COURTHOUSE, BATTLE OF (1781). One of the major military engagements of the American Revolution, fought between an American Army under General Nathanael Greene and a large British force under General Cornwallis (1781). Although neither side won a decisive victory, General Cornwallis was eventually forced to retreat to the Atlantic coast, thus preparing the way for the great American victory at the *Battle of Yorktown* (1781).

HABEAS CORPUS. A court order directing that a detained person be brought before the court to determine the reasons for the detention. Failure of some colonial courts to grant such Writs of Habeas Corpus was one of the causes of the AMERICAN REVOLUTION (1775-83). The U. S. Constitution guarantees the right of habeas corpus (Art. 1, Sec. 9, Cl. 2) except in cases of rebellion, invasion or danger to public safety. During the WAR BETWEEN THE STATES (1861-65) President ABRAHAM LINCOLN authorized the suspension of the right of habeas corpus by the army in special cases only. In the case of Ex Parte Merryman (1861) the U. S. Supreme Court held that the president could not suspend the right of habeas corpus. The right to suspend, said Chief Justice ROGER TANEY, rests with Congress and not with the president.

HAGUE COURT. Also known as the Hague Tribunal and the Permanent Court of International Arbitration. It was established at the first Hague Conference in 1899 for the settlement of disputes between nations. In 1910 the Hague Court settled the North Atlantic FISHING RIGHTS dispute between the U. S. and Great Britain.

HAITIAN INTERVENTION (1911, 1914). See ROOSEVELT COROLLARY and GOOD NEIGHBOR POLICY

HAKLUYT, RICHARD (1552-1616). English geographer who compiled a history of the voyages and discoveries of English navigators as well as histories of other voyages and discoveries. He was also active in planning and encouraging new exploring expeditions.

HALE, NATHAN (1755-76). Schoolteacher who served in the American Revolution. In 1776 he volunteered for the dangerous mission of getting information about the movements of British forces on Long Island. He was caught by the British and hanged as a spy. It is reported that his last words before his death were: "I only regret that I have but one life to lose for my country." He was 21 years of age when executed.

HALF BREEDS. Name applied to the reform wing of the REPUBLICAN PARTY after 1876 to distinguish it from the STALWART, or conservative wing. The Half Breeds supported the reform program of President RUTHERFORD B. HAYES. (See ELECTION OF 1880)

HAMILTON, ALEXANDER (1757-1804). First Secretary of the Treasury of the U. S. At the CONSTITUTIONAL CONVENTION (1787), where he represented New York State, he took an important part in drawing up the new document. During the debate over ratification of the Constitution in New York, Hamilton wrote a series of newspaper articles (together with JAMES MADISON and JOHN JAY) known collectively as "THE FEDERALIST," in which Hamilton urged ratification of the Constitution.

In 1789 Hamilton became the first Secretary of the Treasury under President GEORGE WASHINGTON. As a result of Hamilton's financial reports, Congress passed a tariff (1789) and a WHISKEY TAX (1791), established the BANK OF UNITED STATES (1791), and undertook to pay the national debt as well as state debts incurred during the Revolution. (See ASSUMPTION ACT) He also established the decimal system of our national currency. During his term as Secretary of the Treasury Hamilton was recognized as one of the leaders of the FEDERALIST PARTY. He resigned as secretary in 1795 but continued to remain influential in politics without holding public office. Hamilton's opposition to the ambitions of AARON BURR created intense personal hostility between the two men. In 1804 Hamilton was killed in a duel with Burr.

HAMILTON, ANDREW (1676-1741). One of the greatest lawyers in the English colonies before the American Revolution. He successfully defended JOHN PETER ZENGER (1734) in a case involving the principle of FREEDOM OF THE PRESS.

HAMILTON'S FINANCIAL PLANS. See HAMILTON, ALEXANDER

HAMMER V. DAGENHART (1918). See CHILD LABOR

HAMPTON ROADS CONFERENCE (1865). Meeting of President Lincoln and representatives of the Confederate government. The conference was called to bring the WAR BETWEEN THE STATES (1861-65) to an end through a negotiated peace treaty. The conference adjourned without reaching an agreement.

HANCOCK, JOHN (1737-1793). Colonial merchant and patriot. Before the American Revolution he developed a highly successful shipping business in Massachusetts. In 1768 one of his ships, the *Liberty*, was seized by British customs agents on charges of smuggling and violation of the NAVIGATION ACTS. Thereafter Hancock played a leading role in arousing colonial resistance to British rule. He was chosen president of the SECOND CONTINENTAL CONGRESS (1775-77) and was the first signer of the DECLARATION OF INDEPENDENCE (1776).

HANNA, MARCUS A. (1837-1904). Generally known as "Mark" Hanna. He was a successful Ohio businessman turned politician. Beginning in 1894 he worked to win the Republican presidential nomination for his protégé, WILLIAM MC KINLEY, and succeeded in having him nominated and later elected. (See ELECTION OF 1896) After McKinley's election, Hanna was elected to the U. S. Senate (1897), where he became a staunch advocate of the interests of big business.

HAPPY WARRIOR. See SMITH, ALFRED E.

HARDING, WARREN G. (1865-1923). Twenty-ninth president of the U. S. In 1920 he was nominated by the REPUBLICAN PARTY and in his campaign called for a "return to normalcy." His running mate for the vice-presidency was CALVIN COOLIDGE. In the ELECTION OF 1920, Harding defeated JAMES M. COX, the DEMOCRATIC PARTY nominee. In 1923, during a speaking tour, Harding became ill and died shortly thereafter. Vice-President Coolidge succeeded to the presidency.

During Harding's brief term in office (1921-23) Congress passed the National Budget Act (1921) and the FORDNEY-MC CUMBER TARIFF ACT (1922). The WASHINGTON DISARMAMENT CONFERENCE (1921-22) was held in the nation's capital. Harding's ad-

173

ministration was clouded by the TEAPOT DOME oil lease scandal, a Veteran's Bureau scandal, irregularities in the office of the ALIEN PROPERTY CUSTODIAN as well as other government irregularities.

HARPER'S FERRY RAID. See BROWN, JOHN

HARPER'S WEEKLY (1857-1916). Famous illustrated New York magazine published during and after the War Between the States. It achieved nationwide circulation and exerted a powerful influence on public opinion. One of its famous staff members was THOMAS NAST, whose biting cartoons led to the exposure and overthrow of the TWEED RING in New York City.

HARRIMAN, EDWARD H. (1848-1909). Railroad executive and financier. At the height of his business career he obtained control of the SOUTHERN PACIFIC RAILROAD and Central Pacific Railroad. His efforts to obtain control of the Chicago, Burlington and Quincy Railroad leading into Chicago led to a tremendous financial struggle between Harriman and his business rival, JAMES J. HILL. In his later years Harriman used his vast fortune for many philanthropies.

HARRIS, TOWNSEND (1804-78). First American consul-general sent to Japan (1856) after the opening of Japan by COMMODORE MATTHEW C. PERRY. Harris was popular with the Japanese and succeeded in negotiating another favorable trade treaty. Before his appointment to Japan, Harris was one of the leaders in the movement to establish the free College of the City of New York (CCNY).

HARRISON, BENJAMIN (1833-1901). Twenty-third president of the U. S. Harrison was the grandson of former President WILLIAM HENRY HARRISON. In 1888 he was named REPUBLICAN PARTY candidate for the presidency and defeated GROVER CLEVELAND in the ELECTION OF 1888. In the ELECTION OF 1892, however, Cleveland defeated Harrison's hopes of a second presidential term. During Benjamin Harrison's one term as president the first PAN AMERICAN CONFERENCE was held in Washington D. C. (1889) and the HOMESTEAD STRIKE (1892) rocked the nation. Congress passed the

MC KINLEY TARIFF ACT (1890), the SHERMAN SILVER PURCHASE ACT (1890) and the SHERMAN ANTI-TRUST ACT (1890).

HARRISON, WILLIAM HENRY (1773-1841). Ninth president of the U. S. During his service in the army he defeated the Indians led by TECUMSEH and his brother "The Prophet" at the BATTLE OF TIPPECANOE (1811). As brigadier-general in the WAR OF 1812 he fought the British along the Canadian border and won a number of notable victories. The WHIG PARTY nominated him for president in the ELECTION of 1836 but he was defeated by MARTIN VAN BUREN. In the ELECTION OF 1840, however, he defeated Van Buren and became president. He died one month after his inauguration (April 4, 1841). Harrison's tenure of office was the shortest of any president in our history. Vice-President JOHN TYLER succeeded Harrison as president.

HARTFORD CONVENTION (1841). Meeting of New England Federalists to protest the continuance of the WAR OF 1812. The convention passed a number of resolutions announcing the rights of states to nullify Congressional laws. It also drew up seven proposed amendments to the U. S. Constitution aimed at strengthening the political power of the commercial Northeastern states against the power of the agricultural South and West. The ending of the War of 1812 completely discredited the Hartford Convention and the FEDERALIST PARTY that had sponsored it.

HARVARD COLLEGE. The first college in the Thirteen Colonies, established in Massachusetts in 1636 for the education of young men for the ministry. John Harvard, a Massachusetts citizen, contributed his library to the new institution and the college was named after him.

HAT ACT (1732). One of many restrictive manufacturing and trade acts passed by the British Parliament. The Hat Act forbad the export of felt hats from one colony to another, to a foreign country or to England.

HATCH ACT (1939). Prohibited federal administrative employees from active participation in any Congressional or presidential election campaigns and provided severe penalties for anyone who used political pressure on federal jobholders. In 1940 the act was extended to include state and local employees whose salaries were derived in whole or in part from the federal treasury.

HAWAIIAN ISLANDS. Before 1898 the U. S. signed a reciprocal trade agreement with the native Hawaiian government and obtained rights to a coaling station at Pearl Harbor. In 1893 the native queen Liliuokalani was deposed, largely through the influence of American sugar plantation owners who wanted the U. S. to annex Hawaii. President GROVER CLEVELAND opposed annexation. After the outbreak of the SPANISH-AMERICAN WAR (1898), however, Congress annexed Hawaii by a joint resolution. Hawaii became an incorporated territory in 1900. The PEARL HARBOR ATTACK (1941) by the Japanese led to U. S. entry into WORLD WAR II. Hawaii was admitted as the 50th state of the Union in 1959.

HAWKINS, SIR JOHN (1532-95). English adventurer and sea captain who raided Spanish treasure ships sailing from the New World to Spain. During the attack of the SPANISH ARMADA (1588) Hawkins fought brilliantly and was rewarded with knighthood.

HAWLEY-SMOOT TARIFF (1930). Passed during the Republican administration of President HERBERT HOOVER. Under Republican leadership, tariff rates were raised to the highest level in our history. The "flexible clause" of the FORDNEY-MC CUMBER TARIFF ACT of 1922 was retained in the new tariff law. (See TARIFF LEGISLATION)

HAY BUNAU-VARILLA TREATY (1903). Signed by the U. S. and Panama immediately after Panama rebelled (see PANAMA REVOLUTION) from Colombia. This treaty guaranteed the independence of Panama and provided for a cash payment of $10,000,000 and a rental of $250,000 annually by the U. S. to Panama in return for a U. S. leasehold on the Canal Zone, a strip of land ten miles wide across the Isthmus of Panama. The U. S. was also given the right to fortify the Canal Zone area.

HAYES, RUTHERFORD B. (1822-1893). Nineteenth president of the U. S. In 1876 he was nominated for the presidency by the REPUBLICAN PARTY. In the ELECTION OF 1876 a bitter dispute developed over the counting of conflicting electoral votes but Hayes was finally elected by a single electoral vote. (See ELECTORAL COMMISSION ACT) During Hayes' single term as president the RECONSTRUCTION ERA came to an end with the removal of all federal troops from the South (1877) and the BLAND-ALLISON SILVER PURCHASE ACT (1878) was passed by Congress.

HAY-HERRAN TREATY (1903). Signed by U. S. and Colombia. This treaty gave the U. S. a leasehold on a six-mile-wide strip of land across the Isthmus of Panama. At this time, all of Panama belonged to Colombia. However, the Colombian government failed to ratify this treaty and it never went into effect. (See PANAMA REVOLUTION)

HAY, JOHN (1838-1905). One of President Lincoln's private secretaries. In 1898 he became Secretary of State under President McKinley and continued to serve under President Theodore Roosevelt until 1905. Hay was responsible for the OPEN DOOR POLICY (1899), the HAY-PAUNCEFOTE TREATY (1901) with Great Britain, the HAY-HERRAN TREATY (1903) with Colombia and the HAY BUNAU-VARILLA TREATY (1903) with Panama. These treaties paved the way for the construction of the PANAMA CANAL.

HAYMARKET RIOTS. On May 4, 1886 an outdoor labor meeting was held in Haymarket Square, Chicago, to protest against police violence toward strikers. During the meeting a bomb was hurled into a group of policemen, killing a number of them. The bomb thrower was never identified but eight labor agitators who had advocated the use of violence were tried for murder. Four were hanged, three were imprisoned and one committed suicide. A number of years later Governor JOHN P. ALTGELD of Illinois pardoned the three imprisoned men, and this action aroused so much criticism that he was thereafter ruined politically.

HAY-PAUNCEFOTE TREATY (1901). Signed by U. S. and Great Britain. This treaty put an end to the CLAYTON-

BULWER TREATY (1850) that provided for joint ownership of any interocean canal. The new Hay-Pauncefote Treaty provided that such a canal was to be built and controlled exclusively by the U. S. but that the canal would be open to ships of all nations on an equal basis.

HEAD RIGHT SYSTEM. Colonial system of granting persons a tract of land for every settler transported to the colonies. This land was given either to the settler or to the person who paid his ship passage money. On the basis of the Head Right System a few people, particularly in Virginia and other Southern colonies, accumulated vast tracts of land.

HEARST, WILLIAM RANDOLPH (1863-1951). Owner of the New York *Journal* and other newspapers which became known as the Hearst chain. Before and during the SPANISH-AMERICAN WAR (1898) Hearst engaged in a circulation battle with JOSEPH PULITZER'S New York *World,* using sensationalism, boldface headlines and special features to gain new readers. This type of newspaper publishing became known as YELLOW JOURNALISM. The slanted reporting of events before the Spanish-American War by Hearst and Pulitzer did much to arouse the war spirit in the U. S.

"HE KEPT US OUT OF THE WAR." See ELECTION OF 1916

HELDERBERG WAR. See ANTI-RENT WAR

HELPER, HINTON R. (1829-1909). See "IMPENDING CRISIS"

HENNEPIN, FATHER LOUIS (1640-1701). French Franciscan friar and explorer. In 1679 he joined LA SALLE's exploring expedition along the Great Lakes and Mississippi River. Father Hennepin explored the upper region of the Mississippi Valley, discovered St. Anthony's Falls (present site of Minneapolis), was captured by the Sioux Indians but was rescued. He was the first to publish a description of Niagara Falls.

HENRY, FORT. Military fortification on the Tennessee side of the Mississippi River, held by the Confederate forces at the beginning of the WAR BETWEEN THE STATES (1861-65). It was captured by GENERAL ULYSSES S. GRANT (1862) commanding a Northern Army, and Commodore Foote, commanding a gunboat flotilla on the Mississippi River.

HENRY, PATRICK (1736-99). American colonial lawyer, orator and leader of the Southern radical group who favored war with England. He was a delegate to the Virginia HOUSE OF BURGESSES (1765-74), where he made a famous speech (1765) denouncing the STAMP ACT. In the debate over resistance to British laws (1775) he is reported to have made another famous speech ending with the words: "Give me liberty, or give me death!" During the American Revolution, Patrick Henry, as governor of Virginia (1776-79) authorized the GEORGE ROGERS CLARK military expedition (1778) to the old NORTHWEST TERRITORY. After the Revolution, Henry opposed ratification of the Constitution (1789) because he believed that it infringed on states' rights and provided no guarantee of individual liberties.

HEPBURN ACT (1906). Passed by Congress during President THEODORE ROOSEVELT's administration for the purpose of strengthening the power of the INTERSTATE COMMERCE COMMISSION. Under the Hepburn Act sleeping car companies, express companies, pipeline companies and railroad terminals were placed under the supervision of the I. C. C. Free railroad passes were specifically forbidden and the I. C. C. was empowered to fix fair and reasonable railroad rates subject to approval of the federal courts. (See RAILROAD LEGISLATION)

HERKIMER, GENERAL NICHOLAS (1728-77). See ORISKANY, BATTLE OF

HESSIANS. Soldiers from the German state of Hesse, hired by the British to fight against the colonists during the AMERICAN REVOLUTION (1775-83). Soldiers hired from other German states were also called Hessians. Such soldiers who fought for hire were also called mercenaries.

HICKOK, JAMES B. (1837-76). Popularly known as "Wild Bill" Hickok. He became famous as a marshal in such frontier towns as Fort Riley and Abilene (1866-71). Many tales, some of them exaggerated, were spead about his marksmanship and capture of outlaws. He toured the East with "Buffalo Bill" (WILLIAM F. CODY) in "Wild West" shows (1872-73), later went back West and was himself killed by an outlaw.

HIGHER LAW. See SEWARD, WILLIAM H.

HILL, JAMES J. (1838-1916). Nicknamed the "Empire Builder" because of his efforts to develop the Northwest region of the U. S. As railroad promoter he built the Great Northern Railroad, extending from Duluth to Seattle (1893). Hill fought a long and successful financial battle with his rival EDWARD H. HARRIMAN for control of the Chicago, Burlington and Quincy Railroad leading into Chicago. In 1901 Hill and J. P. MORGAN organized the Northern Securities Company as a holding company for the Great Northern Railroad and the Northern Pacific Railroad. The U. S. Supreme Court, in the famous Northern Securities Case (1904), ordered the company dissolved because it violated the SHERMAN ANTI-TRUST ACT.

HINDENBURG LINE. Heavily fortified military line established by the German Army in France during WORLD WAR I (1914-18). In 1918 the American Army pierced the line during the Meuse-Argonne Campaign. This was one of the factors that led to the surrender of Germany.

HIROSHIMA. Japanese city of approximately 400,000 inhabitants. In August, 1945, during WORLD WAR II, a U. S. bombing plane dropped the first atomic bomb on the city, killing or wounding almost half the city's population.

HISTORIANS, AMERICAN. During the first half of the 19th century American historical writing was a combination of history and literature. As a result our early historians such as William Prescott, John Lothrop Motley, Francis Parkman and George Bancroft rank high in American literature as well as in historical research. After the War Between the States (1865), historical writings emphasized the importance of careful research rather than literary quality. Nonetheless the works of James Ford Rhodes, John Bach McMaster and Henry Adams are very readable. In the 20th century American historical research was dominated by the work of Edward Channing, Frederick Jackson Turner and Charles A. Beard.

HOE, RICHARD (1812-86). Inventor of the steam cylinder press (1846) for high-speed printing of newspapers. The first Hoe press was used by the Philadelphia *Public Ledger,* which printed 8,000 papers in an hour (1847).

HOLMES, OLIVER WENDELL, JR. (1841-1935). Son of the famous poet Oliver Wendell Holmes. He was appointed Associate Justice of the U. S. Supreme Court by President Theodore Roosevelt in 1902 and served until 1932, when he retired at the age of 90. Holmes was noted for his liberal opinions on such matters as child labor laws and freedom of speech. (See ABRAMS V. U. S. and SCHENCK V. U. S.) He developed the RULE OF REASON in cases affecting large corporations and monopolies prosecuted under the anti-trust laws.

"HOLY EXPERIMENT." See PENNSYLVANIA COLONY

HOME OWNERS LOAN ACT (1933). See HOUSING LEGISLATION

HOMESTEAD ACT (1862). Provided that any adult citizen who had not fought against the Union in the War Between the States (1861-65) could get 160 acres of public Western land provided he lived on it, cultivated it for five years and paid a small recording fee ($26 to $34). Under another provision of the act, a citizen could obtain 160 acres after a half year of residence on the land for a payment of $1.25 per acre. These liberal terms encouraged westward migration after 1865. Other important Homestead Acts were passed in 1904, 1906 and 1909. (See PUBLIC LAND ACTS)

HOMESTEAD STRIKE (1892). One of the bitterest strikes in the annals of the American labor movement. This strike, against the Carnegie Steel Corporation in Homestead, Pennsylvania, lasted for five months. In it there was much violence between armed company detectives and the strikers. The Pennsylvania state militia was called out to open the strike-bound plant. This broke the strike, ended the resistance of the steel workers and destroyed the power of their union, the Amalgamated Association of Iron and Steel Workers.

HOOD, GENERAL JOHN B. (1831-79). See NASHVILLE, BATTLE OF

HOOKER, GENERAL "FIGHTING JOE" (1814-79). See CHANCELLORSVILLE, BATTLE OF

HOOKER, THOMAS (1586-1647). Puritan clergyman in MASSACHUSETTS BAY COLONY who left the colony and migrated west with a group of followers. Hooker and his group established a settlement at Hartford (1636) on the Connecticut River. Other settlements were established at Windsor and Wethersfield. Later the three towns joined to form a single Connecticut Colony. Hooker was responsible for the writing of the FUNDAMENTAL ORDERS OF CONNECTICUT (1639), the first written constitution in America.

HOOVER, HERBERT (1874-   ). Thirty-first president of the U. S. In 1928 he was nominated for the presidency by the REPUBLICAN PARTY and in the ELECTION OF 1928 won a landslide victory against ALFRED E. SMITH, his DEMOCRATIC PARTY opponent. In 1929 the stock market crash ushered in the GREAT DEPRESSION, which lasted through Hoover's term of office. In the ELECTION OF 1932 Hoover was defeated for the presidency by FRANKLIN D. ROOSEVELT, the Democratic candidate.

During Hoover's single term in office, Congress passed the NATIONAL ORIGINS IMMIGRATION ACT (1929), the AGRICULTURAL MARKETING ACT (1929), the HAWLEY-SMOOT TARIFF ACT (1930) and the law establishing the RECONSTRUCTION FINANCE CORPORATION (1932). In foreign affairs the U. S. participated in the LONDON NAVAL CONFERENCE (1930), announced a moratorium (1931) on foreign debt payments to the U. S. (see WAR DEBTS), and announced the STIMSON DOCTRINE (1932) after Japan's invasion of Manchuria.

HOOVER MORATORIUM (1931). See WAR DEBTS

HOPKINS, HARRY L. (1890-1946). Intimate friend and personal adviser of President Franklin D. Roosevelt during the early years of the NEW DEAL. Hopkins administered the Federal Emergency Relief Administration and the Works Progress Administration. (See UNEMPLOYMENT LEGISLATION) He was Secretary of Commerce from 1938 to 1940. After the outbreak of World War II in Europe, Hopkins administered the LEND LEASE ACT (1941) and was chairman of the War Production Board (1941). (See WARTIME AGENCIES, WORLD WAR II)

HORNBOOK. Used by colonial children when learning to read. It consisted of a slab of wood on which was attached a single piece of printed paper. This was covered with a transparent sheet of material, called "horn," to protect the paper. After the child had learned the contents of one sheet, it was removed and another was put in its place.

HORSES. The Spanish explorers and CONQUISTADORES were the first to bring horses to the Western Hemisphere. The Indians soon learned how to ride them and the animal became one of the most important means of land transportation for the Indians of the Great Plains. (See INTERIOR PLAINS)

HORSESHOE BEND, BATTLE OF (1814). Military victory of American forces led by ANDREW JACKSON during the WAR OF 1812 against the CREEK INDIANS in the Mississippi Territory. As a result of their defeat, the Creeks agreed to give up a large part of the Mississippi Territory.

"HOUSE DIVIDED" SPEECH (1858). One of Lincoln's famous speeches, delivered at the Illinois Republican State Convention that nominated him for U. S. Senator. In this speech Lincoln used the biblical phrase: "A house divided against itself cannot stand" and added, "I believe this government cannot endure permanently half slave and half free . . . it will become all one thing or all the other."

183

HOUSE, COLONEL EDWARD M. (1858-1938). Personal friend and adviser of President WOODROW WILSON. In 1914 and 1915 President Wilson sent him to Europe to try to end hostilities there (World War I). After the U. S. entered World War I (1917) Colonel House was special assistant to the president. At the end of the war House accompanied Wilson to Paris to serve as adviser during the writing of the VERSAILLES TREATY.

HOUSE OF BURGESSES (1619). The first representative assembly to meet in America. The House of Burgesses first met in a church in Jamestown, Virginia, and included representatives of the LONDON COMPANY, of the governor of Virginia and of settlers in the colony.

HOUSING LEGISLATION. Beginning with the NEW DEAL administration of President Franklin D. Roosevelt in 1933, Congress for the first time passed a series of measures aimed at improving the housing conditions of the "one-third of a nation" who President Roosevelt said were "ill-housed." In 1933 Congress passed the Home Owners Loan Act to stop home foreclosures. The National Housing Act was passed in 1934 to provide government insured loans for private housing. In 1937 Congress passed the Wagner-Steagall Housing Act to encourage slum clearance projects, and in 1938 passed the Steagall National Housing Act to provide further government insured loans for new home construction.

HOUSTON, SAM (1793-1863). American military, frontier and political leader. He was elected to Congress from Tennessee in 1823 and 1825 and to the governorship of the state in 1827. He resigned in 1829 and moved to Oklahoma and then to Texas. Here he became the leader of the American settlers in the TEXAS WAR OF INDEPENDENCE (1836) from Mexico. Shortly after his great victory over the Mexicans in the BATTLE OF SAN JACINTO (1836) he was elected first president of the Texas Republic (1836). After Texas was admitted to the Union (1845) Houston was the first U. S. senator to represent his state in the Senate, where he served for 14 years. He was also governor of Texas when the people of that state voted to secede from the Union (1861). Houston refused to follow the secession policy of his state and was removed from the governorship (1861).

HOWE, ELIAS (1819-1867). Inventor of the sewing machine (1846) which made possible the rapid and inexpensive manufacture of clothing, shoes and other products that require sewing.

HOWE, ADMIRAL RICHARD (1726-99). Commander of the British fleet in American waters during the early years of the AMERICAN REVOLUTION. He was the brother of Sir WILLIAM HOWE, commander of the British Army in America during the Revolution.

HOWE, SIR WILLIAM (1729-1814). See SARATOGA, BATTLE OF; BRANDYWINE, BATTLE OF; GERMANTOWN, BATTLE OF

HUDSON, HENRY (? -1611). English explorer employed by the DUTCH EAST INDIA COMPANY (1609) to explore the east coast of North America for a possible NORTHWEST PASSAGE to the Far East. Hudson explored the east coast of what is now the United States and sailed his ship, the *Half Moon,* into New York harbor (1609) and up the Hudson River. On a later voyage for England (1610) he again tried to find a Northwest water passage around the North American continent. He found Hudson Bay but perished when his crew mutinied and set him adrift in an open boat.

HUERTA, VICTORIANO (1854-1916). See WATCHFUL WAITING and TAMPICO INCIDENT

HUGHES, CHARLES E. (1862-1948). Investigated corrupt practices of insurance companies in New York (1905), as a consequence of which he was elected governor of New York State (1906). President Taft appointed him Associate Justice of the U. S. Supreme Court in 1910. He resigned this post to become the Republican Party candidate for the presidency in the ELECTION OF 1916. After his defeat, in one of the closest elections in our history, he returned to private law practice. Later he was appointed Secretary of State by President Harding. He also served under President Coolidge. As Secretary of State he took a leading role at the WASHINGTON DISARMAMENT

185

CONFERENCE (1922). He served as an international judge at the HAGUE COURT (1926-30) and the WORLD COURT (1928-30). In 1930 President Hoover appointed him Chief Justice of the U. S. Supreme Court, a position he held until his retirement in 1941.

HUGUENOTS. French Protestants who left their native country for the New World after 1685 because of religious persecution at home. Most of the Huguenots settled in South Carolina, but a few went to New York and Massachusetts.

HULL, CORDELL (1871-1955). Secretary of State under President Franklin D. Roosevelt. He was one of the leading authors of the GOOD NEIGHBOR POLICY for Latin America and of the RECIPROCAL TARIFF ACT (1934). He was negotiating with Japanese representatives in Washington D. C. when Japan bombed PEARL HARBOR (1941), bringing the U. S. into WORLD WAR II. In 1945 Hull was awarded the NOBEL PEACE PRIZE.

HULL HOUSE. See ADDAMS, JANE

HULL, CAPTAIN ISAAC (1773-1843). See "CONSTITUTION" AND "GUERRIERE"

HULL, GENERAL WILLIAM (1753-1825). Leader of an American expedition to invade Canada during the War of 1812. Instead of a successful invasion, Hull surrendered Detroit to a British force without any attempt at a determined defense. Hull was court martialed and was saved from execution only by his military record in the American Revolution.

HUNKERS. Conservative wing of the Democratic Party in New York State in the 1840's, as distinguished from the more liberal BARNBURNERS faction. The name "Hunker" was derived from "hanker" and referred to the hankering or eagerness of this group for political jobs. As conservatives, the Hunkers deplored the constant anti-slavery agitation in the state and favored a policy of internal improvements. The Hunkers were generally in control of New York State politics until 1848. In the national ELECTION OF 1852, the Hunkers were themselves split by political differences into "Hards" who opposed Franklin Pierce, the Democratic Party candidate for president, and "Softs" who favored his election.

HUNTINGTON, COLLIS P. (1821-1900). See SOUTHERN PACIFIC RAILROAD

HURON INDIANS. When the first French explorers found this tribe, the Hurons were living on the Canadian side of Lake Huron and had already been in frequent wars with the Iroquois Indians of New York. Because the Iroquois first obtained possession of the white man's guns, they practically wiped out the Huron Tribe (1648-50). (See IROQUOIS WAR)

HUTCHINSON, MRS. ANNE (c.1591-1643). Member of the Massachusetts Bay Colony during its early years. She came into conflict with the religious leaders of the colony because her beliefs differed from those of its Puritan rulers. She and her followers left Massachusetts Bay and established a settlement at Portsmouth, which later joined other neighboring settlements to form the colony of Rhode Island. Mrs. Hutchinson later moved to Pelham Bay Park in New York City, where she and almost her entire family were killed by Indians.

HUTCHINSON, THOMAS (1711-80). One of the most important colonial governors of MASSACHUSETTS BAY COLONY, and a descendant of ANNE HUTCHINSON. He was appointed royal governor in 1771 and was vigorously opposed by such radicals as SAMUEL ADAMS and JAMES OTIS. Hutchinson opposed the principle behind the STAMP ACT but insisted on its enforcement. This, in part, led to the burning of his home by a colonial mob in 1765. His insistence on strict enforcement of British laws made him very unpopular; and his refusal to clear the tea-laden ships in Boston harbor in 1774 led to the BOSTON TEA PARTY.

"I DO NOT CHOOSE TO RUN." See COOLIDGE, CAL-VIN and ELECTION OF 1928

"I HAD RATHER BE RIGHT THAN BE PRESIDENT." See CLAY, HENRY

"I HAVE NOT YET BEGUN TO FIGHT." See JONES, JOHN PAUL

IMMIGRATION. For almost 150 years (1789-1921) there were practically no important restrictions on immigration to the U. S. In the first half of the 19th century almost 3,000,-000 immigrants came to the U. S. because of famine, political unrest, religious persecution or poverty in Europe. The immigration figures soared in the second half of the 19th century as 17,000,000 foreigners arrived. Recruiting of immigrants in Europe was carried on by steamship companies and American manufacturers seeking a source of cheap labor. Most of the 19th century immigrants came from the countries of northern and western Europe such as England, Ireland, Germany, Norway, Scotland and Holland. A few came from the Far East.

The crest of the immigration wave was reached in the first decade of the 20th century, when an average of almost 1,000,000 people arrived each year. Most of the immigrants of the early 20th century came from the countries of southern and eastern Europe such as Russia, Italy, Poland, Austria-Hungary and the Balkans. They came mainly to escape political tyranny, religious persecution and poverty. In 1921 the U. S. began its policy of severe immigration restrictions. (See IMMIGRATION LEGISLATION)

IMMIGRATION LEGISLATION. Prior to 1862 the U. S. placed no restrictions on IMMIGRATION. Beginning in 1862, however, Congress passed legislation excluding convicts, lunatics, contract laborers, polygamists and diseased persons. In 1882 Chinese immigration was stopped (CHINESE EXCLUSION ACT); in 1907 Japanese im-

188

migration was ended by the GENTLEMEN'S AGREE-
MENT; and in 1917 all persons unable to read some language were excluded. Beginning in 1921 Congress began
to restrict immigration on a quota basis (DILLINGHAM
ACT, 1921; JOHNSON-REED ACT, 1924) and in 1929
fixed the maximum number that could enter in any one
year (NATIONAL ORIGINS ACT, 1929; MC CARRAN-
WALTER ACT, 1952). At present, immigration is restricted
under quotas to an annual number of 154,658.

IMPEACHMENT OF PRESIDENT JOHNSON. In 1867
President ANDREW JOHNSON dismissed Secretary of
War Edwin M. Stanton without asking Senatorial consent.
The House of Representatives impeached the president for
violation of the TENURE OF OFFICE ACT and for bringing disgrace and ridicule on Congress. (See COVODE
RESOLUTION, 1868) Johnson was tried by the Senate
with Chief Justice SALMON P. CHASE presiding. Although the violation of the Tenure of Office Act was the
basic reason given for the impeachment, the fundamental
reason was the violent political hostility between Johnson
and the radical Republicans (see STEVENS, THADDEUS)
in Congress over southern RECONSTRUCTION policies.
The impeachment vote was one vote short of the two-
thirds necessary to convict under the Constitution.

"IMPENDING CRISIS" (1857). Written by Hinton R. Helper
of North Carolina, attacking slavery as a hindrance to the
economic development of the South. Slavery, said Helper,
competed with the labor of the poor free whites in the South
and made it impossible for the Southern whites to emerge
from their poverty.

IMPERIALISM. Policy of overseas territorial expansion that
became a national issue during and after the SPANISH-
AMERICAN WAR (1898). Influenced by this policy, the
U. S. acquired PUERTO RICO, the PHILIPPINE
ISLANDS, GUAM and the HAWAIIAN ISLANDS. (See
EXPANSIONISTS and MAHAN, ALFRED T.)

IMPRESSMENT. During the 18th and 19th centuries Great
Britain followed a policy of forcibly seizing men to serve in
the British Navy. Those taken included their own seamen,
who were taken off British merchant ships and forced into

189

the navy. During England's wars with Napoleon (1803-1815) Great Britain also impressed into her naval service seamen taken from American ships. (See "CHESAPEAKE" AFFAIR, 1807) Some of these men were British deserters but others were American citizens. This indiscriminate impressment policy was one of the factors that led to the WAR OF 1812.

INAUGURATION. Ceremonies held in Washington D. C. during which the president is sworn into office. The first inauguration, scheduled for March 4, 1789, was delayed by poor weather and difficult traveling conditions. Washington was inaugurated as first president on April 30, 1789. All other presidents until 1937 were inaugurated on or about March 4th. AMENDMENT 20 (1933) changed the date of the presidential inauguration to January 20th.

INCAS. Indian tribe that had established a highly civilized kingdom in the mountains of Peru before the discovery of America. The Incas knew how to build huge stone temples, carve gold ornaments, irrigate the soil and use domesticated animals such as llamas and alpacas. In 1531 a Spanish expedition led by FRANCISCO PIZARRO, a Spanish conquistador, reached Peru, destroyed the power of the Incas and claimed the region for Spain.

INCOME TAX. The first income tax was levied by Congress during the War Between the States (1861-65) to raise more revenue for the conduct of the war. It was repealed after the war. In 1894 the WILSON-GORMAN TARIFF ACT was passed. One of its provisions levied a 2% tax on incomes over $4,000 per year. This section of the law was declared unconstitutional by the Supreme Court (Pollock vs. Farmers' Loan and Trust Co., 1895) because it violated the constitutional provision that direct taxes must be based on the size of population (Art. 1, Sec. 2). In 1913 AMENDMENT 16 became part of the U. S. Constitution. Under this amendment direct taxes based on income, without regard to size of population, could be levied by Congress.

INDENTURED SERVANTS. Also called "bound labor." This referred to people in Europe who agreed to work for landowners in colonial America for a number of years in return for payment of their passage to the colonies. After working for the agreed length of time, indentured servants became independent. Most indentured servants were landed in the Middle Colonies.

INDEPENDENT TREASURY SYSTEM (1840). To avoid re-establishing the very unpopular Second BANK OF U. S., whose charter expired in 1836, and to avoid Jackson's mistake of depositing federal money in state banks, Congress passed a law establishing an Independent Treasury System. Under this law, federal funds were to be deposited in the Treasury in Washington D. C. and in federal sub-treasuries to be set up in various cities of the country. This sub-treasury system continued until the Federal Reserve System was established in 1913. (See FEDERAL RESERVE ACT)

INDIAN POLICY. During colonial times the colonists attempted to buy land from the Indians, as did WILLIAM PENN and PETER MINUIT, or to drive the Indians away. After the U. S. became a united nation the general government policy was to sign treaties with the Indian tribes (see INDIAN TREATIES) removing them more or less forcibly from land east of the Mississippi River to land west of the river. By 1846 practically all Indian tribes had been removed from the eastern region. After the War Between the States (1865) numerous INDIAN WARS broke out as a result of pioneer encroachments on Indian territory. More Indian treaties were signed, establishing Indian reservations, but invariably the treaties were violated by both the white settlers and the Indians. By the DAWES ACT (1887) the U. S. began to break up tribal reservations and give small land allotments to individual Indian families. In 1924 all Indians became U. S. citizens by act of Congress.

INDIAN TREATIES. In most instances the treaties provided for the voluntary movement or forced removal of Indians from one land area to another farther west to make room for white settlers. (See INDIAN POLICY) For example, during President Jackson's administration more than 90 Indian treaties were signed. These and later treaties were frequently violated by unauthorized white settlers as well as by the Indians. One of the important agreements signed with the Indians was the TREATY OF GREENVILLE (1795) with the Indians of the Northwest Territory.

INDIAN WARS. Conflicts between white settlers and the

Indians were part of our history from earliest colonial times to about 1890 when the FRONTIER came to an end. Some of the bloody colonial Indian wars included the Pequot War, 1637, KING PHILIP'S WAR (1675-77), and Lord Dunmore's War, 1774. In the early 19th century Indian tribes resisted the American policy of moving them west of the Mississippi River. (See INDIAN POLICY) This resulted in many conflicts such as the war with TECUMSEH and his Indian Confederation (BATTLE OF TIPPE-CANOE, 1811) the CREEK WAR (1811) the BLACK HAWK WAR (1832) and the SEMINOLE WARS (1817-18 and 1835-43). After the WAR BETWEEN THE STATES (1865) the continued westward movement of American settlers resulted in further Indian conflicts such as the Apache War (1875-76) in New Mexico and Arizona (see COCHISE and GERONIMO), the SIOUX WAR (1875-76) in the Dakotas and the Nez Perce War (1877) in the Pacific Northwest. In many of these wars, massacres and atrocities were committed on both sides.

INDUSTRIAL REVOLUTION. Change in the methods of manufacturing in which machines in factories replaced the use of hand labor in the home. The industrial revolution began in Great Britain in the middle of the 18th century. During the WAR OF 1812 American imports of British manufactured goods were cut off. As a result Americans began to build their own factories. Thus the industrial revolution began in the U. S., and it has continued to the present day. The rapid economic changes since the War Between the States (1865) are sometimes called the NEW INDUSTRIAL REVOLUTION.

INDUSTRIAL WORKERS OF THE WORLD (I.W.W.). Radical labor organization founded in 1905 for the purpose of unionizing unskilled workers in the mining, lumbering and textile industries. Their platform included the use of sabotage as a weapon against industry. One of the important leaders of the I.W.W. was William "Big Bill" Haywood. Because of the efforts of the I.W.W. to foment strikes during World War I, it was labeled as unpatriotic and many states passed legislation outlawing it.

INFANT INDUSTRIES. Name applied to newly established industries. In 1816 Congress passed a protective tariff (see

TARIFF OF 1816) to protect American infant industries from the competition of imported manufactured goods. These infant industries, which included the manufacture of woolen goods, leather, soap, iron, paper, glass and gunpowder had sprung up in the U. S. in the years preceding and during the WAR OF 1812, when foreign trade was curtailed or completely cut off by the Napoleonic Wars in Europe (1804-14), the EMBARGO ACT (1807), the NON-INTERCOURSE ACT (1809) and our own war with Great Britain (1812-14).

INJUNCTION. Court order forbidding the commission of an act such as a strike or violation of contract. Disobedience of a court injunction is considered "contempt of court" and may be punished by imprisonment. The most famous use of a court injunction was during the PULLMAN STRIKE (1894) in which labor leader EUGENE V. DEBS was jailed for contempt because he violated a court injunction. Under the NORRIS-LA GUARDIA ANTI-INJUNCTION ACT (1932) courts were restricted in their power to issue injunctions to halt labor strikes, boycotts or union picketing.

INSULAR CASES (1901). Series of cases decided by the U. S. Supreme Court involving the rights of people living on our island possessions. The basic issue in the cases was whether the rights listed in the U. S. Constitution applied to the people on our island possessions. In a number of decisions (DeLima v. Bidwell; Downes v. Bidwell), the Supreme Court held that the Constitution did not immediately apply to them and that Congress had the power to determine the rights of inhabitants on our possessions. In effect this meant that the "Constitution did not follow the flag."

INTER-AMERICAN DEFENSE PACT (1947). See RIO PACT

INTERIOR PLAINS. Also called Great Plains. The Western region of the U. S., extending approximately from the 100th meridian to the Rocky Mountains. It is elevated land that rises gradually from 1,000 to 5,000 feet as it extends west; a generally treeless region with enough rainfall for grass but not enough for raising annual farm crops safely. Before the coming of the white man, the Interior Plains teemed with wild game such as deer, antelope, turkey, geese and

193

millions of wild buffalo. The PLAINS INDIANS used the wild game as a source of food, and the hides for clothing. As the white man moved west and destroyed the huge buffalo herds (see CODY, WILLIAM F.) the Plains Indians lost their source of food supply. After the settlement of the west in the late 19th century the region became an area of cattle and sheep ranches.

INTERNAL IMPROVEMENTS. Name given to roads and canals built during the early 19th century. Efforts to have such internal improvements constructed with federal funds were opposed by the New England states and favored by Western states. The BONUS BILL (1817), providing a network of roads and canals to be built with federal funds, was vetoed by President JAMES MONROE because he believed it to be unconstitutional. Monroe favored a constitutional amendment authorizing federal internal improvements.

INTERSTATE COMMERCE ACT (1887). Also called the Cullom Act. It was passed by Congress to regulate interstate railroad abuses. The law forbad rebates, long and short haul discrimination, pooling agreements, favoritism in rate making and unreasonable freight rates. The act also set up a five-man INTERSTATE COMMERCE COMMISSION to administer the law. This act was the first important change in the traditional American policy of LAISSEZ-FAIRE, or no government interference with business. Because of legal technicalities, the law did not prove to be wholly effective. However, subsequent legislation tightened loopholes in this first act. (See RAILROAD LEGISLATION, ELKINS ACT, MANN-ELKINS ACT, HEPBURN ACT)

INTERSTATE COMMERCE COMMISSION (I.C.C.) 1887. Federal agency established under the INTERSTATE COMMERCE ACT to regulate railroads. The powers of the I.C.C. were later extended to include sleeping car, express, pipeline, and railroad terminal companies (HEPBURN ACT, 1906), interstate buses and trucks (MOTOR CARRIER ACT, 1935) and inland and coastwise shipping lines (TRANSPORTATION ACT, 1940).

INTOLERABLE ACTS (1774). Also called Coercive Acts. They were laws passed by the British Parliament as a result of colonial defiance of the Tea Tax, and the BOSTON TEA PARTY. The Boston Port Bill closed the port of Boston until the destroyed tea was paid for and defiance of British laws ended. The Massachusetts Government Act reduced the power of the colony's local government. The Quartering Act made local officials responsible for finding quarters for British troops. The QUEBEC ACT added western territory north of the Ohio River to the Canadian province of Quebec, thus wiping out the claims of some of the colonies to this region. The Administration of Justice Act provided for the trial in England instead of Massachusetts of royal govern‑ ment officials accused of serious crimes.

"I ONLY REGRET THAT I HAVE BUT ONE LIFE TO LOSE FOR MY COUNTRY." See HALE, NATHAN

IRON ACT (1750). One of the laws passed by the British Parliament to restrict the growth of manufacturing in the American colonies. The law restricted the manufacture of goods made of iron; only raw pig iron could be produced. The purpose of this law was to protect the interests of British manufacturers of iron tools and implements.

"IRON HORSE." Nickname of the early railroads during the 19th century.

IROQUOIS INDIANS. Indian group in central New York State, made up of related Indian tribes, including the Mohawks, Oneidas, Onondagas, Cayugas and Senecas. As a group they were known as the "Iroquois League" or the "Five Nations." During the FRENCH AND INDIAN WARS between England and France and during the American Revolution the Iroquois generally sided with the English while the Algonquins and Hurons sided with the French.

IROQUOIS WAR (1642-53). War between the Iroquois of New York and the Hurons in Canada. The Iroquois were armed by the Dutch of New York, who hoped to eliminate the French from the Indian fur trade by destroying the Hurons, their source of supply. The Iroquois raided Montreal, Fort Richelieu and Huron Indian territory. Most of the HURONS were massacred. The French finally signed a peace treaty with the Iroquois in 1653.

195

"IRREPRESSIBLE CONFLICT." See SEWARD, WILLIAM H.

ISOLATION. U. S. policy of forming no alliances or political entanglements with foreign nations in peacetime. President Washington first suggested the policy of isolation in his FAREWELL ADDRESS (1796) and President Monroe announced it as our basic policy in the MONROE DOCTRINE (1823). Although the policy of isolation was partially shattered after the Spanish-American War (1898), when we acquired Puerto Rico, Guam and the Philippine Islands, and in World War I (1917-18) when we entered the European war, it was generally revived after the wars were over and peaceful conditions returned. Efforts to get the U. S. to join the LEAGUE OF NATIONS and the WORLD COURT (see ROOT FORMULA) after World War I failed, thus reviving our policy of peacetime isolation. However, at the end of World War II (1945) the U. S. joined the UNITED NATIONS and subsequently formed alliances with Latin American (see RIO PACT, 1947), European (see NORTH ATLANTIC TREATY ORGANIZATION, 1949) and Pacific Nations (SOUTHEAST ASIA TREATY ORGANIZATION, 1954). Thus the American policy of peacetime isolation officially came to an end in 1945.

IWO JIMA, BATTLE OF (1945). U. S. military and naval forces attacked the heavily fortified island of Iwo Jima near the Japanese home islands in the last year of WORLD WAR II. After a bloody battle the U. S. captured the islands from the Japanese defenders. The U. S. then used Iwo Jima as an air base for the bombing of Japanese cities.

I. W. W. (See INDUSTRIAL WORKERS OF THE WORLD)

JACKSON, ANDREW (1767-1845). Seventh president of the U. S. During the WAR OF 1812 he was commander of militia that defeated the Indians in the CREEK WAR (1813-14). In 1815 he organized the defense of New Orleans and decisively defeated the British. (See BATTLE OF NEW ORLEANS) In the ELECTION OF 1824 he was one of four candidates for the presidency. Because no candidate received a majority of the electoral votes the House of Representatives chose JOHN QUINCY ADAMS as president. In the ELECTION OF 1828, however, Jackson was elected president and he was re-elected four years later. (See ELECTION OF 1832) Jackson was the first so-called "common man" to become president. He was called "Old Hickory" by his friends and "King Andrew" by his enemies. His two presidential terms and the succeeding years are known as the era of JACKSONIAN DEMOCRACY.

During his presidency Jackson made widespread use of the SPOILS SYSTEM to reward his friends and supporters. He vetoed the recharter of the Second BANK OF U. S. (1832). When South Carolina announced its nullification of the TARIFF OF 1832, Jackson threatened to use force if necessary to collect the tariff in South Carolina. (See FORCE ACT, 1833) However, the COMPROMISE TARIFF (1833) settled the crisis. Jackson issued the SPECIE CIRCULAR (1836), paid off the entire national debt, and affirmed the supremacy of the federal government in no uncertain terms.

JACKSONIAN DEMOCRACY. Refers to the political, economic and social changes that occurred in the U. S. during Jackson's presidency and the years that followed. Religious and property qualifications for voting were abolished in almost all states. The convention system of nominating candidates for political office replaced the caucus system. The "common man" could vote and also hold public office. Social movements began for the improved treatment of criminals, the insane, the blind and the deaf. The movements for free public elementary education and for women's rights also began during the Jacksonian Era. (See DIX, DOROTHEA; WILLARD, FRANCES E.; STANTON, ELIZABETH CADY; MANN, HORACE)

JACKSON, GENERAL THOMAS J. (1824-63). Also known as "Stonewall" Jackson. He was a brilliant and daring military leader of Confederate forces during the WAR BETWEEN THE STATES (1861-65) and fought in many of the battles and campaigns in Virginia, including the First and Second BATTLE OF BULL RUN and the BATTLE OF FREDERICKSBURG. He died in the BATTLE OF CHANCELLORSVILLE (1863), accidentally shot by one of his own men.

JAMESTOWN. First permanent English settlement established in the New World in 1607 under a charter granted to the LONDON COMPANY by King James I. The colony started with 104 settlers but disease and starvation reduced the number to 60. However, the strict rule of Captain JOHN SMITH and the arrival of new settlers and supplies saved the colony. It became the nucleus of the Virginia colony.

JAPANESE DISCRIMINATION. During the first decade of the 20th century the San Francisco School Board began a policy of segregating Japanese, Chinese and Korean children in separate schools. The policy was changed only by the intervention of President THEODORE ROOSEVELT. (See GENTLEMEN'S AGREEMENT) In 1913 and after, California legislation made it difficult for Orientals to buy or lease land for farming. Such discrimination aroused Japanese public opinion against the U. S. (See JAPAN, U. S. RELATIONS WITH)

JAPANESE EMBARGO. See JAPAN, U. S. RELATIONS WITH

JAPAN, U. S. RELATIONS WITH. In 1854 MATTHEW C. PERRY arranged the first trade treaty with Japan (Treaty of Kanagawa). TOWNSEND HARRIS was our first official representative to Japan. In the late 19th and early 20th centuries, relations between Japan and the U. S. were unfriendly because of Japanese objections to the U. S. OPEN DOOR POLICY in China (1899), our Japanese immigration policy (see GENTLEMEN'S AGREEMENT, 1907) and the discrimination against Japanese residents in California. (See JAPANESE DISCRIMINATION) During World War I (1914-18), Japan presented her TWENTY-ONE DEMANDS (1915) to China but withdrew them after the U. S. objected. In 1917 the LANSING ISHII AGREEMENT settled some U. S.-Japanese problems. During World War I Japan joined the Allied Powers against Germany. At the WASHINGTON DISARMAMENT CONFERENCE (1922) Japan signed the FIVE POWER PACT, Four Power Pact, and Nine Power Pact. Japan's invasion of MANCHURIA in 1932 resulted in the U. S. announcement of the STIMSON DOCTRINE. Japan's undeclared war on China, beginning in 1937, led the U. S. to impose an embargo on certain exports to Japan. The Japanese attack on PEARL HARBOR (1941) led to the U. S. declaration of war. At the end of WORLD WAR II (1945) Japan was forced to give up all her Far Eastern territorial conquests and a number of Japanese were tried for war crimes. In 1951 the Japanese signed a treaty with the U. S. which subsequently led to a mutual agreement to resist Communist aggression in the Far East.

JAVA SEA, BATTLE OF (1942). Japanese naval victory in the early part of WORLD WAR II over outnumbered British and Dutch naval forces in the western Pacific Ocean. This victory made possible the Japanese invasion and conquest of the Dutch East Indies islands.

JAY, JOHN (1745-1829). American political leader when the republic was established. He was the author of five of the FEDERALIST papers advocating ratification of the Constitution in New York State. He was appointed first Chief Justice of the U. S. Supreme Court (1789-95) and handed down the important Chisholm v. Georgia decision (1793) which led to the ratification of AMENDMENT 11. In 1794 he negotiated the JAY TREATY with Great Britain.

JAY TREATY (1794). In an effort to settle a number of disputes between the U. S. and Great Britain, President Washington sent JOHN JAY to England. An agreement known as the Jay Treaty was reached. Under it, Great Britain agreed to withdraw her garrisons from fur-trading posts in the NORTHWEST TERRITORY, to arbitrate boundary disputes, to pay American shipowners for the

199

illegal seizure of American ships and to open some trading ports in the British colonies to American trade. The U. S. agreed to compensate British merchants for unpaid Revolutionary debts and to admit British trading vessels into American ports. The treaty was very unpopular in the U. S. because it failed to mention the British impressment of American sailors or to provide payment for slaves carried off by the British during the American Revolution. However, Congress ratified the treaty in 1795.

JAZZ AGE. Decade following World War I (1918) during which jazz as a musical form became very popular. The Jazz Age coincided with the PROHIBITION ERA and the popularity of the party-loving girl known as the "flapper."

JEFFERSONIAN DEMOCRACY. Refers to Jefferson's political ideas and to changes in government made during his presidency (1801-09). His political ideas are embodied in the DECLARATION OF INDEPENDENCE, which he wrote. He also believed in freedom of religion, abolition of slavery, public education, strict interpretation of the Constitution, an agricultural society and government by the average man rather than by the rich and well-born. His democratic changes in government while president included the ending of glittering presidential receptions, the delivery of written rather than oral messages to Congress, and informality in conducting the business of the presidency.

JEFFERSON, THOMAS (1743-1826). Third president of the U. S. and known as the "Sage of Monticello." He was a member of the SECOND CONTINENTAL CONGRESS (1775), author of the DECLARATION OF INDEPENDENCE (1776), and author of the clause in the NORTHWEST ORDINANCE (1787) forbidding slavery in the Northwest Territory. He was the first Secretary of State under President Washington (1789-93), leader of the ANTI-FEDERALIST PARTY, and vice-president from 1791 to 1801. Jefferson and JAMES MADISON jointly drew up the VIRGINIA AND KENTUCKY RESOLUTIONS (1798) as a protest against the ALIEN AND SEDITION LAWS (1798). Jefferson ran for president in the ELECTION OF 1800 and received the same number of votes as AARON BURR. By vote of the House of Representatives, Jefferson was chosen third president. He was re-elected for a second term in the ELECTION OF 1804.

During Jefferson's term as president, JOHN MARSHALL rendered his famous decision in the case of MARBURY V. MADISON (1803), the Library of Congress and the West Point Military Academy were established, the LOUISIANA TERRITORY was purchased from France (1803), the LEWIS AND CLARK EXPEDITION explored the new territory (1804-06) and ZEBULON PIKE continued to explore the new region (1805-06). In foreign affairs, a naval expedition was sent against the BARBARY PIRATES (1801) and an EMBARGO ACT was passed (1807) and was replaced two years later by a NON-INTERCOURSE ACT (1809).

JESUIT MISSIONARIES. Members of a Catholic organization, many of whose members accompanied English, French and Spanish explorers to the New World. The Jesuits established missions in Canada along the St. Lawrence River, the Mississippi River and the Great Lakes as well as in Florida, California and Mexico. The major purpose of the Jesuit missionaries was to bring Christianity to the heathen Indians.

JOHN BROWN'S RAID (1859). JOHN BROWN, an ardent abolitionist, and a number of his followers seized the U. S. arsenal at Harper's Ferry, Virginia to obtain rifles in order to start a slave rebellion. Brown and his followers were quickly captured by a company of U. S. Marines commanded by Colonel ROBERT E. LEE. Tried for treason, Brown was found guilty and hanged. The raid was a minor incident but it served to inflame the South and arouse bitter hostility between pro-slavery and anti-slavery factions.

"JOHNNY APPLESEED." See CHAPMAN, JOHN

JOHNSON, ANDREW (1808-75). Seventeenth president of the U. S. He was appointed military governor of Tennessee during the WAR BETWEEN THE STATES (1861-65). In the ELECTION OF 1864 he was chosen vice-president and a few weeks later became president after Lincoln was assassinated (1865). As a result of his bitter clashes with Congress over RECONSTRUCTION policies and his removal of Secretary of War EDWIN M. STANTON, Johnson was impeached. (See IMPEACHMENT OF JOHNSON) He was not nominated for the presidency in 1868 but served again in the Senate in 1875. During his presidential term Congress passed the FREEDMEN'S BUREAU Act (1865), the Negro CIVIL RIGHTS Bills (1866) and the RECONSTRUCTION ACT (1867), over Johnson's veto. In addition, the states ratified AMENDMENT 13 (1865) and AMENDMENT 14 (1868). The MAXIMILIAN AFFAIR (1864-67) in Mexico and the ALASKA PURCHASE (1867) occurred during Johnson's presidency.

JOHNSON DEBT DEFAULT ACT (1934). Passed by Congress during the world wide economic depression. This Act provided that no U. S. loans were to be made to European countries that had defaulted on their war debts to the U. S. Since Finland was the only country that continued to pay its debts, all other countries were ineligible for further loans.

JOHNSON, HIRAM (1866-1945). Governor of California and member of the U. S. Senate. He was nominated for the vice-presidency by the PROGRESSIVE PARTY convention in 1912 as THEODORE ROOSEVELT'S running mate. Although a Republican, Johnson strongly opposed President HERBERT HOOVER's policies and gave vigorous support to FRANKLIN D. ROOSEVELT's NEW DEAL program. After World War I Johnson was one of the leaders of the Senate isolationist group. (See ISOLATION). He opposed U. S. membership in the LEAGUE OF NATIONS, the WORLD COURT and the UNITED NATIONS.

JOHNSON-REED IMMIGRATION ACT (1924). Replaced the DILLINGHAM ACT (1921). Because the 1910 census date of the Dillingham Act permitted many immigrants from southern and eastern Europe to enter the U. S., the Johnson-Reed Act changed the census date to 1890 and reduced the quota of immigrants to 2% of the nationals residing in the U. S. in that year. The law did not apply to any independent countries in North and South America, whose citizens could enter the U. S. without restrictions. Persons barred from U. S. citizenship (Japanese, Chinese and other Orientals) were entirely excluded. The Johnson-Reed Act was superseded by the NATIONAL ORIGINS LAW of 1929. (See also IMMIGRATION LEGISLATION)

JOHNSTON, GENERAL ALBERT S. (1803-62). See SHILOH, BATTLE OF

JOHNSTON, GENERAL JOSEPH E. (1807-1891). Confederate commander during the WAR BETWEEN THE STATES (1861-65). He took part in the first BATTLE OF BULL RUN (1861), the PENINSULAR CAMPAIGN (1862), the VICKSBURG campaign (1863) and the Atlanta campaign (1865) against General Sherman. After hearing of General ROBERT E. LEE's surrender to Grant, Johnston surrendered to General WILLIAM T. SHERMAN (1865) near Durham, North Carolina.

JOINT STOCK COMPANIES. Business ventures organized in the 17th and 18th centuries in England, France and Holland for the purpose of establishing settlements or trading posts in the New World and the Far East to trade in furs, spices and other commodities. Examples of such companies were the VIRGINIA COMPANY OF LONDON (1606), the COMPANY OF NEW FRANCE (1627), the DUTCH WEST INDIA COMPANY (1621) and the MASSACHUSETTS BAY COMPANY (1629).

JOLIET, LOUIS (1645-1700). See MARQUETTE, FATHER JACQUES

JONES ACT (1916). Gave the Philippine Islands more self-government than they' had under the PHILIPPINE GOVERNMENT ACT of 1902. Under the Jones Act, the Filipino Senate and Assembly were to be elected by the Filipinos. The right to vote was given to all adults who could read and write. However, the governor was still appointed by the president of the U. S. The Jones Act was superseded in 1934 by the TYDINGS-McDUFFIE ACT.

JONES ACT (1917). Passed by Congress to give PUERTO RICO more self-government than it had received under the FORAKER ACT of 1900. Under the Jones Act, Puerto Ricans were made citizens of the U. S. and were given the right to elect members of the upper house of their legislature. However, any laws passed by the Puerto Rican legislature could be vetoed by the governor of Puerto Rico (appointed by the president of the U. S.) or rejected by the Congress of the U. S.

JONES, JOHN PAUL (1747-92). U. S. naval captain in the AMERICAN REVOLUTION (1775-83) and commander of the *Bonhomme Richard*. Jones was famous for his brilliant raids and naval victories over superior British naval forces. His most famous achievement was the victory of the *Bonhomme Richard* over the larger and more heavily armed British frigate *Serapis* (1779). It is said that during the battle he replied to a British demand for his surrender by shouting: "I have not yet begun to fight." Although his own ship was sunk in the battle, Jones succeeded in capturing the *Serapis*.

JUDICIAL REVIEW. The power of the U. S. Supreme Court to pass on the constitutionality of laws passed by Congress or by the legislatures of the states. The right of judicial review is not specifically granted to the Supreme Court in the Constitution. In the case of MARBURY V. MADISON (1803), however, Chief Justice JOHN MARSHALL specifically asserted that judicial review was a necessary function of the courts. Thereafter the power of declaring state and federal laws unconstitutional was generally accepted as a basic principle of our government.

JUDICIARY ACT (1789). One of the first laws passed by Congress under the new Constitution. It organized the U. S. Supreme Court and established lower federal courts throughout the country.

JUDICIARY ACT (1801). Passed after the REPUBLICAN PARTY victory in the ELECTION OF 1800 but before the new president (Jefferson) and Congress were to meet on March 4, 1801. The old Congress, in which the FEDERALIST PARTY still had a controlling vote, passed the Judiciary Act, which established 16 new federal judgeships. Outgoing President JOHN ADAMS naturally filled these posts with Federalist appointees. The Republicans called them the "MIDNIGHT JUDGES." The Act was repealed by Congress after Jefferson became president.

JUDICIARY REORGANIZATION BILL (1937). After numerous NEW DEAL laws had been declared unconstitutional by the U. S. Supreme Court (NATIONAL INDUSTRIAL RECOVERY ACT, 1933; AGRICULTUR-AL ADJUSTMENT ACT, 1933; Guffey-Snyder Coal Act, 1935), President FRANKLIN D. ROOSEVELT proposed a radical reorganization of the Supreme Court. He advocated the appointment of one new judge for every judge over 70 years of age who did not retire voluntarily. The maximum number of new judges that could be appointed would be six. Roosevelt's proposal, named the "court-packing plan" by his critics, was assailed as an attempt to destroy our system of "checks and balances." A number of deaths and retirements from the Supreme Court bench soon after the plan was announced made Roosevelt's proposal unnecessary, and Congress rejected the bill.

KALAMAZOO CASE (1874). Decided by Michigan Supreme Court. This case established the principle that state tax money may be used to support public high schools and colleges. This decision started the precedent, later followed by other states, of establishing tax-supported public high schools and colleges and led to the tremendous growth of the public high school system in the U. S.

KANAGAWA, TREATY OF (1854). See PERRY, MATTHEW C.

KANSAS-NEBRASKA ACT (1854). Introduced by STEPHEN A. DOUGLAS, the law provided for the repeal of the MISSOURI COMPROMISE (1820) and stated further that the people of the Kansas-Nebraska Territories were to organize their areas on the principle of POPULAR (squatter) SOVEREIGNTY. This meant that the people in the territories, and not Congress, were to decide the question of slavery in the territories. Although the bill split both the Democratic and Whig Parties, it was passed and signed by President FRANKLIN PIERCE. Its enactment resulted in the growth of hostility between free and slave interests and led to Civil War in Kansas. (See BLEEDING KANSAS)

KEARNY, COLONEL STEPHEN W. (1794-1848). U. S. military commander during the MEXICAN WAR (1846-1848). Kearny led an American military force overland from Missouri to the New Mexico Territory. He took control of the New Mexico Territory without meeting resistance and then continued west to California, where he joined Commodore R. F. Stockton in taking control of that state (1847). A dispute developed between Kearny and Colonel JOHN C. FREMONT which led to the court martial of Fremont. Fort Kearney in Nebraska, although incorrectly spelled, is named in honor of Colonel Kearny.

KEATING-OWEN CHILD LABOR LAW (1916). See CHILD LABOR

KELLOGG-BRIAND PACT (1928). Also called the "Pact of Paris." It was arranged by Secretary of State Frank B. Kellogg and French Foreign Minister Aristide Briand. Signatory nations agreed to "outlaw war as an instrument of national policy." More than 60 nations, including the U. S., signed the pact. When Japan invaded China in 1931 the U. S. announced the STIMSON DOCTRINE (1932) in which the U. S. declared it would recognize no territory seized by any country that had signed and then violated the Kellogg-Briand Pact.

KENNEDY, JOHN F. (1917-   ). Thirty-sixth president of the U. S. He served in Congress, beginning in 1946. In the ELECTION OF 1960 he was nominated by the DEMOCRATIC PARTY to run for president and defeated his Republican rival, Richard Nixon, by a very narrow margin. In domestic affairs, Kennedy's administration saw the launching of the PEACE CORPS and the enactment of the TRADE EXPANSION ACT (1962). In foreign affairs Kennedy sought to find a formula to stop Communist aggression in Europe, Asia, and Cuba. (See CUBAN QUARANTINE)

KEY, FRANCIS SCOTT (1779-1843). During the WAR OF 1812 the sight of the American flag flying over Fort McHenry after an all-night bombardment by the British fleet inspired Francis Scott Key to write the "Star Spangled Banner." The tune was based on a popular English song "To Anacreon in Heaven." In 1916 President Wilson proclaimed the "Star Spangled Banner" the national anthem.

"KING ANDREW." See JACKSON, ANDREW

KING COTTON. Phrase used by Southerners before the WAR BETWEEN THE STATES (1861-65) to indicate the importance of cotton to the South and to the whole nation. Southern plantations were providing more than three-fourths of the world's supply of raw cotton before 1861. (See PLANTATION SYSTEM)

KING GEORGE'S WAR (1744-48). See FRENCH AND INDIAN WARS

KING PHILIP'S WAR (1675-76). One of the many wars (see INDIAN WARS) waged between settlers and Indians in early colonial times. King Philip, chief of one of the New England Indian tribes, started a war against the Massachusetts settlers in order to stop further encroachments on Indian land and to obtain food for his starving people. Both sides were responsible for massacres of men, women and children and the burning of towns and settlements during the many raids that characterized the war. In 1676 King Philip was finally ambushed and shot.

KING, RUFUS (1755-1827). Member of the CONSTITUTIONAL CONVENTION (1787) that drew up the Constitution, and one of the strongest supporters in Massachusetts for its ratification. He was the FEDERALIST PARTY candidate for vice-president in the ELECTION OF 1804 and the ELECTION OF 1808 and for president in the ELECTION OF 1816. However, he was defeated on each occasion.

KING'S COLLEGE. Established in New York City in 1754 by a grant from King George II. During the American Revolution the name was changed to Columbia University.

KINGS MOUNTAIN, BATTLE OF (1780). One of the major military engagements of the AMERICAN REVOLUTION (1775-83). A force of western pioneers in Tennessee and western North Carolina crossed the mountains and inflicted a total defeat on a larger British force at Kings Mountain near the Carolina border.

KING WILLIAM'S WAR (1689-97). See FRENCH AND INDIAN WARS

"KITCHEN CABINET." Applied to a number of President Jackson's political friends, including Amos Kendall of Kentucky and William B. Lewis of Tennessee. Instead of asking his cabinet for advice, President JACKSON (1829-1837) frequently followed the advice of these friends, who were called the "kitchen cabinet" by Jackson's political enemies.

KLONDIKE GOLD RUSH. In 1896 news of the discovery of gold at Dawson, Canada, near the Alaska border caused a rush of thousands of adventurers and miners to the Klondike region of Canada (1897-98). Many of the men in the gold rush suffered severe hardships from the cold and lack of supplies. Few found the gold for which they had come. (See GOLD RUSH)

KNIGHTS OF LABOR, NOBLE ORDER OF. One of the first large labor organizations in the U. S. It was originally organized in 1869 by Uriah S. Stephens as a secret society. Subsequently it accepted as members all workers, skilled and unskilled, citizens and aliens, Negro and white. Its aims were an eight-hour day, prohibition of child labor, laws to improve working conditions, equal pay for men and women, arbitration of labor disputes and restrictions on immigrant contract laborers. At the height of its popularity (about 1885) the Knights of Labor, under the leadership of Terence V. Powderly, had a membership of about 750,000. After 1886 the organization declined rapidly in membership because of internal wrangling and the rise of a new labor organization called the AMERICAN FEDERATION OF LABOR.

KNIGHTS OF ST. CRISPIN. Early labor union organization formed in the shoe manufacturing industry about 1867. At the peak of its strength (1870) the organization had about 50,000 members. Thereafter it declined in strength as new labor organizations developed. (See KNIGHTS OF LABOR)

KNOW-NOTHING PARTY. Small political organization formed in the 1840's and 1850's which opposed unrestricted immigration and was prejudiced against all foreigners, particularly Irish and German Catholic immigrants. The group called itself the Native American Party (1845) but because of its secret organization, secret meetings, and the unwillingness of its members to divulge party secrets, it became popularly known as the Know-Nothing Party. In 1855 it abandoned its policy of secrecy and called itself the American Party. The party platform called for long residence requirements for citizenship and the election of native Americans to political offices. In the ELECTION OF 1856 the American Party nominated MILLARD FILLMORE for the presidency, won a small popular vote and carried the state of Maryland. The Know-Nothing movement continued until the outbreak of the War Between the States (1861).

KNOX, PHILANDER C. (1853-1921). Secretary of State under President William H. Taft. Knox tried to increase American influence and trade in China and provide loans to the Chinese governments. By these devices he hoped to maintain the OPEN DOOR POLICY in China. He also continued the policies of his predecessor JOHN HAY, to protect American financial interests in Latin America. This policy became known as DOLLAR DIPLOMACY.

KNOXVILLE ROAD (1791). One of the important early roads west of the Appalachian Mountains used by settlers moving west. The Knoxville Road, an extension of the WILDERNESS ROAD through Tennessee, was completed about 1795.

KOREAN WAR (1950-53). On June 24, 1950 Communist troops and tanks of North Korea invaded South Korea (Republic of South Korea). President Truman ordered American forces to come to the aid of South Korea. On the day following the invasion, the United Nations Security Council (with Soviet Russia absent) declared North Korea to be an aggressor. It voted to place the U. S. and GENERAL DOUGLAS MAC ARTHUR in charge of U. N. fighting forces in Korea. Although the U. S. contributed the largest share of men and equipment for the war, more than a dozen U. N. member nations provided troops and other assistance. Just as the U. N. forces seemed on the verge of ending the war victoriously, Communist China began to help North Korea with arms, equipment and troops. The war having reached a stalemate near the 38th parallel in June, 1951, a truce was declared. After two years of negotiation an armistice was signed but no permanent peace treaty could be agreed upon.

KOSCIUSKO, THADDEUS (1746-1817). Polish general who volunteered to help the colonies in their struggle for liberty during the AMERICAN REVOLUTION (1775-83). He took a leading part in the BATTLE OF SARATOGA (1777) and helped the Continental Army under General NATHANAEL GREENE in the South. After the American

Revolution Kosciusko returned to Europe to fight for Polish independence.

KU KLUX KLAN (K.K.K.). Secret association organized (1866) in a number of Southern states after the WAR BETWEEN THE STATES (1865) to intimidate the Negro, re-establish white supremacy and get rid of CARPETBAG state governments. The K.K.K. dressed its members in white robes and hoods to frighten the superstitious Negro but the organization also resorted to floggings and outright murder. Although the K.K.K. was officially disbanded in 1869 it has been revived many times to assert white supremacy in the South. In 1870 and 1871 Congress passed a number of KU KLUX KLAN LAWS to end the unlawful activities of the organization.

KU KLUX KLAN LAWS. Passed in 1870 and 1871 to put an end to acts of violence, terrorism and intimidation used by the KU KLUX KLAN to deprive the Southern Negro of his rights under AMENDMENT 14 and AMENDMENT 15. A number of provisions of these K.K.K. Acts were voided by the U. S. Supreme Court because they invaded the reserved powers of states to protect the general welfare of their citizens.

LABOR LEGISLATION. The first direct effort of Congress to legislate for the welfare of labor was the ADAMSON ACT (1916) establishing an eight-hour day for workers on interstate railroads. The CLAYTON ANTI-TRUST ACT (1914) aided labor by declaring that labor was not a commodity and that labor unions did not come under the provisions of the anti-trust laws. The first Congressional legislation for all interstate workers was passed with the beginning of the NEW DEAL administration (1933) of FRANKLIN D. ROOSEVELT. The SOCIAL SECURITY ACT (1935) and the FAIR LABOR STANDARDS ACT (1938) ushered in a new era for American workers. During the GREAT DEPRESSION (1929-35) Congress also provided direct aid to unemployed workers through the establishment of various emergency agencies. (See UNEMPLOYMENT LEGISLATION and LABOR UNION LEGISLATION)

LABOR MANAGEMENT REPORTING AND DISCLOSURE ACT (1959). Also called Landrum-Griffin Act. It was passed to eliminate a number of abuses in labor union organizations and in labor union practices. The law establishes a so-called "bill of rights" for union members, who are guaranteed freedom of speech and assembly and the right to sue the union. Rules are set up for fixing union dues, initiation fees and assessments, and protecting the worker against improper disciplinary action by the union. Unions must file financial reports annually showing how membership dues are spent. Communists and convicted criminals are barred from holding union office. Union elections must be held in accordance with regulations specified in the law.

LABOR UNION LEGISLATION. In the early 19th century many unions were declared illegal because they were classified as conspiracies under the English COMMON LAW (see COMMONWEALTH V. HUNT). After the War Between the States (1865) unions were not considered illegal but in the DANBURY HATTERS CASE (Loewe v.

Lawler, 1908), a union boycott was held to be a conspiracy in restraint of trade under the SHERMAN ANTI-TRUST ACT (1890). Under the CLAYTON ANTI-TRUST ACT (1914) unions were excluded from the scope of the anti-trust laws. The NORRIS-LA GUARDIA ANTI-INJUNC-TION ACT (1932) limited the use of injunctions against labor unions. Beginning with the NEW DEAL administration of FRANKLIN D. ROOSEVELT, labor unions were aided directly by the NATIONAL INDUSTRIAL RECOVERY ACT (1933) which recognized the right of collective bargaining. After this law was declared unconstitutional (Schecter v. U. S., 1935), Congress enacted the NATIONAL LABOR RELATIONS ACT (1935) under which labor unions became a major factor in the nation's economy. The rapid growth of labor union power and the development of labor union abuses, however, led to Congressional legislation to limit the power and activities of unions. Such restrictive legislation included the TAFT-HARTLEY ACT (1947) and the LABOR MANAGE-MENT REPORTING AND DISCLOSURE ACT (1959).

LABOR UNIONS. A small number of unions were organized before the War Between the States (1861) in large Eastern cities. In many states laws restricted the activities of unions on the legal theory that they were conspiracies (see COMMONWEALTH V. HUNT). In the latter half of the 19th century the tremendous expansion of industry, frequent depressions, gradual ending of the free land era, and the overwhelming power of large corporations led workers to organize national labor unions. The first national union was the KNIGHTS OF LABOR, organized in 1869. The unionization of skilled workers such as printers, railroad engineers and cigar makers led to the formation of the AMERICAN FEDERATION OF LABOR (1886) as well as a number of large independent unions. In the 20th century the labor movement continued to grow slowly until the beginning of the NEW DEAL era (1933). Favorable Congressional legislation (NATIONAL INDUSTRIAL RECOVERY ACT, 1933; NATIONAL LABOR RELA-TIONS ACT, 1935) and the organization of the CONGRESS OF INDUSTRIAL ORGANIZATIONS (1935) resulted in tremendous expansion of union membership among skilled and unskilled workers, particularly in large industries. The merging of the American Federation

213

of Labor and Congress of Industrial Organizations into one organization (1955) called A.F.L.-C.I.O. served to strengthen the American labor movement.

LAFAYETTE, MARQUIS DE (1757-1834). French nobleman who came to America during the AMERICAN REVOLUTION (1775-83) to help the colonies fight for their independence. He was wounded at the BATTLE OF BRANDYWINE (1777), was with Washington at VALLEY FORGE (1777-78) and played a major role in the victory at the BATTLE OF YORKTOWN (1781).

"LAFAYETTE, WE ARE HERE." Attributed to U. S. General JOHN J. PERSHING in an address at the grave of LAFAYETTE in 1917. The phrase came to symbolize U. S. aid to France in WORLD WAR I (1917-18) in return for French aid to the THIRTEEN COLONIES during the AMERICAN REVOLUTION (1775-83). At the end of World War I, the delay in bringing American soldiers back to the U. S. led to the paraphrase of the statement by American DOUGHBOYS: "Lafayette, we are *still* here."

LAFITTE, JEAN (c.1780-c.1825). Pirate leader of the early 19th century whose headquarters were in the swampy marshlands called Barataria Bay, south of New Orleans. During the BATTLE OF NEW ORLEANS (1815) he spurned the generous offer of the British to help them seize the city. Instead, Lafitte joined ANDREW JACKSON and the American forces in the successful defense of New Orleans. For his valuable aid, President JAMES MADISON granted Lafitte and his band complete pardons.

LA FOLLETTE, ROBERT M. (1855-1925). Leader of the PROGRESSIVE MOVEMENT in the first quarter of the 20th century. As governor of Wisconsin he sponsored a program of progressive legislation (called Wisconsin Idea) including railroad regulation, use of the direct primary and tax revision. As U. S. senator (1906-1924) he sponsored the LA FOLLETTE SEAMEN'S ACT (1915), organized the Republican League (1911) and became the recognized leader of the Progressive movement. He supported THEODORE ROOSEVELT as PROGRESSIVE PARTY candidate in 1912, voted against a declaration of war in 1917 and against joining the LEAGUE OF NA-

TIONS and WORLD COURT after WORLD WAR I (1918). In 1924 he revived the Progressive Party and polled almost 5,000,000 votes as its presidential candidate.

LA FOLLETTE SEAMEN'S ACT (1915). Regulated conditions of employment on American merchant ships. The law abolished desertion from a merchant ship as a crime and improved working conditions on American vessels.

LA GUARDIA, FIORELLO H. (1882-1947). As congressman from New York he was one of the sponsors of the NORRIS-LA GUARDIA ANTI-INJUNCTION ACT (1932). In 1933 he was elected mayor of New York City and served for three terms. Features of his colorful career as mayor were his campaigns against municipal corruption, substandard housing and gambling. He was nicknamed "Little Flower," a literal translation of his first name.

LAISSEZ-FAIRE. French phrase meaning "let alone" or "keep hands off." As applied to government it refers to a policy of no interference with business by government regulations. Laissez-faire economists believed that if the government did not interfere, the national economy would work out its own problems in the long run with the greatest benefit to all and without limiting anyone's freedom of action. The policy of laissez-faire was substantially the policy of the U. S. government toward business until 1887, when the INTERSTATE COMMERCE ACT was passed.

LAKE ERIE, BATTLE OF (1813). See PERRY, OLIVER H.

"LAME DUCK" AMENDMENT. See AMENDMENT 20

"LAME DUCK" CONGRESS. Prior to the enactment of AMENDMENT 20 (1933), national elections for Congress during presidential election years were held in November but the successful candidates took office on March 4th of the following year. As a result, congressmen defeated in the November elections continued to legislate for the nation until March 4th. These were called "lame duck" congressmen.

LANCASTER TURNPIKE. Construction of this early road was begun in 1792 and completed in 1794. It was about 60

215

miles long and extended from Philadelphia, Pennsylvania to Lancaster, Pennsylvania.

LAND GRANT COLLEGES. See MORRILL ACT (1862)

LAND ORDINANCE (1785). Passed by Congress under the ARTICLES OF CONFEDERATION. The ordinance divided the NORTHWEST TERRITORY into townships six miles square. Townships were then divided into 36 sections each one mile square (640 acres). One section in each township was set aside for the support of public education. All other land was to be sold to the public at not less than $1 per acre. This law was the forerunner of the NORTH-WEST ORDINANCE passed two years later.

LANDRUM-GRIFFIN ACT (1959). See LABOR MAN-AGEMENT REPORTING AND DISCLOSURE ACT

LANGLEY, SAMUEL P. (1834-1906). American inventor and pioneer in the development of the airplane. With the help of a Congressional appropriation he twice tried to launch a motorized airplane and twice failed. (See WRIGHT BROTHERS)

LANSING ISHII AGREEMENT (1917). Signed by the U. S. and Japan. The agreement reaffirmed the U. S. OPEN DOOR POLICY in China with respect to international trade but the U. S. also recognized Japan's special interests in China. (See JAPAN, U. S. RELATIONS WITH)

LA SALLE, ROBERT (1643-87). French explorer who led an expedition from Canada down the Mississippi to the mouth of the river (1682). He claimed for France the entire region drained by the Mississippi River and named it Louisiana in honor of his king, Louis XIV. LaSalle returned to France and was given authority to establish a settlement at the mouth of the Mississippi River. He tried to reach the river by sailing through the Gulf of Mexico but could not find it. After he had failed to locate it a number of times, LaSalle's men mutinied and killed him.

LAWRENCE, CAPTAIN JAMES (1781-1813). American naval commander during the war with the BARBARY PIRATES (1801-05) and during the WAR OF 1812.

While in command of the *Chesapeake,* (1813) he engaged the British frigate *Shannon* in battle (1813). During the fighting Lawrence was mortally wounded. It is reported that his last words were, "Don't give up the ship."

LEAGUE OF NATIONS. International world peace organization established after World War I under a charter called the COVENANT OF THE LEAGUE OF NATIONS. The chief purpose of the League was to maintain international peace. It also sought to improve world health standards, labor standards, international trade and world social conditions. Although WOODROW WILSON was one of the leading planners of the League, the U. S. Senate refused to approve our membership in it. The League of Nations came to an unofficial end with the outbreak of World War II in Europe (1939).

LECOMPTON CONSTITUTION (1857). State constitution written by the pro-slavery settlers in the Kansas Territory. This constitution, permitting slavery in Kansas, was approved by Congress (1858). However it was resubmitted to popular vote of the people of Kansas and was rejected. In 1861 Kansas was admitted to the Union as a free state under the WYANDOTTE CONSTITUTION.

LEE, RICHARD HENRY (1732-94). Virginia delegate to the SECOND CONTINENTAL CONGRESS. On June 7, 1776 he introduced a resolution calling for a DECLARATION OF INDEPENDENCE from Great Britain. On the basis of this resolution a committee was formed to write the Declaration of Independence. In 1799 Lee introduced a resolution in Congress honoring GEORGE WASHINGTON. It read: "A citizen, first in war, first in peace, and first in the hearts of his countrymen."

LEE, ROBERT E. (1807-1870). Leader of the Virginia militia that captured John Brown after his raid on Harper's Ferry Arsenal. (See JOHN BROWN'S RAID, 1859) Lee was supreme commander of the armies of the Confederacy during the WAR BETWEEN THE STATES (1861-65). He led the Confederate forces at the BATTLE OF ANTIETAM (1862), BATTLE OF CHANCELLORSVILLE (1863), BATTLE OF GETTYSBURG (1863), and many other military engagements. He won many victories

217

and was often forced to retreat, but he never surrendered until Appomattox, in 1865. (See APPOMATTOX COURTHOUSE) Because of his brilliant military strategy he is considered the greatest general on either side during the war.

LEGAL TENDER ACT (1862). See GREENBACKS

LEGAL TENDER CASES. A number of U. S. Supreme Court decisions involving the Legal Tender Act (1862) passed by Congress during the War Between the States. At first the court held that the act permitting the payment of debts with GREENBACKS was unconstitutional (Hepburn v. Griswold, 1870). In the following year the court reversed itself and held that the Legal Tender Act was a valid exercise of Congressional power in time of national emergency (Knox v. Lee, 1871).

LEISLER'S REBELLION (1689). When the Glorious Revolution (1689) that led to the overthrow of King James II began in England, political changes also occurred in the colonies. In New York, the flight of the royal governor, Nicholson, was the signal for a brief rebellion led by a merchant named Jacob Leisler. In 1691 a new royal governor, Colonel Henry Slaughter, arrived in New York, took control of the colonial government and seized Leisler and his confederates. Leisler was tried for treason and hanged.

LEND LEASE ACT (1941). Early in 1941, World War II was in progress in Europe and in Asia but the U. S. was still neutral. In order to help those nations fighting the totalitarian dictatorships (see ROME-BERLIN-TOKYO AXIS) Congress abandoned our neutrality policy (see NEUTRALITY ACT of 1939) and passed the Lend Lease Act. It provided for the sale, lease or loan of U. S. war materials to any nation whose defense was necessary for our own national security.

L'ENFANT, PIERRE CHARLES (1754-1825). Came to America from France with LAFAYETTE and served as an engineer in the American Revolution. President Washington commissioned L'Enfant to draw up plans for a new national capital at Washington D. C. Although L'Enfant's original plans were modified in some details, the major features of the modern city of Washington D. C. were his.

"LETTERS FROM A FARMER IN PENNSYLVANIA." See DICKINSON, JOHN

"LETTERS FROM AN AMERICAN FARMER." See CREVECOEUR, ST. JOHN DE

LETTERS OF MARQUE AND REPRISAL. See PRIVATEERS

LEWIS AND CLARK EXPEDITION (1804-06). Exploring expedition of about 50 soldiers led by Meriwether Lewis, President Jefferson's secretary, and Lieutenant William Clark, brother of GEORGE ROGERS CLARK. The expedition, which started out in 1804, followed the Missouri River north and west, crossed the Rocky Mountains and then followed the Columbia River to the Pacific Ocean. An Indian woman named Sacajawea served as guide and interpreter for the expedition during part of the journey. The expedition returned to St. Louis in 1806 with a vast store of information about the Louisiana Territory. The expedition was also one of the factors in future U. S. claims to the OREGON TERRITORY.

LEWIS, JOHN L. (1880-   ). Important 20th Century labor leader. He was president of the UNITED MINE WORKERS (U.M.W.) from 1920 to 1960. In 1935 Lewis organized the Committee for Industrial Organizations to unionize workers in mass production industries. Originally the committee was a part of the AMERICAN FEDERATION OF LABOR. In 1937, however, the committee split from the A.F.L. and Lewis became president of a new organization called CONGRESS OF INDUSTRIAL ORGANIZATIONS (C.I.O.). In 1942 Lewis broke with Philip Murray, the new president of the C.I.O., and the United Mine Workers withdrew from the organization.

LEXINGTON, BATTLE OF (1775). Scene of the first bloodshed of the AMERICAN REVOLUTION. A force of British soldiers on their way to seize military supplies at Concord were met by colonial MINUTEMEN at Lexington. The British opened fire and a number of the colonists were killed.

LEYTE GULF, BATTLE OF (1944). Part of the U. S. Naval campaign during WORLD WAR II (1941-45) to win back the Philippine Islands from the Japanese. In 1944 the U. S. and Japanese fleets met in Leyte Gulf off the coast of the Philippine Islands and the Japanese suffered a crushing naval defeat. The landing of U. S. Marines and troops in the Philippine Islands followed the naval victory and resulted in U. S. reconquest of the islands.

LIBERAL REPUBLICAN PARTY. Organized about 1872 by the liberal wing of the Republican Party, in protest against the corruption in local and national government and the continued harsh RECONSTRUCTION policies in the South. At its Cincinnati Convention in 1872 the party drew up a platform calling for CIVIL SERVICE REFORM as well as an end to Southern reconstruction. HORACE GREELEY, editor of the New York *Tribune,* was named as their presidential nominee. Although Greeley was also supported by the Democratic Party, he was defeated in the ELECTION OF 1872 by ULYSSES S. GRANT, the Republican candidate.

"LIBERATOR." See GARRISON, WILLIAM LLOYD

"LIBERTY AND UNION." See WEBSTER-HAYNE DEBATE

LIBERTY PARTY. One of many small political parties organized by the ABOLITIONISTS before the War Between the States (1861). The Liberty Party, advocating the abolition of slavery, nominated James Birney for president in the ELECTION OF 1840 and the ELECTION OF 1844, but his vote was very small. Most Liberty Party members joined the FREE SOIL PARTY when it was organized about 1848.

LIMA CONFERENCE (1938). See PAN AMERICAN CONFERENCES

LINCOLN, ABRAHAM (1809-1865). Sixteenth president of the U. S. In his younger days he was a store clerk, postmaster, surveyor and lawyer. He was a captain of volunteers in the BLACK HAWK WAR (1832), served in the Illinois state legislature and the U. S. House of Representatives. He soon became one of the leaders of the

Republican Party in Illinois. In 1856 Lincoln opposed STEPHEN A. DOUGLAS for election to the U. S. Senate. During this campaign the famous LINCOLN-DOUGLAS DEBATES on slavery brought Lincoln national prominence, although he was defeated for the Senate seat. In the ELECTION OF 1860 the REPUBLICAN PARTY nominated Lincoln for the presidency and he became known as the "rail splitter" candidate. A split in the DEMOCRATIC PARTY resulted in the election of Lincoln to the presidency.

During Lincoln's presidency the Southern states seceded from the Union (1861) and organized the CONFEDERATE STATES OF AMERICA. The WAR BETWEEN THE STATES began (1861) and continued for four years. During the war, Congress passed the HOMESTEAD ACT (1862), the MORRILL ACT (1862) and the NATIONAL BANK ACT (1863). In 1863 Lincoln issued the famous EMANCIPATION PROCLAMATION. Lincoln was re-elected president in the ELECTION OF 1864 but one month after his second inauguration (April 14, 1865) he was assassinated by the half-mad actor JOHN WILKES BOOTH. Lincoln was succeeded to the presidency by Vice-President ANDREW JOHNSON.

LINCOLN-DOUGLAS DEBATES (1858). Series of debates between STEPHEN A. DOUGLAS (Democrat) and ABRAHAM LINCOLN (Republican) during their campaign for election to the U. S. Senate from Illinois. Lincoln pointed out Douglas' contradiction in favoring POPULAR SOVEREIGNTY under the KANSAS-NEBRASKA ACT (1854) and at the same time defending the DRED SCOTT DECISION (1857) which held that people in a territory could not exclude slavery. (See FREEPORT DOCTRINE) Douglas won the Senatorial election but Lincoln defeated him for the presidency two years later. (See ELECTION OF 1860)

LITERACY TEST ACT (1917). Congress passed a number of laws (1896, 1913, 1915) requiring ability to read some language as a prerequisite for the admission of aliens to the U. S. These bills were vetoed by Presidents Cleveland, Taft and Wilson. In 1917, however, the Literacy Test Act was passed over President Wilson's veto. The law in effect today requires an alien to read at least 30 words of any language as a prerequisite for admission to the U. S.

LITERACY TESTS FOR VOTING. After the War Between the States (1865), many Southern states required the passing of literacy tests to determine voting eligibility. The purpose of this requirement was to stop the Negro from voting. (See AMENDMENT 15) A number of Northern states also established literacy tests for voting, New York State being the first to do so in 1923. However, the purpose of the tests in the North was to eliminate indiscriminate voting by illiterates.

LITERATURE, AMERICAN. The early literature of America before 1830 consisted of religious writings by such clergymen as JONATHAN EDWARDS and COTTON MATHER, the political writings of such historical figures as THOMAS PAINE and ALEXANDER HAMILTON (See "FEDERALIST") and the beginnings of creative literature by BENJAMIN FRANKLIN and the poet Philip Freneau.

The Nationalist Period (1830-1890) was the start of a truly creative era in American literature. The first half of the period, known as the Golden Age (1830-65), was the high point of American literary achievement in the 19th century. It included the prose writings of James Fenimore Cooper, Nathaniel Hawthorne, Washington Irving, Ralph Waldo Emerson, Herman Melville and the poetry of Edgar Allan Poe, William Cullen Bryant, Henry Wadsworth Longfellow, John Greenleaf Whittier, Walt Whitman and James Russell Lowell.

The second half of the Nationalist Period, known as the GILDED AGE, took its name from a book by Mark Twain (pen name of Samuel Clemens) and Charles Dudley Warner. The Gilded Age also saw the publication of novels by Booth Tarkington and short stories by Bret Harte, Joel Chandler Harris, O. Henry (pen name of William Sydney Porter) and other local-color writers.

The period after 1890 is known as the Age of Realism. It featured the writings of such economic realists (see MUCKRAKERS) as Upton Sinclair and Ida Tarbell, and the novels of social realists such as Theodore Dreiser and Sinclair Lewis. Modern American literature has been enriched by the poetry of Carl Sandburg, Edgar Lee Masters and Edna St. Vincent Millay, the dramas of Eugene O'Neill and the novels of Ernest Hemingway and William Faulkner.

LITTLE BIG HORN, BATTLE OF (1876). See SIOUX WAR

"LITTLE FLOWER." See LA GUARDIA, FIORELLO

LIVINGSTON, EDWARD (1764-1836). Secretary of State (1831-33) under President Jackson and author of Jackson's NULLIFICATION PROCLAMATION (1832) to South Carolina. Livingston's most significant contribution was his work in drawing up a criminal code which was used by many states as the basis of their own laws.

LIVINGSTON, ROBERT R. (1746-1813). New York delegate to the SECOND CONTINENTAL CONGRESS (1775) and member of the committee that drafted the DECLARATION OF INDEPENDENCE (1776). He was appointed minister to France (1801) by President THOMAS JEFFERSON and negotiated the treaty that culminated in the LOUISIANA PURCHASE (1803). Livingston helped to finance ROBERT FULTON's experiments that resulted in the construction of the first successful steamboat, the *Clermont*.

LOBBYING ACT (1946). Under this act, all organizations or groups of persons who seek to influence the votes of Congress on any issue before it are required to register, provide a statement of purposes, and present periodical records of their expenditures.

LOCHNER VS. NEW YORK (1905). A New York State law fixing maximum working hours for bakers was declared unconstitutional by the U. S. Supreme Court. The court held the law exceeded the POLICE POWERS of the state and interfered with the individual's right to "freedom of contract" under AMENDMENT 14. The decision in this case was reversed in subsequent decisions of the Supreme Court.

LOCOFOCOS. Name applied in the 1830's to a New York City faction of the Democratic Party that opposed the dominance of TAMMANY HALL by wealthy and privileged men and favored reform of the city government. The revolt of this radical group from Tammany reached its climax at a Tammany meeting in 1835. When the gas lights were turned off during the meeting, the reform group continued by the light of candles and matches (called locofocos); hence the name. Before the election of 1840 the Locofocos returned to the Democratic Party.

LODGE, HENRY CABOT (1850-1924). U. S. senator from Massachusetts. After World War I (1918) he opposed President WOODROW WILSON's plan to have the U. S. join the LEAGUE OF NATIONS. Lodge was willing to vote for League membership but only with reservations to protect American interests. President Wilson refused to approve these reservations and the Senate rejected the VERSAILLES TREATY and our proposed membership in the League.

LOGAN, JOHN A. (1826-86). One of the Radical Republican Congressmen who led the campaign to impeach President ANDREW JOHNSON. His powerful influence in Republican Party circles made him the PARTY BOSS of Illinois. He was a member of the STALWART faction of the Republican Party that opposed the reform programs of Republican presidents after the War Between the States (1861-65). In the ELECTION OF 1884 the Republican Party nominated Logan for the vice-presidency and JAMES G. BLAINE for the presidency. Neither was elected.

LONDON COMPANY (1606). A private stock company organized in England and chartered by King James I for the purpose of establishing a settlement in the New World. The charter guaranteed the rights of Englishmen to all who settled in America. The London Company organized the expedition that established the first permanent English colony in America at JAMESTOWN, Virginia, in 1607.

LONDON NAVAL CONFERENCE (1930). Meeting of Great Britain, U. S. and Japan in London, at which it was agreed to extend for five additional years (to 1936) the Ten Year Naval Holiday established at the WASHINGTON DISARMAMENT CONFERENCE (1922). However an escalator clause gave the three signatory nations the right to increase the size of their navies if nations who did not sign the treaty (particularly France and Italy) increased their naval forces.

LONE STAR REPUBLIC. Name of the Texas republic that was established after a successful revolt from Mexico (1836). It was called the Lone Star Republic because of the single star in its flag. (See TEXAS)

LONG DRIVE. The movement of cattle to market in the mid-19th century by driving them north from Texas (see CATTLE KINGDOM) across the open plains to railroad shipping points such as Abilene and Dodge City, Kansas. The picturesque cowboys played the leading role in these long and hazardous cattle drives. As many as 300,000 head of cattle per year were taken on the long drive to a railhead before being shipped to slaughterhouses in Chicago or to the East.

LONGHORNS. Cattle raised by Western ranchers, particularly in Texas, in the middle of the 19th century. Because of their long horns and tough meat, the longhorn cattle were valuable mainly for hides. Scientific cross breeding changed the longhorn into the valuable beef-producing steers of modern Western ranches.

LONG ISLAND, BATTLE OF (1776). One of the early battles of the AMERICAN REVOLUTION. During the battle the British commander Sir William Howe and a large military force engaged General WASHINGTON and a smaller colonial force in battle. Washington was forced to abandon Brooklyn and move across the East River to Manhattan.

LONG RIFLE. A weapon with a long barrel made in colonial times by gunsmiths of Pennsylvania. Its accuracy made it a favorite of colonial hunters, trappers and frontiersmen.

LOOSE INTERPRETATION OF THE CONSTITUTION. Theory that the powers of Congress, particularly the "elastic clause," should be intepreted liberally so as to meet the needs of a growing nation. ALEXANDER HAMILTON and the FEDERALIST PARTY favored this interpretation from the beginning of our nation's Constitutional history, whereas THOMAS JEFFERSON and the old REPUBLI-CAN PARTY favored a strict interpretation. The Supreme Court, as a result of JOHN MARSHALL'S decisions, generally followed the loose or liberal interpretation.

LOPEZ EXPEDITIONS (1849-50). A series of FILIBUSTER-ING EXPEDITIONS against Cuba led by General Narciso Lopez, a Spanish refugee living in the U. S., together with a number of Southern adventurers. The Lopez Expeditions were motivated by a desire to free Cuba from Spanish rule and also by the hope of Southern EXPANSIONISTS to annex Cuba to the U. S. as a slave state. Lopez led three expeditions, all of which failed. On the last expedition Lopez and his followers were captured by the Spanish authorities. Lopez and some of his men were executed.

LOST COLONY. During one of SIR WALTER RALEIGH's efforts to establish a colony in the New World, a small group of English settlers were left on Roanoke Island off the Virginia coast, in 1587. The vessels that brought them then sailed to England for supplies, but war with Spain (SPANISH ARMADA, 1588) delayed their return. When the supply ships returned to Roanoke in 1591 there was no trace of the settlers but the word "Croatoan" was carved on a doorpost. The word probably referred to an island off the coast of Virginia. This group of about 100 persons who disappeared is known as the Lost Colony.

"LOST STATE." See FRANKLIN, STATE OF

LOUISIANA PURCHASE (1803). In 1800 Napoleon, ruler of France, acquired the LOUISIANA TERRITORY from Spain. In 1802 the right to use the port of New Orleans and the lower Mississippi River (granted to the U. S. by the Spanish in the PINCKNEY TREATY, 1795) was terminated by Napoleon. ROBERT R. LIVINGSTON, our representative in France, was directed by President THOMAS JEFFERSON to find out whether Napoleon would sell New Orleans and the West Florida territory directly east of the Mississippi River. Because of impending war with England, Napoleon offered to sell to the U. S. the entire Louisiana Territory, extending from the Mississippi River to the Rocky Mountains. In 1803 a Treaty of

Purchase, providing for an American payment of $15,000,-000, was signed and the Louisiana Territory became a part of the U. S. This new territory more than doubled the area of the U. S.

LOUISIANA TERRITORY. After the LOUISIANA PURCHASE (1803) it was found that none of the boundaries of the territory except the Mississippi River was clearly defined. The northern boundary was later fixed by treaty with England (1818) and the boundary between Spanish Texas and the Louisiana Territory by the Adams-Onis Treaty through which the U. S. purchased the Florida Territory from Spain in 1819. (See FLORIDA PURCHASE)

LOVEJOY, ELIJAH P. (1802-37). ABOLITIONIST leader in the early 19th century. He published an abolitionist newspaper in Alton, Illinois, where his printing presses were destroyed three times and he was finally killed by a pro-slavery mob.

LOYALISTS. Also called Tories. They were American colonists who remained loyal to England after the Declaration of Independence (1776). At the beginning of the AMERICAN REVOLUTION about one-third of the colonists were opposed to independence. As the Revolution progressed, many of these Loyalists left for Canada. Of the ones who remained in the Thirteen Colonies, many lost their property, were persecuted and were imprisoned.

LUNDY'S LANE, BATTLE OF (1814). Military engagement near the Niagara River between British and American forces during the WAR OF 1812. Neither side won a decisive victory in the battle.

"LUSITANIA." British merchant ship which was torpedoed off the Irish coast by German submarines on May 7, 1915 during WORLD WAR I (1914-18). More than 1,100 English citizens and more than 100 American citizens lost their lives in the sinking. The U. S. protested the sinking as a violation of international law. Anti-German feeling in the U. S. ran high but despite public demands for a declaration of war this country remained neutral for two more years.

227

LYON, MARY

LYON, MARY (1797-1849). Founder of the Holyoke Female Seminary (Massachusetts) for the education of women (1837). It was one of the first women's colleges established in the U. S. Today it is called Mount Holyoke College.

MAC ARTHUR, GENERAL DOUGLAS (1880-   ). Commander of U. S. forces in the Far East during WORLD WAR II (1941-45). Before the last American forces in the Philippine Islands were forced to surrender to the Japanese, MacArthur was ordered to escape to Australia. From there he organized and directed the operation of the campaigns in the Far East which eventually resulted in the reconquest of the Philippine Islands and the unconditional surrender of Japan (1945). After the war MacArthur remained in Japan as Supreme Allied Commander of the U. S. occupying forces. In the KOREAN WAR (1950-53), MacArthur was put in charge of American and United Nations forces. During the fighting he urged American bombing of Communist airfields in China, a policy which President HARRY S. TRUMAN opposed. Because of this difference of opinion in military strategy MacArthur was removed from command.

MACASSAR STRAIT, BATTLE OF (1942). One of the early naval and air battles waged in the South Pacific during WORLD WAR II. The engagement between Japan and Allied sea and air forces took place during the Japanese invasion of the Dutch East Indies islands. It resulted in severe losses for the Japanese but did not stop their invasion and conquest of the islands.

MAC DONOUGH, CAPTAIN THOMAS (1783-1825). American naval commander who defeated an invading British fleet on Lake Champlain (1814) during the WAR OF 1812.

MACON ACT (1810). Passed by Congress during the Napoleonic Wars between Great Britain and France to replace the NON-INTERCOURSE ACT (1809). The Macon Act permitted American foreign trade with all countries for one year. If either Great Britain or France ended its decrees relating to the seizure of neutral ships and the other did not do the same within three months, no

229

American ships would be permitted to trade with the offending nation. Like its predecessors, the EMBARGO ACT (1807) and the Non-Intercourse Act, the new Macon Act failed to stop the seizure of American neutral ships.

MADISON, JAMES (1751-1836). Fourth president of the U. S. As a delegate to the CONSTITUTIONAL CONVENTION (1787) many of his suggestions were included in the final draft of the Constitution. He, together with ALEXANDER HAMILTON and JOHN JAY, wrote the "FEDERALIST" essays explaining the Constitution. He became THOMAS JEFFERSON's Secretary of State (1801-09) and in the ELECTION OF 1808 was himself chosen president. He was re-elected for a second term in the ELECTION OF 1812. During his two terms, the construction of the CUMBERLAND ROAD was begun (1811), the Second BANK OF U. S. was established (1816), and our first protective tariff was passed (1816). In foreign affairs the U. S. fought the WAR OF 1812 with England and signed the TREATY OF GHENT (1814) when the war was over. Because Madison contributed so much to the nation's basic document, he is known as the "father of the Constitution."

MAFIA INCIDENT (1891). A number of Italians suspected of being members of the Mafia (or Black Hand), a secret society, were tried for murder in New Orleans and were acquitted. However, a mob lynched most of the suspects. The Italian government demanded an indemnity which the U. S. paid in 1892.

MAGDALENA BAY INCIDENT (1912). When a Japanese company planned to buy land near Magdalena Bay in Lower California (Mexican territory), the U. S. protested because it violated the MONROE DOCTRINE which now applied to Asiatic as well as European powers. This became known as the Lodge Corollary (see Senator HENRY CABOT LODGE) to the MONROE DOCTRINE. The planned purchase was dropped by the Japanese.

MAGELLAN, FERDINAND (c.1480-1521). Portuguese navigator who sailed to the New World for Spain in 1519 in search of a water route to the Far East. Magellan's ships succeeded in sailing around the tip of South America and across the Pacific Ocean. Magellan was killed by the poisoned arrow of a native in the Philippine Islands but one of his ships, the *Victoria,* continued around Africa and returned to Spain in 1522. It was the first ship in the history of mankind to sail completely around the world.

MAHAN, ALFRED T. (1840-1914). American historian who, through his writings, emphasized the importance of sea power in war and peace. He thus influenced the development of a large American navy and our policy of IMPERIALISM in the late 19th and early 20th century. His most famous work was *The Influence of Sea Power Upon History* (1890).

"MAKE THE WORLD SAFE FOR DEMOCRACY." In his message to Congress calling for a declaration of war on April 2, 1917, President WOODROW WILSON stated that one of the reasons for declaring war on Germany was that "the world must be made safe for democracy."

MANHATTAN PROJECT (1942). See ATOM BOMB

MANIFEST DESTINY. The belief of some American political leaders (see EXPANSIONISTS) before the War Between the States (1861) that the U. S. was destined to stretch from the Atlantic Ocean to the Pacific. Many of our territorial acquisitions in the West were justified on the basis of this belief in Manifest Destiny. Some extreme believers in Manifest Destiny thought that the U. S. would eventually expand to include Canada and Mexico.

MANILA BAY, BATTLE OF (1898). At the outbreak of the SPANISH-AMERICAN WAR (1898) Commodore GEORGE DEWEY, commander of the American fleet in the Pacific Ocean, was ordered to attack the Spanish fleet at Manila Bay in the Philippine Islands. On April 30, 1898 the naval battle began. It ended very quickly with the destruction of the Spanish fleet, while the American ships and personnel suffered practically no damage. Manila was blockaded and subsequently American troops took the city with little opposition.

MANILA PACT (1954). See SOUTHEAST ASIA TREATY ORGANIZATION

231

MANN-ELKINS ACT (1910). The INTERSTATE COMMERCE COMMISSION was given power to regulate and supervise telegraph, telephone and cable companies. In 1934 this power was transferred to the Federal Communcations Commission. (See FEDERAL COMMUNICATIONS ACT)

MANN, HORACE (1796-1859). One of the most important 19th century leaders in the campaign to establish improved free public schools. As secretary of the Massachusetts Board of Education he issued a number of educational reports recommending the establishment of more free schools, improvements in the training of teachers, and the addition of new subjects to the school curriculum.

MARBURY V. MADISON (1803). One of the landmarks in the history of the U. S. Supreme Court. Marbury had been appointed a federal judge by President JOHN ADAMS on March 2, 1801. (See MIDNIGHT JUDGES) THOMAS JEFFERSON, who became president two days later, refused to have the appointment papers delivered. Marbury sued for a writ of mandamus to get the papers delivered. JOHN MARSHALL, who wrote the decision, decided against Marbury. However, the important part of Marshall's decision was his statement that the JUDICIARY ACT of 1789 empowering the court to issue a writ of mandamus was contrary to the Constitution and therefore void. This was the first case in which the Supreme Court assumed the power to declare a law of Congress unconstitutional.

MARCY, WILLIAM L. (1786-1857). Important Democratic Party leader in New York State in the first half of the 19th century and a leading member of the so-called ALBANY REGENCY. He was elected to the U. S. Senate in 1831 and in a speech defending one of the political appointments made by President Jackson (1831) made the famous statement: "To the victor belong the spoils of the enemy" from which the term SPOILS SYSTEM was derived. Marcy also served as Secretary of War during the MEXICAN WAR (1846-48) and Secretary of State when the GADSDEN PURCHASE was negotiated (1853). When the Albany Regency split, Marcy led the HUNKER faction of the Democratic Party in New York State.

MARION, FRANCIS (1732-1795). American military leader in South Carolina during the AMERICAN REVOLUTION (1775-83). Because of superior British military forces in the South, Marion used surprise attacks, quick raids and guerilla tactics to harass the British. By using these tactics successfully Marion became known as the "Swamp Fox."

MARNE, BATTLE OF (1918). Major military engagement of WORLD WAR I (1917-18) in which American forces, together with Allied troops, forced the German Armies to retreat from the Marne River back to the HINDENBURG LINE.

MARQUETTE, FATHER JACQUES (1637-75). French JESUIT MISSIONARY. He came to the New World to set up a mission near the Great Lakes, where he hoped to convert the Indians to Christianity. In 1673 he and a fur trader named Louis Joliet set out to find the "great river" that the Indians had described to them. Marquette and Joliet found the great Mississippi River and paddled two-thirds of the way down before turning back. Father Marquette died on the journey but Joliet returned safely.

MARSHALL, GEORGE C. (1880-1959). Served in World War I (1917-18) as an aide to General JOHN J. PERSHING. During World War II (1941-45) he devised the plan to conquer Germany through an Allied landing on the shores of France. After the war he was appointed ambassador to China (1945-47) in which capacity he tried but failed to bring the Chinese Civil War to an end. He was severely criticized in the American press when the Communists eventually conquered all of mainland China. In 1947 he was appointed Secretary of State by President HARRY S. TRUMAN and devised the MARSHALL PLAN to provide aid to European democracies in resisting the growth of Communism. In 1953 he was awarded the NOBEL PEACE PRIZE.

MARSHALL, JOHN (1755-1835). Recognized as the greatest Chief Justice of the U. S. Supreme Court (1801-35). He was one of the U. S. commissioners sent to France on the mission that ended in the XYZ AFFAIR (1797), was a member of Congress and Secretary of State under President JOHN ADAMS, who subsequently appointed Marshall to

233

the position of Chief Justice. During Marshall's 34 years as head of the Supreme Court he raised the prestige of the court to a point where it was recognized as the equal of the executive and legislative branches of government. His many judicial decisions were based on a broad interpretation of the Constitution with the aim of strengthening the national government, and strong opposition to the doctrine of STATES RIGHTS. In the case of MC CULLOUGH V. MARYLAND (1819) he announced the doctrine of broadly interpreting the powers of Congress. In MARBURY V. MADISON (1803), he first stated the right of the Supreme Court to declare a Congressional law unconstitutional, and, in FLETCHER V. PECK (1810), to declare a state law unconstitutional. In the DARTMOUTH COLLEGE CASE (1819) he affirmed the sanctity of contracts, and in GIBBONS V. OGDEN (1824) gave a broad interpretation to Congressional power to regulate interstate commerce. Marshall also presided at the treason trial of AARON BURR, where Marshall's insistence on evidence of overt acts to prove treason resulted in Burr's acquittal.

MARSHALL PLAN (1947). Five-year program of action proposed by Secretary of State GEORGE C. MARSHALL to provide loans to European countries to help them rebuild their wartorn economies quickly and thus prevent the spread of COMMUNISM. In return for Marshall Plan aid, European nations accepting it were to control inflation and lower tariff barriers. Sixteen nations accepted this aid, including West Germany and Italy, two of our former enemies in World War II (1941-45). (See FOREIGN AID PROGRAM)

MARTIN VS. HUNTER'S LESSEE (1816). One of the landmark cases in Supreme Court history, it involved the confiscation of land grants in Virginia. It was decided in the Virginia state court of appeals and then brought to the Supreme Court. The question at issue was the right of the federal Supreme Court to hear appeals from state courts. Justice Story of the Supreme Court wrote the decision, in which he strongly affirmed the right of the Supreme Court to review the decisions of state courts when they involved constitutional questions.

MARYLAND. One of the original THIRTEEN COLONIES established in 1634 on the basis of a royal charter granted to GEORGE CALVERT, the first Lord Baltimore. His object was to establish a haven for persecuted Catholics. In 1649 the Maryland Colony enacted a TOLERATION ACT that granted freedom of worship to all who believed in Jesus Christ.

MASON AND DIXON LINE. During colonial times the overlapping territorial claims of the Maryland and Pennsylvania Proprietors (see PROPRIETARY COLONIES) caused many disputes between them. In 1763 two surveyors, Charles Mason and Jeremiah Dixon, began the work of fixing a permanent boundary. After four years of surveying they established the boundary as it is today, and it became known as the Mason-Dixon Line.

MASON, CAPTAIN JOHN (1586-1635). See NEW HAMPSHIRE COLONY

MASSACHUSETTS BAY COLONY (1630). Established by PURITANS who came to America under a charter granted to the MASSACHUSETTS BAY COMPANY. Under the leadership of JOHN WINTHROP the colony was founded as a refuge from religious persecution. (See BIBLE COMMONWEALTH)

MASSACHUSETTS BAY COMPANY (1629). By the king's charter the Company received a grant of land in the New World to establish a trading settlement. The members of the company, however, planned the colony as a religious and political refuge rather than as a commercial venture. (See MASSACHUSETTS BAY COLONY) Because the charter did not specify where the company's meetings were to be held, it moved all of its activities to Massachusetts Bay and thus converted the company into a colony.

MATHER, COTTON (1663-1728). Puritan minister who became one of the leading clergymen in the MASSACHUSETTS BAY COLONY. He took a leading role in the Salem WITCHCRAFT TRIALS (1692), in the founding of Yale College and in encouraging the use of the highly unpopular smallpox vaccination.

MAXIMILIAN AFFAIR (1864-67). While the U. S. was engaged in the WAR BETWEEN THE STATES (1861-65),

Napoleon III, Emperor of France, established Archduke Maximilian (brother of the Austrian Emperor) as Emperor of Mexico. Although this was a direct violation of the MONROE DOCTRINE, the U. S., torn by war, could do no more than refuse to recognize the new Mexican government. At the end of the war the U. S. demanded the immediate withdrawal of French troops. Napoleon III, fearing war in Europe, withdrew the French forces and Maximilian's government was overthrown by a Mexican uprising. Maximilian was executed.

"MAYFLOWER." The ship that brought the first 102 Puritans from England to Cape Cod, where they established the PLYMOUTH COLONY in 1620. The voyage took two months. Before landing the passengers drew up the MAYFLOWER COMPACT, providing for majority rule in the new colony.

MAYFLOWER COMPACT (1620). Temporary agreement signed by the Puritans on their ship the "MAYFLOWER" before they landed at Plymouth. The document provided that they agreed to "enact . . . just and equal laws . . . for the general good of the colony." This was the first statement by settlers in the Western Hemisphere that they planned to make their own laws and live by majority rule.

MAYSVILLE ROAD BILL (1830). Provided for the construction of a road in Kentucky at federal expense. President ANDREW JACKSON vetoed the bill because it was a local project and would result in the use of federal funds at a time when the national government could ill afford it.

MC ADOO, WILLIAM G. (1863-1941). Secretary of the Treasury in President Woodrow Wilson's cabinet. During WORLD WAR I (1917-18) McAdoo was appointed director general of all U. S. railroads. (See RAILROAD LEGISLATION) At the National Democratic Convention in 1924 McAdoo was a leading candidate for the presidential nomination. However, the supporters of ALFRED E. SMITH deadlocked the convention and forced the nomination of a "dark horse" named John W. Davis.

MC CARRAN INTERNAL SECURITY ACT (1951). Passed by Congress over President Truman's veto, this act provided that all Communist and Communist-front organizations must register with the Department of Justice. No Communist could be admitted to the U. S., and resident alien Communists may be deported under the act.

MC CARRAN-WALTER IMMIGRATION ACT (1952). Replaced the NATIONAL ORIGINS ACT of 1929. The McCarran Act codified the old immigration laws and made a few changes. Total allowable immigration was fixed at 154,658. National origins provisions of the 1929 law were retained. Pacific areas, including Japan, received a quota of 2,000 immigrants. All Orientals in the U. S. were made eligible for citizenship by naturalization. Aliens dangerous to national security were to be excluded or deported. (See IMMIGRATION LEGISLATION)

MC CARTHYISM. See JOSEPH MC CARTHY

MC CARTHY, JOSEPH (1908-57). In 1954 he became a controversial national figure because of his unorthodox and irresponsible methods of conducting Senatorial investigations of Communist infiltration into government, industry, unions and schools. His methods were labeled "witchhunts" and came to be known as "McCarthyism." In 1952 he was censured by the Senate and his influence declined.

MC CLELLAN, GENERAL GEORGE B. (1826-1885). Union Army commander during the WAR BETWEEN THE STATES (1861-65). McClellan's PENINSULAR CAMPAIGN to capture Richmond (1862) failed when his army was repulsed by General ROBERT E. LEE. At the BATTLE OF ANTIETAM (1862) McClellan's forces again met a Confederate Army led by General Lee. Neither side won a victory but Lee was forced to retreat to Virginia. In the ELECTION OF 1864, while the war was still in progress, McClellan was nominated for the presidency by the northern Democratic Party in opposition to Abraham Lincoln, the Republican Party candidate. McClellan was badly defeated in the election.

MC CLURE'S MAGAZINE. Founded in 1893 by Samuel S. McClure (1857-1949) and edited by him at the turn of the 20th century. His magazine specialized in articles exposing the corrupt and ruthless methods of big business and its

237

effects on government. The magazine enjoyed a wide circulation and had as contributing writers such well-known MUCKRAKERS as Ida Tarbell, Ray Stannard Baker and Lincoln Steffens.

MC CULLOCH V. MARYLAND (1819). Landmark case in the history of the U. S. Supreme Court. McCulloch, cashier of the Baltimore branch of the BANK OF U. S., refused to pay a $15,000 tax levied on the bank by the state of Maryland. The question at issue was the right of a state to tax an agency established by the national government. In his decision, Chief Justice JOHN MARSHALL stated that Congress had the power to charter the bank, which was constitutional under the implied powers of Congress. In addition he held that states could not tax a federal agency because this would make it possible for states to hinder the legitimate functions of the national government and could even force the agency out of business. "The power to tax," wrote Marshall, "involves the power to destroy." The Maryland tax was therefore unconstitutional.

MC HENRY, FORT. See KEY, FRANCIS SCOTT

MC KINLEY TARIFF (1890). As a result of the Republican victory in the ELECTION OF 1888, the Republican Congress passed the McKinley Tariff Act. The law established one of the highest tariffs in our history up to that time, and also included a plan for reciprocal tariff reductions. Government bounty payments were provided for American sugar growers to help and encourage American sugar production. (See TARIFF LEGISLATION)

MC KINLEY, WILLIAM (1843-1901). Twenty-fifth president of the U. S. As congressman he sponsored the famous MC KINLEY TARIFF ACT (1890). In 1896 he was nominated by the REPUBLICAN PARTY for the presidency, to run against WILLIAM JENNINGS BRYAN, the Democratic candidate. In one of the most famous campaigns (see ELECTION OF 1896) involving the issue of "free silver" (see BIMETALLISM), McKinley was elected on the gold standard platform. In the ELECTION OF 1900 McKinley again defeated Bryan. However, on Sept. 6, 1901 McKinley was shot by Leon Czolgosz, an anarchist, and died eight days later.

During McKinley's presidency (1897-1901), Congress passed the DINGLEY TARIFF ACT (1897) and the GOLD STANDARD ACT (1900). Other important events during his term were the SPANISH-AMERICAN WAR (1898), the acquisition of the PHILIPPINE ISLANDS, PUERTO RICO and GUAM (1898), the annexation of the HAWAIIAN ISLANDS (1898) and the announcement of the OPEN DOOR POLICY for China (1900).

MEADE, GENERAL GEORGE G. (1815-72). One of the Union generals during the WAR BETWEEN THE STATES (1861-65). He commanded the Union Army at the BATTLE OF GETTYSBURG (1863), and forced the Confederate forces under General ROBERT E. LEE to retreat to Virginia. Meade's victory was the turning point of the war. He remained in command of the Army of the Potomac until the end of the war.

MEAT INSPECTION ACT (1906). Established a federal system of inspection of meats packed for shipment in interstate commerce. The enactment of the law was due, in part, to the publication of Upton Sinclair's novel *The Jungle,* which revealed the unsanitary conditions existing in the meat-packing industry. (See MUCKRAKERS)

MELLON, ANDREW W. (1855-1937). Banker and statesman. He was Secretary of the Treasury for ten years (1921-31) under Presidents HARDING, COOLIDGE and HOOVER. In that post he reduced the national debt by one-third. He established the Mellon Institute in Pittsburgh, provided the funds for the founding of the National Gallery of Art in Washington, D. C., and also contributed many of its world famous paintings.

MENENDEZ, PEDRO (1519-74). Spanish naval captain and governor. In 1565 he established the colony of ST. AUGUSTINE in Florida. This was the first permanent settlement by Europeans on land that later became the U. S. After the colony was established Menendez attacked a French settlement in Florida, at Fort Caroline, and massacred practically all the inhabitants.

MENNONITES. Also called Pennsylvania Dutch. A Protestant sect that takes the Bible as the only rule of faith. A small group of Mennonites led by Francis Daniel Pastorius (1651-1720) came to the Pennsylvania colony from Germany as early as 1683. Later others came from Russia, Switzerland and other European countries. In the 19th and 20th centuries problems have resulted from the refusal of the Mennonites to bear arms or take oaths of allegiance, because it is contrary to their religious principles. The conservative wing of the Mennonites is called "Amish."

MERCANTILISM. Economic theory popular in Europe from about 1500 to 1800, which held that a nation's wealth and power depended on the amount of gold and silver it possessed. To obtain these precious metals, a nation must sell more than it buys in international trade. It must also use the resources of its colonies for that purpose, place restrictions on colonial trade and make sure that only its own ships are used in trade. The British Trade Acts and NAVIGATION LAWS in colonial times were justified on the basis of Mercantilism.

MERCHANT MARINE. Refers to privately owned freight and passenger ships. In the early years of the republic, American shipping was one of our important industries. The EMBARGO ACT (1807) and the WAR OF 1812 almost ruined American shipping companies. After the war the shipping industry rapidly revived. The first regular transatlantic ship line was begun in 1818 with fast sailing vessels called PACKETS that crossed the Atlantic in about one month. The period from 1840 to 1860 was the Golden Age of the American clipper (sailing) ships (see "FLYING CLOUD"). The introduction of faster steam-driven ships by British companies brought the era of American clipper ships to an end before 1860. From the end of the War Between the States (1865) to the beginning of World War I (1914), American shipping declined because of foreign ship competition and America's interest in industrial expansion. During World War I (1917-18) the U. S. government built a huge fleet of merchant ships to carry troops and supplies to Europe. At the end of the war the U. S. tried to dispose of its fleet of ships (MERCHANT MARINE ACT, 1920) but was successful in part only. American ship companies could not compete with foreign lines because of higher U. S. construction and labor costs. Beginning in 1928 (Jones-White Merchant Marine Act) Congress tried to stimulate the growth of our merchant marine as a national defense measure by providing mail subsidies. The MER-CHANT MARINE ACT of 1936 established a Maritime Commission and provided further mail subsidies and loans to American shiplines. During World War II (1941-45) the U. S. again built a vast fleet of freighters to carry troops and supplies to the farflung areas of the world where America and her allies were fighting. After the war most of these ships were taken out of service, tied up in inland waterways, or sold for scrap.

MERCHANT MARINE ACT (1936). Also called Ship Subsidy Act. Because of high construction costs and high seamen's wages, American merchant ships could not compete with foreign shipping. To stimulate construction of American ships Congress under this law established the U. S. Maritime Commission (U.S.M.C.) with power to pay subsidies to American shipbuilders to make up the difference between the low cost of building ships in foreign shipyards and the higher costs of construction in the U. S. Subsidies were also paid to make up the difference between costs of operation.

MERGENTHALER, OTTMAR (1854-1899). Invented the linotype machine (1885) which made possible the rapid setting of printing type. The invention resulted in the printing of inexpensive newspapers, magazines and books.

MESSAGE TO GARCIA. Romantic legend made popular (1899) by a writer named Elbert Hubbard. According to Hubbard's story, an American military officer named Rowan, after enduring countless hardships, carried a message from President McKinley to Garcia, a Cuban revolutionary leader. In reality Lieutenant Rowan went to Cuba at the outbreak of the SPANISH-AMERICAN WAR (1898) to get information about the size of the Spanish forces in the area. He met Garcia and made his way back to Washington D. C. carrying a message *from* Garcia.

MEUSE ARGONNE, BATTLE OF (1918). One of the last major military engagements of WORLD WAR I. During the campaign, American forces advanced through the heavily fortified Argonne Forest (See HINDENBURG LINE) and reached the key city of Sedan on the Franco-

German border. Before the campaign was over, Germany asked for an armistice, which brought the war to an end (Nov. 11, 1918).

MEXICAN CESSION. See GUADALUPE HIDALGO, TREATY OF

MEXICAN WAR (1846-48). Conflict between U. S. and Mexico resulting from Mexico's refusal to recognize the U. S. annexation of TEXAS and the dispute over the southern boundary of Texas. The war was unpopular with the WHIG PARTY in New England that feared any newly acquired territory from Mexico would increase the power of the slave states. The war included three successful campaigns: General ZACHARY TAYLOR's invasion of northern Mexico, General WINFIELD SCOTT's capture of Vera Cruz and Mexico City and a combined sea and land invasion of California by Commodore Stockton, Captain JOHN C. FREMONT and Colonel STEPHEN KEARNY. The TREATY OF GUADALUPE HIDALGO (1848) brought the war to an end.

MEXICO, U. S. RELATIONS WITH. Mexico gained its independence from Spain by a revolution in 1821. From 1846 to 1848 the U. S. fought the MEXICAN WAR over the Texas boundary and Texas annexation. By the TREATY OF GUADALUPE HIDALGO (1848), ending the war, Mexico ceded a huge tract of land to the U. S. By the GADSDEN PURCHASE (1853) the U. S. bought an additional tract of land from Mexico. In 1864 the MAXIMILIAN AFFAIR began and came to an end in 1867 without U. S. intervention. In the early 20th century, relations with Mexico were strained by the TAMPICO INCIDENT (1914), the raids of Pancho Villa (1916) and the U. S. policy of refusing to recognize "government by assassination." (See WATCHFUL WAITING) In 1917 the Mexican government seized oil lands owned by Americans in Mexico. Through the efforts of our ambassador, Dwight W. Morrow (1927), American oil companies were partly compensated for their losses. Since 1933, under the U. S. GOOD NEIGHBOR POLICY, relations with Mexico have grown more cordial. Mexico, together with other Latin American countries, joined the U. S. during WORLD WAR II (1941-45) in a declaration of war against the Axis

Powers. Mexico was one of the signatories of the ACT OF CHAPULTEPEC (1945) and the RIO PACT (1947).

MIDDLE PASSAGE. See TRIANGULAR TRADE

MIDNIGHT JUDGES. Judges appointed by President JOHN ADAMS to federal judgeships under the JUDICIARY ACT of 1801. Because Adams was supposed to have signed the appointment papers on the night before his presidential term expired, the Republicans called these federal appointees the "midnight" judges. The appointment of William Marbury led to the famous U. S. Supreme Court case, MARBURY V. MADISON (1803).

MIDWAY, BATTLE OF (1942). One of the major battles in the Pacific Ocean between U. S. and Japanese naval and air fleets during WORLD WAR II. By defeating the Japanese forces the U. S. halted the Japanese attempt to seize the Midway Islands. This battle is called the turning point of the Pacific war because it halted further large-scale advances or conquests by the Japanese in the Pacific.

MILES, GENERAL NELSON A. (1839-1925). U. S. Army officer. He fought at the Battles of ANTIETAM, FREDERICKSBURG and CHANCELLORSVILLE during the WAR BETWEEN THE STATES (1861-65). In the SIOUX WAR (1875-76) he led the forces that finally subdued the Indians, and in 1886 he forced the surrender of GERONIMO, the Apache Indian chief. During the famous PULLMAN STRIKE (1894), General Miles was in command of the federal troops at the strike scene. During the SPANISH-AMERICAN WAR (1898) he invaded and took control of PUERTO RICO.

MILLIONAIRE'S CLUB. Name applied to U. S. Senate before enactment of AMENDMENT 17. Prior to 1913 senators were chosen by state legislatures, whose decisions were sometimes influenced by big business interests.

MINING FRONTIER. Western frontier that began with the GOLD RUSH of 1859. News of the discovery of gold and silver in Nevada and Colorado brought a wave of adventurers to the region. Rough mining towns sprang up overnight in the western mountain regions of Montana, Colorado, Idaho, Nevada and Arizona.

MINORITY PRESIDENTS. Because of the Electoral College system of electing presidents, it is possible for a candidate to become president by getting a majority of the electoral votes without getting a majority of the popular votes. This usually happens when there is a split in one major political party and more than two major candidates are nominated. Abraham Lincoln (see ELECTION OF 1860), Benjamin Harrison (see ELECTION OF 1888) and Woodrow Wilson (see ELECTION OF 1912) were minority presidents.

MINT ACT (1792). On the recommendation of Secretary of the Treasury ALEXANDER HAMILTON, Congress established a U. S. Mint with power to manufacture gold, silver and copper coins based on the decimal system.

MINT, U. S. Established by the MINT ACT (1792). Its functions are to coin money, prepare official medals, refine and sell gold for commercial use and assay mineral ores for a fee. Three mints are in operation today, the largest in Philadelphia (established 1793), one in San Francisco (1854) and one in Denver (1906).

MINUIT, PETER (1580-1638). First director general (1626-31) of the Dutch colony of NEW NETHERLAND, established under the charter of the DUTCH WEST INDIA COMPANY. Minuit arranged for the purchase of Manhattan Island from the Indians for beads and trinkets worth about $24.

MINUTEMEN. Name applied to the first colonial Revolutionary soldiers loosely organized as a militia to repel any use of force by the British. They were called "minutemen" because they were supposed to be ready to leave their homes and fight at a moment's notice. (See BATTLE OF LEXINGTON)

MISSIONARY RIDGE, BATTLE OF (1863). Military engagement during the WAR BETWEEN THE STATES (1861-65). In 1863 General ULYSSES S. GRANT and his Union Army attacked the Confederates under General BRAXTON BRAGG on a land elevation called Missionary

Ridge, outside the city of Chattanooga, Tennessee. The Confederate Army was forced to retreat after putting up stubborn resistance.

MISSOURI COMPROMISE (1820). When Missouri asked to be admitted as a state in 1819 Congress and the nation became bitterly divided over the question of permitting or prohibiting slavery in the new state. A compromise was reached by which Missouri was admitted as a slave state and Maine was admitted as a free state. In addition, the Missouri Compromise provided that any new states carved out of the Louisiana Territory north of the 36° 30′ line of latitude were to be free states. Any new states south of the line were to be slave states. (See SLAVERY LEGISLATION)

MISTER REPUBLICAN. See TAFT, ROBERT A.

MITCHELL, JOHN (1870-1919). See ANTHRACITE COAL STRIKE (1902)

MOLASSES ACT (1733). Passed by British Parliament, it levied a high tax on sugar and molasses imported from non-British-owned areas. The purpose of the law was to stop colonial trade with French colonies in the West Indies and give British West Indies colonies a monopoly of the sugar trade. In general the law was evaded in the 13 English colonies by means of smuggling.

MOLLY MAGUIRES. A secret society of Pennsylvania coal miners during the early 1870's. Their methods included the destruction of property, physical violence and murder. The methods of the Molly Maguires were exposed by a PINKERTON DETECTIVE. Fourteen of the leaders were sent to jail and ten were hanged.

"MONITOR" AND "MERRIMAC" (1862). First battle in history between two iron-clad ships occurred during the War Between the States (1861-65). A Confederate ironclad ship, the *Merrimac,* (rechristened *Virginia*) engaged in battle with a Northern ironclad vessel, the *Monitor,* built by John Ericsson. Neither vessel could sink the other, and both withdrew.

245

MONMOUTH, BATTLE OF (1778). During the AMERI-
CAN REVOLUTION (1775-83), General Washington
tried to stop General Clinton and his British forces from
crossing New Jersey into New York. Washington failed in
part because the American general, Charles Lee, failed to
follow Washington's orders to advance.

MONROE DOCTRINE (1823). Announced by President
JAMES MONROE in his annual message to Congress, it incorporated many of the ideas of JOHN QUINCY ADAMS,
his Secretary of State. The Doctrine declared that the U. S.
would not interfere in the affairs of Europe (see ISOLA-
TION), that the American continents were no longer open
to European colonization, and that the U. S. would not interfere with existing European colonies in the Western
Hemisphere. Any attempt by a European nation to interfere
in the Western Hemisphere would be considered a threat to
our own national safety. The doctrine was announced in
order to stop the Quadruple Alliance from attempting to
recover the former Spanish colonies in Latin America. It
was also aimed at stopping further Russian expansion from
Alaska south along the west coast.

MONROE, JAMES (1758-1831). Fifth president of the U. S.
Monroe, together with ROBERT LIVINGSTON, negotiated
the LOUISIANA PURCHASE (1803). President JAMES
MADISON appointed Monroe Secretary of State (1811)
and in the ELECTION OF 1816 Monroe was elected president by a tremendous majority vote. He was returned to the
presidency again in the ELECTION OF 1824. Monroe's first
term in office is sometimes known as the ERA OF GOOD
FEELINGS. During his presidency the FLORIDA PUR-
CHASE (1819) from Spain was arranged, and the
MISSOURI COMPROMISE (1820) over slavery was
passed. In foreign affairs, the RUSH-BAGOT TREATY
(1817) provided for an unfortified Canadian border, and the
TREATY OF 1818 settled a boundary dispute with
Canada. In 1823 Monroe announced the famous MONROE
DOCTRINE as a guiding principle of our foreign policy.

MONSTER, THE. During and after the PANIC OF 1819,
many rural inhabitants blamed the hard money policy of the
Second BANK OF U. S. for their financial troubles.
THOMAS H. BENTON, a Missouri political leader, named

the bank "The Monster" and the epithet came into common use, particularly in the West.

MONTCALM, GENERAL LOUIS (1712-59). French commander sent to defend Canada against the British during the FRENCH AND INDIAN WAR (1754-63). In 1759 the British under General JAMES WOLFE attacked the city of Quebec, defended by Montcalm. In the ensuing battle, on the Plains of Abraham near the city, both Montcalm and Wolfe were killed. However, the British captured the city.

MONTEREY, BATTLE OF (1846). Military victory of U. S. forces at the beginning of the MEXICAN WAR (1846-48). An American Army under General ZACHARY TAYLOR crossed the Rio Grande River and defeated a Mexican force at Monterey in northern Mexico.

MONTEZUMA (c.1480-1520). Ruler of the AZTEC Indians when Mexico was invaded by CORTEZ, the Spanish conquistador. Montezuma tried to stop Cortez by sending him gifts of gold and silver. When this failed, the Aztecs tried to fight the Spaniards but they were no match for Spanish horsemen and firearms. Montezuma was killed by the Spaniards when they captured the Aztec capital in Mexico City.

MONTGOMERY CONVENTION (1861). See CONFEDERATE CONSTITUTION

MONTGOMERY, GENERAL RICHARD (c.1738-1775). Leader of a colonial military force that captured Montreal (1775) at the beginning of the AMERICAN REVOLUTION. General Montgomery was killed during the unsuccessful battle to capture Quebec.

MONTICELLO. Virginia home of THOMAS JEFFERSON, third president of the U. S. The home was designed by Jefferson himself and was built by his slaves under his direction. The home has been restored and is visited by thousands of tourists each year.

MORAVIANS. Protestant sect, some of whose members established settlements in colonial Pennsylvania (Bethlehem,

1744), Georgia (Savannah, 1735), and North Carolina (Winston Salem, 1753). Many of the Moravians lived in communal groups for a short time. Today the Moravians are known as the Evangelical United Brethren Church.

MORGAN, DANIEL (1736-1802). See COWPENS, BATTLE OF (1781)

MORGAN, JOHN P. (1837-1913). One of America's great financiers and founder of the world-famous banking firm of J. P. Morgan and Co. (1895). In 1895, during a U. S. Treasury crisis, Morgan supplied the government with gold in return for government bonds. Morgan played a leading role in organizing the U. S. Steel Corporation (1901) and the International Harvester Corporation (1902). Together with JAMES J. HILL, Morgan formed the Northern Securities Corporation during a financial battle with EDWARD H. HARRIMAN for control of the railroads in the Pacific Northwest. The holding company was ordered dissolved by the Supreme Court in 1904 (Northern Securities Case). Many of Morgan's financial methods were revealed during the PUJO COMMITTEE investigation (1912) of the so-called "Money Trust." Morgan amassed a huge fortune during his lifetime. He used part of it to endow the Morgan Library and to contribute to the Metropolitan Museum of Art in New York City.

MORMONS. Also known as the Church of the Latter-Day Saints. A religious sect founded by JOSEPH SMITH in 1830. One of their religious beliefs was polygamy. This and other Mormon customs made them unpopular. After Joseph Smith was killed (1847) by an anti-Mormon mob, BRIGHAM YOUNG, their new leader, led them west to Great Salt Lake, Utah—then in Mexican territory. Here the Mormons prospered. After Utah became a state (1896), the Mormons gave up their polygamous family customs.

MORRILL ACT (1862). Provided free grants of federal land to each state to establish colleges devoted chiefly to the study of agriculture and mechanic arts. Under the act each state received 30,000 acres of government land for each senator and representative in Congress. Sixty-nine universities were established, including colleges in Alaska,

Hawaii and Puerto Rico. Because of their origin these institutions have become known as Land Grant colleges.

MORRILL TARIFF (1861). Under this act, tariff rates on imports were raised generally from 5% to 10% to provide funds to help finance the WAR BETWEEN THE STATES (1861-65). The Morrill Tariff rates were gradually increased during and after the war until 1869. In 1870 tariff rates were reduced moderately. (See TARIFF LEGISLATION)

MORRIS, GOUVERNEUR (1752-1816). During the AMERICAN REVOLUTION (1775-83) he espoused the colonial cause, although many members of his well-to-do family were LOYALISTS. At the CONSTITUTIONAL CONVENTION (1787) he supported a strong central government and he was on the committee that prepared the final draft of the Constitution. Morris was appointed U. S. minister to France (1792-94), was elected to the U. S. Senate (1800-03) as a FEDERALIST PARTY member, and was closely associated with the planning of the ERIE CANAL in New York State (1817-25).

MORRIS, ROBERT (1734-1806). Helped raise money for loans to the Second Continental Congress during the AMERICAN REVOLUTION (1775-83) in order to finance the war. Morris became Superintendent of Finance in 1781 when the ARTICLES OF CONFEDERATION went into effect. He was one of the delegates to the CONSTITUTIONAL CONVENTION (1787), where he favored the establishment of a strong federal government.

MORSE, SAMUEL F. B. (1791-1872). Artist and inventor, who perfected the electric telegraph. Congress provided Morse with $30,000 to build the first telegraph line from Baltimore to Washington D. C. The first message sent over the wires (1844) was the famous biblical quotation: "What hath God wrought?"

MOTOR CARRIER ACT (1935). Provided that all interstate trucks and buses were to be regulated by the INTERSTATE COMMERCE COMMISSION. Rates, schedules and procedures were to be subject to I.C.C. supervision.

MOTT, LUCRETIA (1793-1880). One of the leaders of the 19th century FEMINIST MOVEMENT. She and ELIZABETH CADY STANTON organized the first Women's Rights Convention in 1848. In addition to her work for women's rights she also lectured on behalf of temperance, the rights of labor and the abolition of slavery. Her home was used as one of the key stations in the UNDERGROUND RAILROAD for escaping Negro slaves.

MOUNT VERNON CONVENTION (1785). Meeting of Virginia and Maryland delegates at the home of George Washington to discuss the dispute between the states over the navigation of the Potomac River. Following this successful conference, Virginia issued a call to all states to send delegates to a convention to meet at Annapolis in 1786 to consider changes and improvements in trade regulations between states. (See ANNAPOLIS CONVENTION)

MUCKRAKERS. Name applied by President THEODORE ROOSEVELT to a group of magazine and book writers such as Lincoln Steffens, Upton Sinclair, Ida Tarbell and Thomas Lawson, who exposed the power, corruption and selfishness of men in politics, business and finance. Many of the articles written by the muckrakers appeared in McCLURE'S, *Everybody's* and *Cosmopolitan* Magazines.

MUGWUMPS. Nickname of Independent Republicans who, in the ELECTION OF 1884, refused to support JAMES G. BLAINE, the regular Republican presidential candidate, but instead threw their support to GROVER CLEVELAND, the Democratic candidate. Critics of the Mugwumps said that they sat on the political fence with their "mugs" on one side and their "wumps" on the other.

MULLIGAN LETTERS. In 1876 James Mulligan, a bookkeeper, charged that JAMES G. BLAINE, then Speaker of the House of Representatives, had tried to use his official position for personal gain through the manipulation of railroad bonds. One of the most damaging letters written by Blaine ended with the sentence: "Burn this letter." The disclosure of the Mulligan letters cost Blaine the Republican presidential nomination in 1880. However, Blaine was nominated in 1884 but lost in a very close election. (See ELECTION OF 1884)

MURFREESBORO, BATTLE OF (1862). Major military engagement in Tennessee during the WAR BETWEEN THE STATES (1861-65). The Confederate Army under General Braxton Bragg was forced to retreat after suffering heavy losses inflicted by General William S. Rosecrans and the Union Army.

NARVAEZ, PANFILO DE (1470-1528). Spanish explorer and adventurer. He explored Florida and established a settlement there. When his search for gold in Florida failed, Narvaez set out for Mexico but his expedition was shipwrecked and only a few members of the expedition, including CABEZA DE VACA, survived.

NASHVILLE, BATTLE OF (1864.) One of the last major battles in the west during the WAR BETWEEN THE STATES (1861-65). General John Schofield, in command of Union forces, inflicted severe casualties on the Confederate Army under General John Hood. This led to the eventual surrender of Confederate forces in Tennessee.

NAST, THOMAS (1840-1902). Newspaper cartoonist of the 19th century. Nast is credited with originating the tiger as the symbol of TAMMANY HALL, the elephant as the symbol of the REPUBLICAN PARTY and the donkey, of the DEMOCRATIC PARTY. Nast's cartoons about the corruption of the TWEED RING (1869-72) in New York City helped arouse public indignation and eventually led to the downfall of WILLIAM M. TWEED.

NATCHEZ TRACE. Early 19th century road extending from Natchez, Mississippi northeast through Tennessee and Kentucky into Ohio. It was used as an overland return route for farmers and traders who floated their crops and livestock on FLATBOATS down the Ohio and Mississippi Rivers.

NATIONAL BANKING ACT (1863). Passed by Congress as a means of raising additional funds to finance the WAR BETWEEN THE STATES (1861-65). Under the act, private citizens could obtain charters to start National Banks provided the banks invested at least ⅓ of their money in U. S. bonds. By depositing these bonds with the U. S. Treasurer the National Banks could then receive national bank currency up to 90% of the value of the bonds. Thus the U. S. government created a ready market for government bonds and a National Bank currency that gradually replaced state bank notes. (See BANKING LEGISLATION)

NATIONAL CONSERVATION COMMISSION (1908). Following the White House Conference of Governors (1908) held by President THEODORE ROOSEVELT, a federal commission under the chairmanship of GIFFORD PINCHOT was organized. Its functions were to make a survey of the nation's natural resources, encourage the organization of local conservation groups and recommend steps to be taken to conserve the nation's mineral, timber, soil and water resources. (See CONSERVATION MOVEMENT)

NATIONAL HOUSING ACT (1934). See HOUSING LEGISLATION

NATIONAL INDUSTRIAL RECOVERY ACT (N.I.R.A.) 1933. Passed by Congress during the GREAT DEPRESSION (1929-35) soon after FRANKLIN D. ROOSEVELT became president. Private industries were empowered to draw up codes of fair competition which were to include the abolition of child labor, the establishment of maximum hours and minimum wages, and fair price agreements among businessmen. The act was to be administered by the National Recovery Administration (N.R.A.) whose symbol was the "Blue Eagle." In 1935 the Supreme Court declared the law unconstitutional. (See SCHECTER V. U. S.)

NATIONALIST ERA (1814-24). During the era following the WAR OF 1812 Americans generally transferred their primary loyalty from their state or section to allegiance to the nation as a whole. The spirit of nationalism was evident in the decline of bitter party rivalries during President JAMES MONROE's administration (ERA OF GOOD FEELINGS), JOHN MARSHALL's historic judicial decisions supporting a strong national government, the purchase of Florida (1819) (see FLORIDA PURCHASE), the announcement of the MONROE DOCTRINE (1823), the MISSOURI COMPROMISE (1820), the recharter of the BANK OF U. S. (1816), the enactment of our first truly protective tariff (1816), the construction of the national (CUMBERLAND) ROAD (1815-18), the admission of new western states such as Indiana (1816), Mississippi (1817), Illinois (1818), and Alabama (1819) which owed their existence to the national government, and the continued westward expansion of the nation.

NATIONALITY ACT (1940). Established new requirements by which aliens could become naturalized citizens. Under this act an alien may file a Declaration of Intention after two years of residence in the U. S. Two years later a Petition of Naturalization may be filed. However the minimum residence requirement is five years. A Petition of Naturalization is approved if the applicant can read and speak English, is of good moral character, and swears allegiance to the U. S. Alien women do not become citizens if they marry U. S. citizens or if their husbands become naturalized citizens. The requirement that a Declaration of Intention be filed has recently been dropped.

NATIONAL LABOR RELATIONS ACT (1935). Also known as the Wagner-Connery Act. The law established a National Labor Relations Board (N.L.R.B.) with power to stop unfair labor practices of employers, to hold elections to determine which of rival unions the workers want to act as their bargaining representatives, and to insure the principle of collective bargaining between unions and employers. The Supreme Court declared the law constitutional in 1937 (N.L.R.B. v. Jones and Laughlin Steel Corp.)

NATIONAL LABOR UNION. Organized about 1866, this was one of the first national labor organizations established in the U. S. At the height of its power it had more than 500,000 members. The attempt of the union to enter politics in 1872 as the National Labor Reform Party failed and the organization gradually disintegrated.

N.L.R.B. V. JONES AND LAUGHLIN STEEL CORPORATION (1937). See NATIONAL LABOR RELATIONS ACT

NATIONAL ORIGINS ACT (1929). Provided that the total number of aliens to be admitted each year was to be limited to 150,000. Each country could send a number of immigrants equal to the percentage which the people of its origin bore to the total number of people of European origin in the U. S. according to the census of 1920. (See IMMIGRATION LEGISLATION)

NATIONAL PROGRESSIVE REPUBLICAN LEAGUE. Organized in the first quarter of the 20th century by pro-

254

gressive Republicans as a protest against the conservative policies of the REPUBLICAN PARTY in Congress. One of the leaders was Senator ROBERT LA FOLLETTE of Wisconsin. In the ELECTION OF 1912 the league supported THEODORE ROOSEVELT for president. (See PROGRESSIVE MOVEMENT 1900-17)

NATIONAL REPUBLICAN PARTY. Developed from a split in the old REPUBLICAN PARTY after the victory of JOHN QUINCY ADAMS in the ELECTION OF 1824. The National Republican Party was made up of supporters of HENRY CLAY and John Quincy Adams who opposed the doctrine of STATES RIGHTS.

NATIONAL SECURITY ACT (1947). Abolished the separate War and Navy Departments and established a single Department of Defense headed by a single cabinet member. The new department is separated into divisions for the navy, army and air force.

NATIONAL UNION PARTY (1866). Minor political party organized by President ANDREW JOHNSON and others who favored moderation in the treatment of the defeated South after the WAR BETWEEN THE STATES (1865) in contrast to the radical RECONSTRUCTION program of the Republicans. The National Union Party was badly defeated by the Republicans in the Congressional election of 1866.

NATIVE AMERICAN PARTY. See KNOW-NOTHING PARTY

NAT TURNER REBELLION (1831). A brief uprising of Negro slaves in the South led by a Negro preacher named Nat Turner. About 60 white people were killed before the rebellion was suppressed. Southerners blamed radical Northern ABOLITIONISTS for the revolt.

NATURALIZATION ACT (1795). Established a five-year residence requirement for aliens who wished to become citizens. The law, passed during President GEORGE WASHINGTON's second presidential administration, changed the two-year residence requirement that had been established by a Congressional act of 1790.

255

NATURALIZATION ACT (1798). Part of the FEDERAL-IST PARTY program during the presidency of JOHN ADAMS, to weaken Jefferson's REPUBLICAN PARTY. This act increased the residence requirement for aliens who wanted to become citizens from five (see NATURALIZA-TION ACT OF 1795) to 14 years. The law was aimed at new immigrants, most of whom were Republican Party supporters. After the election of THOMAS JEFFERSON to the presidency, Congress reduced the residence requirement back to five years (1802).

NAVAHO INDIANS. Mixed Indian tribe originally located in Colorado, Arizona and New Mexico. They made constant war on American settlers after the U. S. acquired their territory from Mexico (see TREATY OF GUADALUPE HIDALGO) until subdued by an expedition (1863-64) led by KIT CARSON.

NAVAL HOLIDAY. See WASHINGTON CONFERENCE and FIVE POWER NAVAL PACT

NAVIGATION ACTS. Series of laws passed by the British Parliament restricting the trade of its colonies. The Navigation Act of 1660 provided that all goods sent to or shipped out of British colonies must be transported on British-owned ships. Specified articles including tobacco, sugar, cotton and indigo, grown or made in British colonies, could not be sold directly to foreign countries but must first be shipped to England.

The Navigation Act of 1663 provided that all foreign ships going to English colonies must first stop in England and there be reloaded and shipped in English ships. (See MERCANTILISM)

NECESSITY, FORT (1754). Built by George Washington and the Virginia militia near Uniontown, Pennsylvania, early in the FRENCH AND INDIAN WAR (1754-63), after Washington learned that the French had captured the English fort at the junction of the Allegheny and Monongahela Rivers. (See FORT DUQUESNE) Washington was forced to surrender Fort Necessity to the French when it was attacked (1754).

NEUTRALITY ACT (1794). Passed by Congress to reinforce President Washington's PROCLAMATION OF NEUTRALITY (1793) during the war between England and France. The Neutrality Act prohibited American citizens from enlisting in a foreign army or providing armed vessels for use by foreign nations at war.

NEUTRALITY ACT (1937). Also known as the "Cash and Carry" Law. It forbad American shipments of arms or other goods to countries at war unless payments were made in cash and goods were transported in foreign ships. Because of the outbreak of the Civil War in Spain (1937), the war between Japan and China (1937) and the outbreak of WORLD WAR II in Europe (1939), Congress passed a new NEUTRALITY ACT in 1939.

NEUTRALITY ACT (1939). Passed by Congress soon after the start of World War II in Europe (1939). This act repealed the embargo on arms shipments established under the NEUTRALITY ACT OF 1937 but continued the "cash and carry" principle. All trade with nations at war was to be paid for in cash and transported in foreign ships. In addition American ships were forbidden to enter the war zone in European waters. The Neutrality Act of 1939 was repealed in 1941 by the LEND LEASE ACT.

NEW AMSTERDAM. See STUYVESANT, PETER

NEW COLONIAL POLICY (1763-1776). Colonial policy of the English king and Parliament after the end of the FRENCH AND INDIAN WAR (1763). The new policy consisted of stricter enforcement of laws and the levying of new taxes to pay for the cost of maintaining British troops in the colonies. The Grenville Acts (see GRENVILLE, GEORGE) and TOWNSHEND ACTS were part of this new colonial policy.

NEW DEAL. Era of FRANKLIN D. ROOSEVELT's first two terms as president (1933-41). It is derived from Roosevelt's speech accepting the presidential nomination in 1932 in which he said: "I pledge myself to a new deal for the American people." A feature of the New Deal was the many new laws passed by Congress to help or regulate industry, agriculture, labor, banking, the stock market,

257

labor unions, public utilities and unemployment. (See NEW DEAL LEGISLATION)

NEW DEAL LEGISLATION. The many laws passed by Congress during FRANKLIN D. ROOSEVELT's first two terms as president (1933-41). Among the most important laws were the following: In the field of labor the New Deal Congress passed the NATIONAL LABOR RELATIONS ACT (1935), the SOCIAL SECURITY ACT (1935), and the FAIR LABOR STANDARDS ACT (1938). In the field of agriculture the New Deal Congress passed the FARM MORTGAGE MORATORIUM ACT (1935), the SOIL CONSERVATION AND DOMESTIC ALLOTMENT ACT (1936), the Farm Security Administration Act (1937), the BANKHEAD-JONES FARM TENANT ACT (1937), and the AGRICULTURAL ADJUSTMENT ACT (1938). In the field of currency and credit the New Deal passed the repeal of the GOLD STANDARD (1933), the GOLD RESERVE ACT (1934), and the SILVER PURCHASE ACT (1934). Banking and stock exchange laws included the SECURITIES AND EXCHANGE ACT (1934) and the Glass-Steagall BANKING ACTS OF 1933 and 1935. Public utility and transportation laws included the TENNESSEE VALLEY AUTHORITY ACT (1933), the EMERGENCY RAILROAD TRANSPORTATION ACT (1933), the MOTOR CARRIER ACT (1935) and the WHEELER-RAYBURN PUBLIC UTILITY HOLDING COMPANY ACT (1935). Housing laws included the NATIONAL HOUSING ACT (1934), the WAGNER-STEAGALL HOUSING ACT (1937) and the STEAGALL NATIONAL HOUSING ACT (1938). Consumer protection laws included the ROBINSON-PATMAN ACT (1936) and the PURE FOOD, DRUG, AND COSMETIC ACT (1938).

NEW ENGLAND CONFEDERATION (1643). Organized by the colonists of Massachusetts Bay, Plymouth, Connecticut, and New Haven for mutual protection against hostile Indians and rival French and Dutch settlements. The confederation succeeded for a number of years but was disbanded because of colonial jealousies.

NEW ENGLAND EMIGRANT AID COMPANY (1855-57). Also known as the Massachusetts Emigrant Aid Society. It was an anti-slavery association formed for the specific purpose of sending anti-slavery settlers into the Kansas territory in order to make certain it would enter the union as a free state. The activities of the company led to efforts on the part of pro-slavery men from Missouri to send pro-slavery settlers into Kansas. The sending of these opposing groups was responsible in part for the outbreak of Civil War in Kansas. (See BLEEDING KANSAS).

NEW ENGLAND RESTRAINING ACT (1775). One of the last coercive acts passed by the British Parliament before the outbreak of the AMERICAN REVOLUTION (1775). The act restricted the trade of the New England colonies to Great Britain and the British West Indies and forbad further fishing by New England fishermen in North Atlantic waters.

NEW FRANCE. Name applied to all French colonial possessions in the New World during the 16th and 17th centuries. New France included the region surrounding the St. Lawrence River, the Great Lakes and the Mississippi River. Many settlers turned to fur trapping, fur trading with the Indians or fishing in the region of New France.

NEW FREEDOM. See WILSON, THOMAS WOODROW

NEW FRONTIER. Name applied by President JOHN F. KENNEDY to his domestic and foreign program. One of its elements was the organization of the PEACE CORPS (1961).

NEW HAMPSHIRE COLONY. In 1622 SIR FERDINANDO GORGES and Captain John Mason received a grant of land in northern New England. In 1629 the land was divided between the two men, Captain Mason receiving an area he called New Hampshire. He died before a permanent settlement was established on his grant, but a colony was subsequently established at Dover, New Hampshire by Edward Hilton about 1628. Other settlements were established at Portsmouth (1630), Exeter (1638) and Hampton (1638). In 1641 New Hampshire was annexed by the MASSACHUSETTS BAY COLONY but in 1679 New Hampshire became a separate colony under a newly granted royal charter.

NEW HARMONY (1825). A small experimental community established by Robert Owen (1771-1858) in Indiana. This was supposed to be an ideal or "utopian" cooperative community in which the people contributed their services and received what they needed to live. The experiment was finally abandoned in 1828 because of internal dissension in the community.

NEW INDUSTRIAL REVOLUTION. The rapid economic changes that occurred in the U. S. after the War Between the States (1865) and continued into the 20th century. These changes included the growth of huge corporate enterprises, the spread of industries to such new industrial areas as the South (see NEW SOUTH) and the Far West and the use of new industrial methods such as standardization, mass production, the assembly line, and automation. These changes were influenced by thousands of inventions of new industrial machines, new methods of transportation and communication, and the use of new types of power such as electric motors and internal combustion (gasoline and diesel) engines.

NEW JERSEY COLONY. The first settlements in New Jersey were made by the DUTCH WEST INDIA COMPANY and by Swedish settlers. In 1655 these settlements were made part of NEW NETHERLAND colony. After the capture of New Netherland by a British fleet in 1664, it was divided into two areas. The area east of the Hudson River was called New York. The area between the Hudson and Delaware Rivers, called New Jersey, was granted by the Duke of York to two proprietors, LORD JOHN BERKELEY and Sir George Carteret. New Jersey remained under proprietary rule until 1702, when it became a royal colony.

NEW JERSEY PLAN. A proposal made by William Paterson, delegate from New Jersey at the CONSTITUTIONAL CONVENTION (1787). His plan provided for a continuation of the policy of giving each state one vote in Congress as it existed under the ARTICLES OF CONFEDERATION (1781-1789). The plan also provided for increased Congressional powers, such as the right to levy tariffs and other taxes. The New Jersey Plan, which was aimed at protecting the interests of small states, was modified by the

260

GREAT COMPROMISE that was finally adopted by the Philadelphia Convention as part of the Constitution.

NEWLANDS RECLAMATION ACT (1902). Also called the National Reclamation Act. It provided that dams, reservoirs and other irrigation projects were to be built in the arid regions of Western states with money obtained from the sale of public lands. One of the most important projects built under this act was the Roosevelt Dam on the Salt River in Arizona.

NEW NATIONALISM. Phrase coined by THEODORE ROOSEVELT in a speech delivered in 1910. It referred to his belief that the U. S. government should be guided by a more liberal philosophy in protecting human as well as property rights.

NEW NETHERLAND. Colony established by the DUTCH WEST INDIA COMPANY based on a land grant (1621) from the Dutch government. The company started settlements on Manhattan Island in 1624, and along the Hudson River. Under a government established by the company, the colony was inefficiently managed and ran into difficulties with the Indians and the nearby MASSACHUSETTS BAY COLONY. In 1664 the British seized the colony from the Dutch and renamed it New York.

NEW ORLEANS, BATTLE OF (1815). Last battle of the WAR OF 1812 (1812-14) fought 15 days after the TREATY OF GHENT, ending the war, was signed. The American defenders, commanded by ANDREW JACKSON, inflicted a serious defeat on the British invading forces. (See LAFITTE, JEAN)

NEW SOUTH. Refers to industrial development in the Southern states after 1865. (See NEW INDUSTRIAL REVOLUTION) Before the WAR BETWEEN THE STATES (1861-65) the South was almost entirely devoted to the raising of cotton, tobacco, rice and other agricultural products. After the war, however, large industries developed in such cities as Birmingham, Alabama and Atlanta, Georgia. Southern factories began to produce textiles, steel, lumber, paper, furniture, tobacco products and other items.

NEW SPAIN. Name applied to all of Spain's possessions in the New World including South America (except Brazil), Central America, Mexico, many of the West Indies islands, Florida and the southwest quarter of what is now the U. S. Settlers in New Spain established universities, churches, monasteries, large estates and such great cities as Mexico City and Lima, Peru. This huge empire was under Spanish control until revolutions (1810-30) put an end to Spanish rule in most of the New World.

NEW SWEDEN. Under the authority of the New Sweden Company, organized in Sweden in 1637, a small colony was established on the Delaware River. In 1655 PETER STUYVESANT and a company of Dutch soldiers took control of the Swedish colony without a struggle and made it part of NEW NETHERLAND.

NEW YORK. See NEW NETHERLAND

NICARAGUAN CANAL. After the completion of the PANAMA CANAL (1914) the U. S. obtained the right to build a future canal across Nicaragua by the Bryan-Chamorro Treaty (1914). Although it has frequently been suggested that a second canal be built across Nicaragua to provide an alternate route in the event that the Panama Canal is damaged or destroyed in wartime, the canal was never built.

NICARAGUAN INTERVENTION. See ROOSEVELT COROLLARY

NINE POWER PACT (1922). See WASHINGTON DISARMAMENT CONFERENCE

NIZA, MARCOS DE (c.1495-1558). Spanish explorer and missionary. He was leader of an exploring expedition sent from Mexico into Arizona and New Mexico (1539) and wrote an imaginary report of the SEVEN CITIES OF CIBOLA that he found on his journey, and their fabulous wealth. DeNiza had probably heard of the "seven cities" from the Indians and had accepted the story as truth. In 1540 CORONADO used DeNiza as a guide to search for these fabled cities. When they were not found De Niza was sent back to Mexico in disgrace.

262

NOBEL PEACE PRIZE. Americans who have been awarded the NOBEL PRIZE for their contributions to international peace include THEODORE ROOSEVELT (1906), ELIHU ROOT (1912), WOODROW WILSON (1919), Charles G. Dawes (shared, 1925), Frank B. Kellogg (1929), JANE ADDAMS and Nicholas Murray Butler (1931), CORDELL HULL (1945), John R. Mott and Emily Balch (1945), RALPH BUNCHE (1950) and General GEORGE C. MARSHALL (1953).

NOBEL PRIZE. Americans have won the NOBEL PEACE PRIZE ten times, the Nobel Prize for literature five times, for physics 14 times, for chemistry nine times and for medicine and physiology 14 times (to 1961).

NOBLE EXPERIMENT. See PROHIBITION

NON-IMPORTATION ACT (1806). Also called the Nicholson Non-Importation Act. It was passed by Congress in retaliation for British seizure of American ships and IMPRESSMENT of seamen during the Napoleonic Wars. The act forbad the importation from England of specified articles such as flax, hemp and tin which could be purchased from other countries or could be produced in the U. S. As a result of diplomatic negotiations between the U. S. and England, the act was suspended until 1807. It was then supplanted by the EMBARGO ACT (1807).

NON-INTERCOURSE ACT (1809). Passed by Congress during the Napoleonic Wars between England and France to replace the EMBARGO ACT (1807). The Non-Intercourse Act stopped all American ships from trading with Great Britain, France or any of their colonies until their restrictions on American trade were lifted.

NORRIS, GEORGE W. (1861-1944). Senator from Nebraska (1913-42). In 1910 he led the fight to reduce the powers of the Speaker of the House of Representatives and specifically the powers of "Uncle" JOSEPH CANNON. In 1932 Norris sponsored the NORRIS-LA GUARDIA ANTI-INJUNCTION ACT and in 1932 was the chief sponsor and supporter of AMENDMENT 20 (Lame Duck Amendment). In 1933 he sponsored the TENNESSEE VALLEY AUTHORITY ACT.

263

NORRIS-LA GUARDIA ANTI-INJUNCTION ACT (1932). Sponsored by Senator GEORGE W. NORRIS and Congressman FIORELLO LA GUARDIA. The act forbad the use of court INJUNCTIONS to stop the unionization of workers who had signed YELLOW DOG CONTRACTS or to stop peaceful strikes, picketing or boycotts.

NORTH ATLANTIC TREATY ORGANIZATION (N.A.T.O.) 1949. Organized under the North Atlantic Pact. Under this military alliance the U. S. and 13 other nations agreed to regard an attack on one as an attack on all. Members of the pact included the U. S., Canada, Great Britain, France, Italy, Belgium, Holland, Luxembourg, Greece, Turkey, Portugal, Denmark, Iceland and Norway. The pact was aimed primarily at preventing military aggression by the Soviet Union.

NORTH CAROLINA. One of the original THIRTEEN COLONIES. It was originally part of the Carolina grant of land given by King Charles II to eight noblemen. However, the area of North Carolina was settled largely by frontiersmen who migrated south from the Virginia Colony, and by Quakers. In 1729 North Carolina became a royal colony.

NORTHERN PACIFIC RAILROAD. See HILL, JAMES J.; MORGAN, JOHN P.

NORTHERN SECURITIES COMPANY and NORTHERN SECURITIES CASE. See HILL, JAMES J. and MORGAN, JOHN P.

NORTHWEST ORDINANCE (1787). Provided a system of government for the NORTHWEST TERRITORY and for the division of the territory into not less than three and not more than five states. When any of the areas had a population of 60,000 or more, it would be admitted into the Union on an equal basis with the thirteen original states. The ordinance also forbad slavery, guaranteed freedom of religion and trial by jury to all inhabitants, and provided for the encouragement of a system of free public education.

NORTHWEST PASSAGE. A water route around or through the North and South American continents which was sought by many navigators and explorers in the 16th and 17th centuries. (See JACQUES CARTIER, HENRY HUDSON, MARTIN FROBISHER) It was hoped that this water passage would lead to the ocean that washed the shores of China, Japan and the East Indies.

NORTHWEST TERRITORY. Land between the Ohio and Mississippi Rivers which was claimed by the states of Virginia, Connecticut and Massachusetts under their colonial charters. These states relinquished their claims to the Northwest Territory and gave it to the national government under the ARTICLES OF CONFEDERATION. In 1787 Congress passed the NORTHWEST ORDINANCE for the government of the territory and its future admission to the Union as states. Five states were eventually carved out of the territory and admitted into the Union: Ohio (1803), **Indiana (1816), Illinois (1818), Michigan (1837) and Wis**consin (1848).

"NOT WORTH A CONTINENTAL." See CONTINENTAL CURRENCY

NULLIFICATION. The doctrine supported by the South before the WAR BETWEEN THE STATES (1861) which held that states could decide if federal laws were unconstitutional. If found to be unconstitutional the states could then declare them null and void and refuse to obey them. The doctrine of nullification was based on the STATES **RIGHTS DOCTRINE which in turn was based on the** COMPACT THEORY of the Constitution.

NULLIFICATION PROCLAMATION (1832). Presidential proclamation by President ANDREW JACKSON addressed to the people of South Carolina in answer to the state's Ordinance of Nullification. In his proclamation, Jackson defended the principle of federal supremacy, the indivisibility of the federal union and the treasonable character of the Ordinance of Nullification.

NYE COMMITTEE (1934-36). Congressional committee established under Senator Gerald P. Nye to investigate the **profits and the influence of the munitions industry in get-**

265

ting the U. S. into WORLD WAR I (1917-18). Although the results of the committee investigation were inconclusive, it led to the enactment of neutrality legislation (NEUTRALITY ACTS OF 1937 and 1939) designed to keep the U. S. out of future wars.

OFFICE OF ECONOMIC STABILIZATION (O.E.S.). See WARTIME AGENCIES, WORLD WAR II

OFFICE OF PRICE ADMINISTRATION (O.P.A.). See WARTIME AGENCIES, WORLD WAR II

OFFICE OF WAR MOBILIZATION. See WARTIME AGENCIES, WORLD WAR II

OGLETHORPE, JAMES (1696-1785). Wealthy English reformer and member of the British House of Commons for 32 years. In 1732 he and 19 associates were granted a charter to establish a colony in GEORGIA as a refuge for imprisoned debtors and other poverty-stricken Englishmen. In 1733 the colony was founded.

OHIO AND ERIE CANAL. Early 19th century canal built through Ohio connecting Lake Erie with the Ohio River.

OHIO COMPANY (1747). One of many colonial land companies organized for the purpose of getting western land grants from royal colonial governors in order to use the land for speculation and fur trading. The Ohio Company, made up of Virginia planters, was organized by Thomas Lee on the basis of a land grant of 500,000 acres between the Ohio and Mississippi Rivers.

OHIO COMPANY (1786). New England land stock company organized by Benjamin Tupper, Rufus Putnam and MANASSEH CUTLER for the purpose of buying U. S. government land and establishing western settlements in the Ohio Valley. One of the first settlements founded by the Company was at Marietta, Ohio (1788).

OHIO IDEA. See GREENBACKS

OKINAWA, BATTLE OF (1945). One of the last and bloodiest battles between U. S. and Japanese forces in the Pacific area during WORLD WAR II (1941-45). After severe fighting the U. S. forces captured the island, which was then used as an air base to bomb the Japanese home cities only 400 miles away.

OLD COLONIAL POLICY. British policy toward her American colonies before 1763 under which restrictive trade, navigation and manufacturing acts (See IRON ACT, HAT ACT, MOLASSES ACT) were passed but little effort was made to enforce them. This policy was also known as "salutary neglect."

OLD HICKORY. See JACKSON, ANDREW

"OLD IRONSIDES." Nickname of the U. S. frigate *Constitution,* so named because of its many brilliant naval victories during the WAR OF 1812 (1812-14). (See "CONSTITUTION" AND "GUERRIERE") After the war it was saved from being scrapped by public sentiment aroused by a poem written by Oliver Wendell Holmes. By special acts of Congress, the ship was rebuilt many times and is still in existence today.

"OLD ROUGH AND READY." See TAYLOR, ZACHARY

OLIVE BRANCH PETITION (1775). Document written by JOHN DICKINSON, adopted by the SECOND CONTINENTAL CONGRESS and sent to King George III of England. The petition asked the king for a cessation of British military action against the colonies and a peaceful settlement of the differences between England and the colonies. The petition was disregarded by the British government.

OLNEY, RICHARD (1835-1917). Held two posts in President GROVER CLEVELAND's cabinet. As Attorney General (1893-95), Olney obtained the court INJUNCTION in the PULLMAN STRIKE (1894) which broke the strike and resulted in the imprisonment of EUGENE V. DEBS for contempt. As Secretary of State (1895-97), Olney announced, during the VENEZUELA BOUNDARY DISPUTE (1897) with Great Britain, that "the U. S. is practically sovereign on this continent and its fiat is law upon the subjects to which it confines its interposition."

OMAHA PLATFORM (1892). Platform of the POPULIST PARTY, drawn up at the party convention in 1892 in Omaha, Nebraska. The platform included a demand for free and unlimited coinage of silver and gold at a ratio of 16 to 1 (see BIMETALLISM), a graduated income tax, postal savings banks, direct election of senators, government ownership of telegraph, telephone and railroad lines, secret ballot, initiative and referendum, eight-hour day for government employees, immigration restrictions to bar undesirables and a single term for presidents.

"ONE-THIRD OF A NATION." Phrase used by President FRANKLIN D. ROOSEVELT in his second inaugural address (1937). In projecting his future goals for the nation Roosevelt indicated his aim of improving the standard of living of "one-third of a nation ill housed, ill clad, ill nourished."

OPEN DOOR POLICY (1899). Proposed by U. S. Secretary of State JOHN HAY. Under this policy, all nations would have equal trading rights and business opportunities in China except in those areas which had already been established as spheres of influence. In 1900 Hay announced that the great powers had approved the policy. However, subsequent events in China indicated that the policy was not followed in practice by Japan or the nations of Europe. In 1922 the Nine Power Pact, signed at the WASHINGTON DISARMAMENT CONFERENCE, reaffirmed the Open Door Policy.

OPENING OF JAPAN. See PERRY, MATTHEW C.

OPEN RANGE. During the mid-19th century era, when the Western plains were unfenced, huge herds of cattle freely roamed the open range. In the spring the cattle were rounded up, branded and taken on the LONG DRIVE to a railroad cowtown for shipment to the East. The construction of Western railroads, the introduction of BARBED WIRE fences and the dangers of contagious cattle diseases put an end to the open range in the last decade of the 19th century.

ORANGE, FORT. Dutch colonial settlement on the Hudson River at a point where the present city of Albany is located.

It was established by the DUTCH WEST INDIA COM-
PANY soon after the settlement of NEW AMSTERDAM.

ORDINANCE OF NULLIFICATION. See NULLIFICA-
TION PROCLAMATION

ORDINANCE OF SECESSION (1860). Passed by a special
convention in SOUTH CAROLINA after the victory of
ABRAHAM LINCOLN in the presidential ELECTION OF
1860. The ordinance announced the secession of South
Carolina from the Union. By the time Lincoln was inaugurated as president on March 4, 1861, six more Southern states had followed the lead of South Carolina and
had announced their secession.

OREGON TERRITORY. Early in the 19th century, Russia,
Spain, Great Britain and the U. S. claimed the territory.
In 1819 Spain, and in 1824 Russia, gave up their claims
by treaties. The U. S. claimed the Oregon region because of
the discovery of the Columbia River by Captain ROBERT
GRAY (1792), the explorations of the LEWIS AND
CLARK EXPEDITION (1804-06), and fur trading posts
established by JOHN JACOB ASTOR in 1811. Great Britain claimed the territory because of the voyages of Captain
James Cook (1778), Captain George Vancouver (1792)
and British fur trading posts established there. In 1818
Great Britain and the U. S. signed a treaty (TREATY OF
1818) providing for joint occupation of Oregon for ten
years. The treaty was extended indefinitely. In 1846, however, the U. S. and Great Britain signed the OREGON
TREATY, which divided the territory between the two
countries at the 49th parallel of latitude. This line extended
the boundary between the U. S. and Canada established
under the Treaty of 1818 along the same line of latitude.

OREGON TRAIL. One of the major routes used by American
pioneers in the early 19th century to reach the Far West.
The Oregon Trail started at Independence, Missouri and led
west across the Rocky Mountains, then northwest to the
OREGON TERRITORY.

OREGON TREATY (1846). Under the TREATY OF 1818
the Oregon region had been jointly occupied for ten years.
This treaty was extended indefinitely. In the ELECTION

270

OF 1844 American EXPANSIONISTS, using the slogan "Fifty-four forty or fight" called for the annexation of the entire Oregon territory. In 1846, however, Great Britain and the U. S. agreed to divide the territory approximately in half by establishing the 49th parallel as the boundary between the U. S. and Canada. Territory north of the line went to Great Britain, south of the line to the U. S. Great Britain kept all of Vancouver Island in Puget Sound, as well as the right to use the Columbia River.

ORGANIZATION OF AMERICAN STATES (O.A.S.) See PAN AMERICAN CONFERENCES and PAN AMERICAN UNION

ORISKANY, BATTLE OF (1777). Important military engagement during the AMERICAN REVOLUTION (1775-83). It was fought in central New York State between an American force led by General Nicholas Herkimer and a British Army moving down from Canada, led by General Barry St. Leger. As a result of the Battle of Oriskany the British were forced to retreat to Canada. The failure of St. Leger to join General JOHN BURGOYNE indirectly led to Burgoyne's defeat at the BATTLE OF SARATOGA (1777)

OSAGE INDIANS. Tribe that lived in the plains region of Oklahoma Territory. They resisted the advance of Western settlers in the late 19th century but were finally forced to move to government reservations.

OSTEND MANIFESTO (1854). Because of pressure of southern EXPANSIONISTS to make the Spanish-owned island of Cuba a Southern state, a movement began in 1854 (after the "BLACK WARRIOR" INCIDENT) to acquire Cuba from Spain. The U. S. ministers to Spain (Pierre Soule), France (John Y. Mason) and Great Britain (JAMES BUCHANAN) met in Ostend, Belgium and drew up a document later known as the Ostend Manifesto. In this document they stated that Spain should sell Cuba to the U. S. and, if she refused, the U. S. would be justified in seizing it by force. WILLIAM L. MARCY, Secretary of State, refused to adopt the manifesto as official U. S. policy and it was dropped.

OTIS, JAMES (1725-83). American colonial lawyer who gained widespread fame in the colonies by his speeches and writings opposing the use of WRITS OF ASSISTANCE. He based his objections on the natural right of all Englishmen that a man's house cannot be searched without just and specific cause.

"OUR COUNTRY, RIGHT OR WRONG." See DECATUR, STEPHEN

"OUR FEDERAL UNION: IT MUST BE PRESERVED" (1830). During 1830 Congress was stirred by the WEBSTER-HAYNE DEBATE on states rights versus the supremacy of the federal government. During a Democratic Party dinner in Washington D. C. President ANDREW JACKSON proposed the toast, "Our federal Union: It must be preserved." To this, Vice-president JOHN C. CALHOUN replied, "The Union, next to our liberty, most dear."

"OUTLAW WAR AS AN INSTRUMENT OF NATIONAL POLICY." See KELLOGG-BRIAND PACT (1928)

OWEN, ROBERT (1771-1858). See NEW HARMONY

PACKETS. Sailing vessels carrying freight and passengers, used in the early 19th century to cross the Atlantic Ocean on regular sailing schedules. Packet boats made the ocean crossing in about 30 days. Eventually they were driven out of business by the development of the steamship. (See MERCHANT MARINE)

PACT OF PARIS. See KELLOGG-BRIAND PACT (1928)

PAINE, THOMAS (1737-1809). Author of *Common Sense* (1776), a pamphlet that urged the colonists to assert their independence. It was widely read and paved the way for the DECLARATION OF INDEPENDENCE (1776). During the AMERICAN REVOLUTION (1775-83), Paine wrote a series of pamphlets called *The Crisis* to encourage loyalty to and support of the CONTINENTAL ARMY during the darkest days of the Revolution. After the Revolution, Paine returned to Europe, where he wrote *The Rights of Man* (1791-2) and *The Age of Reason* (1794-5), both of which caused considerable controversy.

PALATINES. Name of Protestants in the Palatine district of Germany who fled to England (1709) because of religious persecution. The German Palatines were given permission by the British government to settle in the Hudson valley of the New York Colony (1710). From there the Palatines migrated to the Mohawk Valley of central New York and to southeast Pennsylvania. Another group of Palatines settled in North Carolina.

PALO ALTO, BATTLE OF (1846). One of the early military engagements of the MEXICAN WAR (1846-48). General ZACHARY TAYLOR, commander of the U. S. forces, inflicted a serious defeat on a Mexican Army near Palo Alto, Texas and forced the Mexicans to retreat south toward the border of Mexico.

PANAMA CANAL. As early as 1878 a French organization called the Panama Canal Company started to build a canal across the Isthmus of Panama, but failed. The U. S. obtained the right, by a series of treaties, to build the canal. (See HAY-PAUNCEFOTE TREATY, 1901; HAY BUNAU-VARILLA TREATY, 1903) U. S. construction of the canal began in 1904 and was completed in 1914 under the direction of Colonel George W. Goethals. Dr. WILLIAM C. GORGAS contributed to the successful completion of the canal by his work in controlling yellow fever in the Canal Zone.

PANAMA REVOLUTION (1903). After Colombia rejected the HAY-HERRAN TREATY (1903), giving the U. S. the right to build a canal across Panama, the people of Panama started a revolution against Colombia. The U. S. sent a warship to Panama to insure free transportation across the Isthmus and indirectly to insure the success of the revolution. Other American warships were also sent to Panama by President THEODORE ROOSEVELT. The U. S. immediately recognized the independence of Panama and signed a treaty (HAY BUNAU-VARILLA TREATY, 1903) giving the U. S. the right to build the canal.

PAN AMERICAN CONFERENCES. Originally suggested by SIMÓN BOLÍVAR in 1826. However, the first conference was called at the suggestion of JAMES G. BLAINE, U. S. Secretary of State, and was held in Washington D. C. in 1889. At this conference the PAN AMERICAN UNION (1890) was organized. Subsequent Pan American Conferences have been held at irregular intervals in the capitals of Latin American countries, including Havana, Santiago, Montevideo, Lima and others. The most important conferences were the Montevideo Conference (1933) at which the U. S. announced and clarified its GOOD NEIGHBOR POLICY, the Lima Conference (1938), at which a collective security agreement was signed (Declaration of Lima), the Mexico City Conference (1945), at which a mutual defense agreement was signed (ACT OF CHAPULTEPEC), the Rio Conference (1947), where the RIO PACT for the defense of the Western Hemisphere was signed, and the Bogota Conference (1948), where the Organization of American States (O.A.S.) was formed.

274

PAN AMERICAN UNION. Organization of all nations of Latin America and the U. S., established in 1890 at the First Pan American Conference. (See PAN AMERICAN CONFERENCES) Its purpose was to collect and distribute information about economic, social, cultural and political life of the member nations and thereby create mutual trust and understanding. After the Organization of American States (O.A.S.) was established (1948), the Pan American Union became its general secretariat. The permanent headquarters of the Pan American Union are in Washington D. C.

PANIC OF 1819. Occurred during the presidency of JAMES MONROE. American industries were expanding rapidly. Great Britain began dumping her manufactured goods in U. S. markets at very low prices. "Wildcat" state banks and the Second BANK OF U. S. were pursuing liberal lending policies that encouraged speculation in Western lands. The panic was followed by five years of depressed business conditions, unemployment and low prices.

PANIC OF 1837. Occurred during the presidency of MARTIN VAN BUREN. It was brought on by former President Jackson's SPECIE CIRCULAR (1836); widespread speculation in Western lands, encouraged by so-called "wildcat banks"; a sudden drop in land values; the issue of paper currency by state banks, called "pet banks"; the failure of many of these banks; a severe crop shortage and lack of bank credit. The panic and the depression that followed threw thousands of workers out of jobs and caused widespread hunger and suffering.

PANIC OF 1857. Mainly a financial panic touched off by the bankruptcy of the New York branch of the Ohio Life Insurance and Trust Co. Speculation in railroad stocks and real estate contributed to the panic. The business depression that followed lasted for about two years.

PANIC OF 1873. Occurred during the presidency of ULYSSES S. GRANT. The panic began with the sudden bankruptcy of JAY COOKE and Co. and was followed by the bankruptcy of other banks and corporations. Basically, however, the panic and the six years of depression that followed were caused by agricultural overproduction, industrial over-production, overexpansion of railroad construction and stock market speculation.

PANIC OF 1893. Occurred during President GROVER CLEVELAND'S second term (1893-97). Gold reserves in the U. S. Treasury were falling because of silver purchases made by the government under the SHERMAN SILVER PURCHASE ACT (1890). The bankruptcy of the banking firm named Baring Brothers in England led British stock-holders to sell their American securities, thus draining more gold out of the U. S. All of these factors led to the stock market panic, the bankruptcy of many business firms and the spread of large-scale unemployment in cities. In the farming regions, depressed economic conditions had begun as early as 1887 and became worse after 1893. Basically the panic and the four years of depression that followed were caused by overexpansion of railroad construction, the high rates of the MC KINLEY TARIFF ACT (1890), stock market speculation, and the uncertainty over the free silver (see BIMETALLISM) controversy.

PANIC OF 1907. Sometimes known as the "Rich Man's Panic." It was a brief financial crisis that started with the bankruptcy of the Knickerbocker Trust Co. and a number of other New York banks during President Theodore Roosevelt's administration (1901-09). The panic was at-tributed to stock market speculation, overexpansion of in-dustry and a defective national banking system. The brief panic mainly affected speculators and large investors.

PANIC OF 1929. Most serious financial panic in our history. It ushered in the era of the GREAT DEPRESSION (1929-35), which affected not only the U. S. but the entire world. It began in the U. S. with a stock market crash in October, 1929. Basically, however, the panic was due to excessive stock market speculation, industrial and agricultural over-production, overexpansion of credit and technological un-employment caused by the increased use of machinery in industry.

PAPAL LINE OF DEMARCATION (1493). Imaginary line drawn 100 leagues (about 300 miles) west of Cape Verde Islands by Pope Alexander VI. Portugal was given the right to claim all new land east of the line, and Spain all new land west of the line. In 1494, by the Treaty of Tordesillas, the line was moved to 370 leagues (about 1100 miles) west of Cape Verde Islands, thus giving Portugal the bulge of the South American continent now known as Brazil.

PAPER BLOCKADE. A blockade of a nation's ports that is announced by another nation but is not enforced. During the Napoleonic Wars (1803-15) between Great Britain and France, Napoleon announced a "paper" blockade of Great Britain by the BERLIN AND MILAN DECREES (1806-07).

PARIS PEACE CONFERENCE (1919). Held by the Allied powers at the end of World War I, the conference was dominated by the "Big Four" powers—the U. S., represented by President WOODROW WILSON; Great Britain, by Lloyd George; France by Clemenceau and Italy by Orlando. After much negotiation the conference completed the TREATY OF VERSAILLES, officially ending the war with Germany. One section of the treaty contained the COVENANT OF THE LEAGUE OF NATIONS. Because ratification of the treaty also included membership in the League of Nations, the U. S. Senate rejected it.

PARIS, TREATY OF (1763). Series of agreements signed by Great Britain, France and Spain at the end of the FRENCH AND INDIAN WAR (1754-63). Because the French had been defeated, they were forced to cede Canada as well as all land east of the Mississippi River to Great Britain. Since Spain had entered the war on the side of France, she was forced to cede FLORIDA to Great Britain. The city of New Orleans and French territory west of the Mississippi River (LOUISIANA TERRITORY) were ceded to Spain by France. Great Britain, which had seized Cuba and the Philippine Islands during the war, returned them to Spain. In North America, France was stripped of all territory except the two small islands of St. Pierre and Miquelon, near Newfoundland.

PARIS, TREATY OF (1783). Signed at the end of the AMER-ICAN REVOLUTION (1775-83). The treaty provided for complete independence of the THIRTEEN COLONIES, established the Mississippi River as the western boundary,

277

Canada as the northern boundary and Florida as the southern boundary of the new country. The treaty also gave Americans fishing rights off the Grand Banks of Newfoundland and the right to free navigation on the Mississippi River. The U. S. agreed to permit British creditors to collect just debts owed to British merchants before the Revolution and to urge the states to return property seized from the LOYALISTS during the war.

PARIS, TREATY OF (1898). Treaty ending the SPANISH-AMERICAN WAR (1898). By this treaty Spain ceded PUERTO RICO and GUAM to the U. S. In addition, Spain ceded the PHILIPPINE ISLANDS to the U. S. in return for $20,000,000. Spain also recognized the independence of CUBA.

PARSON'S CAUSE (1763). Famous colonial lawsuit in which a clergyman challenged the right of the Virginia HOUSE OF BURGESSES to reduce his salary as established by British law. The basic issue was the right of the English Parliament to set aside a colonial law. The jury awarded the clergyman one penny in damages.

PARTY BOSS. Although the party boss usually does not run for political office, he is a key figure in deciding who is to be nominated by the political party and in directing the election campaign. After an election victory the party boss is expected to distribute government jobs to his party workers as a reward for their efforts during the election. Party bosses were important figures in the politics of the late 19th and early 20th centuries. (See TWEED, WILLIAM M.; PENROSE, BOISE; CONKLING, ROSCOE; PLATT, THOMAS C.; CAMERON, SIMON; LOGAN, JOHN A.; CROKER, RICHARD)

"PARTY PERFIDY AND DISHONOR." See WILSON-GORMAN TARIFF (1894)

PASTORIUS, FRANCIS DANIEL. See MENNONITES

PATRONAGE. See SPOILS SYSTEM

PATRONS OF HUSBANDRY. Organized by Oliver H. Kelley after the War Between the States (1865) as a social and fraternal organization of farmers. Local groups were called granges and members were known as Grangers. By 1875 the Patrons of Husbandry had 750,000 enrolled members. It soon became known as the Granger Movement. Gradually it changed from a social organization to one that tried to improve the economic status of the farmer. Cooperatives were organized to market crops, buy farm equipment and run grain elevators. The Grangers also started a political campaign against high railroad and grain elevator storage rates. They elected members to state legislatures and had state GRANGER LAWS enacted to regulate railroad rates. These laws were declared unconstitutional by the Supreme Court. (See GRANGER CASES) After 1880 the political influence of the Patrons of Husbandry declined.

PATROON SYSTEM. Landholding system introduced in 1629 by the DUTCH WEST INDIA COMPANY in the NEW NETHERLAND colony to encourage settlements. Large grants of land were offered to members of the company who would bring fifty settlers to the colony within four years. The men—called patroons—who received the land grants owned the land, established their own courts, appointed their own local officials and regulated the lives of the people who settled on their land. Vestiges of the system still existed in New York State in the mid-19th century. (See ANTI-RENT WARS)

PAWNEE INDIANS. Warlike tribe originally found in Texas, Kansas and Nebraska. Although they fought with other Indian tribes, they never made war on the U. S. The Pawnees provided many scouts for the U. S. Army and helped the U. S. in its wars with other Indian tribes. (See PLAINS INDIANS)

PAXTON BOYS (1754). Organization of colonial settlers on the frontier of western Pennsylvania, formed to protect the settlements from Indian attacks. However, the Paxton Boys were also responsible for the massacre of peaceful Indians (Conestoga Massacre, 1763). Because the proprietary legislature of Pennsylvania, representing easterners mainly, failed to provide adequate protection for western settlers, the Paxton Boys threatened to march on Philadelphia, the colonial capital. However, the incipient rebellion in western

279

Pennsylvania was settled peacefully, mainly through the efforts of BENJAMIN FRANKLIN.

PAYNE-ALDRICH TARIFF (1909). After President WILLIAM HOWARD TAFT's victory in the ELECTION OF 1908, the Payne-Aldrich Tariff was introduced in Congress to lower tariff rates and increase the number of articles on the free list. However, the Senate added more than 800 amendments to the bill. As finally passed, the Payne-Aldrich Tariff remained highly protective. (See TARIFF LEGISLATION)

PEACE CORPS (1961). Organization suggested by President JOHN F. KENNEDY and established by Congress. It consisted of a group of young Americans who volunteered to work with native people on construction, medical, agricultural, educational and other projects in underdeveloped areas of the world.

"PEACE WITHOUT VICTORY." Before the U. S. was drawn into WORLD WAR I (1917-18) President WOODROW WILSON sought to bring the war in Europe to an end by suggesting that the warring nations agree to a "peace without victory" for either side (1917). The suggestion did not stop the fighting.

PEARL HARBOR ATTACK (1941). On December 7, 1941 Pearl Harbor, a major U. S. naval and air base in the HAWAIIAN ISLANDS, was attacked without warning by Japanese bombing planes. A large number of American warships and planes were destroyed and more than 3,000 lives were lost. President FRANKLIN D. ROOSEVELT called it "the day which will live in infamy." On the following day Congress declared war on Japan, marking the entry of the U. S. into WORLD WAR II (1941-45).

PENDLETON ACT (1883). Passed by Congress during President CHESTER A. ARTHUR's administration in reaction to the ASSASSINATION of former president JAMES A. GARFIELD two years earlier. The act established a Civil Service Commission which was to conduct competitive examinations for certain "classified" federal jobs. Appointments to jobs were to be made by the commission from eligible lists of successful candidates on the examinations.

The president was given power to extend the list of "classified" federal jobs.

PENINSULAR CAMPAIGN (1862). Campaign during the WAR BETWEEN THE STATES (1861-65) to capture Richmond, Virginia, the capital of the CONFEDERATE STATES. General GEORGE B. MC CLELLAN, commander of the Union Army, landed his forces in Virginia on the peninsula between the York and James Rivers and slowly moved toward Richmond. He was met by the Confederate Armies under General ROBERT E. LEE and General THOMAS J. "STONEWALL" JACKSON and the Union Army was forced to retreat.

PENNSYLVANIA CANAL. Early 19th century canal, completed in 1834. It was built to connect Philadelphia with Pittsburgh in the west. Loaded canal boats were hauled over the mountains by a railway along the route of the canal.

PENNSYLVANIA COLONY. Established by WILLIAM PENN in 1682 as a refuge for QUAKERS and as a business venture. It was known as Penn's "holy experiment" because it admitted all people who believed in one almighty God, and made it possible for settlers to buy land cheaply. It also attracted SCOTCH-IRISH Presbyterians and many Protestants from the German principalities. (See PALATINES)

PENNSYLVANIA DUTCH. See MENNONITES

PENN, WILLIAM (1644-1718). One of the leaders of a Protestant sect in England called QUAKERS. In 1681 Penn obtained a grant of land in the New World from King Charles II for the purpose of establishing a colony for Quakers and a profitable business enterprise at the same time. Penn established the PENNSYLVANIA COLONY and was its proprietor or governor.

PENROSE, BOISE (1860-1921). Republican political PARTY BOSS in Pennsylvania. He was elected to the U. S. Senate in 1896 and served until 1921. He was an important leader in many of the Republican Party national conventions and had an important voice in the choice of party candidates for election.

281

PEQUOT INDIANS. Indian tribe that lived in Massachusetts, Connecticut and eastern Long Island. Because of a number of Pequot raids on early settlements, a Pequot War (1636-37) was waged against them by a force of settlers from Massachusetts and Connecticut, as well as by other Indian tribes friendly to the settlers. As a result of the war practically the entire Pequot tribe was wiped out.

PEQUOT WAR. See PEQUOT INDIANS and INDIAN WARS

PERRY, COMMODORE MATTHEW C. (1794-1858). Commander of an American fleet that made an uninvited visit (1853) to Japan for the purpose of negotiating a trade treaty. By a discreet show of force, Perry convinced the Japanese that a trade treaty would be to their advantage. The Treaty of Kanagawa (1854) provided for the opening of two Japanese ports to American merchants ships, the acceptance of an American consul (see TOWNSEND HARRIS) and the protection of seamen shipwrecked in Japanese waters.

PERRY, CAPTAIN OLIVER HAZARD (1785-1819). U. S. naval officer during the WAR OF 1812 (1812-14). He launched a small American fleet of ships on Lake Erie and defeated a British squadron in the brilliant Battle of Lake Erie (1813). His famous report of victory to General WILLIAM HENRY HARRISON read, "We have met the enemy and they are ours."

PERSHING, JOHN J. (1860-1948). Nicknamed "Blackjack" Pershing. He fought in the SIOUX INDIAN WAR (1890-91), the SPANISH-AMERICAN WAR (1898) and the Philippine Insurrection (1899-1903). In 1916 he was put in charge of the American expedition to Mexico to capture the bandit PANCHO VILLA (1916). During WORLD WAR I (1917-18) Pershing was supreme commander of the AMERICAN EXPEDITIONARY FORCES in Europe. His reputation as a military organizer was justified by his successful molding of an American Army of more than 1,000,000 men into an efficient fighting machine in one year.

PERSONAL LIBERTY LAWS. State laws passed in the 1840's and 1850's by Northern state legislatures to make it difficult for Southerners to recapture runaway slaves. The personal liberty laws were the North's answer to the federal FUGITIVE SLAVE LAWS of 1793 and 1850.

PET BANKS. See PANIC OF 1837

PETERSBURG, BATTLE OF (1864). One of the major military engagements of the WAR BETWEEN THE STATES (1861-65). General ULYSSES S. GRANT, leading the Union forces, planned to capture Petersburg, 20 miles south of Richmond, and thus cut off the Confederate capital. However, the attempt to capture Petersburg failed, despite heavy loss of life. General Grant's army continued to besiege Petersburg and Richmond until April, 1865 when General ROBERT E. LEE and the Confederate Army evacuated both cities in an effort to move south. A few days later General Lee surrendered at APPOMATTOX COURT-HOUSE (1865), bringing the war to an end.

PHILIPPINE GOVERNMENT ACT (1902). Also called the Organic Act of 1902. This law gave the Filipinos the right to elect an assembly which was to cooperate with the Philippine Governing Commission in passing laws for the islands. This law was changed by the JONES ACT OF 1916.

PHILIPPINE INDEPENDENCE ACT (1933). See PHILIPPINE ISLANDS

PHILIPPINE ISLANDS. Acquired by the U. S. after the SPANISH-AMERICAN WAR (1898) by the TREATY OF PARIS (1898). In 1899 a revolt against U. S. rule, led by Emilio Aguinaldo, broke out and was not quelled until 1902. A form of government was set up for the islands in 1901 under the Spooner Amendment. WILLIAM HOWARD TAFT was appointed first U. S. governor of the islands. By subsequent Congressional legislation (see PHILIPPINE GOVERNMENT ACT, 1902; JONES ACT, 1916) the Filipinos were given more self-government. In 1933 Congress offered the Filipinos their independence under the Philippine Independence Act (1933) but it was rejected by the islanders. In 1934 Congress again offered them independence after a ten-year probation period under the TYDINGS-MC DUFFIE ACT. This was accepted by

283

the Filipinos, but the Japanese invasion of the islands during WORLD WAR II (1941-45) delayed the announcement of independence. In 1946 the Philippine Islands finally proclaimed their independence.

PHILIPPINE SEA, BATTLE OF (1944). One of the major sea and air battles of WORLD WAR II (1941-45), fought in the Pacific between U. S. and Japanese naval and air forces. The Japanese suffered a serious naval defeat, losing three aircraft carriers and hundreds of planes. The battle was a preparation for the subsequent invasion of the Philippine Islands four months later. (See LEYTE GULF, BATTLE OF)

PICKETT'S CHARGE. One of the historic incidents in the BATTLE OF GETTYSBURG (1863) during the WAR BETWEEN THE STATES (1861-65). General George E. Pickett, one of the Confederate commanders, was ordered to make a frontal charge on the Union forces on Cemetery Ridge. Thousands of Confederates were killed in the charge but the Southern forces were forced to fall back. On the following day the Confederate Army began its retreat to Virginia.

PIERCE, FRANKLIN (1804-69). Fourteenth president of the U. S. in 1852 a deadlock of DEMOCRATIC PARTY leaders over the choice of presidential candidate led to the nomination of Pierce as a "dark horse." In the ELECTION OF 1852 he won an overwhelming victory over WINFIELD SCOTT, the WHIG PARTY candidate. Pierce was not renominated by his party in the ELECTION OF 1856. During Pierce's term of office, the GADSDEN PURCHASE (1853) was arranged with Mexico, COMMODORE MATTHEW PERRY negotiated a trade treaty with Japan (Treaty of Kanagawa, 1854), the KANSAS-NEBRASKA ACT (1854) was passed by Congress, and civil strife broke out in Kansas over the slavery issue. (See BLEEDING KANSAS)

"PIKE'S PEAK OR BUST." Slogan of many western migrants heading for Colorado in 1859 when gold and silver strikes were reported in the nearby mountains. (See COMSTOCK LODE; GOLD RUSH)

PIKE, ZEBULON (1779-1813). Led two important exploring expeditions in the West. From 1805 to 1806 he explored the headwaters of the Mississippi River. On his second expedition (1806-07) he followed the Arkansas River to the Rocky Mountains, found the Colorado peak that is now named after him (Pike's Peak) and then began to move south, following the Red and Rio Grande Rivers into Spanish territory.

PILGRIMS. Protestant separatists living in Scrooby, England, who were persecuted for their religious beliefs. In 1608 they moved to Holland and then set out to establish a settlement in the New World. However, their ship, the Speedwell, proved to be unseaworthy. It was left at Plymouth, England, and the Pilgrims boarded another ship, the "MAYFLOWER," which sailed for the New World and reached Cape Cod in 1620.

PINCHOT, GIFFORD (1865-1946). Leader in the movement for forest conservation in the early decades of the 20th century. During President THEODORE ROOSEVELT's administration (1901-09), Pinchot was appointed chairman of the National Conservation Commission and head of the newly created National Forestry Service. Through Pinchot's efforts almost 150,000,000 acres of public land were removed from sale and set aside for conservation purposes. After WILLIAM HOWARD TAFT became president (1909-13), Pinchot became involved in a controversy with Richard A. Ballinger, the Secretary of the Interior. (See BALLINGER-PINCHOT CONTROVERSY)

PINCKNEY, CHARLES COTESWORTH (1746-1825). American political leader in the late 18th and early 19th centuries. He was a delegate from South Carolina at the CONSTITUTIONAL CONVENTION (1787), was appointed minister to France (1796) and, together with ELBRIDGE GERRY and JOHN MARSHALL, was involved in the XYZ AFFAIR (1797). He was the candidate of the FEDERALIST PARTY for vice-president in the ELECTION OF 1800 and for president in the ELECTIONS OF 1804 and 1808. On all three occasions he was defeated. Charles Cotesworth Pinckney and THOMAS PINCKNEY were brothers.

285

PINCKNEY, THOMAS (1750-1828). American political leader in the late 18th and early 19th century. He negotiated the PINCKNEY TREATY (1795), giving Americans free navigation rights on the Mississippi River. In the ELECTION OF 1796 he was the FEDERALIST PARTY candidate for vice-president but was defeated for the office by THOMAS JEFFERSON.

PINCKNEY TREATY (1795). Concluded with Spain fixing the boundary between the U. S. and West Florida. (See WEST FLORIDA DISPUTE) The treaty, negotiated by THOMAS PINCKNEY, also gave Americans the right to navigate the entire length of the Mississippi River to its mouth and to use the Spanish-owned port of New Orleans as a free shipping point for American exports. The treaty provided frontiersmen with a water outlet for their products.

PINE TREE FLAG. One of many flags used by colonists in New England during the early years of the AMERICAN REVOLUTION (1775-83).

PINKERTON DETECTIVES. Private detective agency organized by Allan Pinkerton (1819-84), which became famous for solving many train robberies, foiling an attempted assassination of Lincoln just before his inauguration (1861) and spying on the Confederacy during the WAR BETWEEN THE STATES (1861-65). Pinkerton detectives succeeded in gathering evidence that eventually resulted in the break-up of the MOLLY MAGUIRES. The Pinkerton Agency, which specialized in labor disputes and the planting of labor spies in unions, was also involved in the HOMESTEAD STRIKE (1892).

PITCHER, MOLLY (c.1754-1832). During the BATTLE OF MONMOUTH (1778) she carried water for her husband and other soldiers. The legend that she manned her husband's gun when he was wounded is probably untrue. Her real name was Mary Ludwig Hays.

PITTSBURGH OF THE SOUTH. Name applied to the city of Birmingham, Alabama because of the immense iron and steel industry that developed there in the late 19th and 20th centuries. (See NEW SOUTH and NEW INDUSTRIAL REVOLUTION)

PIZARRO, FRANCISCO (c.1470-1541). One of the great Spanish conquistadores of the era of exploration. Pizarro landed in Peru in 1531 with a small expedition and succeeded in conquering the INCA Indians (1532) and making the region a part of the Spanish Empire in the New World.

PLAINS INDIANS. Indian tribes such as the Arapahos, Shawnees, Cheyennes, Pawnees and others that lived on the treeless plains of the West during the 19th century. The Plains Indian used buffalo meat for food and buffalo hides for clothing, tents and tools. By the year 1890 American pioneers, trappers and buffalo hunters had killed off most of the buffalo (see CODY, WILLIAM, F.), thus dooming the traditional life of the Plains Indians.

PLANTATION SYSTEM. Agricultural system, based on the use of slave labor, that dominated the life of the South from colonial days to the WAR BETWEEN THE STATES (1861). Plantations were practically self-sufficient economic units where slaves performed all necessary tasks and raised their own food. In colonial times, plantation owners raised tobacco, rice and indigo for export. In the early 19th century cotton became the most valuable crop. Its importance to the Southern economy was expressed in the phrase "KING COTTON."

PLATT AMENDMENT (1901). Passed by Congress after the SPANISH-AMERICAN WAR (1898). The amendment provided that CUBA could not make any treaty impairing its independence and could not borrow money unless it could be repaid out of regular tax revenue. Cuba was to lease or sell naval and coaling stations to the U. S. We reserved the right to intervene in Cuba to protect its independence against internal disorders or foreign intervention. The Platt Amendment remained in force until 1934, when the U. S. ended it as part of our GOOD NEIGHBOR POLICY.

PLATT, THOMAS C. (1833-1910). One of the important PARTY BOSSES in the REPUBLICAN PARTY in the late 19th and early 20th century. In 1881 he was elected to the U. S. Senate, but, following the resignation of Senator ROSCOE CONKLING, Platt also resigned because of a quarrel with President JAMES A. GARFIELD over federal patronage. Because he followed the lead of Conkling,

287

Platt became known as "Me too Platt." In 1897 Platt was re-elected to the Senate and served until 1909. He supported THEODORE ROOSEVELT for governor of New York State in 1898 and for vice-president in the ELECTION OF 1900.

PLESSY V. FERGUSON. See SEGREGATION

PLYMOUTH COLONY (1620). First settlement made by 102 Pilgrims after reaching the Massachusetts coast on the "MAYFLOWER." Their settlement was made on the basis of a charter granted to the Council of New England (see PLYMOUTH COMPANY). Before landing the Pilgrims drew up the MAYFLOWER COMPACT. During the first winter about half of the colonists died of disease and exposure. In 1691 the Plymouth colony merged with the MASSACHUSETTS BAY COLONY.

PLYMOUTH COMPANY (1606). Private stock company organized in England and chartered by King James I for the purpose of establishing a settlement in the New World. After making a number of unsuccessful attempts to establish a colony, the company was reorganized as the Council of New England (1620) and received a new royal charter. Under this new royal grant the company established the PLYMOUTH COLONY (1620).

POINT FOUR PROGRAM. See FOREIGN AID PROGRAM

POLICE POWERS. The power of a state government to make laws protecting the health, morals and general welfare of the people. Such laws include the regulation of crimes and nuisances. The police powers of a state to regulate industrial abuses (long hours, low wages) have frequently come into conflict with the Constitutional provision that a state may not deprive a person of life, liberty or property without DUE PROCESS OF LAW.

POLK, JAMES K. (1795-1849). Eleventh president of the U. S. At the DEMOCRATIC PARTY convention in 1844 the deadlocked delegates finally nominated Polk, a DARK HORSE, as a compromise candidate. Polk was elected. (See ELECTION OF 1844) During his single term in office the OREGON TREATY (1846) was signed with Great Britain, the INDEPENDENT TREASURY SYSTEM (1846) was established, the WALKER TARIFF (1846), lowering rates, was passed, and the MEXICAN WAR (1846-1848) was successfully concluded.

POLLOCK V. FARMERS' LOAN AND TRUST CO. See INCOME TAX

POLL TAX. Tax established in the South after the WAR BETWEEN THE STATES (1865) requiring a money payment for the privilege of voting. The original purpose of the poll tax was not to raise revenue but to bar impoverished Negroes from voting. Some Southern states continue to impose a poll tax even today.

POLO, MARCO (c.1254-c.1324). Venetian adventurer who traveled from Europe to the Far East and spent 17 years in the service of Kubla Khan, the great Eastern ruler. On his return to Europe in 1295, Marco Polo wrote a book in which he described the magnificent places he had visited and the people he had seen. His fascinating story stirred the interest of Europeans in seeking new trade routes to the "fabulous" East.

PONTIAC (d.1769). Leader of the Ottawa Indians in colonial times. After the end of the FRENCH AND INDIAN WAR (1754-63), Pontiac led an Indian uprising against the British and against American colonial settlements along the frontier. This was known as the Conspiracy of Pontiac (1763-66). For three years frontier settlers lived in a constant state of fear. In 1766 the war came to an end, when Pontiac signed a peace treaty, and he was pardoned by the British.

PONY EXPRESS (1860-62). Private express company that carried mail by a system of pony-mounted relay messengers through the West to the Pacific coast. The line began at St. Joseph, Missouri and extended for almost 2,000 miles through dangerous Indian country to Sacramento, California. A letter took about eight days to reach its destination. The line was organized in 1860 and went out of business in 1862 when the first transcontinental telegraph line was completed.

POPE, GENERAL JOHN (1822-92). See BULL RUN, BATTLE OF

POPULAR SOVEREIGNTY. See KANSAS-NEBRASKA ACT (1854) and BLEEDING KANSAS

POPULATION: GROWTH OF U. S. At the time of the AMERICAN REVOLUTION (1775-83) the U. S. population was about 3,000,000. During the 19th century population grew rapidly because of the high birth rate and the large number of immigrants. (See IMMIGRATION) Since 1920 the population has continued to increase but the rate of increase has slowed down. By the census of 1960 the U. S. population was approximately 180,000,000.

POPULIST PARTY. Also called "People's Party." It was organized in 1891. Its membership included Western and Southern farmers, Western silver mine interests and people who favored currency inflation. The party held its first national convention in Omaha, Nebraska in 1892, where it wrote its official OMAHA PLATFORM. The party nominated JAMES B. WEAVER for the presidency and in the ELECTION OF 1892 he received more than 1,000,000 votes. In the Congressional election of 1894 the Populists increased their strength. In the ELECTION OF 1896 the Populists merged with the DEMOCRATIC PARTY, the latter taking over the major planks of the Populist platform, including the free coinage of silver. (See BIMETALLISM) After the defeat of WILLIAM JEN-NINGS BRYAN, the Populist Party and Democratic Party candidate, in 1896, the Populists gradually disappeared.

POTSDAM AGREEMENT (1945). Memorandum signed by President HARRY S. TRUMAN, British Prime Minister Clement Atlee and Josef Stalin of the Soviet Union in Potsdam, Germany, two months after the surrender of Germany in WORLD WAR II (1941-45). At this conference the four nations agreed on the joint occupation of Germany and the city of Berlin, the trial of German Nazi leaders as war criminals and the establishment of a Council of Foreign Ministers to draw up a peace treaty with the defeated nations.

POTTAWATOMIE MASSACRE (1856). Occurred in the Kansas Territory when five pro-slavery men were murdered at Pottawatomie Creek by JOHN BROWN and his band of ABOLITIONISTS. The incident intensified the rivalry of pro- and anti-slavery settlers in Kansas and led to further bloodshed. (See BLEEDING KANSAS)

POWDERLY, TERENCE V. (1849-1924). See KNIGHTS OF LABOR

PRAYER BAN IN PUBLIC SCHOOLS (1962). U. S. Supreme Court decision in the case of Engel v. Vitale, holding that daily reading in New York State public schools of a 22-word prayer drafted by the state Board of Regents constituted "an establishment of religion" in violation of AMENDMENT I and AMENDMENT 14 of the U. S. Constitution. The court declared that no agency of government, state or federal, may prepare or direct the use of any prayers in a public school. Such a procedure is a violation of the principle of separation of church and state.

PREEMPTION ACTS. The first Preemption Act, passed in 1830, permitted unauthorized settlers on public Western lands to enter claims for as much as 160 acres upon payment of $1.25 an acre. A second Preemption Act in 1841 gave new settlers the same right to 160 acres of public land at $1.25 per acre. In addition the second act provided land grants of alternate sections (one square mile) of land to railroad and canal companies at $2.50 per acre in order to encourage rail and canal construction. The HOMESTEAD ACT (1862), which simplified the method for acquiring government land, reduced the number of preemptors or "squatters."

PRESIDENTIAL SUCCESSION ACTS. In 1883 Congress passed a Presidential Succession Act which provided that if both the president and vice-president die or become disabled, the members of the cabinet succeed to the presidency in the order in which the cabinet offices were established. This act was amended in 1947. The amendment provides that the Speaker of the House of Representatives and the president pro-tem of the Senate succeed the president and vice-president. Thus the present order of succession to the

291

presidency is vice-president, Speaker of the House, president pro-tem of the Senate, and finally the members of the cabinet.

PRIBILOF ISLANDS. See BERING SEA DISPUTE

PRIMOGENITURE. System of land inheritance prevalent in England and in the early English colonies by which all property of a parent was inherited by his eldest son. By 1800 the right of primogeniture was abolished in almost all states.

PRINCE HENRY THE NAVIGATOR (1394-1460). Son of the royal family of Portugal. In 1416 he founded a naval school which developed into an institution for the training of navigators, geographers and explorers. The school's work aroused renewed interest in ocean navigation. In 1420 the Madeira Islands were rediscovered and the west coast of Africa was explored as far south as the Gulf of Guinea. These explorations paved the way for the voyages of BARTHOLOMEW DIAZ (1486) and VASCO DA GAMA (1498) and for CHRISTOPHER COLUMBUS' historic voyage (1492).

PRIVATEERS. Armed ships, privately owned and comissioned by the government by letters of marque and reprisal to make war on enemy ships. More than 2,000 privateers were commissioned by the U. S. government during the AMERICAN REVOLUTION (1775-83). During the WAR OF 1812, American privateers captured hundreds of British vessels. Privateering was abolished by common agreement of the great powers in 1856 by the Declaration of Paris.

PROCLAMATION OF 1763. Royal order issued by King George III of England establishing the land west of the Allegheny Mountains as an Indian reserve. The proclamation forbad colonial settlers to move west of the mountains and ordered settlers who were already there to leave. The proclamation met with sharp disfavor in the American colonies.

PROCLAMATION OF NEUTRALITY (1793). During the war between Great Britain and France that followed the

French Revolution, President GEORGE WASHINGTON issued a Proclamation of Neutrality stating that the U. S. would not take sides in the European war. (See GENET AFFAIR)

PROCLAMATION OF NEUTRALITY (1914). At the outbreak of WORLD WAR I (1914) in Europe, President WOODROW WILSON issued a Proclamation of Neutrality urging Americans to be neutral in thought as well as in actions.

PROGRESSIVE MOVEMENT (1900-17). The era during which a strong movement developed to impose curbs on big business, provide aid to farmers, and workers, protect consumers, institute changes in government to make it more responsive to popular will, and encourage changes in judicial thinking to protect human as well as property rights. The movement started in the West and was most frequently associated with Senator ROBERT M. LA FOLLETTE of Wisconsin, organizer of the NATIONAL PROGRESSIVE REPUBLICAN LEAGUE. Other leaders included HIRAM JOHNSON of California, A. B. Cummins of Iowa and THEODORE ROOSEVELT. (See PROGRESSIVE PARTY)

PROGRESSIVE PARTY. Used by three separate but politically similar organizations. In the ELECTION OF 1912 the REPUBLICAN PARTY was split by the secession of supporters of THEODORE ROOSEVELT. They united with Senator ROBERT LA FOLLETTE's Progressive Republican League to form a Progressive Party (also called Progressive Republican and BULL MOOSE Party) on a platform calling for woman suffrage, conservation, minimum wage laws, abolition of child labor, direct election of senators, initiative, referendum, recall and other reforms. The party nominated Theodore Roosevelt for president. Although he polled more than 4,000,000 votes, he was not elected.

In the ELECTION OF 1924 a new Progressive Party (also known as the Progressive Socialist Party) was revived by Senator LaFollette on a platform calling for public ownership of means of communication, public control of natural resources, increased inheritance taxes and ratification of a proposed Child Labor Amendment. LaFollette polled almost 5,000,000 votes but was not elected.

293

In the ELECTION OF 1948 a third Progressive Party was organized and nominated Henry A. Wallace for president on a platform calling for repeal of the TAFT-HARTLEY ACT (1947), cooperation with the Soviet Union and restoration of wartime price controls. The party polled about 1,000,000 votes and then disintegrated.

PROHIBITION. The temperance or prohibition movement began in the early 1830's. After 1865 the PROHIBITION PARTY (1869), the Women's Christian Temperance Union (1874) and the Anti-Saloon League (1893) took the lead in advocating prohibition laws. At the outbreak of WORLD WAR I (1917) more than 30 states had their own prohibition laws. The need to conserve grain during World War I gave strong patriotic impetus to the prohibition movement and resulted in the ratification of the Eighteenth Amendment (1919) establishing national prohibition. During the PROHIBITION ERA (1920-33) effective enforcement became almost impossible because of popular disregard of the law. President HERBERT HOOVER termed prohibition a "noble experiment" and opposed repeal. After the ELECTION OF 1932, the victory of President FRANKLIN D. ROOSEVELT led to quick ratification of Amendment 21 (1933) ending national prohibition.

PROHIBITION ERA (1920-33). Also called the "Roaring Twenties." It was the era during which the Prohibition Amendment was in effect. During this time the manufacture, sale and transportation of intoxicating liquor was illegal. Nonetheless the era was one of general violation of the amendment during which bootleggers, speakeasies, rum running and bathtub gin were common. It was also an era of gangsterism, rival gang wars and free spending resulting from general economic prosperity.

PROHIBITION PARTY. Organized in 1869 for the purpose of getting legislation passed to prohibit the manufacture, transportation and sale of intoxicating liquor. The party nominated a presidential candidate in every election since 1872 but never polled a large vote. Prior to 1900 their most colorful leader was Neal Dow, but their largest vote was

294

gained in the ELECTION OF 1892 when John Bidwell, their candidate, won almost 300,000 votes. The adoption of the Prohibition Amendment (1919) weakened the party and the repeal of prohibition (Amendment 21, 1933) weakened it further.

PROPRIETARY COLONIES. English colonies that were governed directly or indirectly by such men as WILLIAM PENN (PENNSYLVANIA COLONY) and Lord Baltimore (MARYLAND COLONY) who had received private land grants from the English monarchs. Proprietors had practically the same powers as royal governors appointed by the king. After the American Revolution most of these colonies became part of the 13 original states. (See also SELF-GOVERNING COLONIES and ROYAL COLONIES)

PROVIDENCE (1636). Settlement established by ROGER WILLIAMS and his followers, based on the principles of religious freedom for all and the separation of church and state. Providence became the nucleus of the RHODE ISLAND COLONY.

PUBLIC LAND ACTS. Public Land Acts passed by Congress from 1796 to 1862 established a land price that varied from $1 to $2 an acre and permitted the purchaser of public land to buy tracts varying from 80 to 320 acres (Harrison Land Act, 1800). A number of Public Land Acts gave squatters title to the lands they had settled without authorization. (See PREEMPTION ACTS) Speculation in Western lands led to the proclamation of the SPECIE CIRCULAR (1836) by President ANDREW JACKSON. The most important land legislation was the HOMESTEAD ACT (1862), which fixed the land policy of the government after the WAR BETWEEN THE STATES (1865). Thereafter, special Public Land Laws (Kincaid Land Act, 1904; Forest Homestead Act, 1906) made minor modifications in the provisions of the Homestead Act of 1862 and provided free Western land to railroad companies for the construction of transcontinental rail lines. (See RAILROAD LAND GRANTS) By the year 1916 the sale of public land had practically come to an end.

PUBLIC WORKS ADMINISTRATION (P.W.A.) 1933. See UNEMPLOYMENT LEGISLATION

PUEBLO INDIANS. Tribe living in what is now Arizona, New Mexico and northern Mexico. They were town dwellers who lived in large community homes made of adobe bricks and stone or carved out of cliffs. Entrance to these community houses, called pueblos, was by means of ladders through a roof or upper story.

PUERTO RICO. By the TREATY OF PARIS (1898) ending the SPANISH-AMERICAN WAR, Spain ceded Puerto Rico to the U. S. Congress passed the FORAKER ACT (1900), establishing the island as an unorganized territory with a legislature, and a governor appointed by the president. In 1917 the JONES ACT gave American citizenship and more self-government to the Puerto Ricans. In 1947 they were granted the right to elect their own governors. There are no tariff or immigration restrictions between Puerto Rico and the U. S. Since the end of WORLD WAR II (1945) thousands of Puerto Ricans have migrated to the U. S. to escape overcrowded conditions, unemployment and low living standards on the island.

PUJO COMMITTEE (1913). A congressional committee headed by Representative Arsene Pujo, for the purpose of investigating the "money trust." This referred to the growing consolidations among private banks and financial institutions and their control of private business financing.

PULASKI, CASIMIR (1748-79). Polish soldier of fortune who came to America during the AMERICAN REVOLUTION (1775-83) to fight for our independence. As brigadier-general he fought at the BATTLE OF BRANDYWINE (1777) and the BATTLE OF GERMANTOWN (1777). He was killed during the American attack on the city of Savannah (1779).

PULITZER, JOSEPH (1847-1911). American newspaper owner and editor. He bought the New York *World* from JAY GOULD in 1883. Pulitzer was a leader in introducing new journalistic ideas, such as crusades against corruption, headlines in big type, cartoons, pictures and sensational crime news. This became known as YELLOW JOURN-ALISM. Prior to and during the SPANISH-AMERICAN WAR (1898) Pulitzer engaged in a circulation war with WILLIAM RANDOLPH HEARST's New York *Journal*. Both newspapers sensationalized the events preceding the war and the war itself. In his will, Pulitzer set up a fund to provide Pulitzer Prizes for the best plays, books, cartoons, news articles and other types of creative writing of each year.

PULLMAN STRIKE (1894). Began as a local strike and eventually became a national issue. When a committee of workers protested a wage cut by the Pullman Company they were discharged. The Pullman strike quickly spread to 23 rail lines affecting 27 states and territories, and violence and destruction of property became widespread. A court injunction was issued ordering the strikers to desist from obstructing the movement of the mails and to cease destruction of railroad property. Over the objections of Governor JOHN P. ALTGELD of Illinois, federal troops were ordered to the strike area by President GROVER CLEVELAND to insure uninterrupted movement of the mail. EUGENE V. DEBS and six other strike leaders were jailed for violation of the court injunction. The intervention of federal troops brought the strike to an end.

PURE FOOD AND DRUG ACT (1906). Required the labeling of all containers to indicate the contents, forbad the manufacture or sale of adulterated or misbranded foods or drugs and prohibited the addition of harmful chemicals to foods. The law was superseded in 1939 by the PURE FOOD, DRUG AND COSMETIC ACT.

PURE FOOD, DRUG AND COSMETIC ACT (1938). Also known as the Wheeler-Lea Act. The new law, superseding the PURE FOOD AND DRUG ACT of 1906, forbad the misbranding of foods, drugs and cosmetics, required the listing of ingredients on labels and prohibited false or misleading advertising. The Food and Drug Administration was to enforce misbranding regulations and the Federal Trade Commission was to enforce the advertising regulations.

297

PURITANS. Seventeenth century English religious sect that wanted to "purify" the Established Church of England of its many rituals. They were leaders in the company (see MASSACHUSETTS BAY COMPANY) that established the MASSACHUSETTS BAY COLONY (1630) as a refuge from religious persecution.

QUAKERS. English Protestant sect founded by George Fox (1624-91). It is also known as the Society of Friends. Because of their unusual religious beliefs and practices they were persecuted in England. The PENNSYLVANIA COLONY was established in part as a New World refuge for Quakers by WILLIAM PENN.

QUARTERING ACT (1765). Passed by the British Parliament as part of Prime Minister GEORGE GRENVILLE's program of stricter law enforcement in the colonies. Under this act the colonists were required to provide British soldiers with living quarters wherever barracks were not available.

QUEBEC. Canadian settlement founded by the French explorer SAMUEL DE CHAMPLAIN in 1608. Quebec was also the site of the decisive Battle of Quebec (1759) in the FRENCH AND INDIAN WAR (1754-63).

QUEBEC ACT (1774). One of the so-called INTOLERABLE ACTS passed by the English Parliament, providing that western territory north of the Ohio River be added to the Canadian province of Quebec, thus wiping out the claims of some of the colonies to this region. The British government passed this law as an administrative measure. The colonists, however, interpreted it as a law to punish them.

QUEEN ANNE'S WAR (1701-13). See FRENCH AND INDIAN WARS

QUITRENTS. Payments made in colonial times by farmers to the king or a proprietor for the use of land. Most of these quitrents were abolished after the American Revolution (1783).

QUORUM. The number of members of a legislative body that must be present before any legal meeting can be held. Under the U. S. Constitution (Art. 1, Sec. 5, Cl. 1), a quorum consists of a majority of the members in each house of the legislature.

QUOTAS. See IMMIGRATION LEGISLATION

RAILROAD ABUSES. In the last quarter of the 19th century, railroads engaged in many practices harmful to users of the railroads and to railroad stockholders. These abuses included the issuing of free passes to influential politicians, overcapitalization of railroad property, high freight rates, pooling agreements, rebates, and Long and Short Haul discrimination. All of these abuses were made illegal by subsequent Congressional legislation. (See RAILROAD LEGISLATION)

RAILROAD BROTHERHOODS. Four large railway labor unions organized in the late 19th century. They remained independent of all national organizations, such as the A.F.L. The brotherhoods included the Brotherhood of Locomotive Engineers (1863), Order of Railway Conductors and Brakemen (1868), Brotherhood of Locomotive Firemen and Enginemen (1873) and Brotherhood of Railway Trainmen. The Switchmen's Union is sometimes included as one of the railroad brotherhoods.

RAILROAD LAND GRANTS. To encourage the construction of Western railroads in the mid-19th century, Congress passed a series of laws providing for grants of free public Western lands to railroad companies. From 1856 to 1871 the U. S. government gave away 129,000,000 acres of free land to the railroads. This is equal to four times the size of New York State.

RAILROAD LEGISLATION. During the middle of the 19th century the federal government encouraged the construction of transcontinental rail lines by offering generous grants of free public land to railroad companies. (See RAILROAD LAND GRANTS) The growth of RAILROAD ABUSES led to public demand for laws to regulate railroads. State laws regulating railroads, called GRANGER LAWS, were declared unconstitutional by the Supreme Court. (See GRANGER CASES) As a result, Congress

301

passed the INTERSTATE COMMERCE ACT (1887) to regulate railroads. This law was followed by other legislation aimed at eliminating railroad abuses. (See ELKINS ACT, 1903; HEPBURN ACT, 1906; MANN-ELKINS ACT, 1910, ADAMSON ACT, 1916) During World War I (1917-18) the federal government took over the management of all interstate railroads because of the war emergency. After the war the railroads were returned to private management but competition and high overhead costs put many railroads in financial difficulties. As a result, most Congressional legislation after World War I aimed to help railroads remain financially solvent. (See ESCH-CUMMINS TRANSPORTATION ACT, 1920; WATSON-PARKER ACT, 1926; Emergency Railroad Transportation Act, 1933; RAILROAD RETIREMENT ACT, 1934) During World War II (1941-45) railroads remained under private control and they effectively performed the Herculean task of transporting war material and troops. After World War II, the financial problems of railroads grew steadily worse because of the competition of buses, trucks, airplanes and privately owned automobiles.

RAILROAD RETIREMENT ACT (1934, 1935 and 1937). In 1934 Congress established a pension system for workers on interstate railroads. The U. S. Supreme Court held this law unconstitutional (Railroad Retirement Board v. Alton Railroad, 1935). Congress passed a second Railroad Retirement Act in 1935 (known as the Wagner-Crosser Railroad Retirement Act) eliminating the unconstitutional provisions of the first act and reorganizing the Railroad Retirement Board. (See RAILROAD LEGISLATION)

RAILROADS. Construction of railroads in the U. S. began in 1830 with the opening of a 14-mile rail line near Baltimore, Maryland. By the time the War Between the States began (1861) more than 30,000 miles of railroads had been built, mainly in the Northern and Eastern states. During the war, a beginning was made in the construction of the first transcontinental rail line—a combination of the UNION PACIFIC RAILROAD and the Central Pacific Railroad. Congress encouraged the construction of trans-continental rail lines through liberal grants of free public land to rail companies. (See RAILROAD LAND GRANTS) In 1869 the rail line to the Pacific Ocean was completed. It was followed by the construction of many other transcontinental lines as well as by tremendous expansion of railroads in the East and South. By the year 1900 the U. S. had almost 200,000 miles of rail lines. The pace of railroad construction slackened after 1900. The peak year for railroads was 1920, when 250,000 miles of track were in use.

RAILROAD STRIKE OF 1877. The strike began when the Baltimore and Ohio Railroad announced a 10% wage cut. The strike spread to railroads from New York to California and involved more than 100,000 railroad workers and several thousand miles of rail lines. Violence occurred between strikers and state militia and resulted in many killed and wounded and the destruction of millions of dollars of railroad property. The strike was broken when President RUTHERFORD B. HAYES sent federal troops to the strike areas to guard trains carrying U. S. mail and to see that the trains were not delayed by strikers.

RALEIGH, SIR WALTER (c.1552-1618). English statesman, explorer and favorite of Queen Elizabeth I. He established a colony on Roanoke Island off the Virginia coast (1587) but it completely disappeared. (See LOST COLONY) Raleigh is credited with introducing potatoes and tobacco to England. Because of court intrigue in England, he was beheaded on a charge of treason.

RANDOLPH, EDMUND (1753-1813). Represented Virginia at the CONSTITUTIONAL CONVENTION (1787) where he suggested the VIRGINIA PLAN for Congressional representation. He was a member of President GEORGE WASHINGTON's first cabinet, first as Attorney General (1789-94) and then as Secretary of State (1794-95).

RECIPROCAL TARIFF ACT (1934). Also called Trade Agreements Act. It gave the president power to make reciprocal trade agreements with foreign countries changing existing rates by as much as 50%. These agreements did not need senatorial approval. (See TARIFF LEGISLATION and CORDELL HULL)

RECONSTRUCTION. Process by which the Southern states that had seceded in 1861 were restored to the Union after

303

the end of the WAR BETWEEN THE STATES (1861-65). To effect this return of the states, Congress passed the RECONSTRUCTION ACT, as well as additional legislation to help the newly emancipated slaves. (See CIVIL RIGHTS BILLS) The process of Reconstruction also included efforts to restore the economic and social stability of the South. (See RECONSTRUCTION ERA)

RECONSTRUCTION ACT (1867). Passed by Congress after the WAR BETWEEN THE STATES (1861-65) over President ANDREW JOHNSON's veto. The law provided for the governing of Southern states that had seceded from the Union and the procedure for their readmission to the Union. The Southern states were organized into five military districts (see STATE SUICIDE THEORY) each under an army general with power to maintain order and declare martial law if necessary. In order to be readmitted to the Union each state was to hold a convention and draw up a new state constitution, giving the Negro the right to vote. The new constitutions must be approved by a majority of all voters in the states, and by Congress. In all elections in the South, Negroes were to be given the right to vote but Southerners who had participated in the War Between the States were to be ineligible to vote. The legislatures of the new states were then to ratify AMENDMENT 14. After completing these steps the states were to be readmitted to the Union by vote of Congress.

RECONSTRUCTION ERA (1865-77). The postwar decade following the WAR BETWEEN THE STATES (1861-65) during which the economic, political and social life of the reunited nation was reestablished. It was the era during which the Southern states were readmitted to the Union (see RECONSTRUCTION ACT, 1867), the North experienced tremendous industrial growth, the nation expanded rapidly westward (see PUBLIC LAND ACTS) and corruption in national and local governments was exposed. (See CARPETBAG GOVERNMENTS, TWEED RING, STAR ROUTE FRAUDS, WHISKEY RING)

RECONSTRUCTION FINANCE CORPORATION (R.F.C.) 1932. Government agency established during HERBERT HOOVER's presidency and empowered to lend money to banks, railroads and private corporations that were financially sound but were threatened by bankruptcy because of the financial chaos of the GREAT DEPRESSION (1929-35).

REDCOATS. Name given by American colonists to British troops because of the red jackets worn by the soldiers. They were also called "lobsters" and "bloody backs."

REED, THOMAS B. (1839-1902). Speaker of the House of Representatives during the latter part of the 19th century. Because of his arbitrary rules ("Reed Rules") he became known as "Czar Reed." He introduced the rule that a member who was physically present should be counted present for purposes of establishing a QUORUM. He also refused to recognize motions aimed at obstructing Congressional action.

REED, DR. WALTER (1851-1902). Discoverer of the cause of yellow fever. Working on the theory of a Cuban scientist named Carlos J. Finlay, Dr. Reed conducted experiments in Cuba proving that yellow fever was caused by the bite of an infected female mosquito.

"REMEMBER THE ALAMO." See ALAMO, THE

"REMEMBER THE MAINE." See SPANISH-AMERICAN WAR

REPARATIONS. Payments owed by Germany to the Allied Nations because of damages inflicted by Germany during WORLD WAR I (1914-18). The amounts to be paid were fixed after the war but were reduced under the Dawes Plan (1924) and the Young Plan (1929). Finally the Lausanne Agreement (1932) provided for a final token payment. In 1933 Germany stopped all reparations payments when Adolf Hitler and the Nazis took control of the country. (See WAR DEBTS)

REPUBLICAN PARTY. The first, or old, Republican Party was first known as the ANTI-FEDERALIST PARTY (1789), then as the DEMOCRATIC REPUBLICAN PARTY under President THOMAS JEFFERSON (1801-

09) and finally as Republicans (1809-24). This old Republican Party disappeared when it split into factions in 1824 (see ELECTION OF 1824). The modern Republican Party began in 1854 as a result of the KANSAS-NEBRASKA ACT (1854) which split both the DEMOCRATIC PARTY and the WHIG PARTY. The Republican Party was organized by Northern Whigs, anti-slavery Democrats and members of the FREE SOIL PARTY. These diverse factions united on the principle of no further extension of slavery in the territories. In the ELECTION OF 1860 the Republicans won their first national presidential election with the victory of ABRAHAM LINCOLN. After the WAR BETWEEN THE STATES (1865) the Republicans continued to win national presidential elections for 68 years with only three interruptions (ELECTION OF 1884; ELECTION OF 1892; and ELECTION OF 1912). After the Democratic Party NEW DEAL victory in 1932 the Republicans did not win the presidency again until the victory of DWIGHT D. EISENHOWER in the ELECTION OF 1952. Since 1865 the Republican Party has at various times endorsed high protective tariffs, imperialism, a gold standard, a policy of ISOLATION and minimum government regulation of industry.

RESACA DE LA PALMA, BATTLE OF (1846). One of the major military engagements fought at the beginning of the MEXICAN WAR (1846-48). General ZACHARY TAYLOR and an outnumbered American army defeated a large Mexican force near the Rio Grande River. The Mexicans retreated in confusion, leaving many killed on the battlefield. Others drowned trying to cross the river.

RESTRAINING ACT (1775). Law passed by the British Parliament cutting off the rights of the colonies to fish in Atlantic fishing grounds and limiting colonial trade to England, Ireland and English-owned West Indies islands. The law was passed in retaliation for the colonial boycott of British goods started by the CONTINENTAL ASSOCIATION (1774).

RESUMPTION ACT (1875). Provided for government redemption of all GREENBACK currency in specie (gold or silver). Redemption was to begin after January 1, 1879.

Because few of the greenbacks were presented for redemption and because of the demand by farmers and debtors that they remain in circulation, Congress agreed to permit $346,-000,000 in greenbacks to remain permanently in circulation.

"RETURN TO NORMALCY." See HARDING, WARREN G.

REVERE, PAUL (1735-1818). Colonial silversmith and engraver living in Boston. On April 18, 1775 he and William Dawes set out to warn the countryside and the colonial leaders in Lexington that British troops were heading in their direction. Although Revere was captured by the British before completing his mission, Dawes reached his destination.

REVOLUTION OF 1800. Term applied to the victory of President THOMAS JEFFERSON in the ELECTION OF 1800. It was called a "revolution" because the principles of Jefferson's REPUBLICAN PARTY were the opposite of those held by the FEDERALIST PARTY.

RHODE ISLAND COLONY. Founded by ROGER WILLIAMS and his followers in 1636 after they were banished from the MASSACHUSETTS BAY COLONY for religious differences. The first settlements were established at Providence, Portsmouth and Newport. Settlers were attracted to Rhode Island because it permitted freedom of religion to all. Quakers, Jews and others came to the colony during the 17th century and the colony prospered.

RICH MAN'S PANIC. See PANIC OF 1907

RIO PACT (1947). Also known as the Inter-American Defense Pact. Under this agreement the U. S. and the Latin American republics agreed to the principle that a foreign attack on one nation of the Western Hemisphere would be considered an attack on all. Similarly an attack by one Latin American country on another Latin American country would be considered an attack on all. (See ACT OF CHAPULTEPEC).

307

ROANOKE COLONY (1587). See LOST COLONY

ROARING TWENTIES. See PROHIBITION ERA

ROBINSON-PATMAN ACT (1936). Provided that manufacturers must not quote lower prices to large-scale purchasers than to merchants buying in smaller quantities, since this tended to create monopolies. The act was aimed to limit the growth of chain stores and make it possible for the small businessman to compete with them.

ROCHAMBEAU, JEAN BAPTISTE, COMTE DE (1725-1807). See BATTLE OF YORKTOWN

ROCKEFELLER, JOHN D. (1839-1937). American industrialist and financier. In 1862 he entered the oil refining industry and in 1870 formed the Standard Oil Company of Ohio. This eventually became a huge industrial monopoly controlling more than 90% of the oil refining business in the U. S. (See SOUTH IMPROVEMENT CO.) In 1882 Rockefeller's entire business of producing, refining and transporting petroleum was united into one vast Standard Oil Trust. In 1911 the Supreme Court ordered the dissolution of the company as an illegal holding company (Standard Oil Co. v. U. S.). When Rockefeller retired he was one of the wealthiest men in the world. He used his fortune for many philanthropic projects, including the Rockefeller Institute for Medical Research (1901) and the Rockefeller Foundation (1913).

ROCK OF CHICKAMAUGA. See General George H. THOMAS

ROGERS' RANGERS. See ROGERS, ROBERT

ROGERS, ROBERT (1731-95). Leader of a band of about 200 colonial fighters known as Rogers' Rangers, during the FRENCH AND INDIAN WAR (1754-63). Rogers and his rangers, at the suggestion of Sir JEFFREY AMHERST, the British colonial general, made a 400-mile journey (1759) from Vermont north to the village stronghold of the St. Francis Indians on the St. Lawrence River to retaliate for Indian raids on American settlers. The successful attack on St. Francis reduced the Indian menace for settlers. During the AMERICAN REVOLUTION (1775-83), Rogers was imprisoned by the American colonists as a LOYALIST spy.

ROLFE, JOHN (1585-1622). One of the early settlers (1610) in the English colony at JAMESTOWN. He married the Indian maiden Pocahontas, who was supposed to have saved the life of Captain John Smith. Rolfe introduced the regular cultivation of tobacco in the colony (1612) and developed a method of curing tobacco.

ROOSEVELT COROLLARY (1904). In order to forestall European intervention in Venezuela (1902) and Santo Domingo (1905), President THEODORE ROOSEVELT announced that if any intervention were necessary, the U. S. would do it. This doctrine by which the U. S. assumed the right to intervene in Latin America became known as the Roosevelt Corollary. It was applied when the U. S. intervened in the SANTO DOMINGO DEBT DISPUTE (1905) in Nicaragua (1912 ànd 1926), in Haiti (1911 and 1914) as well as in other Caribbean countries. The Roosevelt Corollary came to an end when the U. S., under the GOOD NEIGHBOR POLICY (1933), renounced the right to intervene.

ROOSEVELT, FRANKLIN D. (1882-1945). Thirty-third president of the U. S. He won a landslide presidential victory in the ELECTION OF 1932 and was re-elected in the ELECTION OF 1936, ELECTION OF 1940 and ELECTION OF 1944. He became the first president to hold the office for more than two terms. He died in the first year of his fourth term and was succeeded by Vice-President HARRY S. TRUMAN (1945). During Roosevelt's twelve years as president he inaugurated the NEW DEAL philosophy of government. Hundreds of New Deal laws were passed by Congress, some of which were declared unconstitutional by the Supreme Court. The most significant and lasting New Deal legislation included the TENNESSEE VALLEY AUTHORITY ACT (1933), the SECURITIES AND EXCHANGE COMMISSION ACT (1934), the SOCIAL SECURITY ACT (1935), the NATIONAL LABOR RELATIONS ACT (1935), the FAIR

309

LABOR STANDARDS ACT (1938), the PURE FOOD, DRUG AND COSMETIC ACT (1938), the Wheeler-Lea Act (1940) and many others. AMENDMENT 20 (1933) and Amendment 21 (1933) were ratified by the states. In foreign affairs the Franklin D. Roosevelt era saw the announcement of the GOOD NEIGHBOR POLICY (1933) for Latin America, U. S. participation in the second London Naval Disarmament Conference (1935), the Japanese attack on PEARL HARBOR (1941), U. S. participation in WORLD WAR II (1941-45) and the planning of the UNITED NATIONS (1945).

ROOSEVELT, THEODORE (1858-1919). Twenty-sixth president of the U. S. At the outbreak of the SPANISH-AMERICAN WAR (1898) he organized the ROUGH RIDERS, who fought in Cuba. After the war Roosevelt was elected governor of New York State (1898). To get him out of the way, a PARTY BOSS named THOMAS C. PLATT had him nominated vice-president in the ELECTION OF 1900. He was elected. On the death of President WILLIAM MC KINLEY, Roosevelt succeeded to the presidency. In the ELECTION OF 1904 he was elected president by a large vote. Roosevelt declined to run again in 1908. In 1912, however, he sought the Republican nomination again on a liberal platform he called the New Nationalism. When the party nominated WILLIAM HOWARD TAFT, Roosevelt organized his own PROGRESSIVE (BULL MOOSE) PARTY. This split in Republican ranks threw the ELECTION OF 1912 to WOODROW WILSON, the Democratic Party candidate.

During Roosevelt's presidency (1901-09) his legislative program became known as the Square Deal and he was called the TRUST BUSTER. Congress passed the NEWLANDS RECLAMATION ACT (1902), the MEAT INSPECTION ACT (1906) and the HEPBURN ACT (1906). In foreign affairs his presidency included the signing of the HAY-PAUNCEFOTE TREATY (1901), the beginning of PANAMA CANAL construction (1904), the development of the ROOSEVELT COROLLARY (1904), the signing of the GENTLEMEN'S AGREEMENT with Japan (1907), the signing of the ROOT-TAKAHIRA AGREEMENT (1908) and the development of a BIG STICK POLICY. Roosevelt received the NOBEL PEACE PRIZE (1905) for his work in bringing the Russo-Japanese War (1904-05) to a close.

ROOT, ELIHU (1845-1937). Secretary of War (1899-1904) and Secretary of State (1905-09). During the presidency of THEODORE ROOSEVELT, Root negotiated the ROOT-TAKAHIRA AGREEMENT (1908) with Japan. He was a member of the HAGUE COURT and was awarded the NOBEL PEACE PRIZE in 1912. He helped draw up the plans for the LEAGUE OF NATIONS and the WORLD COURT. His efforts to get the U. S. to join the World Court through the Root Formula (1929) failed.

ROOT FORMULA. See ROOT, ELIHU and WORLD COURT

ROOT-TAKAHIRA AGREEMENT (1908). Arranged by Secretary of State ELIHU ROOT and Japanese ambassador Takahira. In the agreement the U. S. recognized Japan's special interests in Manchuria and Korea. Japan recognized American ownership of the Philippine Islands. Both countries pledged to maintain Chinese independence and the OPEN DOOR for Chinese trade.

ROSECRANS, GENERAL WILLIAM S. See CHICKA-MAUGA, BATTLE OF and MURFREESBORO, BATTLE OF

ROSS, BETSY (1752-1836). Her full name was Elizabeth Griscom Ross. She made a number of flags during the AMERICAN REVOLUTION (1775-83) but the legend that she designed the first American flag with stars and stripes is historically inaccurate. (See FLAG, AMERICAN)

ROUGH RIDERS. A picturesque volunteer cavalry group of former cowboys and college athletes in the SPANISH-AMERICAN WAR (1898) led by Colonel THEODORE ROOSEVELT and Colonel Leonard Wood. Their exploits in the war were publicized in newspapers and in Theodore Roosevelt's postwar writings.

ROYAL COLONIES. English colonies ruled by royal governors appointed by the English monarchs. In general the gov-

311

ernors allowed the settlers little voice in running the colonies. The important royal colonies included Virginia, North Carolina, South Carolina and Georgia. (See PROPRIETARY COLONIES; SELF-GOVERNING COLONIES).

"RUGGED INDIVIDUALISM." Phrase used by HERBERT HOOVER during the campaign preceding the ELECTION OF 1928. He referred to the American system of free enterprise, individual business initiative and unrestricted competition, as contrasted to the DEMOCRATIC PARTY program of social reform legislation. Hoover was elected in 1928 but was overwhelmingly defeated by FRANKLIN D. ROOSEVELT in the ELECTION OF 1932.

RULE OF REASON. Judicial interpretation by the U. S. Supreme Court in decisions relating to large business corporations and monopolies under the SHERMAN ANTITRUST ACT (1890). Justice OLIVER WENDELL HOLMES, JR. suggested the "rule of reason" in his dissenting opinion on the Northern Securities Case (1904). His doctrine held that size alone does not create an industrial monopoly. In 1911 the Supreme Court applied the "rule of reason" in Standard Oil Co. V. U. S., held the company to be a monopoly, and ordered its dissolution. In the case of U. S. V. U. S. Steel Corporation, however (1911), the court applied the same rule and held the corporation was not a monopoly.

RUM, ROMANISM AND REBELLION. See ELECTION OF 1884

RURAL ELECTRIFICATION ADMINISTRATION (R. E. A.) (1935). Federal agency established to provide federal aid to cities and communities that wished to build or expand their own electric power plants and transmission lines.

RUSH-BAGOT AGREEMENT (1817). Arranged by Secretary of State JOHN QUINCY ADAMS between the U. S. and Great Britain. Under this treaty each country agreed not to maintain military vessels on the Great Lakes or on Lake Champlain. This was the beginning of a policy of keeping the U. S. - Canadian border relatively unfortified, a policy that has continued to the present.

RUTLEDGE, JOHN (1739-1800). He was a member of the STAMP ACT CONGRESS (1765) and played an important role in drafting the Constitution at the CONSTITUTIONAL CONVENTION (1787) as well as in getting South Carolina to ratify it. He served as Associate Justice of the Supreme Court from 1789 to 1791.

SACAJAWEA. See LEWIS AND CLARK EXPEDITION

SAGE OF MONTICELLO. See JEFFERSON, THOMAS

ST. AUGUSTINE (1565). First permanent settlement established by Europeans on territory that later became the U. S. St. Augustine was founded by PEDRO MENENDEZ, a Spanish explorer and governor. It remained a Spanish settlement until the FLORIDA PURCHASE (1819) by the U. S.

ST. LAWRENCE SEAWAY. See WILEY-DONDERO ACT (1954)

ST. LEGER, GENERAL BARRY. See ORISKANY, BATTLE OF

ST. MIHIEL, BATTLE OF (1918). One of the major military engagements of WORLD WAR I (1917-18) in which American forces attacked the fortified German position at St. Mihiel and forced the Germans to retreat. This was the first time since the American declaration of war (1917) that the U. S. Army fought as a separate military unit.

SALOMON, HAYM (1740-85). Jewish businessman in colonial Philadelphia. During the AMERICAN REVOLUTION (1775-83) he helped raise money for loans to the SECOND CONTINENTAL CONGRESS, and contributed generously from his own fortune.

SALUTARY NEGLECT. See OLD COLONIAL POLICY

SAMOA. In 1878 the U. S., Germany and Great Britain signed a treaty by which the U. S. obtained the right to establish a coaling station at Pago Pago on Tutuila, an island in the Samoan group. Great Britain and Germany also obtained control of some islands. In 1888 Germany tried to seize control of the entire island group. A naval battle was avoided (1889) when a hurricane destroyed almost all British, U. S. and German vessels stationed near the islands. A treaty signed in 1899 divided the islands between Germany and the U. S.

SAMPSON, ADMIRAL WILLIAM T. (1840-1902). See SPANISH-AMERICAN WAR

SAN FRANCISCO CONFERENCE (1945). Drew up and approved the charter for the UNITED NATIONS. The conference was attended by delegates from 50 countries.

SAN JACINTO, BATTLE OF (1836). One of the major military engagements of the TEXAS WAR OF INDEPENDENCE from Mexico. SAM HOUSTON, leader of the Texans, decisively defeated a Mexican Army led by General Santa Ana, who was taken prisoner.

SANTA FE TRAIL. One of the major routes used by American pioneers in the early 19th century to reach the Far West. The Santa Fe Trail started at Independence, Missouri, and led west and southwest to Santa Fe, New Mexico. From here pioneers took the northerly Spanish Trail or the southerly Gila Trail to California.

SANTO DOMINGO DEBT DISPUTE (1905). Germany threatened to collect unpaid debts from Santo Domingo by force. President THEODORE ROOSEVELT declared such an act would violate the MONROE DOCTRINE. An American representative, protected by American marines, entered Santo Domingo and supervised the collection of customs, administered its finances and paid its debts. This was the origin of the ROOSEVELT COROLLARY.

SARATOGA, BATTLE OF (1777). Called the "turning point" of the AMERICAN REVOLUTION (1775-83). General John Burgoyne, the British commander, was sent south from Canada to Albany to join two other British commanders— General William Howe and General Barry St. Leger. Neither reached Burgoyne. Howe went south to Philadelphia and St. Leger was forced to retreat after his defeat at the BATTLE OF ORISKANY (1777). Surrounded, and short of supplies, Burgoyne was forced to surrender his army to the American commander, General HORATIO GATES.

SATELLITE COMMUNICATIONS ACT (1962). Because of the earth's curvature, television signals can only be received by television sets within a limited radius of a broadcasting station. However the success of orbiting artificial satellites around the earth has made it possible to bounce television signals off the satellites. This method makes possible the reception of television programs from broadcasting stations thousands of miles away. In 1962 the first direct television broadcast from the U. S. was received in Paris and London and the first direct European broadcasts were received in the U. S. In order to regulate and control the development of this new system of international television broadcasting, Congress passed the Satellite Communications Act. Under this law a private corporation was established to develop, own and operate a television communications satellite system.

"SAVANNAH." Name of the first ship using steam power to cross the Atlantic Ocean (1819). In 1959 the first U. S. ship using atomic power was also named the *Savannah*.

SCALAWAGS. Southern white politicians who, during the RECONSTRUCTION ERA (1865-77), took advantage of the new political power of the emancipated Negro voters to further their own political ambitions. (See CARPETBAGGERS)

SCHECTER V. U. S. (1935). Also known as the Schecter Poultry Case and the "Sick Chicken Case." The Schecter Poultry Company violated the code for the industry established under the NATIONAL INDUSTRIAL RECOVERY ACT (1933). The U. S. Supreme Court in this case declared the act unconstitutional because it gave excessive legislative powers, such as the writing of industrial codes of fair competition, to the executive branch of the government. In addition, these codes regulated intrastate as well as interstate industries.

SCHENCK V. U. S. (1919). Under the ESPIONAGE ACT of 1917 persons who interfered with the war effort by making speeches or writing articles encouraging violation of Draft

Laws (see CONSCRIPTION) were subject to imprisonment. Justice OLIVER WENDELL HOLMES, JR. sustained the constitutionality of the Espionage Act on the grounds that freedom of speech and press may be limited when there is a "clear and present danger" to the nation.

SCHOFIELD, GENERAL JOHN M. (1831-1906). See BATTLE OF NASHVILLE

SCHURZ, CARL (1829-1906). German immigrant to the U. S. in the mid-19th century. He served in the Union Armies during the WAR BETWEEN THE STATES (1861-65) and was elected U. S. Senator (1869-75). He was a leader of the CIVIL SERVICE REFORM movement and helped to organize the LIBERAL REPUBLICAN PARTY (1872). Schurz also served as Secretary of the Interior (1877-81) and as editor of the New York *Evening Post* (1881-83).

SCIOTO COMPANY (1786). See CUTLER, MANASSEH

SCOPES TRIAL (1925). Also called the "Monkey Trial." John Scopes, a school teacher, was tried in Tennessee for teaching the subject of evolution. WILLIAM JENNINGS BRYAN was attorney for the state and Clarence Darrow attorney for the teacher. After a dramatic court battle that was given nationwide publicity, Scopes was found guilty.

SCOTCH-IRISH. A group of settlers who originally came from Scotland, lived for a short time in Ireland and then migrated to the American colonies because of religious persecution. The Scotch-Irish settled mainly in the colonies of New Jersey, Pennsylvania, Maryland, Virginia and the Carolinas.

SCOTT, GENERAL WINFIELD (1786-1866). Served in the WAR OF 1812, the SEMINOLE WAR, the CREEK WAR and the MEXICAN WAR (1846-48). In the Mexican War, Scott captured the seaport of Vera Cruz and then marched his forces inland and captured Mexico City (1847). He was popularly known by army men as "Old Fuss and Feathers." In the ELECTION OF 1852 he was presidential candidate of the dying WHIG PARTY but lost to FRANKLIN PIERCE, the DEMOCRATIC PARTY candidate.

317

SEA DOGS. Name given to English sea captains such as SIR FRANCIS DRAKE, MARTIN FROBISHER and JOHN HAWKINS, who preyed on Spanish treasure-carrying ships during the 17th century.

SEATO. See SOUTHEAST ASIA TREATY ORGANIZATION

SECOND CONTINENTAL CONGRESS. Also known as "Congress" during the AMERICAN REVOLUTION. It met in Philadelphia in 1775, drew up the DECLARATION OF INDEPENDENCE, appointed GEORGE WASHINGTON commander-in-chief of the CONTINENTAL ARMY and acted as the governing body of the THIRTEEN COLONIES during the American Revolution (1775-83). It was basically a revolutionary body, inasmuch as it had no constitutional status until the ARTICLES OF CONFEDERATION went into effect in 1781.

SECTIONALISM. Loyalty to a particular section of the country, such as the North, South or West, instead of loyalty to the nation as a whole. Sectional feelings existed in the U. S. from its very origin. However, they were submerged in a stronger feeling of nationalism that developed after the WAR OF 1812. (See NATIONALIST ERA, 1814-24) After the MISSOURI COMPROMISE (1820), however, sectional feeling grew in intensity as different areas of the nation took sides on such questions as the protective tariff (see TARIFF LEGISLATION), the BANK OF U. S., federal INTERNAL IMPROVEMENTS and the extension of slavery in new territories. (See SLAVERY LEGISLATION) Congressional debates reflected the growth of sectionalism. (See WEBSTER-HAYNE DEBATE, 1830; "SEVENTH OF MARCH" SPEECH, 1850) Eventually sectional rivalry resulted in Southern secession and the WAR BETWEEN THE STATES (1861-65).

SECURITIES AND EXCHANGE ACT (1934). Under this act all stock exchanges were to be licensed by a new agency called the Securities and Exchange Commission (S.E.C.). Later, commodity exchanges and investment trusts were also included under the act. Regulations were established for licensing of stock exchanges, the issue of new securities, the conduct of stock brokers and the control of unrestricted speculation.

SECURITY COUNCIL. The most powerful and therefore the most important body of the UNITED NATIONS. It consists of 11 members: five permanent members (U. S., Great Britain, Soviet Union, Nationalist China and France) and six nonpermanent members elected by the General Assembly for two-year terms. The task of the Security Council is to investigate disputes, recommend settlements and impose sanctions (punishments), including military force, if necessary, against an aggressor nation. A single negative vote by any one of the five permanent members of the council is sufficient to veto any major proposal.

SEDITION ACT (1798). Part of the FEDERALIST PARTY program during the Presidency of JOHN ADAMS, aimed at weakening the REPUBLICAN PARTY. The Sedition Act provided for fines and imprisonment for those who tried to stir up sedition or rebellion in the country by speaking or printing false and malicious statements about the president and Congress. This law aroused stormy criticism because it was considered an unconstitutional restriction on the rights of freedom of speech and the press. The law expired before Jefferson became president in 1801.

SEDITION ACT (1918). Passed by Congress during WORLD WAR I (1917-18). It provided penalties for persons who interfered with the war effort, spoke disloyally about the government of the U. S. or the Constitution, or hindered the production of war materials. EUGENE V. DEBS, the Socialist Party leader, was imprisoned under this act. The law was held to be constitutional in the case of ABRAMS V. U. S. (1919).

SEGREGATION. Although AMENDMENT 14 provided "equal protection of the laws" for all, most Southern states practiced racial segregation of Negroes and whites in schools, railroads, parks and other public places after the WAR BETWEEN THE STATES (1861-65). The Supreme Court decision in Plessy V. Ferguson (1896) declared such segregation legal provided "separate but equal" facilities were provided. In 1954 the court reversed itself in the case of Brown V. Board of Education and held that

319

"separate but equal" facilities constituted illegal segregation and was a violation of the "equal protection of the laws" for all citizens guaranteed under Amendment 14.

SELECTIVE SERVICE ACT (1917). Passed after the U. S. declaration of war·on Germany in WORLD WAR I (1917-18) in order to raise a national army. All men between the ages of 21 and 30 (later changed to 18 to 45) had to register with local draft boards. (See CONSCRIPTION)

SELECTIVE SERVICE ACT (1948). Passed after WORLD WAR II (1941-45). It provided for compulsory military training of all able-bodied men between the ages of 18 and 25. With minor changes this law is now in effect. (See CONSCRIPTION)

SELF-GOVERNING COLONIES. These included the colonies of Massachusetts, Connecticut and Rhode Island, whose governments were based on charters granted by the British monarchs. Under these charters the colonists were permitted to choose their own governors and set up local assemblies to pass local legislation. (See also PROPRIETARY COLONIES and ROYAL COLONIES)

SEMINOLE INDIANS. Originally inhabited the Florida peninsula. After the SEMINOLE WARS (1817-18 and 1835-43) the few remaining Seminoles were moved to Indian territory west of the Mississippi River and were known as one of the FIVE CIVILIZED TRIBES. A small number of Seminoles remained in Florida, where a reservation was established for them.

SEMINOLE WARS. The first Seminole War (1817-18) started because of Indian border raids from Spanish-owned Florida, which the Spanish officials seemed helpless to stop; the escape of slaves into Florida; and the hope of Southern EXPANSIONISTS to acquire Florida as another slave state. General ANDREW JACKSON invaded Florida and defeated the Seminoles. In the following year (1819) the U. S. purchased Florida from Spain. In 1832 the Seminoles were ordered to leave Florida and move to Indian territory west of the Mississippi River (Treaty of Payne's Landing, 1832). When the Seminoles refused, the Second Seminole War (1835-43) began. The Seminoles, led by their chief Osceola, resisted fiercely for eight years, until most of the Indians were exterminated.

SENECA FALLS CONVENTION (1848). See FEMINIST MOVEMENT

SEQUOYAH (c.1770-1843). One of the leaders of the CHEROKEE INDIAN tribe, Sequoyah was part white by birth. He originated a special alphabet of 85 letters which made possible the writing of the Cherokee language. As a result of his work the Cherokees were probably the most civilized Indian tribe in North America.

SEVEN DAYS' BATTLES (1862). During the WAR BETWEEN THE STATES (1861-65) a Union Army led by General GEORGE MC CLELLAN and Confederate forces commanded by General ROBERT E. LEE and THOMAS "STONEWALL" JACKSON engaged in a series of battles which were part of the PENINSULAR CAMPAIGN to capture Richmond, the Confederate capital. Despite heavy Confederate losses, the Union Army was forced to retreat.

"SEVENTH OF MARCH" SPEECH (1850). Address by DANIEL WEBSTER in the Senate, in support of HENRY CLAY's COMPROMISE OF 1850 (Omnibus Bill). Webster pleaded for acceptance of the Compromise as the only way to preserve the Union and the Constitution. His speech is considered to be one of the greatest orations ever delivered in Congress. Because of his support of the Compromise of 1850, which did not forbid slavery in new territories, Webster was branded a traitor by Northern anti-slavery groups.

SEVIER, JOHN (1745-1815). See FRANKLIN, STATE OF

SEWARD, WILLIAM H. (1801-72). During his Senatorial career (1848-60) he was nationally known as an ardent anti-slavery advocate. He foresaw the consequences of the slavery struggle as an "irrepressible conflict" and opposed the COMPROMISE OF 1850 because it violated a "higher law." As Secretary of State in ABRAHAM LINCOLN's cabinet he successfully concluded the TRENT AFFAIR (1861), reached a preliminary agreement with Great Britain over the ALABAMA CLAIMS and took a strong stand in the MAXIMILIAN AFFAIR in Mexico. Seward was wounded in the assassination plot that resulted in Lincoln's death (1865) but continued as Secretary of State under President ANDREW JOHNSON. In 1867 Seward negotiated the ALASKA PURCHASE from Russia.

SEWARD'S ICEBOX. See ALASKA PURCHASE

SHAFTER, GENERAL WILLIAM R. (1835-1906). See SPANISH-AMERICAN WAR

SHARECROPPERS. Landless farmers who are supplied with land, seed and tools to raise a crop. The farmer then pays part of his crop to the man who has leased the land to him. This sharecropping system developed on a large scale in the South after the WAR BETWEEN THE STATES (1861-65) when many freed Negro slaves were without land and many landowners were without workers. Sharecropping on a large scale emerged again during the GREAT DEPRESSION (1929-35) both in the South and in the West. In 1937 Congress passed the BANKHEAD-JONES FARM TENANT ACT to help sharescroppers buy their own farms.

SHAWNEE INDIANS. Tribe that originally inhabited territory in the area that is now the state of Kentucky and were later forced to move west of the Mississippi River. (See PLAINS INDIANS)

SHAYS' REBELLION (1786). Brief rebellion in Massachusetts resulting from the seizure of property and jailing of people who could not pay their debts. Shays and his followers forcibly released some debtors from prison and forced some debtors' courts to close. The rebellion was finally quelled by the state militia. Shays was imprisoned but later pardoned.

SHERMAN ANTI-TRUST ACT (1890). Forbad all "contracts, combinations in the form of trust or otherwise, or conspiracies in restraint of trade or commerce" in interstate and foreign commerce. Under this act the Supreme Court ordered the dissolution of some monopolies (Northern Securities Case, 1904; Standard Oil Co. v. U. S., 1911) but upheld the validity of other large corporations (U. S.

V. KNIGHT, 1895; U. S. v. U. S. Steel Corporation, 1911) by using the RULE OF REASON. A number of labor unions were held to be in restraint of trade under the Sherman Act (Loewe v. Lawler, 1908). (See also CLAYTON ANTI-TRUST ACT)

SHERMAN, ROGER (1721-93). One of the drafters and signers of the DECLARATION OF INDEPENDENCE (1776). He helped draw up the ARTICLES OF CONFEDERATION (1777) and was an important member of the CONSTITUTIONAL CONVENTION (1787).

SHERMAN SILVER PURCHASE ACT (1890). Superseded the BLAND-ALLISON ACT of 1878. The Sherman Silver Purchase Act provided that the government was to buy 4½ million ounces of silver per month in the open market and pay for it with Treasury certificates redeemable in gold or silver. After the act was passed, the value of the metal in a silver dollar fell below the value of gold in a dollar. As a result, people and banks hoarded gold and used their silver certificates and silver coins to pay their debts. This caused the U. S. government's gold reserve to dwindle to the danger point. In 1893 Congress repealed the law.

SHERMAN, GENERAL WILLIAM T. (1820-91). Union Army commander during the WAR BETWEEN THE STATES (1861-65). Sherman fought in the VICKSBURG campaign (1863). When General ULYSSES S. GRANT was promoted to commander-in-chief, Sherman succeeded him as supreme commander in the west. Sherman began a military drive through Georgia (see ATLANTA CAMPAIGN) that was noteworthy for its ruthless devastation. He captured and destroyed Atlanta (1864) and started his famous march of destruction eastward to the sea. His army reached and captured Savannah on the Atlantic coast, then moved north through South Carolina and North Carolina to defeat a Confederate Army under General JOSEPH E. JOHNSTON at Durham, North Carolina (1865). By this time General ROBERT E. LEE's surrender to Grant at APPOMATTOX COURTHOUSE had brought the war to an end. Sherman is credited with the famous quotation "War is hell." However, his exact words were, "There's many a boy . . . who looks on war as all glory, but boys, it is all hell."

SHILOH, BATTLE OF (1862). One of the major military engagements of the WAR BETWEEN THE STATES (1861-65) fought at Shiloh in western Tenneseee. A Confederate Army led by General Albert S. Johnston launched a surprise attack on the Union Army led by General ULYSSES S. GRANT. After a two-day battle which resulted in many casualties, and the death of General Johnston, the Confederate Army was forced to retreat.

SHINPLASTERS. Fractional paper currency issued during the WAR BETWEEN THE STATES (1861-65) because people hoarded all metallic coins. To replace nickels, dimes and other hoarded coins the government issued fractional paper money in denominations of five cents, ten cents and so on.

"SHOT HEARD ROUND THE WORLD." See CONCORD, BATTLE OF

"SICK CHICKEN CASE." See SCHECTER V. U. S. (1935)

SILVER PURCHASE ACT (1934). Established a policy of backing our paper money with a reserve of three-fourths gold and one-fourth silver, based on their respective values. The president was given power to buy silver in the open market up to this bullion ratio and to have the Treasury Department issue silver certificates against all silver purchases. The purpose of the act was to raise prices during the depression by inflating the currency.

SIMS, ADMIRAL WILLIAM S. (1858-1936). Commander of U. S. naval forces in the Atlantic Ocean during WORLD WAR I (1917-18). He was president of the Naval War College both before and after the first World War.

SIOUX INDIANS. Also called Dakota Indians. Despite many treaties with the U. S., the Sioux in 1862 massacred a large white settlement in Minnesota. The Sioux were moved to a reservation in South Dakota, but the discovery of gold in the area a few years later resulted in renewed clashes between the Sioux and white settlers. During the SIOUX WAR (1875-76) that followed, General GEORGE A. CUSTER and his company were wiped out at the Battle of Little Big Horn (1876). Eventually the Sioux were removed to reservations in Minnesota, Montana, the Dakotas and elsewhere in the West.

SIOUX WAR (1875-76). Because of the gold rush into SIOUX INDIAN territory (Black Hills, South Dakota), the extension of the Northern Pacific Railroad through Indian territory, and the failure of the Interior Department to live up to its promises, the Sioux tribe went on the warpath in 1875. Their famous leaders were Sitting Bull and Crazy Horse. One of the famous incidents of the war was the Battle of Little Big Horn (1876) at which occurred the famous "last stand" of General George A. Custer and his company of 264 men, who were wiped out to the last man. In 1876 the Sioux were finally subjugated by General NELSON A. MILES.

SIX-SHOOTER. Gun that could fire six shots without reloading. This weapon, known as the Colt revolver, was invented by SAMUEL COLT in 1836. The six-shooter was developed primarily to meet the needs of the pioneers, who did not have time to reload rifles when fighting off Indian raiders.

SLATER, SAMUEL (1768-1835). Called the "father of the American factory system." He was an English textile worker and mechanic who came to New York in 1789. Great Britain had forbidden the export of textile machinery or the plans for making the machines. Slater built a number of textile machines from memory and with the financial help of a rich merchant set up the first American textile factory in Pawtucket, R. I. in 1790.

SLAVERY COMPROMISE. Agreement reached at the CONSTITUTIONAL CONVENTION (1787) with respect to the counting of slaves for representation in Congress. The compromise that was incorporated into the Constitution provided that five slaves were to be counted as three persons in determining representation in Congress and in levying direct taxes. These provisions of the Constitution came to an end in 1865 when AMENDMENT 13 abolished slavery in the U. S.

SLAVERY LEGISLATION. Under the original U. S. Constitution slavery was recognized by the SLAVERY COM-

325

PROMISE. In addition, before 1808 Congress was forbidden to interfere with the slave trade. The invention of the COTTON GIN (1793) made slavery one of the pillars of the Southern PLANTATION SYSTEM. In 1808 Congress prohibited the further importation of slaves and in 1820 made slave trading punishable by death. In efforts to solve the question of slavery extension in the territories, Congress passed a number of laws, including the MISSOURI COMPROMISE (1820), the COMPROMISE OF 1850, and the KANSAS-NEBRASKA ACT (1854). Despite this legislation, the slavery issue led indirectly to the WAR BETWEEN THE STATES (1861-65). During the war, all slaves in seceding states were freed by the EMANCIPATION PROCLAMATION (1863). After the war AMENDMENT 13 abolished slavery throughout the U. S.

SLAVE TRADE. The first shipload of slaves to reach the English colonies arrived in Virginia in 1619. British, Dutch French, Portuguese, Spanish and American colonial shipowners engaged in the slave trade, from which tremendous profits were derived. The TRIANGULAR TRADE of colonial New England shipowners included the shipment of slaves from West Africa to the New World. England was the first to make the slave trade illegal, in 1807. In 1808 the Congress of the U. S., at the suggestion of President THOMAS JEFFERSON, enacted a law putting an end to the slave trade. However, some shipowners engaged in the illegal but profitable smuggling of slaves into the U. S. In 1820 Congress made slave trading punishable by death. Similar laws of European nations practically put an end to the importation of Negro slaves in the Western Hemisphere. (See SLAVERY LEGISLATION)

SLIDELL MISSION. In 1845 John Slidell was sent to Mexico by the United States government to see if a peaceful solution to the Texas boundary dispute could be reached. Slidell was also instructed to offer to buy the New Mexico and Upper California territories from Mexico. The Mexican government refused to discuss any of these matters.

SMITH ACT (1940). Also known as the Alien Registration Act. Made it a crime to teach or advocate the overthrow of our government by force and violence. The act also requires the fingerprinting and registration of all aliens. A

326

number of American COMMUNIST PARTY members were successfully prosecuted (1947) and jailed under this act after World War II.

SMITH, ALFRED E. (1873-1944). Known as the "Happy Warrior." Elected governor of New York State four times, he gained a nationwide reputation for his liberal state reform legislation and genial vote-getting personality. In the ELECTION OF 1928 the DEMOCRATIC PARTY nominated him to run for the presidency against HERBERT HOOVER, the REPUBLICAN PARTY candidate. Smith was the first man of the Catholic faith to be nominated for the presidency by a major political party. He was badly defeated in the election. It was the first national election since the WAR BETWEEN THE STATES (1865) in which the SOLID SOUTH did not vote unanimously for the Democratic Party candidate.

SMITH, CAPTAIN JOHN (1580-1631). One of the leaders of the English settlement at JAMESTOWN in 1607. He began to trade with the Indians and subsequently became the leader of the settlement. His strict rule of "no work, no food" carried the colony during the "starving time" and saved it from failure. A legend, which may be true, tells of an incident in which his life was saved by the Indian maiden Pocahontas.

SMITH, JOSEPH (1805-44). Founder of the MORMON religious sect. Smith claimed he received divine revelations which he wrote in the Book of Mormon. On the basis of those revelations Smith founded the Church of the Latter-Day Saints (1830), commonly called Mormonism. Smith was murdered by an anti-Mormon mob in 1844 and BRIGHAM YOUNG succeeded to the leadership of the Mormons.

SMITH-LEVER ACT (1914). Provided for the establishment of a nationwide "county agent" service working through the Department of Agriculture to help farmers with their problems and provide them with the latest scientific farming information.

SMUGGLING. Quite common in the English colonies because of colonial efforts to evade strict British NAVIGA-

TION ACTS and Trade Laws. The smuggling of slaves into the U. S. after 1808 (see SLAVE TRADE) was profitable but dangerous.

SOCIAL DEMOCRATIC PARTY. See DEBS, EUGENE V. and SOCIALIST PARTY

SOCIALIST PARTY. When organized in 1898 it was known as the Social Democratic Party but changed its name to Socialist Party in 1900. Its early leaders included Morris Hillquit and EUGENE V. DEBS. In the elections of 1900, 1904, 1908, 1912 and 1920 the party nominated Eugene V. Debs for the presidency. In the ELECTION OF 1920 Debs and the Socialist Party polled almost 1,000,000 votes, despite the fact that Debs was in jail for violation of the ESPIONAGE ACT. In 1919 the radical wing of the Party seceded and formed the American COMMUNIST PARTY. After 1929 Norman Thomas became the Socialist Party leader and perennial candidate for the presidency. The Socialist Party platform called for social, political and economic reforms such as unemployment and old age insurance, regulation of corporations, protection of the rights of labor, the right to unionize and the abolition of child labor.

SOCIAL SECURITY ACT (1935). Established a Federal Social Security Board (S.S.B.) to administer the provisions of the act. The law provided for a system of old age insurance for workers who reached the age of 65, and survivors' insurance for children and spouses of insured workers who died before reaching 65. Money for the pension system comes from a social security tax on workers and employers. The law also provided for a federal payroll tax to be returned to the states that set up systems of unemployment insurance. Finally, the law provided for federal grants to states to help blind, crippled or dependent children and dependent mothers. Later amendments to the Act expanded and liberalized these social security provisions.

SOD HOUSE. Prairie home built by Western homesteaders in the 19th century. Since there were no forests on the western plains (see INTERIOR PLAINS), the pioneers made their homes by plowing up the sod, cutting it into strips and laying the strips one on another like bricks.

SOIL BANK. See AGRICULTURAL ADJUSTMENT ACT (1938)

SOIL CONSERVATION ACT (1935). Established a permanent Soil Conservation Service in the Department of Agriculture for the purpose of training farmers in approved methods of preventing soil erosion.

SOIL CONSERVATION AND DOMESTIC ALLOTMENT ACT (S.C.A.D.A.) (1936). Passed by Congress after the AGRICULTURAL ADJUSTMENT ACT of 1933 was declared unconstitutional by the Supreme Court. Under this new law the federal government entered into contracts with farmers to pay them for soil erosion work on land not used for raising crops. (See FARM LEGISLATION)

SOIL CONSERVATION SERVICE. See SOIL CONSERVATION ACT (1935)

SOLID SOUTH. In most elections since the end of the WAR BETWEEN THE STATES (1865) all of the Southern states voted solidly for the DEMOCRATIC PARTY. This solidity developed because of Southern hostility to the REPUBLICAN PARTY, which was blamed for the harsh RECONSTRUCTION laws passed by Congress after 1865. In recent national elections the Solid South has shown signs of breaking up. In the ELECTION OF 1928, HERBERT HOOVER, and in the ELECTION OF 1960, Richard Nixon, both Republican presidential candidates, carried some of the Southern states.

SONS OF LIBERTY. Colonial organizations in New York City, Boston and other cities that protested against the British STAMP ACT (1765), by parades and acts of violence against stamp agents.

SOONERS. The official date for the opening of the Oklahoma territory to homesteaders was April 22, 1889. A few settlers rushed into the territory "sooner" than the official opening date. These were called "Sooners" and Oklahoma became known as the "Sooner State."

329

SOUTH CAROLINA. One of the original THIRTEEN COL-ONIES. In the years before the WAR BETWEEN THE STATES (1861-65) it was the stronghold of the slave-owning cotton plantation aristocracy. JOHN C. CALHOUN was its most illustrious spokesman. In 1832 South Carolina passed the Ordinance of Nullification, declaring the TARIFF OF 1828 and the TARIFF OF 1832 null and void, and threatening secession. In 1861 South Carolina was the first state to secede from the Union when it passed the ORDINANCE OF SECESSION.

SOUTHEAST ASIA TREATY ORGANIZATION (S.E.A.T. O.) (1954). Organized under the Manila Pact of 1954. This organization is a military alliance formed for the purpose of stopping further Communist territorial expansion in Southeast Asia. The alliance includes the U. S., Great Britain, France, the Philippine Republic, Thailand, Pakistan, Australia and New Zealand.

SOUTHERN ARISTOCRACY. Small group of wealthy Southern plantation owners before the WAR BETWEEN THE STATES (1861-65) who lived in mansions and owned large plantations worked by hundreds of slaves. (See PLANTATION SYSTEM) In 1860 there were about 5,000 such large plantation owners of a total Southern population of 6,000,000 whites and 4,000,000 Negro slaves.

SOUTHERN PACIFIC RAILROAD. One of the early trans-continental rail lines extending from New Orleans to the Pacific Coast. Built with the aid of federal RAILROAD LAND GRANTS, it consisted of a number of smaller lines that were merged about 1865 to form the Southern Pacific line. In 1884 the Southern Pacific and the Central Pacific Railroads were combined under the control of Leland Stanford and Collis P. Huntington. (See HARRIMAN, EDWARD H.)

SOUTH IMPROVEMENT COMPANY (1871). Organized by JOHN D. ROCKEFELLER by consolidating the Standard Oil Company and a number of other oil companies for the purpose of obtaining freight rebates from the Pennsylvania Railroad. Not only did the South Improvement Company get rebates on its own oil shipments but also on the oil shipments made by rival companies. These

330

rebates aroused so much public protest that the Pennsylvania legislature revoked the charter of the South Improvement Company.

SPANISH-AMERICAN WAR (1898). The basic causes of the war were the disruption of American investments in Cuban sugar plantations resulting from a Cuban revolt. the newspaper rivalry of JOSEPH PULITZER and WILLIAM RANDOLPH HEARST, the publication of the DELOME LETTER and the sinking of the battleship *Maine* in Havana Harbor with a loss of 260 Americans. "Remember the Maine" became the slogan of those who favored war with Spain. In April, 1898 President WILLIAM MC KINLEY asked Congress for a declaration of war against Spain, despite Spain's offer to accede to almost every demand of the U. S. Congress declared war in 1898. High lights of the brief war were the victory of Commodore GEORGE DEWEY at the BATTLE OF MANILA BAY, the capture of Santiago by General William R. Shafter, the crippling of the Spanish fleet in Cuban waters by Admiral William T. Sampson and the invasion of Puerto Rico by General NELSON A. MILES. On August 12, 1898 hostilities ceased and two months later the TREATY OF PARIS, ending the war, was signed.

SPANISH ARMADA (1588). Also called the "Invincible Armada." A huge fleet of about 130 ships carrying 30,000 men was sent by the Spanish monarch, King Philip II, to destroy English sea power and invade England. The Spanish Armada was defeated and destroyed in part by the British fleet commanded by Charles Howard and in part by sea storms. SIR FRANCIS DRAKE, JOHN HAWKINS and MARTIN FROBISHER also fought in this victorious British sea battle.

SPANISH TRAIL. One of the routes used by American pioneers in the early 19th century to reach the Pacific coast. The Spanish Trail led from Santa Fe, New Mexico, west to California. (See SANTA FE TRAIL)

SPECIE CIRCULAR (1836). Order of President ANDREW JACKSON directing that in all future sales of public lands, payment was to be accepted in gold and silver only. The purpose of the circular was to stop payments for public

331

lands with paper money issued by state banks. By this order Jackson hoped to stop the widespread speculation in public lands. (See PANIC OF 1837)

SPOILS SYSTEM. Also called "Party Patronage." It was a policy of giving government jobs to political party workers after an election victory. During President ANDREW JACKSON's administration (1829-37) government employees of the rival party (NATIONAL REPUBLICAN PARTY) were summarily dismissed soon after the presidential inauguration and were replaced by members of the DEMOCRATIC PARTY. This procedure, which had been going on in state governments for many years (see ALBANY REGENCY), derived its name from a statement made by Senator WILLIAM L. MARCY in 1831 that "to the victor belong the spoils of the enemy." The Spoils System continued until Congress passed the PENDLETON ACT (1883).

SQUARE DEAL. See ROOSEVELT, THEODORE

SQUATTERS. People who settle on public land to which they do not have title of ownership. During the WESTWARD MOVEMENT in the 19th century, thousands of squatters went West and settled on any desirable piece of land without getting a clear title to it from the government. In 1830 and again in 1841 Congress passed a series of PREEMPTION ACTS, giving title to squatters under certain conditions. (See PUBLIC LAND ACTS)

SQUATTER SOVEREIGNTY. See KANSAS-NEBRASKA ACT

STALWART. Popular name applied to the conservative wing of the REPUBLICAN PARTY after 1876 to distinguish it from the HALF BREEDS or reform wing. The Stalwarts were led by ROSCOE CONKLING of New York, SIMON CAMERON of Pennsylvania and JOHN A. LOGAN of Illinois. They opposed the reform program of President RUTHERFORD B. HAYES.

STAMP ACT (1765). Passed by the British Parliament as part of Prime Minister GEORGE GRENVILLE's program of raising more colonial revenue. The act required all legal documents, newspapers, almanacs and other similar papers to have stamps placed on them. The act aroused so much opposition in the colonies (see STAMP ACT CONGRESS) that it was repealed the following year.

STAMP ACT CONGRESS (1765). One of the evidences of growing colonial resistance to British policies. A convention of delegates from nine colonies met in New York City to protest against the levy of the stamp tax. (See STAMP ACT, 1765) The Stamp Act Congress issued a declaration stating that only colonial governments, not the British Parliament, could levy taxes on the colonists.

STANDARD OIL COMPANY. See ROCKEFELLER, JOHN D.

STANFORD, LELAND (1824-1893). See SOUTHERN PACIFIC RAILROAD

STANTON, EDWIN M. (1814-69). Replaced SIMON CAMERON as Secretary of War in President ABRAHAM LINCOLN's cabinet in 1862. After Lincoln's assassination (1865) it was charged that Stanton suppressed evidence that might have saved Mrs. Mary E. Surrat from being hanged as one of the conspirators. Stanton remained in President ANDREW JOHNSON's cabinet and Congress passed the TENURE OF OFFICE ACT (1867) mainly to keep Stanton in the cabinet. Johnson's removal of Stanton from office in violation of the Tenure of Office Act led to the IMPEACHMENT OF JOHNSON (1868).

STANTON, ELIZABETH CADY (1815-1902). One of the leaders in the struggle for women's rights, including the right to vote, own property, attend universities and engage in professions. She was one of the important figures in the 19th century FEMINIST MOVEMENT, was one of the leading organizers of the Seneca Falls Convention (1848) for women's rights, and was president of the National Women's Suffrage Association (1869-90).

STAR ROUTE FRAUDS (1881-83). Political scandal that was exposed during President JAMES A. GARFIELD's and President CHESTER A. ARTHUR'S administrations. The frauds consisted of raising mail rates illegally on certain

333

routes in the South and Far West and in receiving government payments for fictitious delivery of mail.

STAR SPANGLED BANNER. See KEY, FRANCIS SCOTT

STATES RIGHTS DOCTRINE. Political theory held by many Southerners before the War Between the States (1861-65). The States Rights Doctrine held that the U. S. Constitution was a compact among the states (see COMPACT THEORY), that the states could declare acts of Congress null and void if these acts violated the Constitution (see NULLIFICATION), and that the states had the right to secede from the Union. The States Rights Doctrine was stated in the VIRGINIA AND KENTUCKY RESOLUTIONS (1798), by the resolutions of the HARTFORD CONVENTION (1814), by JOHN C. CALHOUN's EXPOSITION AND PROTEST (1828) and by the South Carolina ORDINANCE OF NULLIFICATION (1832). John C. Calhoun was the South's leading expounder of the States Rights Doctrine.

STATE SUICIDE THEORY. Proposed after the WAR BETWEEN THE STATES (1861-65) by Senator CHARLES SUMNER as a basis for readmitting the seceded states into the Union. Under this theory the Southern states lost their statehood by secession and reverted to the status of territories. The former states could return to the Union only with the consent of Congress. This differed from ABRAHAM LINCOLN's theory that individuals had seceded and therefore the president, not Congress, could pardon individuals and restore the South to the Union.

STEAGALL NATIONAL HOUSING ACT (1938). See HOUSING LEGISLATION

STEPHENS, ALEXANDER H. (1812-83). Vice-president of the CONFEDERATE STATES OF AMERICA during the WAR BETWEEN THE STATES (1861-65). He was head of the peace mission known as the HAMPTON ROADS CONFERENCE that met in 1865. At the end of the war Stephens was imprisoned for a few months, was elected to the Senate from Georgia but was not permitted to take his seat in the Senate.

STEPHENS, URIAH S. (1821-82). In 1869 he organized a group of Philadelphia tailors into a secret union. This became the foundation of the Noble Order of the KNIGHTS OF LABOR, one of the earliest national labor organizations in the U. S. Stephens was head of the Knights of Labor until 1879, when he was succeeded by Terence V. Powderly.

STEUBEN, BARON VON (1730-94). Prussian nobleman and soldier of fortune who came to America during the AMERICAN REVOLUTION (1775-83) to help train the CONTINENTAL ARMY. He was with General GEORGE WASHINGTON at VALLEY FORGE and played an important role in the BATTLE OF MONMOUTH (1778) and the BATTLE OF YORKTOWN (1781).

STEVENS, THADDEUS (1792-1868). At the end of the WAR BETWEEN THE STATES (1861) Congressman Stevens opposed President ABRAHAM LINCOLN's moderate RECONSTRUCTION program for the South. Stevens announced his CONQUERED PROVINCE THEORY and insisted that the South should be treated as a defeated enemy. Stevens led the movement in Congress for the enactment of a harsh Reconstruction program, proposed AMENDMENT 14, and was one of the leaders in the IMPEACHMENT OF JOHNSON (1868).

STIMSON DOCTRINE (1932). In 1931 Japan invaded and conquered the northeast Chinese province of Manchuria. The U. S. declared this to be a violation of the KELLOGG-BRIAND PACT (1928). Secretary of state Henry L. Stimson announced that the U. S. would not recognize any territorial changes made in violation of the pact. This policy became known as the Stimson Doctrine.

STIMSON, HENRY L. (1867-1950). The only man who has thus far served in the cabinet of four different presidents. He was Secretary of War (1911-13) under President WILLIAM H. TAFT, Secretary of State (1929-33) under President HERBERT HOOVER, Secretary of War (1940-45) under President FRANKLIN D. ROOSEVELT and President HARRY S. TRUMAN. He was chief U. S. delegate to the LONDON NAVAL CONFERENCE

(1930) and formulated the famous STIMSON DOCTRINE (1932).

STOWE, HARRIET BEECHER (1811-96). Author of the famous novel Uncle Tom's Cabin (1852), an imaginary tale of slave life under the Southern PLANTATION SYSTEM. The novel had a profound influence on Northern opinion, and was widely read and translated.

STRAWFOOT. Young recruit during the WAR BETWEEN THE STATES (1861-65). Farm boys who enlisted sometimes had trouble distinguishing their left from their right foot. By tying hay on the left foot and straw on the right, and by chanting "hay foot, straw foot," drill sergeants could teach their recruits proper marching procedure. (See DOUGHBOYS and G.I.'s)

STRICT INTERPRETATION OF CONSTITUTION. See LOOSE INTERPRETATION OF THE CONSTITUTION

STUART, JAMES E. (1833-64). Best known as "Jeb" Stuart. During the WAR BETWEEN THE STATES (1861-65) he served with great distinction at the first BATTLE OF BULL RUN (1861), the second BATTLE OF BULL RUN (1862), the BATTLE OF ANTIETAM (1862), the BATTLE OF FREDERICKSBURG (1862), the BATTLE OF CHANCELLORSVILLE (1863) and in the WILDERNESS CAMPAIGN (1864-65). In this last campaign Stuart was killed during the fighting. Stuart's cavalry command was famous for its raids deep inside the Union lines, for the valuable information obtained from these raids and for its brilliant cavalry charges during battle.

STUYVESANT, PETER (1592-1672). The last Dutch governor of NEW AMSTERDAM. When a fleet of English ships appeared in New York harbor in 1664 he was forced to surrender the colony. The British took possession of the settlement and renamed it New York.

SUBMARINE WARFARE. Submarines or U-Boats (undersea boats) used by combatants in WORLD WAR I (1914-18) and WORLD WAR II (1939-45) to sink enemy merchant ships. During World War I German submarines sank merchant ships without regard to the lives of crew and passengers. (See LUSITANIA) The U. S., as a neutral, protested the German policy of unrestricted submarine warfare. After changing the policy for a short time (Sussex Pledge), Germany in 1917 renewed its unrestricted submarine warfare, and this led to a U. S. declaration of war. In World War II unrestricted submarine warfare was practiced by both sides from the very beginning of hostilities. (See ATLANTIC, BATTLE OF THE)

SUGAR ACT (1764). Passed by the British Parliament as part of Prime Minister GEORGE GRENVILLE'S colonial program of stricter law enforcement and more tax income. The Sugar Act lowered the duty on foreign molasses to discourage smuggling from the French West Indies islands, but raised the duty on refined sugar and other foreign goods.

SUMNER, CHARLES (1811-74). Senator from Massachusetts and vigorous anti-slavery leader. After the War Between the States (1865), Sumner and THADDEUS STEVENS led the movement to pass the harsh RECONSTRUCTION program for the readmission of the Southern states to the Union. (See STATE SUICIDE THEORY) Sumner was also one of the leaders in the IMPEACHMENT OF PRESIDENT JOHNSON (1868).

SUMTER, FORT. Federal fortification in the harbor of Charleston, South Carolina. On April 12, 1861, the fort, under the command of Major Robert Anderson, was attacked by a military force under General GUSTAVE BEAUREGARD. This signaled the beginning of the WAR BETWEEN THE STATES (1861-65).

SUSSEX PLEDGE (1916). See SUBMARINE WARFARE

SUTTER'S MILL. Site of the first discovery of gold in California (1848) near Sacramento. The news of the discovery reached the East coast of the United States within a short time and led to the great California GOLD RUSH (1849).

"SWAMP FOX." See MARION, FRANCIS

TAFT-HARTLEY ACT (1947). Also known as the Labor Management Relations Act. This law was a supplement to the NATIONAL LABOR RELATIONS ACT (1935). The Taft-Hartley Act forbad closed shops, secondary boycotts and jurisdictional strikes by unions. It also limited high union initiation or membership dues or union contributions to political campaign funds. If a union threatened a strike it was required to give 60 days' notice to an employer. In the event of a strike that threatened the national health or safety, the federal government could ask for a court injunction postponing the strike for 80 days. President HARRY S. TRUMAN vetoed the act but Congress passed it over his veto.

TAFT, ROBERT A. (1889-1953). Son of president WILLIAM HOWARD TAFT. Robert Taft was recognized as the Congressional spokesman of the REPUBLICAN PARTY after WORLD WAR II (1945) and was known as "Mr. Republican." During his term of office in the Senate he sponsored the TAFT-HARTLEY LAW (1947). He was a leading advocate of an ISOLATION policy before World War II but became a supporter of the UNITED NATIONS after the war.

TAFT, WILLIAM HOWARD (1857-1930). Twenty-seventh president of the U. S. and tenth Chief Justice of the U. S. Supreme Court, the only man to have held both posts. In 1908 the REPUBLICAN PARTY, influenced by THEODORE ROOSEVELT, nominated Taft for the presidency. In the ELECTION OF 1908 Taft defeated WILLIAM JENNINGS BRYAN, the Democratic Party candidate, by a large popular vote. In 1912 Taft was again nominated by the Republicans, but his differences with Theodore Roosevelt led to a Republican Party split. This resulted in a victory for WOODROW WILSON, the Democratic Party candidate in the ELECTION OF 1912. In 1921 Taft was appointed Chief Justice of the Supreme Court, which post he held until he retired in 1930.

During Taft's term as president (1909-13), Congress established the Postal Savings Banks and the Parcel Post system, passed the PAYNE-ALDRICH TARIFF ACT (1909) and the MANN-ELKINS ACT (1910). The Supreme Court ordered the dissolution of the Standard Oil Company monopoly (1911) and the reorganization of the Tobacco Trust (1911).

TALLMAGE AMENDMENT (1819). Amendment to a bill to admit Missouri as a state in the Union. The Tallmage Amendment provided for the prohibition of further importation of slaves into Missouri after its admission as a state. The defeat of the amendment in the Senate set the stage for the MISSOURI COMPROMISE (1820).

TAMMANY HALL. Originally the New York Tammany Society was a social, cultural and patriotic organization. AARON BURR was one of its early leaders. After the election of ANDREW JACKSON (1829) to the presidency, Tammany became one of the most powerful political groups in New York City, representing the city Democratic Party machine. Except for a few intervals when reform mayors were elected (SAMUEL J. TILDEN, 1872; Seth Low, 1901; FIORELLO LA GUARDIA, 1932) the government of New York City was controlled by Tammany Hall. Some of the most corrupt eras in the city's history, such as the rules of "Boss" WILLIAM M. TWEED, RICHARD CROKER and James J. Walker were the result of Tammany control.

TAMPICO INCIDENT (1914). An American fleet was sent to Tampico, Mexico to protect American lives and property. A number of American sailors were arrested by the Huerta government of Mexico. The American admiral demanded their release and an apology. The Huerta government submitted to most of these demands. However, the arrival of a German vessel carrying arms and ammunition for the Huerta government led President WOODROW WILSON to order U. S. naval forces to occupy Tampico. As a result of the mediation of the ABC POWERS (Argentina, Brazil, Chile) and the meeting at the Niagara Falls Convention (1914), Huerta resigned, Carranza became the new president of Mexico and the U. S. withdrew its forces from Tampico.

TANEY, ROGER B. (1777-1864). Chief Justice of U. S. Supreme Court (1836-64). Taney's decisions enforcing the FUGITIVE SLAVE LAWS made him unpopular with antislavery factions in the North. His most famous decision was the DRED SCOTT CASE (1857). During the WAR BETWEEN THE STATES (1861-65) Taney opposed President ABRAHAM LINCOLN's suspension of the writ of HABEAS CORPUS.

TARIFF LEGISLATION. From 1789 to 1815 Congress levied revenue tariffs only. (See TARIFF OF 1789) In 1816 Congress enacted the first protective tariff. (See TARIFF OF 1816) From 1828 to 1861, the tariff was a sectional issue. (See SECTIONALISM) In general, the South opposed the protective tariff and the North favored it. (See TARIFF OF ABOMINATIONS, 1828; COMPROMISE TARIFF, 1833; WALKER TARIFF, 1846) During the WAR BETWEEN THE STATES (1861-65), Congress enacted high tariff laws to raise revenue for the conduct of the war. The era of high protective tariffs began with the MC KINLEY TARIFF (1890) and continued to remain high (DINGLEY TARIFF, 1894; PAYNE-ALDRICH TARIFF, 1909; FORDNEY-MC CUMBER TARIFF, 1922; HAWLEY-SMOOT TARIFF, 1930) with only a few brief interruptions when the tariff was lowered somewhat. (See WILSON-GORMAN TARIFF, 1894; UNDERWOOD TARIFF, 1913) In 1934 the NEW DEAL Congress passed the RECIPROCAL TARIFF ACT which led to a gradual reduction in tariff rates. Most of our present tariff rates, however, remain high. In 1962 Congress passed the TRADE EXPANSION ACT.

TARIFF OF ABOMINATIONS (1828). So called by the South. This tariff increased rates beyond those of the TARIFF OF 1816 and 1824. The new tariff aroused tremendous hostility in the South, and led to threats of Southern boycotts of Northern manufactured goods. (See SECTIONALISM: TARIFF LEGISLATION)

TARIFF OF 1789. First tariff in our history. It was proposed in HAMILTON'S FINANCIAL PLANS for raising revenue for the federal treasury. The law placed duties on about 30 articles, including molasses, hemp and steel. (See TARIFF LEGISLATION)

TARIFF OF 1816. First protective tariff in our history. After the WAR OF 1812 (1814) new industries, particularly in woolen, cotton and iron manufacturing, asked Congress for protection against the dumping of foreign manufactured goods. Congress passed the Tariff of 1816. The South, hoping the tariff would stimulate the growth of manufacturing in its section, favored it, but this hope failed to materialize. By 1828 the South called the protective tariff a TARIFF OF ABOMINATIONS. (See TARIFF LEGISLATION)

TARIFF OF 1832. Reduced the rates of the earlier TARIFF OF ABOMINATIONS (1828). However, the new tariff remained high. It was this tariff of 1832 that South Carolina declared null and void and threatened secession if it were enforced in that state. (See NULLIFICATION PROCLAMATION) The controversy was settled by the enactment of the lower COMPROMISE TARIFF OF 1833. (See TARIFF LEGISLATION)

TAXATION WITHOUT REPRESENTATION. This argument was used by the American colonists in protesting taxes levied by the British Parliament before the AMERICAN REVOLUTION (1775). The colonists recognized many of the taxes as reasonable but objected to paying them because they were passed by the British Parliament, in which the colonists were not represented.

TAYLOR, ZACHARY (1784-1850). Twelfth president of the U. S. Taylor served with WILLIAM HENRY HARRISON in a number of Indian campaigns, in the WAR OF 1812, and in expeditions against the BLACK HAWK INDIANS and SEMINOLE INDIANS. During the MEXICAN WAR (1846-48), Taylor won a notable victory at the BATTLE OF BUENA VISTA (1847) and earned the nickname of "Old Rough and Ready." Taylor was nominated for the presidency by the WHIG PARTY in the ELECTION OF 1848 and was elected mainly because of his military record. He died in office after serving little more than one year.

TEA ACT (1770). After the repeal (1770) of the TOWNSHEND ACTS (1767), the British Parliament passed the Tea Act, which continued the tax on tea imported by the American colonists. This Tea Act led to the BOSTON TEA PARTY (1773).

TEAPOT DOME SCANDAL (1924). Albert Fall, Secretary of the Interior under President WARREN G. HARDING, leased government-owned oil lands in Wyoming (called Teapot Dome) to oilman Harry F. Sinclair. Fall also leased Elks Hill oil lands in California to Edward L. Doheny, another oil man. Subsequently it was learned that Fall had received about $400,000 in interest free "loans" from Sinclair and Doheny. Fall was tried, convicted and jailed for accepting bribes, and the oil leases were cancelled.

TECUMSEH (c.1768-1813). Leader of an Indian Confederation that sought to stop further westward expansion of American settlers into the NORTHWEST TERRITORY in the early 19th century. During the WAR OF 1812 (1812-14) Tecumseh's Indian Confederation joined with the British against the U. S. He was killed and his Indian Confederation, together with a British Army, were defeated by an American force under General WILLIAM HENRY HARRISON at the Battle of the Thames River (1813) in Canada.

TELLER RESOLUTION (1898). Passed by Congress, stating that the U. S. intended to recognize Cuba's independence after the restoration of peace on the island. (See SPANISH-AMERICAN WAR, 1898) The purpose of this resolution was to allay fears of many anti-imperialist Americans that the U. S. intended to wage war on Spain in order to annex Cuba.

TENNESSEE VALLEY AUTHORITY ACT (1933). Authorized the establishment of a Tennessee Valley Authority (T.V.A.) with power to plan and develop the entire Tennessee River Valley area with respect to water power, soil conservation, rural electrification, forest conservation, flood control and river navigation. The T.V.A. area included sections of seven different states. Under powers granted by Congress, the T.V.A. built dams, power plants, electric transmission lines and housing projects. In 1936 the Supreme Court held the T.V.A. was constitutional. (See ASHWANDER V. T.V.A.)

TENURE OF OFFICE ACT (1867). Passed by Congress over President ANDREW JOHNSON's veto. The act provided that the president could not dismiss a federal official without the consent of the Senate. When Johnson dismissed Secretary of War EDWIN M. STANTON without the Senate's approval, the House of Representatives impeached the president. (See IMPEACHMENT OF JOHNSON) The Tenure of Office Act was repealed in 1887. In 1926 the Supreme Court held that the president could remove federal officials without the consent of the Senate.

TEXAS. Second largest state in the U. S., admitted as a state in 1845. During its long and colorful history Texas has been under five flags. It was a Spanish province (till 1821), a Mexican province (1821-36) (see MOSES AUSTIN, SAM HOUSTON), an independent republic (1836-45) (see TEXAS WAR OF INDEPENDENCE, LONE STAR REPUBLIC), a state in the U. S. (1845-61), a state in the **CONFEDERATE STATES OF AMERICA** during the WAR BETWEEN THE STATES (1861-65) and finally a restored state in the Union.

TEXAS ANNEXATION (1845). In the ELECTION OF 1844 the DEMOCRATIC PARTY succeeded in electing JAMES K. POLK as president on a platform calling for the annexation of Texas. In 1845 Congress, by a joint resolution, annexed Texas to the U. S. on the following conditions: Four additional states might be carved out of Texas territory; slavery was to be prohibited north of the 36° 30′ line of latitude in Texas territory; and Texas was to pay her own public debts. The terms of the resolution were accepted by Texas and it became a state in 1845.

TEXAS WAR OF INDEPENDENCE (1836). Fought between Americans who had settled in the Mexican province of Texas (see MOSES AUSTIN) and the Mexican government. It began when the Mexican government forbad the further importation of slaves into Texas and restricted the political rights of the Texans. After a few brief battles (see ALAMO) and a major Texan victory at the BATTLE OF SAN JACINTO (1836) the war came to an end. (See SAM HOUSTON) The Texans established an independent nation called the LONE STAR REPUBLIC.

THIRTEEN COLONIES. The English colonies that united to fight in the AMERICAN REVOLUTION (1775-83), signed the DECLARATION OF INDEPENDENCE (1776) and subsequently formed the United States of America (1783). These included most, but not all, of the British colonies in North America. The Thirteen Colonies included NEW HAMPSHIRE, MASSACHUSETTS, CONNECTICUT RHODE ISLAND, New York (see NEW NETHERLAND), NEW JERSEY, PENNSYLVANIA, DELAWARE, MARYLAND, VIRGINIA, NORTH CAROLINA, SOUTH CAROLINA and GEORGIA.

THOMAS, GENERAL GEORGE H. (1816-70). Known as the "Rock of Chickamauga." He was one of the Union Army commanders during the WAR BETWEEN THE STATES (1861-65). At the BATTLE OF CHICKAMAUGA (1863) General Thomas and his forces saved the remainder of the Union Army by putting up a stubborn resistance against the Confederate Army of General Braxton Bragg.

TICONDEROGA, FORT. Important colonial fort on Lake Champlain in upper New York State. During the FRENCH AND INDIAN WAR (1754-63) the French seized the fort and renamed it Fort Carillon. In 1759 the British, under JEFFREY AMHERST, recaptured it. At the beginning of the AMERICAN REVOLUTION (1775-83), the fort was captured by ETHAN ALLEN and his Green Mountain Boys with practically no resistance from the British garrison. In 1777 the British under General John Burgoyne recaptured the fort on their way south and just before their surrender at the BATTLE OF SARATOGA (1777).

TIDEWATER. Coastal region of the Southern states extending inland to areas reached by ocean tides or to the "fall line" of rivers. The area was the region of large plantations (see PLANTATION SYSTEM) and the stronghold of the Southern slave-holding aristocracy before the WAR BETWEEN THE STATES (1861-65).

TILDEN, SAMUEL J. (1814-86). Successfully prosecuted members of the corrupt TWEED RING in New York City. He was elected governor of New York State (1874) and was nominated for the presidency by the DEMOCRATIC PARTY in 1876. In the ELECTION of 1876 the conflicting electoral returns from a number of states left the election undecided. A Congressional electoral commission decided all of the electoral votes in favor of RUTHERFORD B.

HAYES, the REPUBLICAN PARTY candidate, who thus became president. (See ELECTORAL COMMISSION ACT)

"TIPPECANOE AND TYLER TOO." See ELECTION OF 1840

TIPPECANOE, BATTLE OF (1811). Military engagement between a confederation of Indians and an American force led by WILLIAM HENRY HARRISON, governor of the Indiana Territory. Neither side won a decisive victory but Harrison's reputation for bravery spread through the country and was a major factor in his nomination for the presidency by the WHIG PARTY in the ELECTION OF 1840.

TOLERATION ACT (1649). Enacted by the MARYLAND Colony, guaranteeing religious freedom to all Christians. This included Catholics as well as all Protestant sects.

TOLLS EXEMPTION ACT (1912). See CANAL TOLLS CONTROVERSY

TOOMBS, ROBERT (1810-85). Southern political leader before and during the WAR BETWEEN THE STATES (1861-65). He was Secretary of State in the CONFEDERATE STATES OF AMERICA but resigned to fight with the Southern armies. After the war he fled to England but returned in 1867. He remained an influential figure in Georgia state politics.

"TOO PROUD TO FIGHT" (1915). Before the U. S. entered WORLD WAR I President WOODROW WILSON, in a public address, stated one of the reasons for his neutrality policy. He said, "There is such a thing as a man being too proud to fight."

TOPEKA CONSTITUTION (1855). Free soil advocates in the Kansas Territory during the Kansas Civil War (See BLEEDING KANSAS) refused to recognize the legality of the elected anti-slavery legislature, claiming it was chosen by fraud. The free soil group held its own convention and drew up a pro-slavery constitution for Kansas called the Topeka Constitution. However, it was never accepted by

345

Congress. (See LECOMPTON CONSTITUTION and WYANDOTTE CONSTITUTION)

TORIES. Supporters of the 18th century English party which was usually on the side of the British monarchs. In colonial America the name "Tory" was applied to those who supported the British. During the AMERICAN REVOLUTION (1775-83) those who remained loyal to the British were also called Tories or LOYALISTS.

TOSCANELLI, PAOLO (1397-1482). Italian geographer and cartographer of the 15th century. Columbus, on his first voyage across the Atlantic Ocean, used one of his maps.

"TO THE VICTOR BELONG THE SPOILS OF THE ENEMY." See MARCY, WILLIAM L.

TOWNSHEND ACTS (1767). British laws which levied a tax on tea, paper, glass, lead and painters' colors imported into the colonies. The tax money was to be used to pay the salaries of royal officials in the colonies. Because of colonial opposition, all the taxes except the tax on tea were repealed in 1770.

TRADE EXPANSION ACT (1962). Gave the President new powers to reduce tariff rates on imports to the U.S. This authority was granted by Congress in order to provide the President with a bargaining lever for mutual tariff concessions by members of the European Common Market, and other free nations of the world. The act also provided for financial trade adjustment assistance to American companies and workers injured by increased imports of competitive products resulting from tariff reductions.

TRANSPORTATION ACT (1940). Also known as the Wheeler-Lea Act. The law provided that all coastal, intercoastal, and interstate water carriers were to be under the jurisdiction of the INTERSTATE COMMERCE COMMISSION.

TREATIES OF 1778. Two treaties signed by the U. S. and France during the AMERICAN REVOLUTION (1775-83). The first treaty was a trade and commercial agreement between the two nations. The second treaty (see TREATY

OF ALLIANCE) established an alliance between the U. S. and France.

TREATY OF . . . See heading under name of treaty.

TREATY OF ALLIANCE (1778). Signed by the U. S. and France during the AMERICAN REVOLUTION (1775-83). The treaty provided that if France entered the war against Great Britain, neither France nor the U. S. would make a separate peace without the consent of the other nor would a treaty be signed until the independence of the U. S. was established. As a result of this treaty, France entered the war against Great Britain and provided the U. S. with substantial aid in men and materials during the Revolution. The treaty was ended by the U. S. in 1800 by an arrangement called the CONVENTION OF 1800 or Treaty of Morfontaine. (See FRANCE, U. S. RELATIONS WITH)

TREATY OF 1818. Settled a dispute between the U. S. and Great Britain over the northern boundary of the LOUISIANA TERRITORY. The treaty fixed the boundary at the 49th parallel and also gave the U. S. fishing rights along the coasts of Labrador and Newfoundland. Furthermore, the treaty provided for joint occupation of the OREGON TERRITORY by the U. S. and Great Britain for a ten-year renewable period.

"TRENT" AFFAIR (1861). During the WAR BETWEEN THE STATES (1861-65), two Confederate envoys to Great Britain and France, James Mason and John Slidell, were forcibly removed from a British ship, the *Trent* by a Union warship. The incident almost led Great Britain to declare war on the North. However, President ABRAHAM LINCOLN ordered the release of the two men and the incident was closed.

TRENTON, BATTLE OF (1776). General GEORGE WASHINGTON and a small American force crossed the ice-clogged Delaware River from Pennsylvania to the city of Trenton, N. J. There they attacked a small force of HESSIAN soldiers. The surprise attack resulted in an important though minor American victory. (See AMERICAN REVOLUTION)

347

TRIANGULAR TRADE. Most commonly refers to the colonial shipment of molasses and sugar from the West Indies to New England where it was manufactured into rum, the barter of New England rum for Negro slaves in West Africa and the shipment of slaves from West Africa to the West Indies. The movement of slaves from Africa to the West Indies islands was called the "Middle Passage." Other triangular trading routes in colonial times ran from New England to European ports, to the West Indies and back to New England.

TRIPOLI WAR. See BARBARY PIRATES and STEPHEN DECATUR

TRUMAN DOCTRINE (1947). When Greece was threatened with political and military control by the Soviet Union, President HARRY S. TRUMAN declared that the U. S. must support free peoples who are resisting attempted subjection by armed minorities or by outside pressures. On the basis of this Truman Doctrine, Congress voted financial and military aid to Greece and Turkey.

TRUMAN, HARRY S. (1884-   ). Thirty-fourth president of the U. S. As senator from Missouri he gained national prominence as chairman of a Senate committee investigating national defense expenditures. At the DEMOCRATIC PARTY convention in 1944 he was nominated for the vice-presidency and, together with FRANKLIN D. ROOSE-VELT, won in the ELECTION OF 1944. On Roosevelt's death in 1945 Truman became president. In the ELECTION OF 1948 he was the Democratic Party candidate and won a surprising victory.

In domestic affairs, Truman's presidency saw Congress pass the G. I. BILL OF RIGHTS (1944) for war veterans, unify the army, navy and air force into a single Department of Defense (1947), adopt a new PRESIDENTIAL SUCCESSION ACT (1947) and end wartime price and wage controls. However Truman's Fair Deal policies of civil rights legislation, national health insurance and a new federal farm program were blocked by Congress. In foreign affairs, Truman authorized the use of the first ATOMB BOMB against Japan during WORLD WAR II (1941-45), and approved the POTSDAM AGREEMENT (1945). The MARSHALL PLAN (1947) for foreign aid, the NORTH

ATLANTIC TREATY ORGANIZATION (1949) and the POINT FOUR PROGRAM (1949) were all adopted by Congress. In 1950 Truman ordered American forces to resist Communist aggression in Korea, thus precipitating the KOREAN WAR (1950-53).

TRUST BUSTER. Applied to President THEODORE ROOSEVELT because of his outspoken criticism of industrial monopolies and his efforts to get strict enforcement of the SHERMAN ANTI-TRUST ACT (1890).

TURNPIKES. In colonial times and in the early 19th century, private companies built roads and turnpikes for the use of which wagons and carriages paid tolls. One of the most successful of these toll roads was the Philadelphia-Lancaster Turnpike (1794) in Pennsylvania.

TWEED RING. Group of corrupt New York City politicians led by WILLIAM MARCY TWEED, the leader of TAMMANY HALL. After the War Between the States (1861-65) the Tweed Ring stole millions of dollars from the city treasury by means of padded city contracts. As a result of articles and cartoons (see THOMAS NAST) in the city's newspapers and magazines the corrupt methods of the Tweed Ring were exposed. Many members of the ring, including Tweed, were tried, convicted and sent to jail. (See SAMUEL J. TILDEN)

TWEED, WILLIAM MARCY (1823-78). Also known as "Boss" Tweed. As New York City Commissioner of the Department of Public Works (1870) he engaged in a series of frauds that involved millions of dollars of city funds. He and his associates became known as the TWEED RING. He was tried for fraud, escaped to Spain while out of prison on bail, was returned to the U. S. and died in jail.

TWENTY-ONE DEMANDS (1915). During WORLD WAR I (1914-18) Japan presented twenty-one demands to the Chinese government which would have given Japan special economic, territorial and military privileges in China and would have put an end to the American OPEN DOOR POLICY. The U. S. protested and Japan withdrew the demands.

TYDINGS-MC DUFFIE ACT (1934). Provided that the U. S. would grant independence to the PHILIPPINE ISLANDS at the end of a ten-year period. Tariffs on Philippine goods sent to the U. S. were to be imposed gradually. Because of WORLD WAR II (1941-45), the declaration of Philippine independence which under this act was to take place in 1945 was postponed for one year. On July 4, 1946 the independence of the Philippine Republic was officially proclaimed.

TYLER, JOHN (1790-1862). Tenth president of the U. S. The WHIG PARTY nominated him for vice-president in the ELECTION OF 1840, together with WILLIAM HENRY HARRISON as president. Both were elected. On Harrison's death in April, 1841, Tyler succeeded to the presidency. Among the highlights of his administration were the enactment of the Tariff of 1842, the signing of the WEBSTER-ASHBURTON TREATY (1842) with Canada, and TEXAS ANNEXATION (1845). Because of Tyler's opposition to the policies of his own Whig Party, he did not run for president in the election of 1844.

U-BOATS. See SUBMARINE WARFARE.

UNCLE SAM. Name of the symbol representing the U. S. It probably originated during the WAR of 1812. A New York merchant named Samuel Wilson was known among his employees as "Uncle Sam." He labeled his packages U. S. and it soon came to represent the United States. The first cartoon of a man named Uncle Sam to represent the U. S. appeared in 1852. THOMAS NAST, the famous cartoonist of HARPER'S WEEKLY, added whiskers to the Uncle Sam cartoon.

"UNCLE TOM'S CABIN" (1852). See STOWE, HARRIET BEECHER

"UNCONDITIONAL SURRENDER" GRANT. Name applied to General ULYSSES S. GRANT during the WAR BETWEEN THE STATES (1861-65). During Grant's siege of Fort Donelson (1862) he answered a request of the Confederate commander for terms of surrender by writing, "No terms other than unconditional and immediate surrender can be accepted."

UNDERGROUND RAILROAD. Method and route used by runaway slaves to escape to Canada before the WAR BETWEEN THE STATES (1861-65). Runaway slaves were hidden in the homes of ABOLITIONIST sympathizers during the daytime and were moved north at night a few miles at a time until they reached the Canadian border.

UNDERWOOD TARIFF (1913). Passed during President WOODROW WILSON's administration. On the average the Underwood Tariff reduced the rates of the earlier PAYNE-ALDRICH TARIFF (1909) by about 10%. The Underwood Tariff also levied a graduated INCOME TAX on the basis of the recently ratified AMENDMENT 16 (1913). (See TARIFF LEGISLATION)

UNEMPLOYMENT LEGISLATION. When FRANKLIN D. ROOSEVELT became president after the ELECTION OF 1932, the GREAT DEPRESSION (1929-35) had left about 10,000,000 workers unemployed. Under the NEW DEAL legislative program, Congress passed laws to provide some kind of work for the unemployed and at the same time tried to stimulate industrial production. In 1933 the Public Works Administration (P.W.A.) was organized to start a long-term program of public works projects such as dams, roads and public buildings. In the same year the Civil Works Administration (C.W.A.) was established to provide immediate employment on any kind of government work and the Federal Emergency Relief Administration (F.E.R.A.) was set up to give direct aid to states for needy people. In 1934 the CIVILIAN CONSERVATION CORPS (C.C.C.) was organized to provide work for unemployed young men. In 1935 the Works Progress Administration (W.P.A.) was established to develop a public works program requiring small expenditures for materials and large expenditures for wages. Finally in 1935 the SOCIAL SECURITY ACT was passed. One of its major provisions established an unemployment insurance system to be administered by individual states with federal cooperation.

UNESCO. United Nations Educational, Scientific and Cultural Organization. It is a UNITED NATIONS agency whose task is to encourage cultural and scientific cooperation among the nations of the world.

UNION PACIFIC RAILROAD (1869). Rail line running from Omaha, Nebraska west to Ogden, Utah. Construction of the road began in 1865 and was completed in 1869. It was part of the first transcontinental railroad to span the West. The Central Pacific Railroad continued from Ogden, Utah to California on the Pacific coast to form the first transcontinental rail line to the Pacific. (See RAILROAD LAND ACTS)

UNITED MINE WORKERS OF AMERICA (U.M.W.). Industrial union organized in 1890. Under the presidency of John Mitchell the miners won higher wages and improved working conditions in the bitter ANTHRACITE COAL STRIKE (1902). In 1920 JOHN L. LEWIS became president of the union. When Lewis organized the CONGRESS

OF INDUSTRIAL ORGANIZATIONS (1935), the U.M.W. was one of the first unions to join.

UNITED NATIONS (U.N.) 1945. International peace organization whose charter was written at the SAN FRANCISCO CONFERENCE (1945). The U. N. consists of a General Assembly, SECURITY COUNCIL, Military Staff Committee, Secretariat, Economic and Social Council (ECOSOC), Trusteeship Council, International Court of Justice as well as scores of specialized agencies. Among these special organizations are the World Health Organization (W.H.O.), International Labor Organization (I.L.O.), United Nations Educational, Scientific and Cultural Organization (UNESCO) and many others. The permanent home of the U. N. is in New York City. The U. S. is a charter member of the organization.

U.S. V. BUTLER (1936). See AGRICULTURAL ADJUSTMENT ACT OF 1933

U. S. V. KNIGHT (1895). The U. S., acting under the SHERMAN ANTI-TRUST ACT (1890), prosecuted the American Sugar Refining Company as a monopoly. The Supreme Court held that sugar refining, of itself, was manufacturing, not interstate commerce. Therefore it was not subject to federal regulation. This decision seriously impaired the effectiveness of the Sherman Anti-Trust Act. However, the court modified its ruling in 1899 in the case of ADDYSTON PIPE AND STEEL CO. V. U. S.

VALLEY FORGE. Winter headquarters (1777-78) of General GEORGE WASHINGTON and the colonial army during the AMERICAN REVOLUTION (1775-83). Lack of supplies, food, clothing, shoes and proper barracks resulted in bitter hardships for the American soldiers. It was the darkest hour of the American Revolution.

VAN BUREN, MARTIN (1782-1862). Eighth president of the U. S. He was vice-president during ANDREW JACKSON's second presidential term. In the ELECTION OF 1836 Van Buren was chosen president but he was defeated for a second term in the ELECTION of 1840 by WILLIAM HENRY HARRISON. During Van Buren's term as president, the PANIC of 1837 ushered in a period of hard times. The INDEPENDENT TREASURY SYSTEM was established (1840). Van Buren was called the "Wizard of Kinderhook" because of his political shrewdness.

VANDERBILT, COMMODORE CORNELIUS (1794-1877). American financier and businessman. During the GOLD RUSH to California (see FORTY-NINERS) Vanderbilt established a shipping line (1851) from the East to the West coast, including an overland trip across Nicaragua. After the WAR BETWEEN THE STATES (1861-65) he consolidated a number of short rail lines to form the New York Central Railroad, stretching from New York City to Chicago (1873). His efforts to seize control of the ERIE RAILROAD failed, however, mainly because of his business rivalry with JAY GOULD and JIM FISK.

V-E DAY and V-J DAY. See WORLD WAR II

VENEZUELA BOUNDARY DISPUTE (1895). Dispute between Venezuela and Great Britain over the boundary between Venezuela and British Guiana. The discovery of gold in the disputed area led to a diplomatic crisis in which Great Britain refused to arbitrate. In 1895 Secretary of State RICHARD OLNEY stated that Great Britain's at-

354

tempt to enlarge her territory in South America was a violation of the MONROE DOCTRINE. A threat of war between the U. S. and Great Britain developed, but in 1897 Great Britain agreed to arbitrate the dispute. By a treaty, most of the disputed territory was awarded to Great Britain.

VENEZUELA DEBT DISPUTE (1902). When Venezuela was unable to pay her debts to Great Britain, Germany and Italy, these countries established a blockade of Venezuelan ports. President THEODORE ROOSEVELT urged arbitration of the dispute and threatened to send the U. S. fleet to Venezuela if arbitration were not accepted. The three great powers agreed to arbitration and the size of the Venezuelan debt was reduced to less than one-fourth of the original demands. The threatened intervention of the U. S. led to the announcement of the ROOSEVELT COROLLARY (1905).

VERMONT. First state to be admitted to the Union (1791) after the U. S. was formed by the original THIRTEEN COLONIES. The Vermont region had been claimed both by the New York and the NEW HAMPSHIRE COLONY. The Vermonters, however, wished to be independent of both. In 1777 Vermont declared itself an independent state. During the AMERICAN REVOLUTION (1775-83) Vermonters captured FORT TICONDEROGA (see ETHAN ALLEN) and Crown Point and won a notable victory at the BATTLE OF BENNINGTON (1777).

VERRAZANO, GIOVANNI DA (c.1480-c.1527). Italian navigator in the service of the King of France. Sent to the New World to search for a NORTHWEST PASSAGE to the East, he explored the coast of North America (1524) from the Carolinas to Nova Scotia and was probably the first European to sail into New York harbor.

VERSAILLES TREATY (1919). Drawn up at the Paris Peace Conference (1919) at the end of WORLD WAR I (1914-18). Among its important provisions were the establishment of new nations such as Poland, Finland, Estonia, Latvia, Lithuania, Czechoslovakia, Austria and Hungary from territory taken from the former German, Russian and Austro-Hungarian Empires. In addition the national boundaries of Greece, Rumania, Jugoslavia (Serbia),

355

Belgium, Italy and France were redrawn to include more
territory and more people of similar nationality. The treaty
also placed the blame for starting the war on Germany,
called for the German payment of REPARATIONS for
war damages in Allied countries and included the
COVENANT or constitution of the LEAGUE OF NA-
TIONS. The Versailles Treaty was ratified by all Allied nations except the United States.

VESPUCCI, AMERIGO (1451-1512). Italian navigator who
sailed at different times under the Spanish and Portuguese
flags. In 1501 he explored the coast of South America and
finally reached the conclusion that it was a new continent.
In 1507 a German geographer named Martin Waldseemuller
published a book in which he used Vespucci's first name
as the name for the New World. Thus the continents of
the Western Hemisphere received their name, "America."

VICKSBURG, BATTLE OF (1863). One of the major military engagements of the WAR BETWEEN THE STATES
(1861-65). During the latter part of 1862 General
ULYSSES S. GRANT failed repeatedly in his efforts to
capture the city. In 1863 he began a siege and bombardment of the city that lasted six weeks, after which, on July
4, 1863, the city surrendered. Soon after this victory the
Union forces gained complete control of the Mississippi
River.

"VICTORIA," THE. See MAGELLAN, FERDINAND

VIGILANTES. Unofficial citizens' committees organized in
the Far Western territories to maintain law and order in
the early lawless days of the mining frontier. The usual
punishment by vigilantes was hanging. The most notorious
vigilantes were those organized in San Francisco in 1851
and 1856 to suppress the lawlessness of the BARBARY
COAST. Vigilantes were also organized in the mining towns
of Montana, Nevada and Idaho after the discovery of gold
in those regions in 1861.

VIKINGS. Scandinavian navigators who explored Greenland,
Iceland and the shores of Labrador 500 years before
COLUMBUS found the New World. Although the Vikings
reached North America about 1000 A. D. they established

no permanent settlements and left practically no evidence of their discoveries. (See ERICSON, LEIF)

VILLA, PANCHO (c.1877-1923). Mexican bandit and revolutionary leader. In 1916 he and his followers murdered a number of Americans in Mexico. He then crossed the border into the U. S. and committed a number of additional murders in New Mexico. In 1916 President WOODROW WILSON, with the consent of the Mexican government, sent General JOHN J. PERSHING and a U. S. military force into Mexico in an effort to capture Villa. He was never captured, however, and American armed forces were withdrawn from Mexico in 1917 because of the threat of war with Germany.

VINCENNES. See CLARK, GEORGE ROGERS

VINSON NAVAL ACT (1938). Because of increasing threats of war in Europe and the Japanese invasion of China (1937), Congress authorized the expansion of the U. S. naval forces to establish a "two-ocean navy" and appropriated more than $1,000,000,000 for that purpose.

VIRGINIA AND KENTUCKY RESOLUTIONS (1798). Drawn up by THOMAS JEFFERSON and JAMES MADISON and passed by the Virginia and Kentucky legislatures. The Virginia and Kentucky Resolutions were protests directed against the ALIEN AND SEDITION LAWS (1798). These resolutions stated that Congress had exceeded its power under the Constitution by passing the Alien and Sedition Laws and that our government was based on a COMPACT THEORY between the national government and the sovereign states. The states were therefore not bound by Congressional laws unauthorized by the Constitution.

VIRGINIA CITY. Virginia City, Nevada was founded in 1859, soon after the news spread of the discovery of gold and silver in the region. The most famous silver mine in the area was the COMSTOCK LODE. Virginia City, Montana was founded in 1863. It grew up almost overnight when news of the discovery of gold in the region became public. In their early days, both towns were sprawling, lawless communities typical of the MINING FRONTIER.

VIRGINIA COLONY (1609). Site of the first permanent English settlement in America at JAMESTOWN. It was established and controlled by the LONDON COMPANY, a private stock corporation, to earn profits for investors in England. In 1624 the charter of the London Company was revoked and Virginia became a ROYAL COLONY.

VIRGINIA COMPANY OF LONDON (1606). An organization of Englishmen who received a royal charter (1606) to establish two colonies in North America. The Virginia Company of London was to establish a colony between the latitudes of 34° and 41° north. The Virginia Company of Plymouth was to establish a colony between latitudes of 38° and 45° north. The settlements were to be at least 100 miles apart. In 1609 a new royal charter made the LONDON COMPANY independent of the PLYMOUTH COMPANY.

VIRGINIA PLAN (1787). Also called the "Randolph Plan." Proposal made by EDMUND RANDOLPH, delegate from Virginia, at the CONSTITUTIONAL CONVENTION (1787). His plan provided for a Congress of two branches in which the states would be represented on the basis of their total free population. This plan, which favored the larger states, was modified by the GREAT COMPROMISE that was finally adopted by the convention.

VIRGIN ISLANDS PURCHASE (1917). The U. S. purchased the islands from the Danish government for $25,000,000. The purchase gave the U. S. control of 68 Caribbean islands that could be used as an outer ring of protection for the PANAMA CANAL. By an Organic Act (1936) Congress provided for limited self-government by the islanders.

"VIRGINIUS" AFFAIR (1873). A Spanish gunboat seized the *Virginius,* a ship flying the American flag. It was transporting men and supplies to Cuban rebels who were trying to overthrow Spanish rule on the island. Eight American citizens on the *Virginius* were shot by the Spanish authorities. American public opinion was aroused for a time, but the incident was closed when Spain returned the *Virginius* to the U. S. and paid damages to the families of the executed Americans.

VOTING REQUIREMENTS. Also called suffrage requirements. In colonial times the suffrage, or right to vote, was restricted by religious and property qualifications. After the adoption of the U. S. Constitution (1789) the states retained the right to decide who would have the privilege of voting. Most states retained their religious and property qualifications. During President GEORGE WASHINGTON's administration, for example, less than 10% of the population voted. New Western states admitted to the Union, however, gave the suffrage to all white males regardless of religious or property qualifications. During the era of JACKSONIAN DEMOCRACY (1829-41) most of the Eastern states also dropped their restrictive voting requirements. Amendments to the U. S. Constitution have put certain limitations on the rights of states to restrict suffrage. AMENDMENT 15 forbids the denial of voting rights because of former slave status, race or color. AMENDMENT 19 forbids denial of suffrage because of sex. Individual states, however, still retain specific requirements for voting. All states have minimum age and residence requirements. Some states also have LITERACY TEST and POLL TAX requirements for voting.

WABASH AND ERIE CANAL. Early 19th century canal built to connect the western end of Lake Erie to the Wabash River in Illinois. This canal, together with the ERIE CANAL, made possible the transportation of freight by inland waterways from New York City to New Orleans, Louisiana.

WADE-DAVIS BILL (1864). Passed by Congress during the WAR BETWEEN THE STATES (1861-65) for the readmission of seceded states. The bill provided that a state could set up a new state government and return to the Union when a majority of the white male citizens took an oath of allegiance to support the U. S. Constitution. President ABRAHAM LINCOLN, however, favored a more lenient plan. He blocked the Wade-Davis Bill with a pocket veto.

WAGES AND HOURS ACT (1938). See FAIR LABOR STANDARDS ACT.

WAGNER-CONNERY ACT (1935). See NATIONAL LABOR RELATIONS ACT

WAGNER, ROBERT F. (1877-1949). U. S. Senator from New York (1927-49) for 22 years. During the NEW DEAL administration of President FRANKLIN D. ROOSEVELT, Wagner sponsored or supported many of the laws that have become keystones of American labor policy. These included the NATIONAL LABOR RELATIONS ACT (Wagner-Connery Act, 1935), and the Wagner-Steagall Housing Act (1937). His son, Robert F. Wagner, Jr., was later elected mayor of New York City.

WAGNER-STEAGALL HOUSING ACT (1937). See HOUSING LEGISLATION

WALKER TARIFF (1846). Passed by Congress during President JAMES K. POLK's administration. The Democratic majority in Congress reversed the trend of earlier protective tariffs by providing for tariff reductions in the Walker Tariff. A number of commodities were put on the "free list" and other rates were adjusted with the idea of raising revenue rather than providing protection to American industries. (See TARIFF LEGISLATION)

WALKER, WILLIAM (1824-1860). American adventurer who led a number of private military expeditions (see FILIBUSTERING EXPEDITIONS) to the Caribbean area to seize control of some of the smaller nations. Walker led an unsuccessful filibustering expedition against Lower California in 1853 and a successful one against Nicaragua in 1855, where he set himself up as dictator for two years. In 1860 Walker led another expedition into Honduras, where he was captured and executed.

WANGHIA, TREATY OF (1884). First commercial treaty signed by the U. S. and China opening Chinese ports to American trade. The treaty was negotiated by CALEB CUSHING, the first U. S. Commissioner to China.

WAR BETWEEN THE STATES (1861-65). Also known as the Civil War. It was a military conflict between Northern and Southern states which began with the firing on FORT SUMTER in the harbor of Charleston, South Carolina. This action was caused by the secession of Southern states after the ELECTION OF 1860 in which ABRAHAM LINCOLN became president. The 23 states of the North, with a population of 22,000,000, were opposed by 11 Southern states with a population of 5,500,000 whites and 4,000,000 Negro slaves, organized into the CONFEDERATE STATES OF AMERICA. Except for the Battle of Gettysburg, all of the major military engagements were fought on Confederate soil. Highlights of the war were the unsuccessful PENINSULAR CAMPAIGN (1862) of the North to capture Richmond—the Confederate capital—the BATTLE OF VICKSBURG (1863), the BATTLE OF GETTYSBURG (1863), General WILLIAM T. SHERMAN's march through Georgia (ATLANTA CAMPAIGN) (1864), the BLOCKADE of southern ports and the final surrender of the great Southern commander ROBERT E. LEE to General ULYSSES S. GRANT at Appomattox Courthouse (April 9, 1865). More than 1,000,000 men were killed or wounded during the war.

WAR DEBTS. During and after WORLD WAR I (1917-18) the U. S. loaned about $12,000,000,000 to the Allied nations to finance the war and to stabilize their national finances after the war. Soviet Russia, under Bolshevik rule, repudiated all of its debts to the U. S. Thereafter Allied war debts were reduced by the U. S. Debt Funding Commission (1922), the DAWES PLAN (1924) and the Young Plan (1929). From 1922 to 1931 the debts were paid by the Allies largely out of REPARATIONS collected by them from Germany. Because of the world-wide economic crisis in 1931 (see GREAT DEPRESSION) President HERBERT HOOVER called a one-year moratorium on payments of all war debts due to the U. S. (called Hoover Moratorium). At the end of 1932 a number of Allied nations made token payments to the U. S. but most countries defaulted. The war debts of World War I were never fully repaid.

WAR HAWKS. Southern and Western congressmen such as HENRY CLAY and RICHARD JOHNSTON of Kentucky and JOHN C. CALHOUN of South Carolina who clamored for war with Great Britain (1810-12). They were influenced in large part by the desire to increase the size of the U. S. by seizing Canada from Great Britain and Florida from Spain. (See EXPANSIONISTS) Indian frontier raids and disrespect for the American flag on the high seas were also factors in their demand for war, which was finally declared by Congress in 1812. (See WAR OF 1812)

WAR INDUSTRIES BOARD. See WARTIME AGENCIES, WORLD WAR I

"WAR IS HELL." See SHERMAN, GENERAL WILLIAM T.

WAR LABOR DISPUTES ACT (1943). Also known as the Smith-Connally Anti-Strike Act. It was passed by Congress during WORLD WAR II (1941-45) over President Franklin D. Roosevelt's veto. Under the act the president could seize all plants where labor disputes interfered with the production of war materials or hindered the national war effort. On the basis of this law, President Roosevelt took control of all railroads (1943) to prevent a strike.

WAR OF 1812. Sometimes called the "War for Commercial Independence." The U. S. declared war on Great Britain because of British IMPRESSMENT of American seamen, illegal seizure and search of American merchant ships (see FREEDOM OF THE SEAS), British incitement of Indians on the Western frontier (see TECUMSEH) and the desire of Western and Southern congressmen (see WAR HAWKS and EXPANSIONISTS) for more territory. The war was mainly a series of naval battles in which Americans won notable victories (see "CONSTITUTION" AND "GUERRIERE") but in which the larger British Navy controlled the sea lanes. Efforts by the U. S. to invade Canada by land failed. In one land invasion the British burned the capital buildings in Washington, D. C. The last clash between the U. S. and British forces at the BATTLE OF NEW ORLEANS (1815) was a brilliant American victory. The TREATY OF GHENT (1814) ending the war established peace between the countries but neither side gained anything and the question of "freedom of the seas" remained unsettled.

WAR PRODUCTION BOARD (W.P.B.). See WARTIME AGENCIES, WORLD WAR II

WAR SHIPPING BOARD. See WARTIME AGENCIES, WORLD WAR I

WARTIME AGENCIES, WORLD WAR I (1917-18). In order to conduct the war effort successfully, Congress established a number of special agencies. The War Industries Board provided plans for increasing production of war materials. The Railroad Administration operated the nation's railroads as a government function. The War Shipping Board supervised the construction and use of freighters to carry war materials. The Food Administration encouraged the conservation of food and the Committee on Public Information distributed war information, explained our war aims and encouraged the purchase of war bonds by the public.

WARTIME AGENCIES, WORLD WAR II (1941-45). In order to conduct the war effort successfully and at the same time maintain economic stability at home, Congress established a number of special wartime agencies. The Office of

Price Administration (O.P.A.) established price and rent ceilings and rationed scarce consumer goods. The Office of Economic Stabilization (O.E.S.) established a system of priorities for the use of scarce materials needed in war industries. The War Production Board (W.P.B.) coordinated and speeded up the work of war industries. The Office of Defense Transportation (O.D.T.) coordinated the use of the railroads for wartime needs. The War Manpower Commission (W.M.C.) established regulations for draft deferments for men in essential industries. The Office of War Information (O.W.I.) distributed war information and explained our war aims. The Office of War Mobilization (O.W.M.) coordinated the activities of all of these newly established wartime agencies.

WASHINGTON, BOOKER T. (1856-1915). Negro educator and founder of Tuskegee Institute in Alabama. Born of a slave mother, Washington eventually was graduated from Hampden Institute, Virginia. In 1881 he organized Tuskegee Institute, which he administered for many years and which became nationally famous.

WASHINGTON, D. C. Capital of the U. S. located on the Potomac River between Maryland and Virginia. The location was the result of a compromise agreement between ALEXANDER HAMILTON and THOMAS JEFFERSON over the ASSUMPTION ACT (1790). The capital was planned and designed by the French architect, PIERRE CHARLES L'ENFANT. Construction of the capital buildings was begun in 1793 and Thomas Jefferson was the first president to be inaugurated there (1801). Residents of Washington, D. C. were given the right to vote in national elections by AMENDMENT 23.

WASHINGTON DISARMAMENT CONFERENCE (1922). Called by President WARREN G. HARDING. Three important treaties were signed at the conference. A FIVE POWER NAVAL PACT provided for a ten-year "Naval Holiday" in battleship construction and the establishment of a 5:5:3:1⅔:1⅔ ratio for capital ships among the U.S., Great Britain, Japan, France and Italy. A Four Power Pact signed by the U. S., Great Britain, France and Japan provided for the peaceful solution of Far Eastern rivalries. A Nine Power Pact signed by the five great powers plus

Holland, Belgium, Portugal and China guaranteed the OPEN DOOR in China and her territorial integrity.

WASHINGTON, GEORGE (1732-1799). First president of the U. S., known as the "father of his country." Washington was a member of General EDWARD BRADDOCK's ill-fated expedition to capture FORT DUQUESNE from the French (1755), commander-in-chief of the CONTINENTAL ARMY during the AMERICAN REVOLUTION (1775-83) and chairman of the CONSTITUTIONAL CONVENTION (1787) that wrote the Constitution. He was elected first president of the U. S. in the ELECTION OF 1788, was re-elected for a second term in the ELECTION of 1792 and set the precedent which lasted until 1940, of a president's serving no more than two terms.

During his eight years as president, the First BANK OF U. S. was chartered (1791), a national mint was established (MINT ACT, 1792), the BILL OF RIGHTS was added to the Constitution (1791) and the WHISKEY REBELLION (1794) in Pennsylvania was suppressed. In foreign affairs, Washington issued the PROCLAMATION OF NEUTRALITY (1793) and resolved the GENET AFFAIR (1793). The JAY TREATY (1794) was signed with England and the PINCKNEY TREATY (1795) with Spain. In his FAREWELL ADDRESS (1796) Washington urged no entangling alliances (see ISOLATION) with foreign nations.

WASHINGTON, TREATY OF (1871). See ALABAMA CLAIMS

WATAUGA ASSOCIATION (1772). Political organization formed by settlers in eastern Tennessee before the AMERICAN REVOLUTION (1775-83). The association was under the leadership of James Robertson and its purpose was to provide protection against Indian raids. In 1776 it voluntarily dissolved and became part of the state of North Carolina. In 1784 the members of the former Watauga Association joined the new state of FRANKLIN, which became the state of Tennessee in 1796.

WATCHFUL WAITING (1913). President WOODROW WILSON's policy toward Mexico after the assassination of Mexican President Francisco Madero (1913) and the assumption of power by Victoriano Huerta. Wilson refused either to recognize the new Huerta government or to intervene in Mexican affairs. In 1914, after the TAMPICO INCIDENT, Huerta resigned and fled to Europe. He was succeeded by Venustiano Carranza, who promised to respect American lives and property in Mexico. The U. S. therefore recognized the Carranza government (1915). A Mexican revolution in 1920 again raised the question of American recognition of the new revolutionary government. The U. S. recognized the new government in 1923.

WATER POWER ACT (1920). Established a Federal Power Commission (F.P.C.) with authority to issue 50-year licenses to private corporations for the construction of dams, reservoirs and electric power transmission lines on government-owned public lands. The commission was to regulate the electric power rates charged by these private corporations and all stocks and bonds issued by them.

WATSON-PARKER ACT (1926). Also called the Railway Labor Act. It abolished the Railroad Labor Board that had been established under the ESCH-CUMMINS ACT OF 1920 and replaced it with a National Mediation Board to settle railway labor disputes through conciliation, mediation and arbitration. The Watson-Parker Act also provided for a 30-day "cooling off" period before a railroad strike could legally be called. (See RAILROAD LEGISLATION)

"WAVING THE BLOODY SHIRT." Popular phrase used to describe the political campaign policy of the REPUBLICAN PARTY after the WAR BETWEEN THE STATES (1861-65). Leaders of the party reminded voters that the DEMOCRATIC PARTY was the party of disloyalty, rebellion and war and that the Republican Party had saved the Union.

WAYNE, ANTHONY (1745-96). Also known as "Mad Anthony" Wayne because of his quick temper. He was an officer in the AMERICAN REVOLUTION (1775-83), fought at the BATTLE OF BRANDYWINE (1777), the BATTLE OF GERMANTOWN (1777), and the BATTLE OF MONMOUTH (1778), and in 1779 captured Stony Point from the British. In 1792 he was appointed commander of American Armies and conducted a campaign against the Indians in the NORTHWEST TERRITORY. At the BATTLE OF FALLEN TIMBERS (1794) he defeated the Indians decisively and in the following year arranged the TREATY OF GREENVILLE (1795), which opened new land in the Northwest Territory to American settlers.

WEAVER, JAMES B. (1833-1912). Leader of the GREEN-BACK movement. In the ELECTION OF 1880 he was the unsuccessful GREENBACK PARTY candidate for president. Weaver was one of the founders of the FARMERS' ALLIANCE in 1887. When the Alliance merged with the newly organized POPULIST PARTY, Weaver was nominated as the latter's presidential candidate in the ELECTION OF 1892 and polled about 1,000,000 votes. In the ELECTION OF 1896 Weaver supported WILLIAM JENNINGS BRYAN and the free silver platform of the Democratic Party.

WEBSTER-ASHBURTON TREATY (1842). For many years the boundary between the state of Maine and Canada was disputed. These differences almost led to the use of military force. (See AROOSTOOK WAR) In 1842, however, DANIEL WEBSTER, the U. S. Secretary of State, and Alexander Ashburton, the British Foreign Secretary, arranged a treaty settling the boundary between Maine and Canada, as well as the boundary west of the Great Lakes from Lake Superior to the Lake of the Woods.

WEBSTER, DANIEL (1782-1852). One of the greatest orators in the annals of Congressional history. He became well known as the attorney for the college in the DARTMOUTH COLLEGE CASE (1819) and for the bank in the MC CULLOCH V. MARYLAND case (1819). He represented the state of Massachusetts as WHIG PARTY member in Congress with few interruptions from 1813 to his death in 1852. During his long and distinguished period of service, he defended the indestructibility of the Union in the famous WEBSTER-HAYNE DEBATE (1830) and supported the COMPROMISE OF 1850 in his brilliant "SEVENTH OF MARCH" SPEECH. As a result of his support of this compromise, anti-slavery men branded him a traitor to the cause of liberty. As Secretary of State (1841-43) under President WILLIAM HENRY HARRISON, he negotiated the WEBSTER-ASHBURTON TREATY (1842). Webster was nominated for the presidency by the WHIG PARTY but was badly defeated in the ELECTION OF 1836.

WEBSTER-HAYNE DEBATE (1830). Famous Senatorial debate between Senator Robert Y. Hayne of South Carolina and DANIEL WEBSTER of Massachusetts. The debate started over a resolution by Senator Foote of Connecticut to restrict temporarily the sale of federal public lands. It was quickly changed into a verbal battle over the questions of STATES RIGHTS and NULLIFICATION. Hayne defended the Southern position of states' rights and nullification, while Webster, in a masterful reply, upheld the doctrine of the supremacy of the national government over the states. His speech ended with the words, "Liberty and Union, now and forever, one and inseparable."

"WE HAVE MET THE ENEMY AND THEY ARE OURS." See PERRY, CAPTAIN OLIVER HAZARD

WEST COAST HOTEL V. PARRISH (1937). U. S. Supreme Court decision upholding a Washington state minimum wage law under the POLICE POWERS of a state. In earlier decisions, similar state legislation had been declared unconstitutional. (See ADKINS V. CHILDREN'S HOSPITAL, 1923)

WEST FLORIDA DISPUTE. After the LOUISIANA PURCHASE (1803), a dispute developed between the U. S. and Spain over ownership of West Florida. This was territory along the Gulf coast between the Perdida and the Mississippi Rivers. The U. S. claimed it was part of the Louisiana Purchase, while Spain claimed it was part of her Florida Territory. In 1810 a number of Southern EXPANSIONISTS led a revolt in West Florida and set up an independent republic in the area. In 1811 President JAMES MADISON, in a proclamation, announced that West Florida was part of the U. S. During the WAR OF 1812 (1812-14) the U. S. seized military control of the area from Spain (1813) and after the war retained control of it. By the FLORIDA PURCHASE (Adams-Onis Treaty, 1819) Spain gave up all claims to West Florida.

WEST VIRGINIA. During the WAR BETWEEN THE STATES (1861-65) the people in the northwestern area of

Virginia were opposed to secession. When the state of Virginia seceded in 1861 the people in the northwest region decided to organize a separate state. In 1863 they were admitted to the Union as the State of West Virginia.

WESTWARD MOVEMENT. Before the AMERICAN REVOLUTION (1775-83), the colonists had moved as far west as the Appalachian Mountains. By the time of the WAR BETWEEN THE STATES (1861-65) settlers had reached the Mississippi River and settled beyond it. The GOLD RUSH to California (1849) created a new FRONTIER on the Pacific coast. The westward movement continued after 1865 and came to an end about 1890 when the last frontier disappeared. This westward movement of settlers was caused by many factors, including economic depressions in the east (see PANICS), expansion of cotton cultivation in the South, liberal land policies of the national government (see PUBLIC LAND ACTS), escape from religious intolerance (see MORMONS), discovery of gold in California, Nevada and Montana, and the building of transcontinental railroads. This westward movement profoundly affected national policies in such fields as immigration, education, labor legislation, the tariff, currency legislation, democratic reforms, regulation of railroads and big business, foreign policies and many others.

"WESTWARD THE COURSE OF EMPIRE TAKES ITS WAY." Quotation attributed to George Berkeley, Bishop of Cloyne, England (1745). Berkeley was referring to the colonies and settlements of the New World.

WEYLER, GENERAL VALERIANO (1838-1930). Spanish commander in Cuba during the Cuban revolution of 1895. General Weyler earned the name of "Butcher" Weyler because of his use of concentration camps for the imprisonment of rebels, women and children. Thousands died in these camps of disease and starvation. News of these atrocities, spread in the U. S. by YELLOW JOURNALISM, aroused public opinion against Spain and helped to bring on the SPANISH-AMERICAN WAR (1898).

WHALING. Important New England industry from colonial times to the middle of the 19th century. The center of the industry was New Bedford, Massachusetts, where the first whaling ship set sail in 1755. Whale oil was used for lamps and for the manufacture of candles until the middle of the 19th century.

"WHAT HATH GOD WROUGHT?" See MORSE, SAMUEL F. B.

WHEELER-LEA ACTS. The Wheeler-Lea Act of 1938 is better known as the PURE FOOD, DRUG, AND COSMETIC ACT. The Wheeler-Lea Act of 1940 is also known as the TRANSPORTATION ACT OF 1940.

WHEELER-RAYBURN ACT (1935). Regulated public utility holding companies by forbidding the pyramiding of such companies beyond the second degree. This was the "death sentence" for all public utility holding companies of the third or any higher degree. The act also required all public utility holding companies to register with the Securities and Exchange Commission and to get its approval for all new issues of securities.

WHIG PARTY (1832-1854). Formed during ANDREW JACKSON's second term as president (1833-1837) from the remnants of the earlier NATIONAL REPUBLICAN PARTY. The Whig Party also included former Southern Democrats who opposed Jackson, and members of the ANTI-MASON PARTY. Although the various factions of the Whig Party had many differences, they were unanimous in their opposition to Jackson. HENRY CLAY of Kentucky, the recognized leader of the Whigs, was nominated three times for the presidency, once by the National Republicans (1824) and twice by the Whigs (1832, 1844). He was defeated on each occasion. However, the Whig Party elected WILLIAM HENRY HARRISON to the presidency in the ELECTION OF 1840 and ZACHARY TAYLOR in the ELECTION OF 1848. Both Whig presidents died during their terms in office. In 1854 the Whig Party fell apart over the question of the extension of slavery in Western territories. Southern Whigs joined the DEMOCRATIC PARTY and Northern Whigs joined the REPUBLICAN PARTY.

WHISKEY REBELLION (1794). Uprising of farmers in western Pennsylvania who refused to pay the federal whiskey tax. The rebellion was easily quelled by a force of militia. The ringleaders were arrested and jailed but later pardoned by President GEORGE WASHINGTON. The whiskey tax was repealed (1802) after THOMAS JEFFERSON became president.

WHISKEY RING (1875). A group of Midwestern businessmen used bribes to evade the payment of the revenue tax on whiskey. A federal revenue officer who was a member of the Whiskey Ring gave gifts to President ULYSSES S. GRANT's private secretary and also gave Grant a gift of a team of horses. Several members of the ring were sent to prison but were later pardoned by Grant.

WHISKEY TAX (1791). See WHISKEY REBELLION

WHITE HOUSE. Official residence of the president of the U. S. in WASHINGTON, D. C. Construction was begun in 1792 and JOHN ADAMS was the first president to reside in it (1800). The White House was burned (1814) during a British invasion of the capital during the WAR OF 1812. After repairs to the building were completed, it was painted white and thereafter became known as the White House.

WHITMAN, MARCUS (1802-47). American missionary who moved west to the Oregon Territory in the first half of the 19th century. Although his primary purpose was to convert the Indians to Christianity, he also encouraged other people to come to Oregon as farmers.

WHITNEY, ELI (1765-1825). Young New England teacher. While visiting in the South he invented the COTTON GIN (1793), which revolutionized the cotton growing (see PLANTATION SYSTEM) and cotton textile industries. Whitney made little money from his "gin." However, he became wealthy when he went into the business of manufacturing rifles and guns (see SIX-SHOOTER) by means of a mass-production system based on standardized and interchangeable parts.

WILDCAT BANKS. See PANIC OF 1819 and PANIC OF 1837

371

WILDERNESS CAMPAIGN (1865). One of the last campaigns of the WAR BETWEEN THE STATES (1861-65). General ULYSSES S. GRANT and a Union Army marched directly on Richmond, the Confederate capital, while General ROBERT E. LEE and a Confederate Army blocked the way. Despite terrible Union losses, Grant continued his campaign and finally captured Richmond. On April 9, 1865 General Lee surrendered to Grant at APPOMATTOX COURTHOUSE, Virginia, thus bringing the war to an end.

WILDERNESS ROAD (1795). Eighteenth century mountain trail and early 19th century road. It led from Virginia across the Appalachian Mountains through the CUMBERLAND GAP into Kentucky. The earliest colonial pioneers used this route to move west of the mountains into Kentucky and Tennessee.

WILEY-DONDERO ACT (1954). Established the St. Lawrence Seaway and Development Corporation under which the U. S. and Canada began construction of the St. Lawrence Seaway project. It was opened to ocean-going vessels in 1959.

WILLARD, FRANCES E. (1839-98). Temperance and WOMEN SUFFRAGE leader in the late 19th century. She helped to organize the WOMEN'S CHRISTIAN TEMPERANCE UNION (1874) and in 1879 became president of the organization. She also campaigned for the extension of the suffrage to women.

WILLIAMS, ROGER (c.1603-1683). Minister in the MASSACHUSETTS BAY COLONY whose ideas were unpopular with the Puritan leaders of the colony. Williams believed in the principle of religious freedom for all and the separation of church and state. In 1635 he was expelled from Massachusetts. He, together with a few followers, established a new settlement at PROVIDENCE (1636) in the present state of RHODE ISLAND, where religious freedom was guaranteed to all.

WILMOT PROVISO (1846). Before the beginning of the MEXICAN WAR (1846) Congress debated a bill to purchase territory from Mexico. David Wilmot, congressman from Pennsylvania, proposed an amendment or proviso to the bill which would forbid slavery in any newly acquired territory. The Wilmot Proviso was defeated in the Senate. However, it reopened the question of slavery in new territories, since the MISSOURI COMPROMISE (1820) had provided a formula only for states carved out of the LOUISIANA TERRITORY.

WILSON-GORMAN TARIFF (1894). The Democratic Party majority in Congress set out to enact a tariff law that would be lower than the high MC KINLEY TARIFF (1890) then in effect. However, the Senate added more than 600 amendments to the proposed law, making the final act almost as high as the McKinley Tariff. President GROVER CLEVELAND labeled the law "party perfidy and dishonor" and refused to sign or veto it. It thus became law without his signature. The Wilson-Gorman Tariff Act also established a national INCOME TAX of 2% on all incomes over $4,000. This provision was later declared unconstitutional. (Pollock v. Farmers' Loan and Trust, 1895).

WILSON, THOMAS WOODROW (1856-1924). Twenty-eighth president of the U. S. In 1910 he was elected governor of New Jersey. Two years later the DEMOCRATIC PARTY nominated him for the presidency. A split in the REPUBLICAN PARTY led to Wilson's victory in the ELECTION OF 1912. He was rechosen for a second term in the ELECTION OF 1916. Wilson called his domestic reform program the "New Freedom." During his presidency Congress passed the UNDERWOOD TARIFF ACT (1913), the FEDERAL RESERVE ACT (1913), the FEDERAL TRADE COMMISSION ACT (1914) and the CLAYTON ANTI-TRUST ACT (1914). In addition, AMENDMENT 16 (1913), legalizing the INCOME TAX, AMENDMENT 17 (1913), providing for direct election of senators, AMENDMENT 18 (1919), establishing PROHIBITION, and AMENDMENT 19 (1920), giving women the right to vote, were ratified by the states.

In foreign affairs, President Wilson's administration saw the opening of the PANAMA CANAL (1914), the enactment of the JONES ACT (1916) for the government of the PHILIPPINE ISLANDS, the enactment of the JONES ACT (1917) for the government of PUERTO RICO, the purchase of the VIRGIN ISLANDS (1917) and the U. S.

373

declaration of war on Germany (WORLD WAR I, 1917-
18). Wilson drew up the FOURTEEN POINTS (1918),
helped to write the TREATY OF VERSAILLES (1919)
and the COVENANT OF THE LEAGUE OF NATIONS
(1919). In 1920 Wilson was awarded the NOBEL PEACE
PRIZE.

WINDMILLS. American homesteaders who settled on the
great Western plains (see INTERIOR PLAINS) in the mid-
19th century found that they had to dig deep wells to get
water. Farmers built windmills with high towers to catch
the wind and use it to pump water to the surface.

WINTHROP, JOHN (1588-1649). Leader of the PURITANS
in England and first governor (1629-49) of the MASSA-
CHUSETTS BAY COLONY. He was a leading advocate
of the NEW ENGLAND CONFEDERATION as a defense
against the Indians and was its first president when it was
organized in 1643.

WISCONSIN IDEA. See LA FOLLETTE, ROBERT M.

WITCHCRAFT TRIALS (1692). Many people in Salem,
Massachusetts were charged with being witches (one who
deals with the devil), were tried by a court and found guilty.
Nineteen persons were put to death for witchcraft before
the royal governor, Sir William Phips, put an end to the
trials.

**"WITH MALICE TOWARD NONE: WITH CHARITY
FOR ALL."** Quotation from President ABRAHAM LIN-
COLN's second inaugural address (1865), in which he out-
lined his policy for bringing the seceded states back into the
Union.

WIZARD OF KINDERHOOK. See VAN BUREN, MAR-
TIN

WOLFE, GENERAL JAMES (1727-59). Commander of
British forces sent to capture Canada from the French during the FRENCH AND INDIAN WAR (1754-63). In 1759
he succeeded in capturing the city of Quebec from the
defending French commander, Louis Montcalm. Both generals were killed in the Battle of Quebec.

WOMAN SUFFRAGE. Before the WAR BETWEEN THE STATES (1861-65) it was the general rule in almost all states that women could not vote. In 1869 the territory of Wyoming permitted women suffrage. When Wyoming became a state (1890), it was the first to permit women to vote. Leaders of the movement to give women the right to vote in the 19th century included SUSAN B. ANTHONY, ELIZABETH CADY STANTON, LUCRETIA MOTT and the GRIMKE SISTERS. Among the early 20th century women suffrage leaders were CARRIE CHAPMAN CATT and Anna Howard Shaw. In 1920 AMENDMENT 19 gave all women the right to vote. (See FEMINIST MOVEMENT)

WOMEN'S CHRISTIAN TEMPERANCE UNION (1874). See PROHIBITION

WOOLENS ACT (1699). Passed by the English Parliament. It forbad the export of woolen goods from one colony to another or to a foreign country. The purpose of this law was to protect the interests of woolen merchants in England.

WORCESTER V. GEORGIA (1832). See CHEROKEE INDIANS

WORKINGMEN'S PARTY (1828). A political party formed in Philadelphia and other Eastern cities by city workers and mechanics. Its pro-labor platform called for equal taxes, public-supported education, election of all public officials and elimination of imprisonment for debt. The party never grew large and succeeded in electing candidates for a few local offices only.

WORKS PROGRESS ADMINISTRATION (W.P.A.). See UNEMPLOYMENT LEGISLATION

WORLD COURT (1920). Also known as the Permanent Court of International Justice. After WORLD WAR I (1918) the World Court was established as the judicial arm of the LEAGUE OF NATIONS. Efforts to get the U. S. to join the World Court through the ROOT FORMULA were rejected by the Senate (1935). After WORLD WAR II (1945) the World Court became an agency of the new UNITED NATIONS. By becoming a charter member of the U. N.

the U. S. automatically became a member of the World Court in 1945.

WORLD WAR I (1917-18). The war had begun in Europe in 1914 but the U. S. did not declare war on Germany until April 6, 1917, three months after Germany announced renewal of her policy of unrestricted SUBMARINE WARFARE. (See LUSITANIA, ZIMMERMAN NOTE) Highlights of American participation included American fighting at Chateau Thierry and in the St. Mihiel-Argonne offensive. After their HINDENBURG LINE collapsed, Germany surrendered in 1918 and the war came to an end. The U. S. did not sign the TREATY OF VERSAILLES (1919) after the war.

WORLD WAR II (1941-45). The war began in Europe in 1939 with Adolf Hitler's invasion of Poland. The U. S. declared war on Japan on December 8, 1941, the day after the Japanese attack on PEARL HARBOR. A few days later Germany and Italy declared war on the U. S. High lights of American participation in the war included the BATTLE OF THE ATLANTIC, the invasion of North Africa (1942), the surrender of Italy (1943), the opening of a "second front" in Europe (1944), the BATTLE OF GUADAL-CANAL (1942), the BATTLE OF LEYTE GULF (1944) and the atomic bombing of HIROSHIMA. The war came to an end with the unconditional surrender of Germany (V-E Day) on May 8, 1945 and of Japan (V-J Day) on August 14, 1945.

WRIGHT BROTHERS. Wilbur (1867-1912) and Orville (1871-1948) Wright experimented with heavier-than-air flying machines and made the first successful airplane flight in 1903 over the sand dunes of Kitty Hawk, North Carolina.

WRITS OF ASSISTANCE. Search warrants used in colonial times by British agents to find smuggled goods. The writs were very general, since they did not include the place to be searched or the goods that were sought. JAMES OTIS gained widespread fame for his speeches and writings opposing the indiscriminate use of Writs of Assistance by the British.

WYANDOTTE CONSTITUTION (1859). After the people of the Kansas Territory rejected the LECOMPTON CONSTITUTION (1858) permitting slavery in Kansas, the free soil faction in the territory drew up the Wyandotte Constitution. Under this constitution, Kansas asked to be admitted into the Union as a free state. Congress approved this new constitution and Kansas entered the Union in 1861.

XYZ AFFAIR (1797). JOHN MARSHALL, ELBRIDGE GERRY and CHARLES C. PINCKNEY were sent to France by President JOHN ADAMS to settle difficulties resulting from French seizure of American ships on the high seas. Persons identified as X, Y and Z, claiming to speak for the French government, asked the American delegates for a bribe before the French government would consider a settlement. This disgraceful incident aroused such animosity that actual fighting between French and American ships occurred on the high seas, although there was no official declaration of war.

YALTA CONFERENCE (1945). Held at Yalta in the Russian Crimea during the last year of WORLD WAR II (1941-45). FRANKLIN D. ROOSEVELT of the U. S., Winston Churchill of Great Britain and Josef Stalin of the Soviet Union agreed on final plans for the defeat of Germany, the control and occupation of Germany after the war and the calling of a new conference at San Francisco (see SAN FRANCISCO CONFERENCE) to draw up a charter for the UNITED NATIONS.

YAZOO LAND FRAUDS. In 1795 the Georgia legislature sold state-owned land in Alabama and Mississippi (Yazoo River District) to four land companies. When fraud involving some of the Georgia legislators was discovered in the transaction, Georgia rescinded the sale. In 1802 Georgia ceded the land to the U. S. government. The holders of the land grants sued. In 1810 the Supreme Court, with Chief Justice JOHN MARSHALL presiding, decided (FLETCHER V. PECK) that the land grants were valid. Despite the opposition of many members of Congress, including John Randolph, the original recipients of the Yazoo land grants were paid $48,000,000 by the U. S. government for their land claims (1814).

YELLOW DOG CONTRACTS. Agreements signed by workers not to join a union as a condition of employment. The Erdman Act (1898) prohibited the use of "yellow dog" contracts by interstate railroad corporations. The U. S. Supreme Court declared this provision of the act unconstitutional because it violated the freedom of contract provision of AMENDMENT 5 and regulated union membership, which was not a part of "interstate commerce"

378

(Adair v. U. S., 1908). However, the NORRIS-LA GUAR-DIA ACT (1932) put an end to yellow dog contracts.

YELLOW JOURNALISM. Also called "yellow press." It refers to newspapers which intentionally feature sensational news with blaring headlines. The term "yellow" was derived from an early newspaper comic strip called "The Yellow Kid." Two of the most famous practitioners of yellow journalism were JOSEPH PULITZER, editor of the New York *World* and WILLIAM RANDOLPH HEARST, editor of the New York *Journal,* particularly before and during the SPANISH-AMERICAN WAR (1898).

YORKTOWN, BATTLE OF (1781). Last major military engagement of the AMERICAN REVOLUTION (1775-83). General GEORGE WASHINGTON and his army, aided by the French General Jean Rochambeau and his forces, surrounded General Cornwallis and his British Army on the Yorktown, Virginia peninsula. A French fleet under Admiral Francois DeGrasse drove off the British fleet trying to bring help to Cornwallis. Surrounded by land and sea, General Cornwallis was forced to surrender his army of more than 6,000 men.

YOUNG, BRIGHAM (1801-77). Leader of the MORMONS. After the violent death of JOSEPH SMITH (1844), leadership of the Mormon Sect was assumed by Brigham Young. He led the Mormons west to Salt Lake City, Utah (1846-47), where they settled. Through Young's tremendous drive and energy, the Mormon settlement became a thriving and prosperous community. Since Young practiced the Mormon custom of plural marriages (polygamy) he was married to 27 women during his lifetime. Yet he was a man of high and unquestioned morality.

YOUNG PLAN (1929). See WAR DEBTS

ZENGER, JOHN PETER (1697-1746). Colonial New York printer and publisher. In 1734 he was arrested and tried for printing articles criticizing the New York colonial governor. He was defended by a famous colonial lawyer named AN-DREW HAMILTON because his case involved the important principle of FREEDOM OF THE PRESS. Zenger was acquitted by a jury in 1735 and the principle of freedom of the press was firmly established as one of our basic liberties. (See AMENDMENT 1)

ZIMMERMAN NOTE (1917). Note from the German foreign minister, Alfred Zimmerman, intercepted and published in the U. S. before we entered WORLD WAR I (1917). The note revealed a plan by which Germany promised Mexico that her former territories (Texas and the Mexican Cession) would be restored to her if, after a U. S. declaration of war on Germany, Mexico declared war on the U. S. The note also sought to get Japan to declare war on the U. S., if and when we declared war on Germany.

The type used in this book is Times Roman
with Times Roman Bold headings.

Typography by Central Typesetting
& Electrotyping Co., Chicago 39, Illinois

Book designed by Donald A. Schrader